Literature and Social Justice

Cognitive Approaches to Literature and Culture Series
Edited by Frederick Luis Aldama, Arturo J. Aldama, and Patrick Colm Hogan

Cognitive Approaches to Literature and Culture includes monographs and edited volumes that incorporate cutting-edge research in cognitive science, neuroscience, psychology, linguistics, narrative theory, and related fields, exploring how this research bears on and illuminates cultural phenomena such as, but not limited to, literature, film, drama, music, dance, visual art, digital media, and comics. The volumes published in this series represent both specialized scholarship and interdisciplinary investigations that are deeply sensitive to cultural specifics and grounded in a cross-cultural understanding of shared emotive and cognitive principles.

Literature and Social Justice

Protest Novels, Cognitive Politics,
and Schema Criticism

BY MARK BRACHER

University of Texas Press ◄◊► *Austin*

Portions of Chapter 1 and Chapter 6 originally appeared in the article "Schema Criticism: Literature, Cognitive Science, and Social Change" in *College Literature* 39.4 (Fall 2012): 84–117.

Excerpts from *The Grapes of Wrath* by John Steinbeck, copyright 1939, renewed © 1967 by John Steinbeck, are used by permission of Viking Penguin, a division of Penguin Group (USA) Inc. and Penguin UK.

Excerpts from *Native Son* by Richard Wright, copyright 1940 by Richard Wright (renewed 1968 by Ellen Wright), are reprinted by permission of Harper-Collins Publishers. Additional permission for *Native Son* by Richard Wright, published by Jonathan Cape, was granted by The Random House Group Limited.

Copyright © 2013 by the University of Texas Press
All rights reserved

First edition, 2013
First paperback edition, 2014

Requests for permission to reproduce material from this work should be sent to:
Permissions
University of Texas Press
P.O. Box 7819
Austin, TX 78713-7819
http://utpress.utexas.edu/index.php/rp-form

♻ The paper used in this book meets the minimum requirements of ANSI/NISO Z39.48-1992 (R1997) (Permanence of Paper).

Library of Congress Cataloging-in-Publication Data
Bracher, Mark, 1950–
    Literature and social justice : protest novels, cognitive politics, and schema criticism / by Mark Bracher.
        p.   cm. — (Cognitive approaches to literature and culture series)
    Includes bibliographical references and index.
    ISBN 978-0-292-74778-4 (cloth : alk. paper)
    ISBN 978-1-4773-0209-5 (paperback)

    1. Protest literature, American—History and criticism.   2. Justice, Administration of, in literature.   3. Social justice in literature.   I. Title.
    PS228.P73B73   2012
    810.9′353—dc23

                                                    2012042771

doi:10.7560/747784

For Tammy

I love thee to the depth and breadth and height
My soul can reach, when feeling out of sight
For the ends of being and ideal grace.
I love thee to the level of every day's
Most quiet need, by sun and candle-light.
I love thee freely, as men strive for right.
I love thee purely, as they turn from praise.
I love thee with the passion put to use
In my old griefs, and with my childhood's faith.
I love thee with a love I seemed to lose
With my lost saints. I love thee with the breath,
Smiles, tears, of all my life . . .
—ELIZABETH BARRETT BROWNING

Contents

Preface   ix

Acknowledgments   xv

PART I. **The Psychological Basis for a Cognitive Politics of Social Justice**

1. Cognitive Science for a New Social Criticism   3

PART II. **The Cognitive Roots of Injustice: Four Person-Schemas**

2. Autonomism versus Situationism: Responsibility for Behavior and Life Outcomes   35

3. Essentialism versus Malleability: Responsibility for Character   75

4. Atomism versus Solidarity: Relation of Self to Others   103

5. Homogeneity versus Heterogeneity: The Structure of Character   140

PART III. **How Protest Novels Work to Replace Faulty Person-Schemas**

6. *The Jungle*   167

7. *The Grapes of Wrath*   193

8. *Native Son*   237

PART IV. **A Radical Cognitive Social Criticism**

9. Schema Criticism: Radical Cognitive Politics   287

viii Literature and Social Justice

Notes 297

Works Cited 303

Index 321

Preface

In "Why Literature Matters," Frederick Luis Aldama asks:

> To what degree can reading works of fiction affect us in a lasting way?
> . . . What happens to our sense of right and wrong after we've finished
> reading [novels about social injustice] and entered the real world again?
> Do we now see the world differently and have a different sense of right
> and wrong? Does this lead to some sort of action? . . . Is it really possi-
> ble for our work as scholars and teachers of literature to influence and
> single-handedly transform the values and attitudes of the many millions
> of people required for real social transformation? (Aldama 253, 270)

Literature and Social Justice offers a scientifically informed, evidence-
based affirmative answer to these crucial questions, arguing that literature has the *potential*—albeit largely unrealized—to produce lasting,
socially transformative psychological changes in readers. Drawing on
cognitive science and other social and behavioral sciences, this book provides empirically grounded support for and elaboration of claims made
by Martha Nussbaum, Elizabeth Ammons, and others that literary texts
have the potential to "transform people" in socially crucial ways (Ammons ix), and it develops a detailed, systematic critical strategy for maximizing and extending this potential.

Social criticism in its various forms, including feminist, gender, queer,
and postcolonialist approaches, has long recognized that social injustice
is grounded in faulty and unjust perceptions, judgments, beliefs, and
feelings about the other, and that correcting these faulty cognitions is
key to reducing injustice. But social criticism to date has lacked an ade-

quate understanding of the nature and functioning of these faulty cognitions, and consequently its attempts to correct them have not been as effective as they could be.

The aim of *Literature and Social Justice* is to present a new, more effective method of social criticism, called "schema criticism." Grounded in cognitive science and American protest novels, schema criticism promises to be significantly more productive in promoting social justice than past and current methods have been, because it makes use of new knowledge concerning the cognitive structures and processes that constitute the psychological roots of unjust and harmful social policies, institutions, systems, and structures. Based on this new understanding of the cognitive roots of injustice, schema criticism adopts the principles of schema therapy and learning theory and adapts them to the task of altering these root cognitive structures in ways that eliminate key misunderstandings concerning other people that give rise to social injustice at all levels and in all areas of the social order, ranging from the capitalist economic system to civil and criminal law, the judicial and penal systems, and U.S. military, welfare, economic, and financial policies, institutions, and systems.

Schema criticism incorporates several key findings of cognitive science in order to produce a more effective social criticism. The first is that the misunderstandings concerning other people that lead to injustice are the result not just of faulty group (ethnic, national, class, gender, sexual orientation) stereotypes but also of much more general stereotypes, or cognitive schemas, concerning human nature, or persons in general. These general person-schemas—or "implicit person theories," as psychologists sometimes call them—form the core of negative group stereotypes, but they also exist and function independently of them, distorting our understanding and actions regarding others even when no specific group stereotypes are operating. Research in cognitive science has identified four faulty person-schemas that distort our understanding of other people in ways that lead to profound injustices in policies, institutions, and systems concerning such issues as commerce, ownership, taxation, government assistance, criminal justice, education, health care, and international relations.

- The *autonomy schema* embodies the assumption that an individual's character is the primary cause of his or her behaviors and life outcomes and that the role of circumstances is negligible. By blinding people to the role of the situation in determining behavior and life outcomes, the autonomy schema leads them to commit what psychologists call the "fundamental attribution error," continually concluding that poor, marginalized, or stigmatized individuals and groups are responsible for their "bad behavior" and inferior stations in life and that people who have exhibited "good behavior" and attained success deserve full credit for their good fortune. This conclusion, in turn, leads to social policies, institutions, and structures that stigmatize, neglect, and/or punish the unfortunate and maintain poverty and inequality in the United States and around the world. Justice requires that the autonomy schema be countered by a *situationism* schema, which takes into account the profound effects that situations have on behaviors and life outcomes.

- The *essentialism schema* holds that individuals are born a certain way, not made the way they are by their formative experiences and environment. By systematically preventing recognition of the formative effects of environment on character, essentialism fosters the view that people are somehow responsible for their own character and are thus fully and solely deserving of whatever benefits they derive from their strengths and virtues and whatever hardships or punishments result from their weaknesses or vices. This view, in turn, leads people to respond to social problems such as poverty, crime, violence, drug abuse, war, and terrorism with (largely ineffective and unjust) vindictive and punitive measures instead of much more effective and just preventive and rehabilitative interventions. To do justice to people, we need to employ a *malleability* schema, which recognizes the significant degree to which people's characters are formed by environmental forces over which they have no control.

- The *atomism schema* frames individuals as fundamentally separate and competitive, and not united and cooperative. This person-schema obscures one's inherent sameness and interconnectedness with all other human beings and supports the view that individuals are essentially and indefeasibly isolated from each other. Seen through the distorting lens of atomism, life is a war of each against all, and any cooperation is merely a means of furthering one's competitive advantage. In producing this vision of persons, the atomism schema potentiates infrahumanization and dehumanization of the other, which further enables various forms of indifference and aggression toward the other, including the Social Darwinism that has plagued the United States in varying degrees for well over a century. For justice to prevail, we need a *solidarity* schema, which allows us to apprehend the ontological, neurological-psychological-emotional, and practical connectedness of all human beings.

- The *homogeneity schema* reduces people to "all good" or "all bad," blocking awareness of the negative qualities of some individuals and groups (usually one's own) as well as the positive qualities of others (usually members of out-groups). This dichotomous categorization of people enables the division of the moral landscape into "us" versus "them," as in the terrorists' division of the world into the faithful and the infidels, and George W. Bush's declarations that "we" Americans are good, peaceful, freedom-loving people, while "they," the "terrorists" and their supporters, are evil people who hate our freedoms. This absolute distinction between "us" and "them" works, like the atomism schema, to deny our common humanity and foster infrahumanization and dehumanization, which are often followed by indifference or violence. Justice requires that we develop a *heterogeneity* schema that provides us with the capacity to recognize the good and the bad in everyone.

These general person-schemas determine our perceptions, judgments, emotions, and actions (including collective actions) regarding other people by controlling the multiple micro-cognitions through which we process information about people. Such acts of micro-processing include expectation, attention, information search, memory encoding, memory retrieval, inference, supposition, emotion, and action-script retrieval. Social criticism must correct faults in these micro information-processing steps if it is to be fully effective. This means that social criticism cannot limit itself simply to critiquing false stereotypes, images, or representations of particular groups. Rather, the faulty general person-schemas that control the micro information-processing routines must be countered with schemas that take account of the crucial information about other people that the faulty schemas systematically and harmfully obscure.

And this means correcting three basic types of knowledge structures, apart from propositional knowledge, that govern these micro acts of information processing: prototypes, exemplars, and information-processing scripts or routines. Cognitive schemas, that is, are composed not just of propositional, declarative knowledge but of other types of knowledge as well, including not only multiple information-processing scripts but also various exemplars and prototypes of concepts, individuals, body images, episodes, life stories, emotions, and actions, all of which can influence each step of information processing, from expectation to action-script retrieval.

Correcting faulty exemplars, prototypes, and information-processing routines cannot usually be accomplished simply by means of evidence, logic, and rational argument. This is because these nonpropositional types of knowledge are based not primarily in semantic memory but rather in episodic and procedural memory. Altering exemplars and prototypes requires accumulating, through multiple experiences, more accurate exemplars (which gradually form prototypes as they accumulate). And correcting faulty information-processing scripts requires constructing and practicing more adequate routines, just as one must do in order to develop an optimal fingering technique for a musical instrument or a more effective swing of a bat, club, or racquet.

From the perspective of this understanding of the cognitive roots of social injustice, literature emerges as a privileged site for promoting social justice by correcting the faulty cognitive structures that are ultimately responsible for injustice. Literature is in a privileged position to foster these corrections because, unlike other discourses, it routinely operates with and on all forms of exemplars and prototypes, as well as leading readers through, or inducing them to perform, each step of information processing.

The question, then, is whether literature actually engages readers in any of the processes that psychologists have found to be necessary for correcting faulty and harmful cognitive schemas. An examination of three major protest novels in light of the understanding of person-schemas just sketched out provides an affirmative answer, revealing that these novels do virtually all of the things that cognitive scientists and schema therapists have found to be necessary and sufficient for altering faulty and harmful cognitive schemas: they provide multiple alternative exemplars in all forms, they engage readers in repeatedly performing more adequate routines for processing information about other people, and they help readers develop metacognition concerning their own social information processing.

The first chapter of *Literature and Social Justice* provides a more systematic and detailed account of the preceding points. The next four chapters, which constitute part II, draw on studies in social cognition, social neuroscience, evolutionary psychology, political psychology, and psychoanalysis to provide extensive expositions of the nature, falseness, harmful social consequences, modes of operation, sources, and corrective measures for the four faulty person-schemas. The three chapters of part III are devoted to demonstrations of how three major American protest novels—Upton Sinclair's *The Jungle*, John Steinbeck's *The Grapes of Wrath*, and Richard Wright's *Native Son*—work to replace the misleading exemplars, prototypes, and information-processing routines of the four faulty person-schemas with more adequate counterparts, a process that constitutes a radical cognitive politics in pursuit of social justice. Part IV consists of the final chapter, which formalizes the schema-changing operations promoted by these novels into a method of social criticism that I call schema criticism, which can be employed not only with protest novels but also with other literary genres and modes of discourse and, most crucially, in direct response to unjust social policies, institutions, systems, and structures as well.

Any number of people, including many scholars and critics, are becoming increasingly frustrated with "academics comfortably situated in their corner of the world destabilizing the symbolic while real oppression and exploitation of real people continue" (Aldama 273). As Elizabeth Ammons laments, "We live in a time of retreat among professional humanists into increasingly conservative, socially disengaged positions that close out the majority of people and mistake rhetoric for action. Skepticism and endless critical thinking for its own sake have become goods in and of themselves, while the power of the humanities to teach us how to change the world for the better gets lost" (Ammons 98). Ammons contends that most humanists do believe that literature can improve life on this planet. "If we did not believe that," she argues, "few of us would devote our energy to the odd lifelong work of reading, teaching, and writing about ideas and words. Yet," she observes, "too many progressive teachers shy away from talking head-on about the power of the humanities, and literature in particular, to contribute to the activist struggle for progressive social change by transforming people's hearts and minds" (Ammons 47). One reason many humanists eschew this urgent task is the lack of a credible strategy by which it might be accomplished (see Harpham, *Humanities* 27). It is my hope and belief that readers will find such a strategy in the following pages.

Acknowledgments

The greatest intellectual debt that I owe for this book is to Martha Nussbaum, whose *Poetic Justice* opened my eyes to fundamental ways in which certain types of literary texts can promote the development of specific cognitive habits and capabilities that are virtual prerequisites for social justice. In addition, many students and colleagues offered helpful encouragement and criticism during the decade-long development of the theory and method of schema criticism presented here. Among the most noteworthy are Tammy Clewell, Ron Corthell, Kevin Floyd, and Bob Samuels. During the final revisions, Patrick Colm Hogan provided invaluable advice and encouragement.

I also thank Hogan and his coeditors Arturo Aldama and Frederick Luis Aldama for endorsing this book for their Cognitive Approaches to Literature and Culture series, and Jim Burr, senior editor at the University of Texas Press, for masterfully shepherding the manuscript through the evaluation and approval process.

I thank HarperCollins and Random House U.K. for permission to reproduce passages from *Native Son*, and Penguin U.S.A. and Penguin U.K. for permission to quote passages from *The Grapes of Wrath*. Portions of Chapter 1 and Chapter 6 appeared in my article "Schema Criticism: Literature, Cognitive Science, and Social Change," published in *College Literature*. I am grateful to this journal and its editor, Graham MacPhee, for permission to reproduce this material here.

Literature and Social Justice

PART I

THE PSYCHOLOGICAL BASIS FOR A COGNITIVE POLITICS OF SOCIAL JUSTICE

CHAPTER 1

Cognitive Science for a New Social Criticism

Deficiencies of Traditional Social Criticism

In the 1970s, spurred by second-wave feminism and a resurgent Marxism, social change emerged as an important goal of literary and cultural criticism, with ideology critique being viewed as the primary means of producing it. Judith Fetterley, to take a prominent feminist example, declared in 1978 that "at its best, feminist criticism is a political act whose aim is not simply to interpret the world but to change it" (Fetterley viii), and by the 1980s, many critics were boldly embracing social change as a central goal of criticism.

Frank Lentricchia's widely read *Criticism and Social Change* (1983) echoed Fetterley in asserting that "the point is not only to interpret texts, but in so interpreting them, to change our society" and maintained that ideology critique, through exposing the social struggles that canonical literature and interpretation worked to obscure, would help readers "spot, confront, and work against the political horrors of one's time" (Lentricchia 10–12). Similar positions were taken by Fredric Jameson in *The Political Unconscious* (1981) and by Terry Eagleton in the "Political Conclusion" to *Literary Theory* (1983) and in *The Function of Criticism* (1984), as well as by other feminists, such as Patrocinio Schweickart, who wrote in 1986 that "the point is not merely to interpret literature in various ways; the point is to *change the world*" (Schweickart 39; emphasis in original). But as these critics and others recognized, if literary study is to contribute to social or political change, it must do so by changing readers: "Literature acts on the world by acting on its readers," as Schweickart put it (39), thus producing "new forms of subjectivity," to use a phrase of Foucault's adopted by Eagleton (*Function* 116).

4 The Psychological Basis for a Cognitive Politics of Social Justice

And ideology critique lacked a theory of subjectivity, as Jameson and others have noted regarding Marxism in particular.

The logical place to look for such a theory was of course psychoanalysis, and Jameson, in particular, explored the possibility of adapting certain psychoanalytic concepts to the needs of social criticism. The main problem with this tack, however, as Jameson observed at the beginning of his essay on Lacan, was "the difficulty of providing mediations between social phenomena and what must be called private, rather than even merely individual, facts" (Jameson, "Imaginary" 338). And such mediations were not forthcoming. Julia Kristeva's claim in *Revolution in Poetic Language* (1974; translated into English in 1984) that disruptive linguistic practices in avant-garde poetry produce new forms of subjectivity having revolutionary ramifications had little evidentiary support, while the work of the most prominent American psychoanalytic critic of the 1970s and 1980s, Norman Holland, purported to demonstrate that reading experiences don't change people or even engage them in collective concerns so much as offer them an opportunity to rehearse their own idiosyncratic identity themes (Holland, "Unity" and "Why"), a conclusion that made the possibility of a psychoanalytic mediation between the psychological and the social appear highly unlikely. Nor has the work of the most prominent psychoanalytic cultural critic of the past two decades, Slavoj Zizek, offered any strategies for producing new forms of subjectivity that would lead to social change. Indeed, as Rita Felski has recently noted, psychoanalysis is not "especially well suited for fine-grained descriptions of the affective attachments and cognitive reorientations that characterize the experience of reading a book or watching a film" (Felski 11).

Despite their not having a comprehensive theory of subjectivity, social critics recognize that faulty knowledge about certain groups of people plays a major role in social injustice, and these critics have worked diligently to identify, expose, denounce, and correct inaccuracies, distortions, and omissions in people's understanding of women and non-heterosexual, non-white, non-European, and non-middle-class people. These efforts have rarely, if ever, produced the desired results, however, and there is good evidence that they are incapable of doing so. The reason is that faulty knowledge and beliefs about other people involve more than falsifiable propositions that are susceptible to correction by rational argument and evidence (see Meyers; Gardner; Levy; and Smith and DeCoster).

Foucault recognized this fact, and it seemed for a time that Foucauldian theory might be able to mediate the psychological and the social in a manner that could constitute a basis for an effective criticism for social change. Foucault appeared to offer a remedy for both the ineffectiveness of ideology critique and its theoretical deficiencies (deficiencies magnified by Foucault's stinging criticism of Marxist notions of history, ideology, and power, all of which he demonstrated to be more multifarious, "micro-physical," and mutually interconstitutive than ideology critique had acknowledged). With regard to literature specifically, while both Marxist and psychoanalytic theories had failed to provide a convincing explanation of how literature or criticism of it could alter readers' forms of subjectivity in ways that would lead to social change, the Foucauldian discourse–knowledge–power triad seemed to provide the basis for such an explanation: discourse (including literature and criticism) not only serves and expresses power, it also embodies and produces it, by constructing and regulating knowledge, a central element of subjectivity and thus a key determinant of behavior.

New Historicist criticism enthusiastically embraced these ideas. Drawing on Foucault's reconceptualization of power as a network of capillary forces with multiple types and points of generation, transmission, and resistance—including discourse, along with other techniques, technologies, apparatuses, practices, and disciplines—rather than as a monolithic force emanating from a single source such as the state, New Historicism offered a significant advance in our understanding of literature's relation to power.[1] More specifically, in focusing on the ways literary texts engage with "the processes by which social subjects are formed, re-formed, and enabled to perform" and in "foreground[ing] the differential subject positions from which readers read, and into which they are maneuvered during the process of reading" (Montrose 16, 26), New Historicist criticism appeared to possess the means by which literary study might promote the new forms of subjectivity that would lead to significant social change.

Here too, however, practice failed to achieve the goal. New Historicist criticism operated on the assumption that "construing literature as an unstable and agonistic field of verbal and social practices" (Montrose 30) would "bring to our students and to ourselves a sense of our own historicity, an apprehension of our positionings within ideology," thus "demonstrating the limited but nevertheless tangible possibility of contesting the regime of power and knowledge that at once sustains us and constrains us" (Montrose 31). The problem with this strategy is that even if criticism does successfully "demonstrat[e] the . . . possibility of con-

6 The Psychological Basis for a Cognitive Politics of Social Justice

testing the regime of power and knowledge," such a demonstration still leaves us a good distance from social change. For *simply being aware* of the historicity—the arbitrariness, contingency, and socially constructed nature—of our social positionings and our subjective dispositions does not in and of itself lead to the sorts of adjustments in emotions and behaviors toward other people that result in social change.

This is the impasse not only of New Historicist criticism specifically but also of Foucauldian theory and practice generally: while it can produce intricate and massive archaeological excavations, which can in turn facilitate the construction of genealogies that reveal the arbitrary and constructed nature of regimes of truth and knowledge that had appeared natural, universal, and/or immutable, such exposure does not by itself even change these regimes, much less alter behavior. And Foucauldian theory is finally incapable of providing a strategy for doing so. The reason lies not only in Foucault's aversion to making normative judgments, which any agenda of social change necessarily presupposes, but also, and more crucially, in the fact that his theory fails to provide an adequate mediation of the psychological and the social. More specifically, Foucauldian theory, like Marxist theory and psychoanalysis, cannot explain how reading and analyzing literary texts and other discourses can produce the sorts of alterations of knowledge and belief that will lead to the kinds of behavioral modifications that result in social change. And in the case of Foucauldian (and Marxist) theory, this inability is based on a more fundamental deficiency: the absence of an account of the operations of the human mind. For although Foucault emphasizes the role of discourse, knowledge, and other implements of power in producing the soul (psyche), he says little about the nature of this psyche or how it variously produces, maintains, transmits, is produced by, and sometimes alters specific forms and elements of discourse, knowledge, and power. As J. M. Balkin has pointed out, "Foucault does not seem to have any theory of internal mental processes or cognitive structure. . . . He simply takes for granted that mechanisms of socialization and cognition supply whatever is necessary for disciplines of power/knowledge to have their requisite effects" (Balkin 267). This is a fatal deficiency,[2] for, as Balkin rightly contends,

> disciplines and practices cannot have these effects unless they are understood and internalized by individuals with a cognitive apparatus. Social construction on the order that Foucault proposes requires elaborate mechanisms of understanding that must perform a great deal of work

in shaping and constituting the individual's identity and thought. Foucault's account lacks any description or concern with these internal cognitive processes [that account for . . .] how each individual processes information. (Balkin 267)

Thus literary criticism after Foucault still lacks a viable, coherent strategy for facilitating social change, because it still lacks an understanding of how discourse — including literature and criticism — can (re)form subjectivity in socially consequential ways.

What Cognitive Science Offers

Cognitive science offers valuable new resources in this regard. Research has clarified four crucial features of social cognition — the processes through which we perceive, understand, and judge other people — that can provide the foundation for a more effective practice of social criticism. This research indicates, first, that the ultimate source of distorted, harmful assessments that people make about each other is not stereotypes per se, but certain faulty "knowledge" or beliefs about "human nature," or persons in general, that both form the core of negative group stereotypes and also operate independently of stereotypes (see Levy; Henry et al.). Second, cognitive research has emphasized that our knowledge of people, including beliefs about human nature or persons in general, exists not just in propositional form but also in multiple other forms that often serve as more powerful determinants of perception, judgment, emotion, and behavior than does propositional knowledge. Third, cognitive science has revealed that knowledge is not simply a static, continuously existing entity stored in some warehouse of memory; rather it is, like memory itself, produced or assembled for the nonce by information-processing routines (themselves the result of countless neural networks distributed throughout the brain) that are activated whenever we assess other people's behavior or character. And fourth, these information-processing routines, along with the multiple other types and forms of knowledge that both govern them and are (re)produced by them, cannot usually be altered solely by the operations of critique — that is, by evidence, argument, or correct propositional knowledge. Rather, they must be altered through cognitive retraining, ideally in conjunction with the development of metacognition. Consider each of these findings in turn.

Fundamental Beliefs about Persons in General, or Human Nature

As noted in the preface, four key faulty assumptions about persons in general, or human nature, have been identified that lead people to support harmful and unjust social policies, institutions, and systems. Once again, these are

1. *Autonomy*: the assumption that an individual's character is the primary cause of his or her behaviors and life outcomes and that circumstances are not a major factor.
2. *Essentialism*: the conviction that upbringing and environment play no significant role in forming one's character and that individuals themselves therefore bear the primary responsibility for the type of person they are.
3. *Atomism*: the view that individuals are fundamentally separate and competitive, not united and cooperative, and that life is thus a war of each against all and that any cooperation is merely a means of furthering one's individual competitive advantage.
4. *Homogeneity*: the belief that people can be adequately categorized as simply good or bad—as in, "We are good, peace-loving people; they are evil people who hate our freedoms."

As I will explain in Chapters 2 through 5, each of these assumptions has been shown to be false and to lead to inaccurate judgments about other people that result in harmful and unjust social actions, policies, institutions, and structures. The degree to which assumptions about human nature can have real-world consequences is not always recognized, but as the following chapters will show, the impact is considerable. As economist Robert H. Frank points out, "Views about human nature are not merely a subject of debate among behavioral scientists. They also have practical consequences, including the way corporations treat their workers and customers, as well as the foreign, economic, and tax policies of a society" (Frank xi). Stephan Chorover traces the consequences of assumptions about human nature even further, arguing in *From Genes to Genocide: The Meaning of Human Nature and the Power of Behavior Control* that such assumptions have "a powerful influence upon social expectations," which "shape the ways in which people in a given social context are treated . . . [and therefore] significantly influence how they behave." Such beliefs are thus "powerful instruments of behavior control . . . [and thus] have been fostered since antiquity for the sole purpose of justifying the power of some people to control the behavior of others" (Chorover 4–5). Chorover notes that "dominant groups will propagate whichever myths about human nature justify [current social] structures as 'natural'" (Chorover 22). From Plato to the present, claims about human nature have been used "to justify as inevitable the concentration of social, political, and economic power in the hands of those who are alleged to be the inherently deserving" (Chorover 26; see also Lewontin et al. 72–74, 239–246). "Of all the ideas by which human behavior can be shaped," Chorover argues, "by far the most important and most persuasive (if not always the most credible) are the ones that purport to define what it means to be a human being" (Chorover 13).

This is not to say that faulty and harmful assumptions about persons are merely the product of the interests of certain groups of people. As we will see in the following chapters, these beliefs also derive from certain innate features of human cognition, as well as from various contingent cultural and psychological factors that are at most only partly and tenuously produced by the power interests of a particular group.

Nor is it to say that to avoid the misunderstandings and injustices that are produced by these false views of human nature we need simply to abandon the idea of a human nature. As Steven Pinker explains in *The Blank Slate: The Modern Denial of Human Nature*, this strategy has been dominant among many intellectuals for decades, due to their belief that "to acknowledge human nature . . . is to endorse racism, sexism, war, greed, genocide, nihilism, reactionary politics, and neglect of children and the disadvantaged" (Pinker viii). Pinker argues convincingly that these feared dangers result from the *mis*recognition rather than the *recognition* of human nature. He points out that the claim that there is no human nature—that humans are a blank slate, an infinitely malleable species—is itself a claim about human nature, which, moreover, "has done harm to the lives of real people" by enabling unrealistic and misguided hopes and social projects (Pinker x–xi). "Everyone has a theory of human nature," Pinker observes, and it's a good thing that we do: "Everyone has to anticipate the behavior of others, and that means we all need theories about what makes people tick" (Pinker 1). In addition, "every society must operate with a theory of human nature" (Pinker 2) as a necessary foundation for its policies, institutions, and systems:

> Our theory of human nature is the wellspring of much in our lives. . . .
> Its assumptions about learning drive our educational policy; its assumptions about motivation drive our policies on economics, law, and crime.

> And because it delineates what people can achieve easily, what they can achieve only with sacrifice or pain, and what they cannot achieve at all, it affects our values: what we believe we can reasonably strive for as individuals and as a society. (Pinker 1)

Indeed, without some theory of human nature, however implicit or unconscious, we would be unable to distinguish a person from a bear, a tree, or a rock and hence would have no basis for discriminatory feelings, thoughts, and actions regarding these different kinds of being. The solution to the problem of the oppressive role played by the concept of human nature is thus not to deny that such a thing as human nature exists, but to correct the faulty beliefs about human nature that are responsible for the oppression.

Types and Forms of Knowledge

Unfortunately, correcting these faulty beliefs cannot be accomplished solely by evidence and argument. The problem is not merely that many people—such as those under the spells of fundamentalist religion on the right or absolute cultural relativism on the left—simply reject evidence and argument, though that is certainly a concern.[3] The real issue is that such faulty assumptions are encoded not just in propositional form but in other modes as well, including concepts, episode scripts, life scripts, prototypic individuals, prototypic images, prototypic emotions, and action scripts.[4] And these other modes of knowledge are more directly linked to emotions, which are not only a form of knowledge themselves but also the proximal motivator and determinant of much human behavior.[5]

This difference between persuading people that their assumptions are untrue, on the one hand, and changing their faulty cognitive apparatuses and hence their behavior, on the other, is quite important and consequential. It is the difference between persuading phobic individuals that they really have nothing to fear and helping them actually get rid of their fear and their phobic behavior, or between convincing depressed people that their lives and prospects are actually pretty good and getting them to stop feeling despair and living fatalistically (see Beck). It is also the difference between persuading white people that African Americans are in no way inferior and changing the way white people process information about African Americans, so that they do not produce flawed and unjust judgments, emotions, and actions regarding them. Studies have shown that white people can be convinced that blacks are their equals, but still produce prejudiced judgments, feelings, and behaviors regarding them. Persuasion may get rid of traditional racism, but it often leaves in place various forms of "modern" racism, including aversive racism (see Jones 126–130).

As the feminist philosopher Diana Tietjens Meyers has noted, one reason prejudice is so intractable is that it operates "without obliging anyone to formulate, accept, or reject repugnant negative propositions about any group's standing" (53). This is because prejudice, as Meyers explains, is enacted largely through other forms of knowledge, including imagery, figurative concepts (e.g., women as "foxes," "chicks," "babes," or "bitches"), prototypic figures such as the saintly mother and the evil witch, and ideal and cautionary narrative prototypes articulating stereotypical relationships and actions of these mythical types. It is these non-propositional forms of faulty knowledge about other people that render faulty and harmful social judgments so difficult to eliminate: "It is not possible to refute [them] with counterexamples or statistics, . . . [because] empirically grounded arguments attacking propositional paraphrases of these figurations fail to make contact with their emotional underpinnings" (Meyers 55–56).

The emotions and other forms of nonpropositional knowledge are key, because social action is often driven much more by these forms of knowledge about other people than by propositional knowledge or beliefs. This point has been powerfully demonstrated in recent books by Drew Westen and George Lakoff. In *The Political Brain: The Role of Emotion in Deciding the Fate of the Nation*, Westen shows that people's positions with regard to social issues and policies, as well as political parties, platforms, and candidates, are determined more by the emotions they feel toward these things than by evidence and logical thought. He argues that the reason right-wing policies and candidates have dominated American politics for the past generation is because they have appealed to voters' emotions, whereas Democrats have based their appeals primarily on reason and evidence: "Republicans understand . . . that reason is a slave to emotion. . . . With the exception of the Clinton era, Democratic strategists for the last three decades have instead clung tenaciously to the dispassionate view of the mind and to the campaign strategy that logically follows from it, namely one that focuses on facts, figures, policy statements, costs and benefits, and appeals to intellect and expertise" (Westen 15). "The brain," Westen explains, "gravitates toward solutions designed to match not only data but desire, by spreading activation to [neural] networks that lead to conclusions associated with positive emotions and inhibiting networks that would lead to negative emotions" (Westen 100). This means that the most effective political persuasion is that which either activates, creates, or reinforces neural networks that produce positive feelings about one's own position and negative feelings about the opponent's (Westen 85). Republicans understand much better than Democrats that the primary way to activate these networks is by using emotion-bearing images and narrative frames and that to create new networks they must identify constituents' key values and principles and "weave them into a story [narrative frame] that resonates with the average American" (Westen 165).

Lakoff makes a similar argument in *The Political Mind: Why You Can't Understand 21st-Century American Politics with an 18th-Century Brain*. Progressives, he declares, have been operating with an outdated, "false view of reason" and have thus "ceded the political mind to radical conservatives" (Lakoff 2). This false view, which assumes "that reason is conscious, literal, logical, unemotional, disembodied, universal, and functions to serve our interests," not only "does not account for real political behavior" (Lakoff 3, 8), but also leads progressives to assume that appeals to facts and logic will carry the day (Lakoff 12). Progressives need to realize that the persuasive power of language comes not primarily from evidence and logic but rather from the "frames, prototypes, metaphors, narratives, images, and emotions" it engages (Lakoff 15). Instead of appealing only to facts and logic, they need to frame and reframe issues in such a manner that reveals the truth about these issues in emotionally compelling ways.

Much of the effort of Lakoff and Westen is devoted to variously repositioning conservative and progressive policies in relation to hegemonic images, narratives, and prototypes. "Schema criticism," in contrast, aims to replace hegemonic images, narratives, and prototypes with more adequate ones. What schema criticism shares with the approaches of Westen and Lakoff is the recognition that attempting to refute or alter faulty propositional knowledge, as social criticism has traditionally done, will not change harmful social attitudes, practices, policies, institutions, systems, and structures as long as other forms of knowledge remain intact and continue to govern people's information processing and hence their emotions and behaviors. Preventing unjust treatment of others, whether in public policies or in private actions, therefore requires a radical cognitive politics: a strategy of intervention that corrects not just faulty propositional knowledge but also the multiple faulty nonpropositional forms of knowledge that constitute the roots of false and unjust perceptions, judgments, feelings, actions, and policies concerning other people.

Both cognitive theory and the practice of cognitive therapy indicate that elimination of unjust attitudes requires, more specifically, modifying four basic types of knowledge, each of which has multiple forms. These four types include:

- Specific instances of individuals, or *exemplars*, which are a function of episodic memory systems,[6]
- General types of individuals, or *prototypes*, which are a function of semantic memory,
- Know-how in the form of *information-processing routines*, which are a function of procedural memory systems, and
- *Propositional knowledge*, including metacognition, which is based in semantic memory.

Exemplars are memories of particular individuals and events, while prototypes are composites (average or standard cases) of multiple exemplars that form in semantic memory when a critical mass of exemplars for a particular category has been encoded in episodic memory.[7] Information-processing routines are a form of procedural knowledge that, like other instances of procedural knowledge such as those involved in playing a musical instrument or driving a car, operate largely automatically and outside of awareness—as exemplars and prototypes tend to do as well. Information-processing routines can, however, be influenced and altered by both semantic knowledge and episodic knowledge—as when, for example, we observe that a young state legislator appears very senatorial (prototype) or reminds us of a young John F. Kennedy (exemplar) and then begin to notice, remember, infer, and/or suppose additional senator-like or Kennedy-like features in the individual, or when we employ metacognition to explicitly formulate (often with the help of teachers or coaches) revisions or alternatives to current procedures (e.g., a different fingering technique on a musical instrument or a different swing of a baseball bat, golf club, or tennis racquet). Conversely, information-processing routines themselves function to produce particular types of exemplars—and hence prototypes as well—by directing attention to certain features, ignoring or discounting other features, and so on.

Together these four types of knowledge constitute cognitive schemas. "Cognitive schemas," in my usage of the term,[8] are functional (rather than neurological) constructs[9] designating the multiple types and forms of previously acquired knowledge concerning a particular category, which are "stored" in multiple systems and locations in the brain and which guide the processing of information about each phenomenon we encounter. Thus whenever we encounter or think of a person (or an object, action, or event), one or more cognitive schemas are activated. These schemas are absolutely essential to our functioning in the world; they are what enable us to quickly identify and appropriately respond to people, objects, and events. But essential as they are, they can also distort our perception and understanding by causing us to ignore important information, to falsely infer, remember, or suppose facts that do not exist, or to connect or dissociate bits of information in tendentious, flawed, and harmful ways.

Some person-schemas are of particular types of people, but others concern people in general. These general person-schemas, or "implicit person theories," as they are sometimes called (see Levy et al. 179), constitute key assumptions about human nature (or human nature in conjunction with the human condition), and they in many ways exert even greater influence on social perception and judgment than particular stereotypes do. The four faulty person-schemas identified above systematically produce misunderstandings of self and others that, in turn, lead to unjust social policies, institutions, and systems. They do so not only directly but also indirectly, through their role in negative group stereotypes as well as in the moral frames discussed by Lakoff (see Reyna et al.; Levy et al.; Henry et al.). The first two schemas listed below, those of autonomy and essentialism, are responsible for the mistaken judgments that individuals deserve full blame for their failures and full credit for their successes, while the last two, those of atomism and homogeneity, blind people to the profound sameness and interconnectedness they share with all other humans and thus validate and reinforce intergroup hatred and selfish, chauvinistic actions and policies:

1. The *autonomy* schema blinds people to the role of circumstances in determining behavior and life outcomes and leads them to continually conclude that poor and marginalized individuals and groups are responsible for their "bad behavior" and inferior stations in life and that people who have exhibited "good behavior" and attained success deserve full credit for their good fortune. This conclusion, in turn, produces social policies that stigmatize, neglect, and/or punish the

unfortunate and maintain poverty and inequality in the United States and around the world (see Fineman; Ryan; and Lewis).

2. The *essentialism* schema systematically prevents recognition of the formative effects of environment on character, promulgating the view that people are somehow responsible for their own character and that their formative experiences and environment played little or no role in determining the type of person they have become. This view, in turn, leads people to respond to social problems such as poverty, crime, violence, drug abuse, war, and terrorism with (largely ineffective) vindictive and punitive measures instead of much more effective and just preventive and rehabilitative interventions (see Levy et al. and Haslam et al.).

3. The *atomism* schema obscures one's inherent sameness and interconnectedness with all other human beings and supports the view that individuals are fundamentally separate and isolated from each other, that life is a war of each against all, and that any act of altruism or cooperation is simply a means to achieve dominance over others. In producing this vision of persons, the atomism schema potentiates infrahumanization and dehumanization of the other, which further enables various forms of indifference and aggression toward the other, including Social Darwinism (see Lukes 30; Iacoboni 152, 155, 271; Haslam; Levy et al.; Cialdini et al.; and Wolgast).

4. The *homogeneity* schema homogenizes self and other into all good or all bad, thus blocking awareness of one's own negative qualities as well as the positive qualities of others who may have evinced negative behaviors or character traits. The schema thus enables categorization of people as either good or bad, and the division of the moral landscape into "us" versus "them," as in the terrorists' division of the world into the faithful and the infidels, and George W. Bush's declarations that "we" Americans are good, peaceful, freedom-loving people, while "they," the terrorists and their supporters, are evil people who hate our freedoms. By enabling an absolute distinction between "us" and "them," the homogeneity schema thus denies our common humanity and, like the atomism schema, fosters infrahumanization and dehumanization and the often-ensuing indifference and violence (see Volkan; Robins and Post; Clarke; and Altman).

These general person-schemas govern both top–down and bottom–up processing of information about other people. They govern top–down processing from within specific stereotypes, such as the dominant ones for a welfare recipient or a homeless person, where they are embedded. That is, exemplars, prototypes, and information-processing routines, along with propositional knowledge, regarding specific categories of people such as the homeless, welfare recipients, and criminals are all influenced by assumptions about human nature embodied in the four general-person schemas (see Henry et al.; Reyna et al.; Levy et al.). Moreover, when no stereotype is operative and bottom–up processing occurs, these general person-schemas themselves function as the templates governing our perception and judgment whenever we apportion responsibility for success or failure and whenever we assess another individual's or group's inherent worth (which we do in part by judging their degree of overlap with ourselves). Altering these flawed and harmful schemas is thus a prerequisite for social justice.

As we have noted, however, altering a cognitive schema requires changing not just its explicit, propositional beliefs but also the three types of implicit knowledge it includes—prototypes, exemplars, and information-processing routines—each of which itself exists in multiple forms, any of which can exert significant distortive pressure on our information processing in any given instance, resulting in harmful and unjust emotions and actions concerning other people.[10]

PROTOTYPES

Much of our perception and assessment of other people is based on prototypes, our constructs of what we take to be the typical member of a particular category. Prototypes function as cognitive templates that guide our perceptions, judgments, emotions, and actions when we are dealing with people who fall into a category with which we are quite familiar. When a prototype is activated, it usually preempts further information processing (e.g., searching for new information, drawing additional or alternative inferences, analyzing the information, etc.) by providing us with a prefabricated assessment of the person along with an emotional response and an action tendency or script.

The most familiar prototypes are stereotypes.[11] Think of our culture's dominant stereotypes for welfare recipients, homeless people, or criminals. The stereotype many white people have of a welfare recipient is a person who is single, black, female, unemployed, lazy, self-indulgent, and overweight, and who lives with her multiple unruly children in the inner city (see Hancock). When a person who is guided by this stereotype thinks of public policy concerning welfare recipients, this prototype will often lead her to assume, without gathering any information whatsoever, that most welfare recipients are lazy, self-indulgent, and irresponsible, with little or no similarity to herself. And as a result of judging welfare recipients to be lazy, irresponsible, and other, the perceiver will experience negative emotions (disdain, contempt, anger, etc.) rather than compassion toward this group and proceed to support public policies that administer discipline and even punishment to them rather than aid. In such instances, the prototype may get the key facts about the welfare recipients at issue completely wrong: only a very small proportion of real welfare recipients actually fit the prototype of being lazy and irresponsible (most welfare recipients are children, many adult recipients are employed, and of the unemployed, most are unable to work or to find a job, etc.), and all of them have the same basic human needs as oneself. And as a consequence of her having gotten these key facts wrong, the perceiver's resulting emotional and behavioral responses—including the public policies that these responses support—are likely to be harmful, unjust, and socially and economically counterproductive.

Prototypes exist in multiple forms, any one of which can function as the default knowledge structure guiding perception, judgment, and action regarding other people. The autonomy prototype, for example, has the following forms:

- *Concepts,* such as autonomy, independence, self-reliance, and self-sufficiency, as well as derogatory counterparts such as laziness, self-indulgence, dependency, and parasitism.
- *Episode scripts,* such as determination-leads-to-success—that is, episodes in which character is shown to determine behavior no matter what the circumstances (*character→ circumstances→behavior*) and behavior is portrayed as determining success or failure no matter what the circumstances (*behavior→ circumstances→ success/failure*).
- *Life scripts,* such as the rags-to-riches life story, in which determination and hard work are shown to overcome all difficult circumstances and, conversely, the vice-to-downfall story, in which failure is shown to be the product of bad character squandering even the most propitious of circumstances.
- *Prototypic individuals,* such as the self-made man and the hero who overcomes all opposition and, conversely, the lazy, self-indulgent ne'er-do-well.
- *Prototypic body images,* such as confident, can-do voices, gazes, postures, and movements—as well as, conversely, their listless, passive, hopeless counterparts.

- *Prototypic emotions,* such as disdain and contempt for unsuccessful people and admiration and pride for successful people.
- *Action scripts* (in the form of social practices and policies) of neglect, discipline, and punishment of the unfortunate (e.g., refusing the jobless unemployment benefits) and further rewards for the fortunate (e.g., reducing their taxes even further).

EXEMPLARS

In some cases, instead of using prototypes, we use particular examples, or exemplars, as templates for perceiving and judging other people. Exemplars are not inherently more (or less) reliable than prototypes as processing guides, for they function in basically the same way as prototypes, often preempting further searching for information and immediately producing an emotional response and an action tendency. Exemplars can come from either direct or secondhand experience. Secondhand exemplars originate from literature, television, movies, folktales, stereotyping statements made by one's family and associates, and so on, and are often actually more numerous and prominent than firsthand exemplars (Linville and Fischer 92–93, 107). This means that the media and popular culture play a major role in the production of exemplars, and thus of prototypes as well (see Zillman and Brosius).

And it also means that literature has at least the potential to make significant contributions to an individual's store of exemplars and prototypes and through them, to his perceptions, judgments, and actions regarding other people. As Patrick Hogan states, "The characters and situations depicted in literature" are exemplars that "can function to guide both understanding and action" (Hogan, "Stories" 40). Hogan reasons that although "exempla[rs][12] from our own lives are likely to have predominant force in guiding ethical and other thought and action, . . . we know literary characters much better than we know almost any real people" and thus that "literary exempla[rs] are likely to have considerable force as well" (Hogan, "Stories" 40). Consequently, Hogan concludes, "literature produces its ethical effects, at least in part, by supplying us with cognitive exempla[rs]. . . . Once triggered, these exempla[rs] serve to guide our response to that person or situation. They serve to highlight certain aspects and obscure others, to fill in details, to associate emotions. . . . [And] the emotional valence of the exempl[ar] motivates spontaneous action toward the . . . person or situation" (Hogan, "Stories" 43, 47).

Exemplars become operative in cases where a fitting prototype is lacking, as well as in cases where a particular exemplar is especially accessible in memory (e.g., because of priming, recency of activation, or frequency of activation and hence chronic accessibility [see Shrum 72ff.]). Thus if a person has a close friend or family member on welfare, or has recently read a memorable account of a (real or fictional) welfare recipient, that single exemplar may override the dominant stereotype and function as a template for perceiving, judging, and responding to other welfare recipients. If the exemplar had to go on welfare because of an illness, a disability, or other circumstances over which he or she had no control, the perceiver will be more likely to at least consider the possibility that other welfare recipients might similarly be victims of circumstance and thus respond to them more with compassion and assistance than with the disdain and neglect or punishment triggered by the dominant cultural prototype, which attributes sole responsibility to the individual and ignores the situation. On the other hand, seeing a homeless black man with a young boy, for example, might remind some moviegoers of the example of Chris Gardner (as recounted in the film *Pursuit of Happyness*), who, although homeless and living in the subway with his young son, worked hard and became a successful stockbroker. On the basis of this exemplar, people may eschew any inquiry into the circumstances of the homeless father before them and simply leap to the conclusion that he could achieve the same success as Chris Gardner if he just worked harder.

Exemplars exist in the same multiple forms as prototypes. They include our episodic memories (which are themselves reconstructed for the nonce whenever they are recalled [see Hogan, *Cognitive* 161]) of particular episodes, life stories, individuals, body images, emotions, and actions. As is the case with prototypes, a faulty belief or "knowledge" such as that of autonomy—the assumption that individual behaviors and life outcomes are determined by character and not circumstances—can operate in each form of exemplar. To illustrate, consider the following exemplars of the autonomy assumption found in the early pages of Upton Sinclair's *The Jungle*:

- *Signifier* of the autonomy concept: powerful, prosperous, successful.
- Autonomy *episode*: Jurgis works hard on the railroad in Poland, earns good money, and through his own efforts and conscientiousness manages to outwit those who attempt to prey upon him and returns to Lithuania still in possession of his earnings.
- Autonomy *life story*: a Lithuanian acquaintance of Jurgis's family emigrates to America and through diligence and hard work prospers there.

- Autonomous *individual*: the successful Jurgis—e.g., Jurgis in the early days of his labor in the meatpacking plant.
- *Body image* of autonomy: the huge and powerful Jurgis standing out in the crowd or effortlessly carrying a quarter of beef.
- *Emotion* presupposing autonomy in self or others: Jurgis's pride in getting a job (a manifestation of the self's supposed autonomy); Jurgis's contempt for men who don't get jobs, readers' admiration for Jurgis, and their indifference or contempt toward the jobless (in response to others' supposed autonomy).
- *Action* responding to supposed autonomy (and entailed by the emotions thereby generated): Jurgis's strutting and swaggering at his own success, scoffing at those who are jobless, and attempting to solve his financial problems simply by working harder; readers' opposition to jobless and other welfare benefits.

Any exemplar of this sort can, like a prototype, function (often outside of our awareness) as a template for our perception of other people, causing us to ignore important information about their circumstances and/or to (inaccurately) interpolate, infer, or suppose key information about their character that is not given, and hence to have unjustified emotions about them that may in turn lead to unjust actions toward them. Thus when such individuals encounter or think about unsuccessful people—homeless people, for example—the activation of any one of these exemplars or prototypes can be sufficient to short-circuit a further information search and analysis and precipitate the conclusion that the plight of these people is their own fault. Such a judgment leads to emotions of indifference, contempt, or anger, which incline one toward actions of neglect, discipline, or punishment.

As noted above, even when people possess accurate abstract knowledge that refutes these exemplars and prototypes—for example, the knowledge that most welfare recipients are white, not black; are children, not adults; are employed (if adult), not unemployed; and live in rural rather than urban areas—the atypical exemplars and false prototypes will often (e.g., as a result of cognitive busyness or of self-affirmation needs) bypass this abstract knowledge and determine people's emotions and actions. And even when information processing is not short-circuited, each processing step can be constrained or misdirected by an atypical exemplar or faulty prototype. Each of the various exemplars and prototypes of the autonomy schema, for example, can prevent people from expecting, seeking, finding, focusing on, inferring, supposing, encoding in memory, or recalling the multiple ways in which a person's behavior and life outcomes are determined by circumstances rather than by the person's character.

INFORMATION-PROCESSING ROUTINES

Prototypes and exemplars produce what is known as top–down, or categorical, processing, in which a current object of perception is forced, Procrustean style, to fit a preexisting model. Not all perception and judgment proceed in a top–down manner, however. In cases where a person cannot be readily assimilated to either a prototype or an exemplar, either because these aren't available or because such assimilation is opposed by cognitive (including emotional and ethical) obstacles, information processing proceeds in a more systematic, bottom–up, manner.

In bottom–up processing, people are judged on the basis of their own actual qualities, rather than on the basis of the typical qualities attributed to a category to which they belong. In such cases, information processing is governed largely by cognitive routines, or scripts, established in one's procedural memory. There are cognitive scripts, for example, that determine what information we expect to find concerning a given phenomenon, what information we pay attention to and what we ignore, how we interpret ambiguous information, what inferences we draw from incomplete information, what suppositions we make in the absence of information, what kinds of information we search for, and what kinds of memories (exemplars) we retrieve.

Such bottom–up processing, however, is unfortunately also vulnerable to distortion and misdirection, and the four faulty person-schemas identified above constitute a major source of distortion. As one research team observes, "Such [person-schemas], although generally unconscious and unarticulated, contain key assumptions that can underlie different patterns of social information processing. . . . Fundamentally different perspectives on human nature are likely to spawn very different mental models about how humans function, and therefore very different [implicit] beliefs about what information is needed in order to understand and predict their behavior" (Levy, Plaks, and Dweck 179).

These schemas can distort the particular procedures of information processing in several different ways. First, a schema's inadequate exemplars or prototypes can unconsciously distort our information processing even if we have consciously rejected them (see Hogan, *Understanding* 47). In addition, a schema's faulty propositional knowledge can prevent even the most diligent investigation from reaching accurate conclusions about a person. Thus, for example, people who believe that disease is caused by sin will never think to look for (and hence will be extremely unlikely to discover) situational (e.g., environmental) causes such as polluted drinking water. And finally, the schema's systematic information-processing routines encoded in procedural memory may be inadequate for the task of acquiring and interpreting all the information necessary for making an accurate and fair assessment of any given individual or group.

Thus in addition to correcting atypical exemplars and false prototypes, it is also important to address faulty information-processing routines directly. Failure to do so is a third reason that the critique of flawed knowledge about people often fails to produce social change. Knowledge of other people is not simply a preconstituted static entity lying in the vaults of memory waiting to be retrieved and then utilized, altered, or destroyed; rather, it is a construct produced by multiple information-processing routines that are activated whenever we assess other people. As J. M. Balkin has pointed out, "The standard view of ideology as a collection of beliefs" does not provide an adequate basis for effectively opposing ideology, because the essence of ideology and the source of its power are "rooted in the very way in which we are able to process information" (Balkin 19). To understand ideology, we have to examine the "psychological and cognitive mechanisms that produce beliefs. . . . We must break down what previous thinkers have called ideology into distinct and analyzable mechanisms"—mechanisms that variously expect, notice, search for, infer, suppose, and remember information that confirms one's preexisting beliefs and screen out information that disconfirms these beliefs (Balkin 44, 1, 58, 102–104; see also Wells), producing what is known as confirmation bias (see Hogan, *Conformism* 74–77).

With regard to the autonomy schema, for example, this means recognizing and addressing the fact that people operating with autonomist processing routines *expect* there to be no significant situational determinants of behaviors or life outcomes, and because of this expectation, they often fail to *notice* situational factors even when they are apparent. As a result, homeless persons are seen as responsible for their fate because of their own supposed shiftlessness or laziness, and situational factors that caused the homelessness—such as an accident or illness that rendered them incapable of working and/or resulted in crippling medical expenses—are overlooked. When people operating with the autonomy schema do notice such situational factors, or are forced to notice them, they often discount the significance of these facts and focus their *attention* on character traits instead. Thus even when people consider a person whose homelessness they know was caused by bankruptcy brought about by overwhelming medical expenses, they may still blame her for this fate, criticizing her for not having better insurance or for not taking better care of herself in the first place.

Because they *expect* behavior and life outcomes to be determined by character traits, in the absence of evidence that such traits played a central role, individuals operating with the autonomy schema will often *search for* such traits—but not for situational determinants. Or they will simply *infer* or *suppose* the existence of character determinants, either because their search for evidence proved unproductive or because they are so confident in their general assumption of autonomy that they don't feel that specific evidence is necessary. They will not, however, make similar inferences or suppositions concerning the situational determinants of behavior or destiny. Thus when there is no clear evidence that a welfare recipient is lazy or self-indulgent, many people will simply infer that she has these traits on the basis of highly ambiguous data, such as the fact that she walks very slowly or spends a lot of time sleeping. And when there is no evidence even of the most ambiguous sort to support the inference that a behavior or life outcome is the result of character rather than situation, the autonomy schema will often fill the gap in information with the supposition that such character traits exist. Thus in the absence of any evidence that a homeless person has squandered his resources on alcohol or drugs, many people will nonetheless conclude that he has.

Often people reach or bolster such a conclusion by *recalling* other examples in which character supposedly determined behavior or life outcome. When they search their memories, they fail to retrieve any exemplars of behavior or destiny being determined by situational factors. They retrieve exemplars of presumably lazy, dissolute, or self-indulgent homeless persons, but no exemplars who were rendered homeless by forces beyond their control. Since the autonomy schema blocks awareness of situational factors, however, there is often no experience of such factors to remember. And on those relatively rare occasions when an individual does notice situational factors, the autonomy schema is likely to either prevent such instances from being *encoded in memory* or cause them to be encoded as special cases that do not disconfirm the principle of autonomy and that are therefore not retrieved from memory in future instances where the memory would be relevant.

Faulty Cognitive Schema—>Faulty Processing—>Misunderstanding—>Injustice

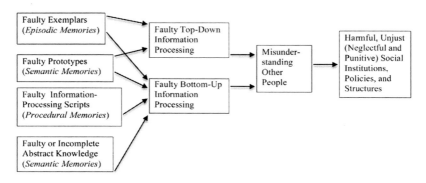

Diagram 1. Faulty information processing and its harmful and unjust consequences

Information processing is thus governed by—and is therefore subject to distortion by—the four basic factors, or forms of knowledge, we have discussed: exemplars, prototypes, information-processing routines, and abstract propositional knowledge. The diagram above indicates how these factors operate to produce faulty judgments that lead to social injustice.

In influencing each step of information processing, these various forms of "knowledge" lead people to continually misperceive and misjudge other people—as when they conclude, for example (in the case of the autonomy schema), that the marginalized and stigmatized individuals and groups they encounter are themselves responsible for their inferior stations in life and thus deserve no assistance, and that people who have attained success deserve full credit for their good fortune and thus should not be subjected to any redistribution of their wealth. These faulty conclusions, in turn, lead them to support social policies that stigmatize, neglect, and/or punish the unfortunate and maintain poverty and inequality (Fineman; Ryan; and Lewis). Correcting people's information processing to take adequate account of the crucial information concerning other people would thus contribute significantly to social justice and is arguably a prerequisite for it (see Ryan). The question, then, is how such faulty, harmful schemas can be corrected or replaced with more adequate person-schemas as default information-processing structures.

Principles of Schema Change

To help answer this question, we move from the laboratories of cognitive science to its clinical wing, where cognitive therapists have successfully addressed a problem very similar to this one, that is, the failure of critique to disable harmful prejudices, stereotypes, ideologies, and power/knowledge formations.

The clinical problem is that certain psychological maladies, such as depression and phobia, often prove highly resistant to traditional forms of therapy based on insight, clarification, or confrontation—practices that closely resemble traditional forms of social criticism. The traditional therapeutic techniques help people acknowledge that, for example, their deep despair about their lives, or their fear of public spaces, is unfounded and irrational, but despite this knowledge, their perceptions, feelings, and behaviors often remain unchanged, just as people who are rationally convinced that certain prejudices or ideological beliefs are invalid often continue to perceive, feel, and respond to others in a prejudiced and harmful manner. Cognitive therapists gradually realized that to overcome their faulty and harmful perceptions, feelings, and behaviors, patients need to change not just their conscious, propositional beliefs but the cognitive schemas that continually reproduce the faulty perceptions, feelings, and behaviors. The result, known in one of its more prominent forms as "schema therapy," is composed of processes that can be adapted by social and cultural critics to alter or replace faulty and harmful collective cognitive schemas.[13]

The general process through which a faulty cognitive schema is replaced involves repeatedly employing, in varying contexts, a more adequate schema. One step toward this end is to help individuals develop metacognition of their own information processing by compelling them to repeatedly apprehend the faulty and harmful nature of their flawed schema in its various elements—that is, its various exemplars, prototypes, and information-processing routines, as well as propositional knowledge. The key activity in this step is to help people identify the important types of information that are excluded when they arrive at certain judgments, emotions, and actions. A second step is to provide these people with exemplars that reveal this crucial excluded information and thus serve as correctives to the faulty exemplars and prototypes. Third, one must help people formulate and perform information-processing routines that provide the crucial information that their current processing is excluding. And fourth, one must get people to repeatedly recognize, interrupt, and override the old, faulty schema elements when they are triggered, and to activate instead the elements of the new, more adequate schema.

Repeated activation of these alternative, corrective schema elements will incrementally establish them as the default structures for processing information, at which point the old schema will no longer be cued and the new schema will be activated automatically instead. The more experiences one has of recognizing and eschewing the propositions, exemplars, prototypes, and processing routines of the old, faulty schema and activating instead the elements of the new, more adequate schema, the more powerful and automatic the new, more adequate schema becomes (see Padesky 277; Horowitz 65–69; Wells 128).

Such repetition is essential because while a single experience may be sufficient to correct faulty propositional knowledge, the nonpropositional forms of knowledge often cannot be changed by a single intervention. This is because unlike propositional knowledge, which is encoded in a "fast-binding" memory system, nonpropositional forms of knowledge and their information-processing mechanisms are based in "slow learning" memory systems that can only be changed incrementally, through multiple repetitions (Smith and DeCoster, 127). More specifically, countering the effects of misleading exemplars usually requires that multiple alternative exemplars be encoded in episodic memory, which takes multiple encounters with alternative exemplars. Similarly, reducing the effects of distorting prototypes generally requires the encoding in episodic memory of a critical mass of alternative exemplars sufficient to produce the development of an alternative prototype in semantic memory. And correcting faulty information-processing routines requires the same sort of practice and repetition that is necessary to correct, for example, a faulty backhand swing or keyboard fingering technique.

To summarize, faulty cognitive schemas can be replaced by employing the following basic principles:

1. Developing metacognition, the awareness of one's own processing activities, their pitfalls, and their consequences—for example, being aware of one's tendency to overlook people's circumstances when judging their behavior or life outcome—through directing attention to the act of information processing. Metacognition can be aided by the acquisition of more adequate and comprehensive propositional knowledge concerning human nature and the human condition,

which can then serve as a standard against which one can assess the comprehensiveness and accuracy of one's information processing.

2. Acquiring more adequate exemplars and prototypes through repeatedly engaging with perceptually salient and emotionally powerful specific instances that include crucial information that one's faulty prototypes and exemplars do not include — e.g., an image of a homeless man that includes information about the circumstances that contributed to his homelessness.

3. Developing more adequate information-processing routines — that is, expectations, attention, inferences, suppositions, and so on that take into account all the relevant information — through enacting them repeatedly, in multiple and various contexts.

Protest Novels as Schema-Altering Apparatuses

What this understanding of schemas and schema change means is that the most effective strategy of social criticism has been right under our noses the whole time — in the form of certain protest novels whose purpose was to change the social order by changing the way people thought and felt about other people. As we will see in part III, these novels possess features that can engage readers in precisely the sorts of cognitive activities that have been found to correct faulty social information processing. Literary texts operate with and on all the forms of knowledge and information-processing activities that constitute cognitive schemas. And certain types of literary texts themselves promote the replacement of certain harmful schemas by (1) demonstrating their faulty and harmful nature (i.e., developing readers' metacognition), (2) providing more adequate exemplars in multiple forms (concepts, characters, episodes, life stories, etc.), and (3) actually engaging, and hence training, readers in more accurate information-processing routines.

Providing Corrective Exemplars and Prototypes

Various studies have shown that even a briefly presented fictional exemplar can alter readers' attitudes and actions toward real people. In one study, University of Kansas psychologist Daniel Batson and his colleagues presented students with a brief fictional interview of a confessed murderer and found that the brief encounter with this exemplar improved the students' attitudes toward murderers in general, as measured one to two weeks later (Batson et al.). In another study, Batson found that after reading a fictional interview with an incarcerated drug dealer, with instructions to imagine the dealer's feelings and life circumstances, students voted to allocate more university funds to help drug addicts (Batson, Chang, Orr, and Rowland). Other studies have found that simply imagining counter-stereotypical exemplars of an out-group can reduce negative, stereotypical judgments of them (Blair, Ma, and Lenton 831, 838; see also Dasgupta and Greenwald).

The novels we will examine work to correct readers' deficient general knowledge of persons in a similar, but much more systematic and thus presumably more powerful, way: by providing multiple new exemplars that embody crucial information that many readers' current exemplars and prototypes omit. In addition, by repeatedly engaging readers in processing numerous emotionally powerful exemplars representing a more adequate understanding of persons, these novels promote the gradual construction of new, more adequate general person–prototypes incorporating the recognition that individuals are situated rather than purely autonomous, malleable rather than immutable, in fundamental solidarity with each other rather than in unmitigated opposition, and internally heterogeneous rather than homogeneous. As we have noted, striking exemplars can themselves substitute for faulty prototypes in guiding information processing, and, moreover, when a critical mass of these exemplars accumulates in readers' episodic memory, they form alternative prototypes that can serve as the default templates of social cognition. These exemplars and their resulting prototypes can then function as templates for our perception and judgment of real people, models of what we expect, attend to, search for, infer, suppose, feel, and do when we deal with actual human beings.

Developing More Adequate Information-Processing Routines

Besides providing more adequate exemplars and prototypes, literature can also correct readers' faulty information-processing routines in several additional ways. It can do so, first, by explicitly articulating in propositional form crucial knowledge about people in general that readers are often blind to. By providing propositional knowledge of situatedness and malleability, for example, a text cues readers to expect, attend to, search for, infer, or suppose such information when assessing characters in the text. Second, a literary text can correct faulty information processing by prompting readers to develop metacognitive knowledge concerning their own deficient information processing. Literature can induce such metacognition by, for example, thwarting readers' expectations about characters or disconfirming their inferences or suppositions about them in ways that are dramatic enough to enter readers' awareness and induce self-reflection, or by portraying obviously flawed information processing on the part of a narrator or character, as when one character commits the fundamental attribution error and blames another character for behavior that was actually determined by the other's situation. A third way in which literature works to correct faulty information-processing routines is by directly guiding readers' information processing through the text's own enactment of specific processing activities, repeatedly engaging readers in more accurate and thorough processing of crucial information about characters in the novel.

A literary text does this first by directing our *attention* and determining our *focus*. A novel, as Martha Nussbaum points out, "tells its readers to notice this and not this" (Nussbaum, *Poetic* 2). Furthermore, when a literary text makes *suppositions*, it engages its readers in making the same suppositions, and when it foreshadows, it elicits specific *expectations* in readers. And when a narrator or character makes an *interpretation* of another character, expresses an *emotion* regarding another character, or engages in an *action* toward another character, readers' mirror neurons make their brains follow suite and simulate the same actions and emotions.[14] In some cases, literary texts also directly instruct readers to *search* their *memories* for certain kinds of experiences, or to *search for* particular types of *information* in the world.

Finally, literary texts can induce readers to engage in more adequate information-processing routines by evoking pro-social emotions, such as compassion and moral outrage at suffering and injustice. Emotions play an important and complex role in information processing. First, they are often the *product* of information processing, with a particular judgment or constellation of judgments producing a particular emotion (see Lazarus and Lazarus; Smith and Kirby). Thus the judgment that people's distress is their own fault will result in emotions of indifference, disdain, contempt, or even anger, while the judgment that their distress is the result of factors over which they had no control will lead to feelings of sympathy (and possibly anger at a responsible third party) (see Weiner, *Judgments* and Bracher, "Teaching"). And since each form of exemplar and prototype (i.e., concept, episode script, prototypic image, etc.) is capable of embodying such a judgment, each is also capable of producing the corresponding emotion. Furthermore, the concurrent experience of a particular emotion with a particular exemplar or prototype produces an association between the two that is encoded in memory and that can thus produce the emotion whenever the exemplar or prototype is activated.

But in addition to being the *effect* of certain (possibly faulty) specific judgments about persons and situations, emotions can also be the *cause* of such appraisals, by biasing each step of information processing in the direction of information that supports the appraisals that constitute the specific emotion (Ekman 126–127). Emotions can bias information processing in at least two ways. They can do so, first, through their associations with particular beliefs (Bower and Forgas 108) and second, through their embodiment of the particular appraisals that give them their specific nature. As Clore and Gasper put it, "emotional feelings provide internal, felt evidence that an object or situation has the attributes implied by the emotion" (Clore and Gasper 28). Anger, for example, embodies the judgments that one has been harmed or threatened, that the source of the harm or threat is an intentional agent, and that this agent acted intentionally or negligently. Thus whenever we feel angry, we assume that someone is responsible and look for someone to blame (Clore and Gasper 33, 39; Hogan, *Understanding* 178; Frijda and Mesquita 65).[15] People operating with the autonomy schema, which include emotions of disdain, contempt, and anger, are thus inclined by those emotions to (mis)attribute responsibility to any party in need— an attribution that then serves as an appraisal that validates and/or reproduces the original negative emotion, resulting in a vicious circle in which the emotion-producing appraisal and the appraisal-producing emotion reproduce each other (see Clore and Gasper 35–36).

Emotions aroused by literature can engage this process in ways that work to replace faulty information-processing routines. A literary text that evokes compassion, for example, will incline readers to expect, search for, infer, recall, and suppose situational causes for problematic behaviors and life outcomes. As Keith Oatley has noted, literature evokes both "fresh" and remembered emotions in readers. "Fresh" emotions, Oatley argues, are produced in two basic ways. First, literary texts engage us in simulating the goals, plans, and actions of characters we identify with, which brings us "to feel in ourselves the emotions that occur with the results of actions that we perform mentally as if in the place of [the] character" (Oatley 116). Second, literary texts can provide "a pattern of appraisal, a pattern of events capable of causing [specific] emotions," which causes readers to "recognize [a character's] predicament, and feel sympathetic emotions for the character" (Oatley 118).[16]

In addition to evoking fresh emotions in these two ways, literary texts can also produce emotions in readers by triggering emotional memories as they read (Oatley 120ff.). These memories can be explicit, involving conscious recollection of specific events, or implicit, in which the emotion is experienced without the conscious recall of the event to which it is attached (Hogan, *What* 51).[17] By eliciting, in one or more of these ways, emotions such as compassion and moral outrage at human suffering that are congruent with the more adequate person-schemas (situationism, malleability, solidarity, and heterogeneity), literature counters the biased information processing of the faulty, harmful schemas (autonomism, essentialism, atomism, and homogeneity) with a corrective emotional bias in an opposite direction. And with sufficient repetition, as noted above, these corrective processing routines become established as the defaults, thus resulting in more adequate and just judgments, emotions, and actions regarding real people.

Conclusion

Together, these various alterations of readers' information-processing structures effected by protest novels constitute a radical cognitive politics, a mode of intervention that works to promote social justice by altering the cognitive roots of harmful and unjust social policies, institutions, systems, and structures, as illustrated in the following diagram.

Reading—>Better Structures—>Better Information Processing—>Better Understanding—>Emotion—>Justice

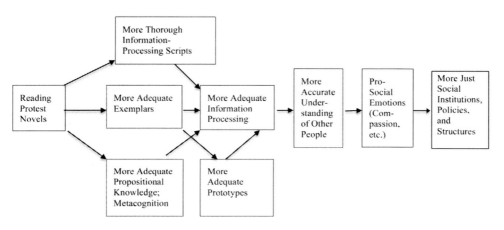

Diagram 2. How reading protest novels corrects faulty information processing and promotes social justice

One reading of any literary text is of course unlikely to provide readers with sufficient repetitions of these various schema-changing activities to fully displace the faulty cognitive schemas with the more adequate ones. For a sufficient number of repetitions to occur so that the more adequate exemplars, prototypes, processing routines, emotions, and metacognition become established as their default social information-processing structures, readers must first of all engage fully in the repetitions offered by the text, something readers who are not focusing on these textual elements—whether because they are inattentive or because they have been trained to focus on other things (style, symbolism, narrative techniques, etc.)—will not do. And second, in order for these new cognitive capabilities to fully develop, readers must exercise them on characters in other texts and on real people as well.

Hence the need for schema criticism. For while a novel itself may not be able to produce or induce all of the textual, intertextual, and extra-textual cognitive activity that is necessary for the full development of more adequate cognitive schemas, it can do so with a little help from schema critics and teachers. Indeed, literature teachers are in a privileged position to promote precisely such activity and thus to actualize the radical cognitive politics of protest novels—and to pursue this cognitive intervention in response to other genres and forms of discourse, and harmful social policies, institutions, systems, and structures as well.

The chapters that follow will explain how the four faulty person-schemas identified above operate, how such cognitive schemas can be changed or replaced, and how three prominent protest novels work to correct or replace these four schemas. Drawing on the techniques of these protest novels as well as the more general principles of schema change discussed above, the final chapter will then outline a new critical methodology, which I call schema criticism, for implementing a radical cognitive politics that works to repair the faulty cognitive schemas that constitute the roots of unjust social policies, institutions, systems, and structures.

PART II

THE COGNITIVE ROOTS OF INJUSTICE: FOUR PERSON-SCHEMAS

CHAPTER 2

Autonomism versus Situationism: Responsibility for Behavior and Life Outcomes

The race is not to the swift,
nor the battle to the strong,
neither yet bread to the wise,
nor yet riches to men of understanding,
nor yet favor to men of skill;
but time and chance
happeneth to them all.
ECCLESIASTES 9:11

The autonomy schema, which constitutes the core of the American Dream and its valorization of independence and self-reliance, leads one to perceive people's character, and not their circumstances, as the chief cause of both their behavior and their life outcomes. The faulty nature of such judgments has been amply demonstrated by numerous empirical studies, and research has also shown that Americans are more prone to this error—which cognitive psychologists call "the fundamental attribution error"—than are people in East Asian cultures.

The autonomy schema produces these faulty judgments by severely limiting the information people expect, seek, attend to, recall, infer, suppose, and remember. It leads people to continually conclude that poor and marginalized individuals and groups are responsible for their inferior stations in life and that people who have attained success deserve full credit for their good fortune. This conclusion, in turn, supports social policies, institutions, and systems that stigmatize, neglect, and/or punish the unfortunate, further reward the affluent, and thus maintain poverty and inequality in the United States and around the world. Correcting Americans' information processing to take adequate

36   The Cognitive Roots of Injustice

account of the situational determinants of behavior and destiny—a recognition that the autonomy schema prevents—would thus contribute significantly to social justice and is arguably a prerequisite for it. Fortunately, research has demonstrated that replacing the autonomy schema with a more adequate one, the "situationism schema," which takes situational determinants of behavior and life outcomes into account, is both possible and effective in reducing neglectful and punitive actions toward stigmatized groups.

The Hegemony of Autonomism

The autonomy schema dominates most Americans' understanding of success and failure. As sociologists Stephen McNamee and Robert Miller observe, "According to the promise implied by the American Dream, you can go as far as your talents and abilities can take you. . . . Presumably, if you work hard enough and are talented enough, you can overcome any obstacle and achieve success. No matter where you start out in life, the sky is ostensibly the limit" (McNamee and Miller 1). The autonomy schema also produces the corollary conviction that failure to prosper is the fault of the individual, not the result of external circumstances. Sociologist Michael Lewis writes that, beginning in the nineteenth century in America, "the dominant interpretation of disadvantage [poverty, unemployment, ill health, etc.] . . . held it the result of personal ineptness or misbehavior and therefore a sign of moral inferiority. . . . To be poor, to have suffered disadvantage, was taken to mean failure to make the most of an abundance of chances; through sloth, venality, or simple ineptitude, one had not exerted sufficient productive effort, and having done less than one might, one had done ill" (Lewis 7). This belief, as McNamee and Miller note, functions to justify inequality: "In the United States, inequality is justified, or 'explained,' [predominantly] by an ideology of meritocracy. America is seen as the land of opportunity where people get out of the system what they put into it. . . . In this formulation, you may not be held responsible for where you started out in life, but you are responsible for where you end up" (McNamee and Miller 3).

Sociologists and historians find that the autonomy belief is particularly powerful among Americans. Sociologist Robert Bellah and his co-authors state that Americans "are united . . . in at least one core belief, even across lines of color, religion, region, and occupation: the belief that economic success or misfortune is the individual's responsibility, and his or hers alone" (vii–viii). As historian Howard Zinn summarizes, Americans believe that "if you work hard enough, you'll make a good living. If you are poor, you have only yourself to blame" (Zinn 3). While this belief is more prominent among conservatives than liberals, "both liberals and conservatives appear to view poverty and disadvantage as a function of qualities characteristic of the disadvantaged poor" rather than of circumstances over which they have no control (Lewis 11).

The Falseness of Autonomism

Despite its widespread acceptance in the United States, the autonomy assumption is profoundly false. Social psychologists and others have long maintained that blaming individuals for their deviant behavior or lack of economic standing is not justified by the facts. In *Blaming the Victim*, psychologist William Ryan observed several decades ago that those who make such attributions "are, of course, ignoring a whole set of factors that ordinarily might be considered relevant—for instance, unequal distribution of income, social stratification, political struggle, ethnic and racial group conflict, and inequality of power. Their ideology concentrates almost exclusively on the failure of the deviant" (Ryan 14).

As Emory law professor Martha Fineman points out, no one is completely autonomous or self-sufficient: "We all live subsidized lives. . . . There is an inherent dependence on society on the part of all individuals. . . . We delude ourselves when we think that many (perhaps any) endeavors in our complex modern society can be undertaken in an autonomous and independent manner. . . . The very idea of an independent individual is fashioned upon unrealistic and unattainable (dare I even say, 'undesirable') premises" (Fineman xvii, 30, 33, 35).

Situational Determinants of Life Outcomes

Studies of the determinants of life outcomes reveal that the factors most Americans assume to be both primary and under an individual's control—"innate talent, hard work, proper attitude, and moral virtue" (McNamee and Miller 16)—are neither. Apart from the fact that individuals are less responsible for such personal qualities than we tend to assume (a point that is the subject of the next chapter), such attributes have been found to play a much smaller role in determining social and economic success than do situational forces over which individuals have little or no control. Chief among the uncontrollable situational factors are the circumstances of one's birth, which one can never control: the economic, social, and political positions of one's parents and the geographical, economic, and political conditions prevailing at one's birth and unfolding during one's lifetime.

The childhood benefits of a privileged birth, which are particularly determinative of one's future success and well-being, include better care, healthier food, better clothing and shelter, more and better education, training, and socialization, and environments that are generally not only safer and more enjoyable but also more developmentally stimulating (see McNamee and Miller 63). Later advantages of a privileged birth include having "friends and relatives in high places, cultural advantages, infusion of parental capital while parents are still alive, insulation against failure, better health and greater life expectancy, and inheritance of bulk estates when parents die" (McNamee and Miller 16–17). In addition, place of birth and upbringing (neighborhood, community, nation, geography) can also play a significant role in determining a person's survival and degree of personal fulfillment, social status, and financial success. Children born in war zones, economically destitute nations, or geographical regions of limited resources are at a clear disadvantage.

The timing of one's birth is also a crucial aspect of the birth lottery. From a purely economic point of view, "the best scenario is one in which a person is part of a small birth cohort and enters the labor force during a period of economic expansion; the worst scenario is one in which a person is part of a large cohort entering the labor force during a period of economic retrenchment" (McNamee and Miller 150). As McNamee and Miller explain, "While individuals have some control over how skilled they are, they have no control over what kinds of jobs are available, how many, and how many individuals are seeking those jobs. These labor-market conditions occur independently of the capacities of discrete individuals—how smart or talented they are, how hard they work, or how motivated they are to get ahead" (McNamee and Miller 161). Today, they observe, many Americans have gotten educations and developed skills that are in excess of the jobs they are actually able to acquire and hold: "Many American workers are all dressed up with no place to go. . . . The simple fact is that there is far more intelligence, talent, ability, and hard work in the population as a whole than there are people who are lucky enough to find themselves in a position to take advantage of these qualities" (McNamee and Miller 161). Thus "getting ahead in terms of occupations people hold and the pay they receive involves an element of luck—being in the right place at the right time" (McNamee and Miller 157).

Luck plays a particularly significant role, McNamee and Miller observe, in the acquisition of wealth: "Striking it rich—be it through inheritance, entrepreneurial ventures, investment, or the lottery—necessarily involves at least some degree of just plain dumb luck" (McNamee and Miller 161). Economist Lester Thurow agrees. "Luck is necessary," he writes. "Talent, drive, and persistence by themselves aren't enough to get wealthy." This is true even of apparently "self-made" individuals who are not born wealthy, as the example of Bill Gates demonstrates. Thurow notes that "there are many other individuals just as smart, just as good businessmen, and just as good at everything else [as Bill Gates] who do not have his wealth. Acquiring wealth is best seen as a conditional lottery. Luck is necessary. One does have to be in the right place at the right time. . . . Ability is not enough" (as quoted in McNamee and Miller, 157).

Situational Causes of Behavior

Americans are even more convinced that non-normative and harmful behaviors, especially criminal acts, are the sole responsibility of the individual. Most Americans believe that all behavior is caused by individuals' dispositions—their character—and that individuals' situations play little or no role in determining their behavior. In attributing behavior to the disposition and character of the person rather than to the situation, they are committing the fundamental attribution error, "the tendency for people to overlook situational causes of actions and outcomes in favor of dispositional ones" (Ross and Nisbett 79).

They are in error because, as philosopher John Doris observes, "behavior is . . . extraordinarily sensitive to variation in circumstance"; not only major situational factors but also "seemingly insubstantial situational factors have substantial effects on what people do" (Doris 28). Indeed, as legal scholars Jon Hanson and David Yosifon note, "the hidden situation can be as powerful as a loaded gun" pointed at someone's head (Hanson and Yosifon, "Situational Character" 55). Nor does the power of a situational factor have to be overwhelming in order to determine the course of an individual's behavior. This is because, as psychologists Ross and Nisbett explain, the individual psyche is a system in a state of tension (Ross and Nisbett 13), with certain parts of the mind/

brain inclining an individual in one direction and other parts pushing him or her in a different direction. When the opposing forces are delicately balanced, a relatively weak situational factor can tip the balance in one direction or the other, just as swaying a single vote in the Supreme Court or Congress can sometimes determine the difference between life and death for masses of people. This means that very important and life-changing actions, such as whether or not a particular individual commits a crime in a given situation, can be determined by apparently insignificant and even invisible situational factors.

Numerous empirical studies have demonstrated that circumstances often trump character in determining people's behavior. Altruistic actions, which are generally assumed to be a function of the actor's character, often are determined more by situation than by character. In a classic study, students at Princeton Theological Seminary were enlisted to give a talk on the biblical parable of the Good Samaritan, in which a man who has been robbed, beaten, and left beside the road to die is given aid by an outcast, while men of social rank and supposedly high character pass the victim by. Each seminarian in the experiment arrived at the experimenter's office, was briefed, and was then dispatched to the meeting room, which was located in another building. Half of the subjects were told that they were running late and had better hurry, while the other half were told that they had more than enough time but might as well head on over to the site anyway. Unbeknownst to the seminarians, a confederate of the experimenter had been stationed along the route to the meeting and lay moaning on the sidewalk in apparent distress, in order to test how many of the seminarians—who were all primed with, and presumably shared the charitable values of, the Good Samaritan story—would act according to these values. The results revealed that character played a decidedly secondary role in determining the seminarians' behavior: while 63 percent of the subjects who were not late for their lecture stopped to help the man, only 10 percent of those who were late did so (Darley and Batson). Numerous other studies have produced similar results concerning the role of the situation in altruistic behavior (see Ross and Nisbett 49).

Research has also revealed that situational factors are the dominant causes of antisocial, unethical, and violent behaviors. In one of the most famous experiments in the history of psychology, Yale psychologist Stanley Milgram found that decent, ordinary individuals, when placed in certain situations, would often engage in harmful, antisocial actions reminiscent of those of Nazi prison personnel. Milgram's experiment, ostensibly a study of how negative reinforcement affected learning, involved placing subjects in the position of administering increasingly powerful electrical shocks to a "learner" each time he gave an incorrect answer. As the apparent force of the shocks (which were faked) mounted with each wrong answer, the learner, who was actually a confederate of the experimenter, expressed increasing distress, including crying out in agony, pleading a risky heart condition, begging the subject to stop the shocks, and finally falling silent in apparent unconsciousness when the voltage dial was turned up to its highest level. As the learner's apparent distress increased, most subjects expressed unease and reluctance to continue administering the shocks. But, upon being instructed by the experimenter to continue, the majority of them did so, despite their fears that they were subjecting the learner to severe pain and perhaps even mortal injury. The numerous versions of this experiment conducted by Milgram, totaling hundreds of subjects, demonstrated that the degree of compliance could be changed significantly by altering a single feature of the situation, such as the apparent institutional auspices under which the experiment was conducted, the professional identity or status of the experimenter, and the physical location of the subject in relation to the experimenter and the "learner." Through these variations, "Milgram was able to demonstrate that compliance rates could soar to over 90 percent of people continuing to the 450-volt maximum or be reduced to less than 10 percent—by introducing one crucial variable into the compliance recipe" (Zimbardo 272).

One of the most powerful situational factors in Milgram's experiment was authority, and numerous subsequent studies have demonstrated how authority can override people's moral scruples and induce them to engage in unethical or antisocial behaviors. In a study conducted at the University of San Diego, law professor Steven Hartwell arranged for his students to provide legal aid to individuals (actually confederates) who came seeking help in a rent dispute. Hartwell was available in an adjoining room to advise his students, and when they sought his input, he told them "to advise the client to lie under oath that she had paid the rent." And although many of the two dozen students thus instructed expressed reluctance to advise their client to perjure herself, all but one of them nonetheless did so (Hanson and Yosifon, "The Situation" 194, n. 242).

In addition to authority, the social roles that situations put people in are also powerful determinants of behavior. The best-known demonstration of this fact is the Stanford Prison Experiment conducted by psychologist Philip Zimbardo in 1971. Zimbardo's experiment took a group of normal young men, without any significant psychopathologies, and randomly placed them as either guards or inmates in a mock prison. Within a few short days these ordinary young men were engaging in behaviors that were so pathological (sadistic, masochistic, manic, depressive) and potentially harmful that the experiment had to be discontinued. Zimbardo reports:

> We were surprised that situational pressures could overcome most of these normal, healthy young men so quickly and so extremely. . . . These young men did not import into our jail any of the pathology that subsequently emerged among them as they played either prisoners or guards. At the start of this experiment, there were no differences between the two groups; less than a week later, there were no similarities between them. It is reasonable, therefore, to conclude that the pathologies were elicited by the set of situational forces constantly impinging upon them. (Zimbardo 196–197)

The Stanford Prison Experiment is thus, as Zimbardo concluded, "a powerful illustration of the potentially toxic impact of bad systems and bad situations in making good people behave in pathological ways that are alien to their natures" (Zimbardo 195).

In another well-known experiment, a third-grade teacher in a small Iowa town informed her students that scientists had found blue-eyed students to be superior to their brown-eyed counterparts and that, consequently, the blue-eyed students would be granted certain privileges while the brown-eyed children would be subject to certain restrictions. The results were similar to those of the Stanford Prison Experiment: by the end of the day, the blue-eyed children had come to engage in aggressive, dominating behaviors toward the brown-eyed children, who quickly began to evince submissive demeanors, underachievement, and depression. When the teacher informed her class the next day that a mistake had been made and that it was actually the brown-eyed children who were superior, the same behaviors quickly manifested themselves, only with the roles reversed. The teacher described the dramatic changes the situation produced in her students: "What had been marvelously cooperative, thoughtful children became nasty, vicious, discriminating little third-graders. . . . It was ghastly!" (Zimbardo 283–284).

Another school experiment produced even more disturbing behavioral changes through manipulation of the situation. To help his high school world history class understand the Holocaust, a California teacher informed them that the following week they would simulate certain features of the Nazi regime. On Monday, he issued strict rules for classroom behavior, including the requirement that students stand at attention when answering questions and that they limit their answers to three words, preceded by "Sir." He introduced a salute, secret handshakes, rigid sitting postures, recruitment of other students, and slogans such as "Strength through discipline." In this situation, the more thoughtful and articulate students soon became passive, and the less verbal, more physical ones became dominant. The students quickly became active contributors to this authoritarian regime, issuing membership cards and expelling some of the brightest students, verbally abusing them as they were ushered out of class. At the end of the week more than two hundred students assembled in the auditorium for what they had been told would be an announcement by a presidential candidate of the formation of a national Third Wave youth movement. "Exhilarated Wave members wearing white-shirted uniforms with homemade armbands posted banners around the hall, . . . [and] muscular students stood guard at the door" while the mass shouted, "Strength through discipline!" (Zimbardo 282) in a demonstration distressingly reminiscent of Nazi youth groups.

These studies and numerous others demonstrate that any one of multiple situational factors can result in significant behavioral effects. In addition to authority and social roles, other situational factors that have been found to influence behavior include social rules, social modeling, peer pressure to conform, group identity, intergroup conflict, labeling, deindividuation of agents, and dehumanization or infrahumanization of the other (see Zimbardo 212ff.; Ross and Nisbett 8, 38, 49, 69–70; Ross and Shestowsky 49).

History, too, has provided striking and often gruesome evidence of the power of these various situational factors to induce decent, ordinary people to engage in horrific behavior. The best-known instance, of course, is that of the agents of the Holocaust, the majority of whom were good citizens and even loving family men before they were placed in their roles as implementers of Hitler's "final solution." Various studies have found that many of the individuals who killed Jews by shooting them or by operating the gas chambers—including those who did so with enthusiasm and pride—led exemplary lives both before and after they committed these horrendous actions. One researcher found that many from a group of Hamburg family men, recruited to massacre Jews in Poland, "posed proudly for photographs of their up-close and personal killing of Jews" (Zimbardo 286). "There was no special selection of these men, nor self-selection, nor self-interest or careerism that could account for these mass murders. Instead, they were as 'ordinary' as can be imagined—until they were put into a novel situation in which they had 'official' permission and encouragement to act sadistically against people who were arbitrarily labeled as the 'enemy'" (Zimbardo 286). Initially, only about half the members of this group were willing to engage in the killing, but eventually, as a result of pressures to conform and peer modeling, 90 percent of the men became personally involved in the killings (Zimbardo 286). Another researcher, who interviewed hundreds of Nazi SS members of all ranks after the war, concluded that although many of them possessed significant authoritarian traits, these traits alone were insufficient to produce their violent and cruel behavior and would have lain dormant under ordinary circumstances. Both before and after their tenure in the concentration camps, these men led normal lives, free of violence. It was the situation of the authoritarian and violent SS subculture that activated these traits and triggered the murderous actions (Zimbardo 287).

Zimbardo and other researchers arrived at similar conclusions regarding the government torturers and death squad members they investigated in Brazil and Greece. They began their research wondering, "What kind of men could do such deeds? Did they need to rely on sadistic impulses and a history of sociopathic life experiences to rip and tear the flesh of fellow beings day in and day out for years on end? Were these violence workers a breed apart from the rest of humanity, bad seeds, bad tree trunks, and bad flowers?" (Zimbardo 287). But although one might reasonably assume that these individuals must have been sadistic psychopaths who enjoyed inflicting pain on others, Zimbardo and his colleagues found that this was not the case. "From all the evidence we could muster," he concludes, "torturers and death squad executioners were not unusual or deviant in any way prior to practicing their new roles, nor were there any persisting deviant tendencies or pathologies among any of them in the years following their work as torturers and executioners" (Zimbardo 290). Their terrible behavior was a function not of some twisted personality but rather of situational factors such as their training, their social role, their group membership, the secrecy of their activities, pressure to produce results, their political ideology, and other situational factors (Zimbardo 290).

Two more recent historical cases of mass violence and inhumanity, the terrorist attacks of 9/11 and the Abu Ghraib prison abuses, reveal the same situational etiology. U.S. government and military officials, as well as many media commentators, attributed both of these actions to the supposed evil or pathological natures of the immediate perpetrators. President George W. Bush (in)famously declared the 9/11 attacks to be the irrational and unexplainable actions of evil people, and Secretary of State Condoleezza Rice insisted that U.S. foreign policy had nothing to do with the attacks and that the hijackers were simply evil people who wanted to kill Americans (Zimbardo 311). Similarly, Secretary of Defense Donald Rumsfeld and a host of other officials pronounced the abuses at Abu Ghraib the work of "a few bad apples." Both of these conclusions were dead wrong.

Los Angeles Times reporter Terry McDermott's investigation of the 9/11 hijackers revealed that these men were unexceptional—not blood-thirsty evildoers or crazy religious fanatics but rather, in the words of *New York Times* reporter Michiko Kakutani, "surprisingly mundane people, people who might easily be our neighbors or airplane seatmates" (Zimbardo 293). What ultimately caused these individuals to engage in their suicide missions was the situation—largely invisible to most Americans, though created in no small measure by American policies and actions—in which they found themselves and which they experienced as intolerable. Ross and Shestowsky conclude regarding these terrorists and terrorists in general:

> We cannot in good conscience claim that the terrorists' choices, which were the product of indoctrination, humiliating circumstances, or culturally prescribed understandings, were freely made or a simple reflection of bad character or evil dispositions, any more than we could make such a claim about actors who committed their crimes at gunpoint or in the face of grievous threats to their families. Indeed, it seems evident that, for the terrorist, the fear of facing a hostile gunman or other threats to life and limb or a threat to the well-being of his family have proven *less* powerful behavioral determinants than the specific set of situational forces and constraints that attended their terrorist acts. (Ross and Shestowsky 1103)

The Abu Ghraib prison abuses were similarly the result primarily of a pathogenic situation rather than pathological personalities. As Zimbardo documents in *The Lucifer Effect*, U.S. military personnel placed as guards at the facility were subjected to the same sorts of situational forces as those in place in the Stanford Prison Experiment, only on a much more massive and powerful scale, and for a much longer period of time than the six days endured by the subjects in the experiment. After extensive research into the psychological profiles of the guards and the conditions to which they were subjected at the prison, Zimbardo concluded that "you could put virtually anybody [in that situation and] get this kind of evil behavior" (quoted in Benforado and Hanson, "Naïve" 552).

Evidence of Autonomy Schema Operation

Given the historical and experimental findings concerning the power of situations to determine behavior, there should be little doubt that circumstances often play a much greater role than character in determining people's actions. As Zimbardo concludes, such evidence compels us "to abandon simplistic notions of the Good Self dominating Bad Situations. . . . Social situations can have more profound effects on the behavior and mental functioning of individuals, groups, and national leaders than we might believe possible. Some situations can exert such powerful influence over us that we can be led to behave in ways we would not, could not, predict was possible in advance" (Zimbardo 211–212). This means, furthermore, that *"any deed that any human being has ever committed, however horrible, is possible for any of us—under the right or wrong situational circumstances"* (Zimbardo 211; emphasis added).

Given this fact, we should practice what psychologist Lee Ross calls "attributional charity" when judging the behavior of other people: we should "start not by blaming the actor for the deed but rather, being charitable, we [should] first investigate the scene for situational determinants of the act" (Zimbardo 212). Yet despite the overwhelming evidence of the powerful role of situations in determining behaviors and life outcomes, most Westerners, and Americans in particular, persist in the fundamental attribution error, attributing people's behaviors and life outcomes to their disposition, or character, rather than to the situation. People continually underestimate the impact that situations have on behavior, even when they are aware of the situational forces that are in play, because the autonomy schema governs all aspects of their information processing and thus overrides any declarative knowledge that contradicts the perception of autonomy.

A number of researchers have noted the role of cognitive schemas in producing the fundamental attribution error. Yaacov Trope explains that our judgments about the determinants of behavior are guided by cognitive schemas and that these "a priori models," or "causal theories," as they are sometimes called,[1] govern every step of information processing about the causes of behavior: "The various stages of inferring dispositions from behavior are presumably guided by perceivers' a priori models of behavior. These models are preexisting causal theories that specify how dispositional and situational factors combine to produce behavior" (Trope 70); they guide our expectations concerning the causes of behavior and "constrain the inferences perceivers can draw from immediate behavior" (Trope 68–69). Consequently, "situational inducements [of another person's behavior] will have little or no effect on their judgments if they believe that this kind of behavior is fully determined by the corresponding personality trait" (Trope 71). Such cognitive schemas "may justify, and actually prescribe, assigning little weight to situational inducements in inferring a target's dispositions from immediate behavior" (Trope 74; see also Gawronski; Reeder).

This autonomist bias—or "dispositionism," as it is often called—has been demonstrated by numerous studies showing "that people automatically—and unconsciously—provide a dispositional interpretation to behavioral information" (Ross and Nisbett 121). Even for behavior that is clearly the result of the situation rather than character, many people will ignore the situational factors and attribute the behavior to character alone (Ross and Nisbett 126). The first dramatic study demonstrating dispositionism involved asking subjects to judge whether an essay or speech supposedly produced by students who were instructed (in a debate or on a final exam) to defend Castro's Cuba or oppose the legalization of marijuana actually reflected the writer/speaker's own attitudes. Even with the knowledge that the situation required the opinion expressed, most subjects judged the expressed opinion to reflect the writer/speaker's true attitude (Ross and Nisbett 126).

In another study, subjects observed a group of confederates being asked if they would volunteer to entertain campus visitors over the weekend. A modest hourly wage was offered as an incentive, with one group being offered three times the amount offered the other group. Over three times as many of the supposedly higher-paid confederates pretended to volunteer, clearly demonstrating that the money, and not the confederates' dispositions, was the major determinant of their behavior. Yet when asked which of the confederates would be more likely to volunteer for a United Way Fund drive, the observing subjects judged

48   The Cognitive Roots of Injustice

that the actors they saw volunteering would be substantially more likely to help, despite the fact that they were no longer being offered money to do so (Ross and Nisbett 126–127).

A third study, discussed above, described to subjects a version of the Good Samaritan experiment and asked them to predict which seminarians would stop to help the person in distress. They predicted that the great majority of seminarians would stop, and that those whose religious beliefs emphasized helping others would stop and help more often. They predicted that the time constraints of the seminarians would have no effect at all on their behavior. These predictions assumed that character or disposition was the sole determinant of behavior and that situation was irrelevant—precisely the opposite, we recall, of what the Good Samaritan experiment actually found. The tenacity of dispositionism was demonstrated by the fact that even when subjects were made to read the Good Samaritan study before taking part in their own experiment, they still dramatically overestimated the role of disposition or character and underestimated the impact of situation on behavior (Ross and Nisbett 131–132). Similar results were obtained from a study in which subjects were shown a film of the Milgram experiment demonstrating the power of situation to determine behavior. Even after viewing this film, the subjects significantly overestimated the amount of shock that the subjects in the film would deliver in the absence of the coercive situational factors that were the main determinants of their behavior (Ross and Nisbett 132).

In perhaps the most compelling demonstration of the power of the autonomy schema, subjects were asked to identify the individuals among their acquaintances who would be most likely and least likely to contribute to a food drive. Half of the individuals in each group were then pressured to contribute by being sent a personalized letter asking them to do so, being given a map showing the location of the food collection point, and receiving a personalized phone call reminding them to contribute. The other half were sent an impersonal "Dear Student" form letter asking for a contribution and were given no map or phone call. The subjects of the experiment predicted that around 16 percent of the "least likely" group and around 80 percent of the "most likely" group would contribute, and that their differing situations would make virtually no difference in their behaviors. In fact, it was the differing situations that made the greatest difference in behavior: in the nonfacilitory situation, only 4 percent of the students donated food (8 percent and 0 percent of the most and least likelies, respectively), while in the facilitory situation 33 percent did so (42 percent and 25 percent of the most and least likelies), demonstrating yet again that situation is often a more powerful determinant of behavior than character and that the autonomy schema consistently blinds people to this fact.

Costs of the Autonomy Schema

While the misjudgments made by the subjects in these experiments were fairly innocuous, the costs of the autonomy schema in real life are huge. There are two main types of cost: (1) the profound injustice that the fundamental attribution error perpetrates on individuals who are blamed and punished for actions and life outcomes that were determined more by their situation than by their character; and (2) the social cost of failing to solve social problems—ranging from poverty, unemployment, and homelessness to crime, substance abuse, war, and terrorism—due to our systematic refusal to acknowledge the primary, situational causes of the behaviors behind these problems and our focusing instead on the character of the immediate perpetrators.

As legal scholars Jon Hanson and David Yosifon declare, "the power of the dispositionist presumption has had, and is now having, an immense effect on both the framing and the resolution of virtually every major social policy debate—from the obesity epidemic to the War on Terrorism" (Hanson and Yosifon, "The Situation" 303). "Attributions matter," Adam Benforado and Hanson observe. "Do the have-nots bring poverty upon themselves because of their lazy dispositions and bad choices, or is poverty a violent situational force that harms its victims and encourages rationalizations among the haves? How one answers those attributional questions has major implications when it comes to what, if anything, we should do about poverty and the impoverished" (Benforado and Hanson, "Attributional" 406). And more often than not, we get these answers wrong, because we arrive at them via the faulty autonomy schema: "Attributional schemas are having a huge influence on many of our most pressing policy debates, . . . [and] attributional schemas that social science appears to have quite clearly discredited [e.g., the autonomy schema] . . . dominate the policy landscape" (Benforado and Hanson, "Naïve" 573). "At almost every turn, dispositionism [the autonomy schema] defines or biases what we see and how we construe what we see: behavior is strongly presumed to reflect freely willed, preference-satisfying individual choice. But as dispo-

50 The Cognitive Roots of Injustice

sitionists, we are . . . consistently wrong" (Hanson and Yosifon, "Situational Character" 3). The dramatic rightward shift in American social policy in recent decades is an example of "the enormity of what [autonomy] schemas and scripts have accomplished" (Chen and Hanson, "Illusion" 148). As Hanson and Hanson observe,

> In our market-based democracy, almost all arrangements are presumed to reflect choices—individual and collective. Laws and legal theories are founded on the premise that the consumer is sovereign. Many of America's most influential religions emphasize "choice" as the determining condition of salvation—our choice or God's. . . . [And] choice-based dispositionism, like the other dispositionist theories justifying oppression throughout our history, is badly flawed. . . . This is not a purely innocent mistake. . . . In all cases, victims are blamed while non-victims are excused, the haves and the have-nots are separated, and the persistent chasm between them (which would otherwise be seen as unjust) is legitimated. As always, the situational influences on the oppressed remain largely ignored, and dispositions are said to determine outcomes. (Hanson and Hanson 445–446)

Autonomism in the Legal System

Psychologists and legal scholars have demonstrated numerous ways in which law and the legal system are dominated and distorted by the false and harmful assumption of dispositionism. Stanford psychologists Lee Ross and Donna Shestowsky declare that the criminal justice system is based on "a lay conception of behavioral causation and the role of free will"—autonomism or dispositionism—"that . . . is neither empirically nor logically defensible, and ultimately is unjust" (1087). More generally, Ross and Shestowsky argue, social psychological research indicates

> that ordinary laypeople called upon to assess misdeeds are apt to show less understanding and empathy than is warranted. This relative lack of empathy is particularly likely in cases where the situational forces in question are not overt threats, opportunities for enrichment, traumas, or deprivations, but rather subtler matters of peer pressure or situations that induce initial small transgressions and then lead, step-by-step, to increasingly serious ones. This situationist research implies that many, if not most, people (including those who sit in judgment of transgressors) could be led, by the right set of subtle and not so subtle situational

pressures and constraints, to commit similar transgressions that they presently are certain they would never commit. (Ross and Shestowsky 1094–1095)

Social science research thus indicates that criminality is less a character trait than a function of the consistent presence of certain situational factors, such as incentives or constraints to behave in illegal ways (Ross and Shestowsky 1098–1099). Hence, "acknowledging the role that situational factors, as opposed to character, play in determining whether a given individual runs afoul of the legal system obliges us to consider deeper issues of justice and fairness, especially in the domain of criminal law" (Ross and Shestowsky 1096). Ross and Shestowsky note that our current assessments of legal responsibility and blame are the result more of our cultural conventions and of our need to justify our punitive practices than of a logical analysis of all the causal factors contributing to a given action (Ross and Shestowsky 1112), and they argue that "a logically coherent account of behavioral causation would compel us to treat transgressors with more compassion than they typically receive" (Ross and Shestowsky 1088). For justice to prevail, they maintain, the criminal justice system must free itself from autonomism:

> The workings of the criminal justice system should not continue to be guided by illusions about cross-situational consistency in behavior, by erroneous notions about the impact of dispositions versus situations in guiding behavior, or by failures to think through the logic of "person × situation" interactions, or even comforting but largely fanciful notions of free will, any more than it should be guided by the once common notions about witchcraft or demonic possession. (Ross and Shestowsky 1114)

Psychologist Craig Haney offers a similar assessment of the pervasive and harmful effects of autonomism in the legal system. Haney notes that although contemporary psychology, as a result of the research discussed above, emphasizes the role of situational factors in determining behavior, the American legal system "remains mired in an antiquated model of behavior that consistently compromises the fairness of legal doctrines and undermines the ability of legal institutions to deliver justice to those most in need of it" (Haney 10). In light of the powerful role of situations in determining human behavior, Haney argues, fairness and justice require some fundamental revisions in the legal system.

First, "considerations of fairness thus would require revised standards of culpability that accounted for the tremendous power of certain contexts and situations to strongly influence and even control behavior. Legal decision makers would need to reflect on whether and when justice was being served by holding persons fully responsible whose primary distinguishing characteristic was their presence in a crime-producing or criminogenic situation" (Haney 34). As a result of this new perspective and understanding, Haney reasons, all legal determinations of criminal responsibility should involve "detailed inquiries into the nature and power of relevant situations" (Haney 37).

Currently, the legal system narrows courtroom inquiry so that it systematically ignores some of the most important causes of the illegal behaviors at issue. "In criminal trials, in particular, where the goal is to affix personal guilt, the identity and state of mind of individual wrongdoers are all that are at issue" (Haney 20). This process, Haney points out, by "continuing to address individuals and not social situations or life circumstances[,] limits [judges' and jurors'] focus to the symptoms rather than the causes of many disputes and leads them to ignore the most important determinants of legally problematic behavior" (Haney 21). In contrast to this approach, "a legal system that recognizes the importance of the situational determinants of behavior would necessarily focus its fact-finding processes less exclusively on individual criminal agents and more on criminogenic conditions" (Haney 21). And as a result of such investigations, "an increasing number of psychologically relevant criminogenic situations would come to be regarded as prima facie coercive," thus absolving perpetrators of much, if not all, of their responsibility and guilt (Haney 37).

The autonomism at the heart of our legal system ensures not only that the allocation of responsibility and blame will be unfair but also that the system will be significantly less effective than it could and should be in reducing crime. High rates of recidivism, Haney observes, are due in significant measure to the autonomy assumption. If situation, rather than character, is the primary cause of crime, incarcerating people who commit criminal acts will not be the most effective means of crime prevention, because so long as the same situations prevail, they will keep producing new "criminals" (Haney 27). Thus "social structural and situational factors [should] be seen not only as significant causal elements to be taken explicitly into account in legal decisions about criminal responsibility, . . . but also as primary targets in any effective program of crime control" (Haney 47).

Haney argues, further, that recognizing the influence of situations on behavior requires a fundamental rethinking of incarceration as a means of crime prevention. Prisons, he explains, are a material embodiment of the autonomist assumption "that the social problem of crime is to be solved primarily through the identification and punishment of the persons who have engaged in it" (Haney 46). But the study of human behavior has refuted this assumption, revealing situational factors to be the primary cause, and this means that "criminal behavior can only be significantly reduced when the contextual, situational, and structural forces that produce it are addressed more directly" (Haney 47).

Finally and most fundamentally, taking full account of situational causes entails the recognition that "due process" and "equal protection under the law" require much greater social and economic equality than is currently in place: these basic rights "can only be guaranteed through attention to the relative equality of social situations. By this view, no legal process is 'due' nor legal rule 'equally protective' unless it incorporates rights to equitable environments and freedom from situations that preempt meaningful choice" (Haney 18).

Harvard Law professor Jon Hanson and his colleagues have reached much the same conclusions regarding law and the legal system. In a series of long articles based on massive research, Hanson et al. demonstrate that "the underlying person schemas and attributional schemas of law and legal institutions reflect strong dispositionist presumptions," that "such dispositionism, though appealing and initially plausible, is badly flawed" (Chen and Hanson 1244), and that consequently virtually every area and aspect of law and the legal system are plagued with severely flawed judgments (Hanson and Yosifon, "Situation" 299), which in turn result in profound injustice and social harm.

Autonomism in Other Institutions, Systems, and Policies

The law is not the only institution that is deeply flawed because of autonomism. As Zimbardo observes, most American institutions, including not only law, but also medicine, education, religion, and psychiatry, are founded on the autonomist assumption that individuals are the sole determinants of their behaviors and life outcomes (Zimbardo x, 7–10, 319–321). And as a result, as Hanson and Yosifon write, "evidence that human animals are situational characters implicates and threatens to delegitimate, not only our favored self-conception, but also our laws, legal theories, and indeed, most of our social systems" (Hanson and Yosifon, "Situational Character" 9).

Through these institutions, as well as directly, the autonomy schema

54 The Cognitive Roots of Injustice

also has a major impact on our social policies. Hanson and Yosifon note "that the fundamental attribution error is playing an immense and influential role in our policymakers' world views and in their policies" (Hanson and Yosifon, "The Situation" 286), and this influence produces great harm. As Benforado and Hanson state, "How one answers . . . attributional questions has major implications when it comes to what, if anything, we should do about poverty and the impoverished," and if autonomism continues to increase its sway, "we can expect significant societal costs as more and more vital decisions for the future of our country are made based on incorrect attributions of causation, responsibility, and blame" (Benforado and Hanson, "Attributional" 406–408).

More specifically,

> if we are basing our laws around a mistaken view of how humans interact with their world, our prescriptions are unlikely to address the symptoms or causes of serious societal problems—much less offer a cure. Indeed, they may themselves be part of the illness. If obese children are obese, not because they are lazy or because their parents are poor guardians, but because of, say, broader economic, social, and legal forces, then a program that tells kids to get off the couch or parents to monitor their children's caloric intake is unlikely to have much beneficial impact on habits or health. If middle-class consumers are on the cusp of insolvency, not because they fritter away their paychecks on flat-screen televisions and other luxury goods, but because of an unexpected job loss or health crisis, then tightening bankruptcy laws may do little more than enrich Bank of America. If corporate leaders are exaggerating earnings, not because they are greedy and immoral, but because of larger market dynamics and a widely held set of legitimating beliefs, then a legal regime that comes down hard on a few "bad apples" is unlikely to get to the root of the problem. And if 100,000 New Orleans residents stay put as Katrina moves in, blaming them for bad choices instead of recognizing their lack of good options will cost lives. (Benforado and Hanson, "Naïve" 504–505)

Shamefully, because of our autonomy bias, we Americans support social policies, institutions, and structures that denigrate and punish those who are dependent or in need, rather than helping them. As Jennifer Hochschild states, "Failure is made more harsh by . . . the belief that success results from actions and traits under one's own control. . . . Americans who do everything they can and still fail may come to understand that effort and talent alone do not guarantee success. But they have a hard time persuading others. After all, they are losers. . . . People who fail are presumed to lack talent or will. . . . Even the poor blame the poor for their condition. . . . Losers even blame themselves" (Hochschild 30–31). Martha Fineman agrees: "We venerate the autonomous, independent, and self-sufficient individual as our ideal. We assume that anyone can cultivate these characteristics, . . . and we stigmatize those who do not" (Fineman 3).

This "blaming the victim," a syndrome identified by the psychologist William Ryan in his popular 1971 book of the same title, is ubiquitous in American society:

> The generic process of Blaming the Victim is applied to almost every American problem. The miserable health care of the poor is explained away on the grounds that the victim has poor motivation and lacks health information. The problems of slum housing are traced to the characteristics of tenants who are labeled as "Southern rural migrants" not yet "acculturated" to life in the big city. The "multiproblem" poor, it is claimed, suffer the psychological effects of impoverishment, the "culture of poverty," and the deviant value system of the lower classes; consequently, though unwittingly, they cause their own troubles. . . . The growing number of families receiving welfare are fallaciously linked together with the increased number of illegitimate children as twin results of promiscuity and sexual abandon among members of the lower orders. Every important social problem—crime, mental illness, civil disorder, unemployment—has been analyzed within the framework of the victim-blaming ideology. (Ryan 5–6, 14)[2]

As a result of the belief in autonomy, Americans are thus prone to "blame the victim" and to unjustly withhold support or even punish people who have met with misfortune through little or no fault of their own, including the poor, the unemployed, the homeless, and the sick. As psychologists Daniel Gilbert and Patrick Malone state, "Juries misjudge defendants, voters misjudge candidates, . . . and, as a consequence, the innocent are executed, the incompetent are elected, and the ignoble are embraced" (Gilbert and Malone 35).

The impact of these misattributions on public policy is considerable, as Fineman explains. "Notions of individual autonomy have been powerfully employed in shaping policy," she states. "The very language of our politics and politicians is mired in a simplistic rhetoric of individual

56 The Cognitive Roots of Injustice

responsibility and an ideology of individual autonomy. . . . The idea of individual autonomy is used as a measure against which to judge the appropriateness of both individual and governmental actions," as well as the functioning of the family, the economy, and the government. More specifically, the hegemony of the autonomy assumption "has served to derail or limit contemporary policy discussions about important issues of public welfare" to the point that it is now, in America, "particularly difficult to assert the claim of any collective responsibility to assure at least a minimal standard of economic and material equality for all citizens," and "the mere invocation of the term 'dependency' prompts and justifies mean-spirited and ill-conceived political responses" (Fineman xvi, 9, 22, 25, 31–34).

In cultures that take more adequate account of the situational constraints on human behavior, the emotional responses to social deviants (including criminals and the social underclass) involve greater compassion and less contempt or anger, and the result is policies, institutions, and systems relying less on punishment and more on prevention and rehabilitation. As Joan Miller explains, the notion of the autonomous individual leads people "to view deviance as arising from dispositional factors within the agent. . . . In contrast, cultural views stressed in many non-Western cultures emphasize the openness and interdependence characterizing the agent's relations with the surround, . . . [and] such cultural conceptions tend to approach deviance in interactional terms, as resulting from some disequilibrium in the agent's relations with the environment" (Miller 963). Ryan concludes "that the ideology of Blaming the Victim so distorts and disorients the thinking of the average concerned citizen that it becomes a primary barrier to effective social change . . . [and] that the injustices and inequalities in American life can never be understood (and, therefore, can never be eliminated) until that ideology is exposed and destroyed" (Ryan xv).

Liberty as well as justice requires that we acknowledge the power of situations to determine behaviors and life outcomes rather than clinging to the illusory notion of freedom offered by our cherished self-image as autonomous, self-determining individuals. As Hanson and Yosifon explain,

> the model of human agency we so often work with—as laypeople, as legal scholars, and as policymakers—is wrong. And not just wrong, but clearly and dangerously wrong. . . . By blinding ourselves to the very forces that impinge upon our freedom, we are surrendering to them.

To be serious about liberty requires that we not unwittingly turn over the situational strings to whoever has the means and ends to manipulate them. Indeed, our greatest dispositional act may be to acknowledge that we are situational characters and to choose to understand and gain some voice and control over the situation that largely controls us. In that very important sense, we do have a choice. (Hanson and Yosifon, "Situational Character" 73–74)

Replacing the Autonomy Schema

Preventing the fundamental attribution error by replacing the autonomy schema at the heart of American ideology with a schema that takes appropriate account of situational constraints on behavior and life outcomes would thus contribute significantly to social justice and is arguably a prerequisite for it. Indeed, given the tremendous suffering and injustice that are perpetrated by faulty, autonomist judgments, there is a pressing need to take all possible measures to correct or replace the autonomy schema that gives rise to them. As Benforado and Hanson declare, "changing the sources of the attributional framework used by policymakers may be the single most important step in developing effective policies in the law and beyond. The costs of inaction are huge" (Benforado and Hanson, "Attributional" 406).

But as we noted in Chapter 1, simply providing people with declarative knowledge of the determinative power of situations rarely succeeds in preventing such faulty judgments. This fact raises two basic questions. First, is it even possible to correct the dispositionist bias and prevent the fundamental attribution error? And second, if it is possible, how can it be done? Fortunately, research has demonstrated that changing the autonomy schema is not only possible but also effective in reducing punitive behavior toward stigmatized groups. One investigation found that the intensive study of social science, which educates students in the environmental or situational causes of people's actions and fates, decreases the tendency to attribute poverty to personal shortcomings (Guimond et al. 132, 137). Another study found that educating students on the structural causes of inequality reduces their tendency to focus exclusively on the dispositional causes of behavior and thereby blame the victims of these conditions (Lopez et al. 321ff.).

These courses appear to have worked in two basic ways to replace students' autonomy schemas with situationism schemas so that they automatically took account of, rather than ignored, the situational causes of behavior and life outcomes. First, the courses undoubtedly provided students with multiple exemplars of situationism. And second, they also, in all likelihood, engaged students in enacting most of the information-processing steps of the situationism schema. In addition to these two practices, the efficacy of which has also received some empirical support (see Stewart et al.) and which we will address in more detail at the end of this chapter, the replacement of faulty schemas can also be advanced by identifying their sources and eliminating or reducing them where possible, while at the same time developing people's metacognition regarding these sources (as well as their modes of operation and harmful consequences). It is to the question of sources that we now turn.

Sources of the Autonomy Schema

Psychologists have determined that the fundamental attribution error results from both nature and culture. The factors attributable to nature include the human perceptual apparatus. One basic reason we emphasize persons more than situations when we attribute causality is the simple fact that the persons involved are often more salient than the situations to which their behavior is responding.

This factor was demonstrated in a number of experiments that varied the visibility of person and situation. One study found that subjects attributed behavior more to a person when he was brightly illuminated or moving than when he was more dimly lit or immobile. Another study demonstrated that when subjects observed an interaction between two persons but could see one better than the other, they attributed greater causal responsibility for the outcome of their interaction to the more visible of the two. And a third experiment revealed that variations of the focus of observers from one person to the other produced corresponding variations in the observers' attributions, with greater causal responsibility being attributed to the more visible person in each case (Ross and Nisbett 140–141). Since many or all aspects of the situation to which any given action is responding are often invisible to observers — because they are either spatially or temporally distant or intangible — the person is frequently the only viable candidate for focus and hence for causal attribution. Thus, Benforado and Hanson explain,

> In our eyes, the welfare recipient buying a wide-screen Magnavox at inflated prices on a rent-to-own credit plan is a foolish consumer mak-

ing another bad decision—a wasteful extravagance for someone struggling to pay the light bill and save for retirement. All of the situational elements that moved her toward renting the TV—the promise from her kids that they will spend more time at home, the deceptive wording of the credit plan, the clever sales techniques of the retailer, the fact that a neighbor has one and "loves" it, the absence of other retailers willing to sell in the inner city, and the optimism that a raise will come through at the end of the year—are not particularly noticeable as we watch her signing on the dotted line. Were we the ones making the purchase, those and other situational elements might seem very relevant (and, indeed, hard to miss), but as mere observers, it is difficult to see anything but a spendthrift exercising her free choice and a retailer responding to the customer's demands. (Benforado and Hanson, "Attributional" 322)

Even when the physical situation is visible to observers, they still may fail to perceive the aspects of the situation that the agent finds most compelling—such as a threat or an opportunity of some sort (see Gilbert 21–22). As psychologist Daniel Gilbert points out, "people often adopt an egocentric point of view and assume that the situation they see is the situation that the actor sees too" (Gilbert 23). For example, when Bigger Thomas, the African American protagonist of *Native Son*, enters the rich white neighborhood of the Daltons and then their house, he sees dangers at every turn, whereas most white people, in the absence of the novel's vision, would see a completely innocuous situation (see Chapter 8).

Egocentrism also accounts for a second cause of dispositionism: inaccurate assumptions about what constitutes a "normal" response to a certain situation. When a person's response to a situation seems normal, we attribute the behavior to the situation. For example, when a person flees a burning building, we attribute the flight to the dangerous situation and not to some special quality of the person. But when a person runs into a burning building, we are likely to attribute that action to some characteristic of the person, such as courage, self-destructiveness, or madness. Our assumptions about what constitutes a normal response are often inaccurate because they are based on our beliefs about what our own response in such a situation would be, and such beliefs are often seriously off target, as demonstrated by subjects of some of the experiments described earlier who were greatly surprised and dismayed that they behaved as they did in those situations. Thus when we judge certain individuals to be aggressive or cowardly because we believe that

60 The Cognitive Roots of Injustice

we would not have acted in such a manner in such a situation, we may be profoundly mistaken on both counts (see Gilbert 24).

Third, the fundamental attribution error can result from our failing to adequately factor in the determinative force of the situation because our minds lack the processing capacity, at the time, to perform this task, which is much more difficult than the automatic action of making inferences about the person. Psychologists have surmised that our initial move in attempting to understand the causes of an action is to posit a corresponding disposition in the actor. Thus with an aggressive act, we initially infer that the actor must be an aggressive person. Only subsequently do we examine the situation to determine whether it warranted the aggression (according to our own standards and expectations); if we judge that it did, then we back away from our initial dispositional inference. But this second action requires more time, effort, and cognitive resources than the initial inference, and in cases where we lack one of these elements, the second step is never taken, or is inadequately executed, and our faulty initial dispositional inference is left uncorrected (see Gilbert and Malone 29).

Our tendency to focus on persons rather than their situations is also due in no small measure to the fact that the human brain has evolved to give precedence to identifying the presence and deciphering the dispositions and intentions of humans (and, to a slightly lesser degree, other animals) in our environment—and, moreover, to err on the side of overattributing rather than underattributing agency, intention, and hostility to other individuals (see Atran). This overattribution of intention and agency—of which autonomism, or dispositionism, is a manifestation as well as a source—had (and in many ways still has) a clear survival value, insofar as failing to detect a hostile intention or disposition would be more likely to be fatal than failing to detect a benign intention or disposition or the absence of intent altogether.

Other fundamental and powerful psychological sources of autonomism derive from the various forms taken by the most basic human psychological need: the need to maintain one's identity, or sense of self (see Bracher, *Social*). This need manifests itself in numerous forms, including the need for self-affirmation, the need for self-efficacy, the desire for social dominance, the need to see the world as fundamentally just, and the need to justify the social system(s) of which one is a part. Each of these basic identity-needs finds support in—and thus helps to motivate—the autonomy schema (see Benforado and Hanson 383–388). First, the autonomy schema allows the fortunate to credit themselves with their good fortune and thus to feel both more morally worthy (the self-affirmation motive) and more powerful (the self-efficacy motive). In addition, autonomist attributions also help legitimize fortunate people's positions of social dominance ("social dominance orientation") by enabling them to conclude that the system is fair (belief in a just world) rather than slanted to give them an unfair advantage over the less fortunate. Indeed, the autonomy schema even provides security for the unfortunate themselves by allowing them to believe that the social system with which they are identified is good and blameless because their own lower status is their own fault (system justification). Thus, one reason the autonomy schema is so powerful is that to doubt the role of individuals' choice in determining their life outcomes would undermine our very sense of self.

In addition to these constraints imposed on cognition by our cognitive hardware and psychological needs, numerous mutually reinforcing material, social, and cultural forces also contribute in a major way to the formation and dominance of Americans' autonomy schema. That culture is a major source of the autonomy schema is demonstrated by studies comparing Americans' causal attributions with those of individuals from East Asian cultures. Such studies consistently reveal that Americans typically judge people to be significantly more responsible for their actions and life outcomes than they in fact are (Choi, Nisbett, and Norenzayan 47). A comparative study of American and Chinese newspaper articles reporting mass murders found that the American reporters attributed greater causality to the personal qualities of the murderers, while the Chinese reporters saw situational factors as the primary causes for these crimes: Americans emphasized personality traits, attitudes, and psychological problems, but the Chinese focused on the murderers' relationships, societal pressures, and economic situations (Morris and Peng 961). Another study found that Hindu Indian adults gave contextual factors more than twice as much weight as did American adults in explaining the causes of certain deviant behaviors (Miller 968). For example, whereas an American explained a neighbor's cheating on her tax return as resulting from the neighbor's character ("That's just the type of person she is. She's very competitive"), an Indian subject explained his being cheated by a housing contractor in terms of the contractor's situation ("The man is unemployed. He is not in a position to give that money") (Miller 968).

The same contrast was found in another study, in which subjects were asked to explain why a lawyer motorcyclist, whose passenger was injured in an accident when the back tire blew out, left the injured man at a hospital and then went on to his court date, rather than staying at the hospital with the passenger, who later died from his injuries. While the Hindu subjects emphasized the lawyer's duty to be in court for his client, his possible nervousness or confusion resulting from the situation, and the possibility that the passenger's injuries might not have appeared to be serious, the American subjects explained his behavior primarily in terms of his character, viewing him as irresponsible or ambitious (Miller 972). That these differences between Americans and Indians are culturally conditioned is further demonstrated by fact that the differences do not appear in attributions made by American and Indian children; they only emerge later, after socialization and enculturation have done their work.

Failure to recognize the other's lack of responsibility can be traced to faulty information processing—specifically, expecting, searching for, attending to, inferring, and supposing causes internal to the agent and thus excluding, marginalizing, or discounting external, situational causes of the agent's behavior. As Miller explains, "The Western cultural emphasis on the agent's autonomy from contextual influences and on individual responsibility for action . . . encourag[es] attributors *to search for* internal factors predicting behavior," while "the more relational conceptions of the person in non-Western cultures" leads them to search for the situational causes of behavior (Miller 963; emphasis added). Hochschild's observation that the American dream, with its presumption of individual autonomy, "leads one to *focus on* people's behaviors rather than on economic processes, environmental constraints, or political structures as the causal explanation for social orderings" (Hochschild 36; emphasis added) identifies another key information-processing mechanism by which the autonomy schema produces its impact: the directing and focusing of attention. This focusing of attention on people's behaviors and away from environmental constraints makes it "extremely difficult for Americans to see that everyone cannot simultaneously attain more than absolute success" (Hochschild 37).

Empirical studies have demonstrated the narrowed focus of Americans in this regard. One study found that Koreans "made more external attributions than Americans because Koreans considered more information than did Americans" (Choi et al. 46). American and Korean subjects were given a short description of a murder and asked to choose which items in a list would be relevant in explaining the act. It was found that Koreans had a more comprehensive view of the causes of behavior than Americans, and that this view resulted in their taking more information into account, which in turn produced more external attributions than Americans produced (Choi et al. 54).

The information-processing effects of the autonomy schema of American ideology are most evident from the fact that the schema not only prevents Americans from attending to and searching for situational causes of behavior, it actually prevents them from acknowledging and correcting for such factors when they are explicitly presented. In the responses to the motorcycle accident described above, it was found that the Americans ignored explicit information about the motorcyclist's situation "to concentrate instead on dispositional properties of the agent, factors that [were not given but] could only be *inferred*"—an information-processing strategy that was driven by "American cultural conceptions of the person" (Miller 972; emphasis added), or more specifically, the autonomy person-schema. Similar blinding effects of the autonomy schema are evident in the finding that when the situational constraints on behavior were made salient, Koreans took this information into account and reduced their internal attributions but Americans *discounted* the information and maintained their internal attributions (Choi and Nisbett 949).

Thus the reason Americans commit the fundamental attribution error and are less accurate than East Asians in their assessment of the causes of behavior is because they systematically ignore situational causes. And the reason they ignore these causes is because their autonomy person-schema embodies the assumption that a person's behavior is caused primarily by the qualities of the person and only slightly, if at all, by the person's situation. As one research team explains,

If a person has a very complex causal theory [i.e., schema] and believes that an event has numerous causes, he or she will try to consider a large pool of information before constructing a convincing causal account. For example, when trying to explain why someone would kill another person, a person with a complex causal theory [schema] will consider many different pieces of information about the perpetrator, the victim, and the context in which the incident occurred. However, if a person has a relatively simple causal theory [schema], the number of different pieces of information he or she considers would be relatively fewer. For instance, if one believes that only internal attributes cause behavior [as the autonomy person-schema has it], then information about the perpetrator's personality would be considered sufficient to satisfactorily explain the incident. Evidence from past studies indicates that the complexity of one's causal theory may be shaped to a substantial degree by the culture to which one belongs. People from East Asian countries tend to possess relatively more complex causal theories than do people from Western cultures. East Asians tend to believe that humans' behavior is the outcome of a complex interaction between personal and situational factors, whereas Americans tend to believe in the dominant power of personal factors. (Choi et al. 47)

These psychologists conclude "that the typical East–West differences in causal attributions derive primarily from East Asians' relative sensitivity to situational influences on behavior" and that this greater sensitivity to situational causes derives from a different person-schema: "a more holistic notion of the person in which the boundary between the person and the situation is rather porous and ill defined" (Choi et al. 57).

The prominence of the autonomy schema in America specifically and the West generally has been attributed to several additional factors. One is geography. Nisbett suggests that autonomism is more suited to the needs of hunting and industrial societies than is situationism (Nisbett, "Essence" 191). Hanson and Yosifon agree that historical geographical factors may have played a role in American dispositionism insofar as the "seemingly boundless land and natural resources, together with growing markets and changing technologies, provided many Americans with a strong perception of self-reliance and self-determination" (Hanson and Yosifon, "The Situation" 261, note).

Social roles that correspond to these geographical conditions have also contributed to the establishment and maintenance of the autonomy schema. Nisbett states that attributional differences between Asians and Westerners may result in part from differences in social reality: "Life is situationally determined for Asians to a greater degree than for Americans so Asians are situationists. Life is a function of choices, preferences, and dispositions for Americans to a greater degree than for Asians so Americans are dispositionists" (Nisbett, "Essence" 184). In addition, Benforado and Hanson argue that many jobs in America in effect train workers in dispositionism and that career advancement in many fields is also organized in such a way as to promote dispositionism (339–341).

Western and American intellectual traditions and institutions also contribute significantly to the establishment of the autonomy schema. As Ross and Nisbett note, "Much of Western culture, from the Judeo-Christian insistence on individual moral responsibility to the intellectual underpinnings of capitalism and democracy in terms of the imperative of freedom of action, emphasizes the causal role of the actor and attributes actions of different kinds to actors of different kinds" (Ross and Nisbett 142).

Zimbardo concurs, noting, "Most of our institutions are founded on [a dispositionist] perspective, including law, medicine, and religion. Culpability, illness, and sin, they assume, are to be found within the guilty party, the sick person, and the sinner. They begin their quest for understanding with the 'Who questions': *Who* is responsible? *Who* caused it? *Who* gets the blame? and *Who* gets the credit?" (Zimbardo 7). The repeated observation of, and participation in, such inquiries plays a major role in inculcating the autonomy schema.

Language, too, may play a significant role in promoting the autonomy schema, as Nisbett argues:

> For Westerners, it is the self who does the acting; for Easterners, action is something that is undertaken in concert with others or that is the consequence of the self operating in a field of forces. Languages capture this different sort of agency . . . : there are many different words for "I" in Japanese and (formerly, at any rate) in Chinese, reflecting the relationship between self and other. So there is an "I" in relation to my colleague, "I" in relation to my spouse, etc. It is difficult for Japanese to think of properties that apply to "me." It is much easier for them to think of properties that apply to themselves in certain settings and in relation to particular people. Grammar also reflects a different sense of how action comes about. Most Western languages are "agentic" in the sense that the language conveys that the self has operated on the world: "He dropped it." (An exception is Spanish.) Eastern languages are in general relatively nonagentic: "It fell from him," or just "fell." (Nisbett, *Geography* 158)

The autonomy schema also receives reinforcement by the fact that in English and other Western languages, "the same adjective that can be applied to the actor's behavior can usually be applied to the actor. Thus, 'hostile' acts are perpetrated by 'hostile' people, 'dependent' acts by 'dependent' people, and so on." Such correlations between actions and situations, in contrast, are only rarely possible in English (Ross and Nisbett 141–142). The ease with which our language allows us to move from categorizing an action to making a corresponding inference about the actor, while simultaneously prohibiting a similar correspondent inference

66 The Cognitive Roots of Injustice

regarding situational determinants of the action (see Ross 61–62), facilitates the dispositionist attributions that reinforce the autonomy schema.

Formal education also inculcates the autonomy schema in the United States. Studies have found "that law school is encouraging dispositionism and punishing those who seek to offer a more situationist account of human behavior—in the law or in the classroom" (Hanson and McCann 1441). Hanson and McCann report that in law schools, "the student who offers [situationist] arguments is met with anything from indifference to [indignation]. The [situationist] arguments themselves are seen as fanciful and dangerous—the product of ignorance, bias, hypersensitivity, and emotion and the stuff of unwarranted intergroup animosity" (Hanson and McCann 1443). Nor is the inculcation of the autonomy schema restricted to legal education; it is also produced by various other education and child-rearing practices, including American history courses from elementary school to college that portray major figures as agents of historical events rather than products of historical circumstances (see Nisbett, *Geography* 127–128).

One of the most visible and powerful contemporary cultural sources of the autonomy schema is autonomist propaganda. As Hanson and Yosifon point out, "large corporate interests have a great deal at stake in maintaining and promoting a dispositionist worldview" because such a view "justifies their profit-seeking behavior as socially beneficial," reduces regulation of their activities and recognition of their liability, and more generally "helps to preserve and legitimate the status quo, in which corporations are the wealthiest and most powerful entities" (Hanson and Yosifon, "The Situation" 225–228). Consequently, advertising is replete with assertions of consumer autonomy. Cigarette advertisements, for example, have historically emphasized the consumer's autonomy and choice, and many other commercial interests do the same (Hanson and Yosifon, "The Situation" 245–249).

In addition to advertising, commercial interests have also promoted autonomism through less overt but nonetheless extremely effective efforts, such as the John M. Olin Foundation's funding of centers, journals, workshops, scholarships, and fellowships to produce autonomist propaganda and propagandists in legal studies and the law (see Hanson and Yosifon, "The Situation" 273ff.). Capitalist interests promote autonomism by attacking individuals who make situationist arguments and predicting loss of freedom and prosperity if the validity of situationism is recognized (see Hanson and Yosifon, "The Situation" 328ff.; Benforado and Hanson, "Naïve Cynicism" 560ff.; and Chen and Hanson, "Illusion" 99ff.). And the hegemony of the autonomy schema in the law is solidified by the appointment of hard-core autonomists to the federal judiciary, as Hanson and Yosifon note. Writing during the last Bush administration, they declare: "At this moment in history, it is difficult to imagine that any federal judge will be appointed or promoted who does not substantially embrace the hard-core dispositionism promoted by President Bush, his advisors, and the Federalist Society" (Hanson and Yosifon, "The Situation" 243).

One of the most pervasive and powerful forces inculcating the autonomy schema during the past half-century is television. The nature of the televisual medium, the format of television programming, and the dominant content of its programs all function in various ways to activate, validate, and reinforce the autonomy schema by providing viewers with multiple autonomy exemplars of all types and by repeatedly guiding viewers through autonomist information-processing routines. The dominant narrative structures of television programming provide exemplars of, and direct attention to, actions and persons rather than the situational forces underlying them. Police dramas and news reports alike focus on criminals, law enforcement officers, lawyers, and other individuals and their actions rather than on the personal circumstances and social situations, policies, institutions, and systems that variously coerce and constrain their actions. Situation comedies, despite the acknowledgment of situation embodied in the genre's name, also emphasize character as determinative of action, by foregrounding character quirks and types. Indeed, the sticky situations in which the characters of these dramas inevitably find themselves are usually presented as partly if not completely generated by the various quirks, flaws, and actions of the characters themselves. Action and character are also the focus of programs involving competition, where sporting events, game shows, cooking contests, fashion-design competitions, and so on emphasize the agent as the major or even sole cause of outcome. Significantly, while sports analyses in American media focus on individual performances as the primary causes of winning and losing, analyses of winning and losing in other cultures often attribute the causes more to the context and the other team (see Nisbett, *Geography* 115–116).

As a visual medium, the very form of television focuses attention on moving bodies in space, leaving out of mind the external causes and constraints of the movement, which are often out of sight if not inherently invisible. Somewhat less concretely, as Jeffrey Scheuer observes, television "*personalizes*, focusing on—and often exaggerating the im-

68 The Cognitive Roots of Injustice

portance of—individuals (heroes and villains, freaks, clowns, and celebrities), who typically seem unaffected by broader social forces" (Scheuer 74–75). As Scheuer explains, "specific persons and events, especially dramatic ruptures and socially fracturing activities—war, crime, natural disaster, competition, immediate physical or emotional conflict—are inherently telegenic," whereas "complex and diffuse social problems, such as the intractable and interconnected pathologies of poverty, dependency, violence, illiteracy, drug abuse, and teen pregnancy, are . . . viewed only from the perspective of isolated 'trees' "—i.e., autonomous individuals (Scheuer 87). The format of television, with its quick cuts and lack of continuity, likewise reinforces the focus of attention on immediate action and the actor performing it, rather than on circumstantial pressures and the actor's ongoing experiences of and responses to those pressures.

By thus engaging viewers in endlessly repeating the inherent perceptual biases discussed above, which focus on action and the actor and overlook or ignore situational factors that are not themselves immediately present, tangible, and dynamic, television functions as a major reason for the autonomy schema's continued hegemony.

Correcting Autonomist Information-Processing Routines

Although developing metacognition of this sort about the sources and functioning of the autonomy schema can contribute to its replacement by enabling people to avoid, resist, compensate for, or decommission some of these sources, addressing its sources is by itself neither necessary nor sufficient to replace the schema. More crucial are the development of more adequate, situationist information-processing scripts and the accrual of a critical mass of more adequate, situationist exemplars of various sorts. Information-processing routines that must be altered in order to correct the faulty processing of the autonomy schema include the following.

- *Expectation and notice.* People operating with the autonomy schema expect there to be no significant situational determinants of behaviors or life outcomes, and because of this expectation they often fail to notice situational factors even when they are apparent (see Hamilton; Wittenbrink et al.; and Gawronski). Thus homeless persons are seen as responsible for their fate because of their supposed shiftlessness or laziness, and situational factors that caused the homelessness—such as an accident or illness that rendered them incapable of working and/or resulted in financially devastating medical expenses—are overlooked. People need to expect there to be significant situational determinants for every behavior and every life outcome, both positive and negative. They should expect that every homeless person, for example, will have encountered one or more situations—such as lack of help from family members or social services, a downturn in the economy, or a bankrupting illness—in the absence of which the person would not be homeless.

- *Attention and focus.* Even when people do notice situational factors, or are forced to notice them, they often discount the significance of these circumstances and focus their attention on character traits instead. Thus when people see a person whose homelessness was caused by bankruptcy resulting from medical expenses, they may still blame the individual for this fate, criticizing her for not having better insurance or for becoming ill in the first place. People must learn to focus on such situational determinants when they are evident.
- *Information search.* Because people expect behavior and destiny to be determined by character traits, in the absence of evidence that such traits played a central role, individuals operating with the autonomy schema will often search for such traits, but they will not search for situational determinants. Thus when people see a homeless man, they may look for signs that he drinks or uses drugs, but they will not look for evidence that he has encountered misfortune. To break free of the autonomist bias, they must develop the habit of searching for such evidence when it is not immediately evident, such as by looking for signs of serious illness or other unavoidable causes of financial ruin.
- *Inference.* In some cases, people will simply infer the existence of character determinants, either because their search for such factors proved unproductive or because they are so confident in their general assumption of autonomy that they don't feel that specific evidence is necessary. They will not, however, draw similar inferences concerning the situational determinants of behavior or destiny. Thus when there is no clear evidence that a welfare recipient is lazy or self-indulgent, many people will simply assume that she is on the basis of highly ambiguous data, such as the fact that she walks very slowly or spends a lot of time sleeping. People must learn to infer the existence of situational determinants of behavior and life outcome when such determinants are not obvious—for example, by wondering whether slow

walking or excessive sleeping may be symptoms of physical or psychological maladies rather than signs of laziness or self-indulgence.

- *Supposition.* When there is no evidence even of the most ambiguous sort to support the inference that a behavior or life outcome is the result of character rather than situation, the autonomy schema will fill the gap in information with the supposition that such character traits exist. Thus in the absence of any evidence that a homeless person has squandered his resources on alcohol or drugs, many people will simply assume that he has. Such supposition must be prevented and replaced with the new default assumption—triggered in the absence of any information about specific situational determinants—that some misfortune or disability must have contributed significantly to the person's homelessness.

- *Memory search.* Often people reach or bolster their conclusion by recalling other examples in which character supposedly determined behavior or life outcome. When they search their memories, they fail to recall any examples of behavior or life outcome being determined by situational forces. They remember examples of presumably lazy, dissolute, or self-indulgent homeless persons, but no examples of people who were rendered homeless by forces beyond their control. People must acquire the habit of questioning the typicality of these memories, resisting drawing general conclusions from them and searching instead for memories in which situational determinants dominate.

- *Memory encoding.* Since the autonomy schema blocks awareness of situational factors, however, there is often no experience of such factors to remember. And on those relatively rare occasions when an individual does notice situational factors, the autonomy schema is likely to either prevent these examples from being encoded in memory or cause them to be encoded as special cases that do not disconfirm the principle of autonomy and that are therefore not retrieved from memory in future instances where the memory would be relevant. Individuals must be helped to encode in their memories the situational determinants of behavior and destiny.

- *Emotions.* The autonomy schema produces feelings of indifference, disdain, contempt, anger, and even hatred for the stigmatized other, and feelings of respect, admiration, and awe for fortunate people. Many Americans, for example, respect and admire wealthy people without knowing anything about them other than their wealth, and not even knowing how they came by that wealth. Individuals should be helped to feel sympathy for the (unfortunate) stigmatized other and indifference or lack of admiration and undue respect—and even resentment—toward the fortunate other, for reaping undeserved benefits from the system.

- *Action script retrieval.* People in whom the autonomy schema is operating respond to the stigmatized other with neglect, punishment, oppression, or persecution. Poor people are left to fend for themselves, and users of illegal drugs and other criminals are punished. Individuals must be helped to retrieve action scripts of support, assistance, and rehabilitation for such people.

Many literary texts are structured in ways that train readers in situationist information processing. As Lucy Pollard-Gott has noted in her article "Attribution Theory and the Novel," novels have a unique power and tendency to focus our attention on elements and complexities of situations that have a powerful impact on people and determine their behaviors but that are often invisible to observers outside of fiction. By focusing our attention on situational factors that we tend to overlook in real life and by making us privy to characters' feelings and thoughts evoked by these situational factors—feelings and thoughts that are generally not available to us in real life—novels lead us to make more situational attributions than we tend to make when observing similar behaviors in similar situations outside the novel (Pollard-Gott 505–506). More specifically, by presenting events from a character's point of view rather than from that of an external observer, and thus making readers more aware of the compelling, behavior-determining force with which certain situational factors influence the character, "novels can . . . induce readers to overcome their typical [dispositionist] attribution biases" (Pollard-Gott 516). And since "well-practiced processes become automatized" (Newman et al. 244), when this new information-processing routine of focusing on situations and their behavior-determining effects on persons is repeated numerous times, it begins to become automatic and to replace the default attention script of the autonomy schema.

Furthermore, the repeated frustration of the autonomist expectation of character-determined behaviors and life outcomes by repeated encounters with situation-determined behaviors and life outcomes will eventually establish the situationist expectation as the default. Similar changes can occur in the other information-processing scripts as novels lead readers through, or induce them to perform, situationist processing in each case. Autonomist information search, inference, and supposition are similarly frustrated by texts that offer no character determinants of behavior and life outcome to be found and/or provide information that blocks autonomist inferences and suppositions of such—as in the Book of Job, which makes it clear both to Job's "comforters" and to contemporary readers that Job's calamities were not due to any actions or shortcomings of his own and powerfully rejects the comforters' autonomist claims to the contrary.

Literary texts can also produce situationist memory searches in readers, either by directly instructing them to remember when they were in a similar situation (as Stowe does in *Uncle Tom's Cabin*) or inducing them to do so by using imagery and details that directly evoke their personal memories or that produce strong emotions in them that then trigger such memories through the principle of "mood-congruent recall." Moreover, by repeatedly eliciting situationist emotions of compassion and empathic anger for the plights of characters, literary texts also gradually develop these emotions of readers as the default, in place of autonomist indifference, disdain, contempt, and hatred. The same is true of action scripts: through positive portrayals of actions of prevention, repair, and assistance in response to problematic behaviors and life outcomes, novels create or strengthen associative networks linking such actions with situationist perceptions and emotions and thus move them toward automaticity and the default position.

Replacing Autonomist Exemplars and Prototypes

In addition to correcting faulty information-processing routines through engaging people in performing more adequate ones, it is also necessary to replace inaccurate, atypical exemplars and prototypes with more accurate ones. Correcting faulty exemplars and prototypes is crucial because, as we saw in the first chapter, these forms of knowledge can lead to faulty judgments in two ways: first, they can short-circuit more systematic information processing by directly activating emotion and action scripts, bypassing information search, careful inference, and so on, and second, they can serve to (mis)direct each step of information processing whenever a person engages in a more systematic and comprehensive assessment of others.

The autonomist prototypes that must be replaced include the following:

- *Concepts* such as "autonomous," "self-reliant," "reliable," "dependable," "perseverant," "courageous," "indomitable," and "steadfast."

Characterizing people with these concepts performatively establishes the power of the autonomy schema, by tacitly assuming, and eliciting implicit agreement, that the category of autonomy is an important and unproblematic category for perceiving and judging people's behavior and character. The same is true of negative signifiers such as "dependent," "needy," "unreliable," "parasitical," "lazy," "self-indulgent," and "cowardly," which not only administer social censure but also reinforce the assumption that autonomy exists, that it is a virtue, that it is a crucial category of appraisal, that its meaning is transparent, and that its attribution is unproblematic. Such concepts must be countered with concepts recognizing the determinative force of situational factors, such as "victim," "unfortunate," "ill-fated," "unlucky," and "star-crossed" (as well as "lucky," "fortunate," etc.).

- *Episode scripts* of competition, perseverance, triumph, and success, as well as intransigence, intractability, and stubbornness. These must be countered with episodes in which effort, ability, and virtue do not win the day, as well as episodes in which people who lack virtue, effort, and ability triumph.
- *Life scripts* such as the rags-to-riches story of the self-made man, survival stories of the frontiersman, the homesteader, and the explorer, and biographies of professional athletes and entertainers recounting their struggles and triumphs—all of them success stories in one way or another. These prototypic narratives must be countered with stories showing individuals approaching life with the best of intentions and equipped with the best of abilities being defeated and even destroyed by forces over which they have no control.
- *Prototypic individuals,* including the frontiersman, the homesteader, the hunter, the fisherman, the explorer, the independent farmer, the successful businessman or entrepreneur, the self-made man, and the autodidact, as well as negative figures such as the drug addict, the drunkard, the welfare cheat, the criminal, the loner, and the sociopath. Such prototypes must be countered by figures embodying the determining force of fortune, including the child born with a silver spoon in her mouth and the child born destitute and victimized by bad luck, violence, or indifference.
- *Body images,* including postures, gazes, facial expressions, movements, and vocal intonations that express self-sufficiency, domination, triumph, complacency, contentment, smugness, and superiority. These must be balanced with postures, gazes, facial expressions, movements, and vocal intonations embodying defeat, exhaustion, and helplessness, revealing the triumph of circumstances over character.

- *Emotions*, including pride, elation, jubilation, confidence, and arrogance in response to one's own good fortune and indifference, disdain, scorn, contempt, anger, and hatred toward unfortunate others. Such emotions must give way to emotions that recognize one's own and others' lack of autonomy, including humility and gratitude for one's own good fortune, and sympathy, fear, sadness, anguish, and empathic anger at the misfortune and injustice suffered by others.
- *Action scripts*, of neglect, oppression, or persecution of victims of circumstance. These must be replaced with scripts of assisting victims and acting to prevent future harm. Such action scripts can be found in all social policies, institutions, systems, and structures that provide assistance to needy people or take steps to prevent suffering or need.

As we will see in Chapters 6 through 8, literary texts can perform each of these schema-altering functions: they can develop metacognition of the nature, sources, and operations of the faulty schema, engage readers in exercising more adequate information-processing routines, and provide readers with more valid exemplars for use as templates for assessing the behaviors and life outcomes of other people. And as we will see in the final chapter, schema criticism can systematize and enhance these processes in practices that constitute a new, more effective methodology for literary, cultural, and social criticism.

CHAPTER 3

Essentialism versus Malleability:
Responsibility for Character

We have made them what they are; . . . it would be cruel to make the fault and punish it too.
HARRIET BEECHER STOWE, *UNCLE TOM'S CABIN*

The essentialism schema, which embodies "the belief that certain characteristics . . . may be relatively stable, unchanging, likely to be present at birth, and biologically based" (Gelman, Heyman, and Legare 757), systematically prevents recognition of the formative effects of environment on character, maintaining the view that people's attributes are inherent rather than a product of their environment, fixed rather than malleable (see Keller 687; Bastian and Haslam 229, 232; Haslam et al. 64).

As one psychological research team explains, "Essentialism is a naïve ontology positing that categories have a deep and unobservable reality, that this reality . . . is unchanging and unchangeable by human intervention, . . . that it has a 'natural' basis, [and that] in the domain of social categories this causal basis may often be understood in a biological fashion" (Haslam et al. 64). The essentialism schema underwrites the belief that "people's qualities are fixed over time and across situations" (Levy, Plaks, and Dweck 191), that "many forms of human behavior are biologically determined," that "the fate of each person lies in his or her genes," "that intelligence is a trait that is strongly determined by genetic predispositions," "that many differences between humans of different skin color can be attributed to differences in genetic predispositions" (Keller 690), that "heroes and champions are born, not made," and that "our leaders, our 'Best,' are in the proper position in society because they have inherited the best genes" (Lerner 13).

Like the autonomy schema, the essentialism schema blocks awareness of the influence of external, environmental forces on people. While the autonomy schema blocks awareness of *current* external determinants of *behavior* and life outcomes, however, the essentialism schema blocks awareness of *past* external determinants of *character*. Also like the autonomy schema, the essentialism schema is more prominent among Americans than among East Asians (Choi, Nisbett, and Norenzayan 58): just as they tend to deny the impact of circumstances on behavior, so also do Americans tend to deny the impact of environmental forces on the formation of character.

Although one research team claims to have identified six factors of essentialism, most researchers recognize innateness and immutability as the core essentialist qualities.[1] And the key issue for social justice is that of immutability/malleability: whether or not a person's personality and character traits are formed, and can be re-formed or trans-formed, by experience. This issue of malleability has been the focus of one of the most interesting research programs related to essentialism, that of Carol Dweck and her colleagues concerning two opposed cognitive schemas, or "implicit person-theories," as they call them. "Entity theory," which embraces the core position of essentialism, and which I will therefore refer to as the "essentialism schema," takes human character to be fixed and innate, while "incremental theory," which I will refer to as the "malleability schema," views human character as malleable and determined to a large degree by a person's formative environment (Levy, Plaks, and Dweck 190–192).[2] People operating with the entity theory agree with the proposition "Everyone is a certain kind of person, and there is not much that can be done to really change that," while people with the incremental theory agree more with the statement "Anybody can change their personality a lot" (Levy, Plaks, and Dweck 191).

Falseness of Essentialism

Essentialism has been disproven in multiple ways. First, geneticists have found that the presence of certain genes, apart from environmental influences on them, determines relatively little about a person's character. Lewontin et al. observe, "We cannot think of any significant human social behavior that is built into our genes in such a way that it cannot be modified and shaped by social conditioning. Even biological features such as eating, sleeping, and sex are greatly modified by conscious control and social conditioning" (Lewontin et al. 267–268). Recent studies have revealed that even among lower animals such as rats, "genes are not destiny" (Begley 169). The finding that a mother rat's treatment of her babies turns certain genes on and others off suggests "that the lives we lead and the behavior of those who care for us can alter the very chemistry of DNA. Genes are not destiny. Our genes, and thus their effects on the brain, are more plastic than we ever dreamed" (Begley 180; see also 10, 169).

The essentialist view of persons is also refuted by developmental studies, which demonstrate that individuals are for the most part made the way they are by their formative environment rather than born to be that way (e.g., "born to be wild," "born to run," "born under a bad sign," etc., as various titles of popular songs would have it). Contrary to the essentialist view, people's temperament, character, and personality are significantly determined by their early experiences and environment. McGill University researcher Michael Meany finds from his study of rats that "when you expose the parent to stress or to adversity, the offspring show increased responses to stress in adulthood," because the caregiving of mother rats is altered by their stress, and her altered care produces a different brain development in the baby rats (Begley 174). The same basic process occurs in humans, where stress from poverty and other environmental conditions increases parental neglect and abuse, which in turn produces increased levels of stress hormones in their children, thus potentially "shap[ing] their brains in undesirable ways, leading to poorer cognition and emotional control" (Begley 176). Thus, as Begley concludes, "How we are treated as babies by the people who care for us the most really does mold at least some aspects of our temperament. Traits as basic as fearfulness, curiosity, openness to new experiences, and neuroticism are not, despite the drumbeat of 'gene of the week' discoveries, woven immutably into our DNA. Nor . . . are they stamped irrevocably into our brain circuits" (Begley 182).

Social psychological studies of children also confirm that factors in the formative environment are the primary determinants of human character. In his book *Raising Children in a Socially Toxic Environment*, Cornell psychologist James Garbarino offers two research findings that reveal

> just how powerful and important social conditions are in shaping individual development. First, genetically identical twins separated at birth and growing up in *similar* communities end up with similar IQs (correlated .88), while genetically identical twins separated but living in *dis-*

similar communities end up with IQs much less alike (correlated .26). Second, children who are developmentally delayed (low Developmental Quotient—DQ) at four months of age and receive no significant remedial intervention are four times as likely to be intellectually delayed (low IQ) at four years of age [as] are similarly delayed children who receive such intervention. (Garbarino, *Raising* 155; emphasis in original)

Psychologists have identified multiple factors in children's formative environments that interfere with optimal development, "including poverty, father absence, low parental education, a rigid and punitive childrearing style, minority group status, parental substance abuse, maternal mental illness, and large family size" (Garbarino, *Raising* 152). A study comparing the IQs of children with varying numbers of these risk factors in their environment found that "children with fewer than three risk factors had above-average IQ scores of 112 [and that] children with four had below average IQ scores of 93" (Garbarino, *Raising* 152). Studies have also found, conversely, that certain positive environmental factors, such as a father who is deeply involved in the child's life or a mother who copes effectively with stress, work to offset the harm produced by the risk factors, and that adding the number of risk factors and subtracting the number of preventive factors produces a score that predicts with significant accuracy the child's chances of intellectual success (Garbarino, *Raising* 154).

Evidence is also compelling and growing that "social toxins" are responsible for most of the character problems for which we continue to blame the individuals who exhibit them. "Social toxins" are "the social equivalents of lead and smoke in the air, PCBs in the water, and pesticides in the food chain." They include "violence, poverty and other economic pressures on parents and their children, disruption of relationships, nastiness, despair, depression, paranoia, alienation—all the things that demoralize families and communities" (Garbarino, *Raising* 4–5). Not only the most vicious criminals but also most other individuals who run seriously afoul of the law are victims, to one extent or another, of what Garbarino calls the "socially toxic environment." "The social world of children," he argues, "the social context in which they grow up, has become poisonous to their development" (Garbarino, *Raising* 4).

The most dramatic evidence of the impact that social toxins can have on temperament, personality, and character is found in the effects of trauma. That environmental forces are capable of overriding and transforming even the most solid character was demonstrated, for example, by a U.S. Army study of psychiatric casualties during World War II, which found that when soldiers were in combat continuously for at least sixty days, their psychiatric casualty rate was 98 percent, demonstrating that "when the experience of violent trauma is intense and chronic, virtually no one is immune" (Garbarino, *Lost* 115).

On the home front, psychiatrist James Gilligan, who as head of the mental health division of the Massachusetts state prison system interviewed and treated hundreds of the most violent criminals incarcerated there, reports that traumatic childhoods were a major determinant of the violent characters of these men. Many of these criminals, Gilligan found, "had been beaten nearly to death, raped repeatedly or prostituted, or neglected to a life-threatening degree by parents too disabled themselves to care for their child" (Gilligan, *Preventing* 36). Gilligan's findings are corroborated by other researchers, one of whom found that out of fourteen inmates on death row for extremely brutal crimes, all except one had been profoundly traumatized when they were children. One's stepfather hit him on the head with a hammer, another's father hit him in the face with a board, a third one was kicked in the head and stomped on and beaten by relatives, another's stepfather placed him on a hot burner, and a fifth's stepfather sodomized him (Currie 83). Thus the violent character of most perpetrators is due not to any innate factors but rather to the traumatizing violence of their childhood environments. As Garbarino puts it, "Inside most of the adolescent and adult perpetrators of violence are traumatized children" (Garbarino, *Lost* 86).

The plasticity of the brain and the malleability of character and personality are also demonstrated by the results of various forms of intervention, including education, training, therapy, and rehabilitation. Simply altering a person's environment, which is a central feature of much education as well as of basic training in the military and rehabilitation for substance abuse, can produce substantial changes not just in behavior but also in character and can, moreover, stimulate the genesis of new neurons as well (Begley 58ff.). The same is true for many of the specific mental exercises and activities that education, training, rehabilitation, and therapy engage their charges in. UCLA neuropsychiatrist Jeffrey Schwartz found, for example, that patients suffering from obsessive-compulsive disorder can reduce their symptoms by practicing mindfulness, in which one dispassionately observes one's thoughts and feelings, standing apart from them instead of merging with them, and telling oneself that the compulsive urges one is experiencing are "in reality just a brain-wiring problem" (Begley 140). Similar training in mindfulness has been found to reduce depression (Begley 146–151). Schwartz concludes from his study that certain kinds of mental activity can alter the metabolism of the brain circuit at the center of obsessive-compulsive disorder: "Mental action can alter the brain chemistry of an OCD patient. The mind can change the brain" (quoted in Begley 141).

Other research has found that certain parts of the brain can be expanded not only by engaging in specific activities but also merely by *thinking* about engaging in them. Neurophysiologist Alvaro Pascal-Leone found not only that piano practice increased the size of the relevant area of the motor cortex but that merely imagining practicing the piano and mentally rehearsing the movements that one's fingers would make in playing a particular piece of music achieved the same result (Begley 152). Attention plays a particularly important role in these changes, because it increases the activity and hence (over time) the strength of the circuits to which it is directed and decreases the activity and strength of the circuits it ignores (Begley 157–158). As one pair of researchers explains, "The pattern of activity of neurons in sensory areas can be altered by patterns of attention. . . . Experience coupled with attention leads to physical changes in the structure and future functioning of the nervous system" (quoted in Begley 159). As Salk Institute researcher Rusty Gage concludes, "The environment and our experiences change our brain, so who you are as a person changes by virtue of the environment you live in and the experiences you have" (quoted in Begley 71). The assumption of a static, immutable character or self is thus without foundation (Begley 71).

Human malleability is evident not only in individual development and transformation but also in "the fates of human societies," as Jared Diamond puts it in the subtitle of his *Guns, Germs, and Steel*. As Diamond observes at the outset of this sweeping historical study, some form of essentialism has, from the sixteenth century to the present, underwritten the dominant explanations for why some societies have outpaced other societies technologically and politically:

> Probably the commonest explanation involves implicitly or explicitly
> assuming biological differences among peoples. In the centuries after
> A.D. 1500, as European explorers became aware of the wide differences
> among the world's peoples in technology and political organization,
> they assumed that those differences arose from differences in innate ability. With the rise of Darwinian theory, explanations were recast in terms
> of natural selection and of evolutionary descent. Technologically prim-

itive peoples were considered evolutionary vestiges of human descent from apelike ancestors. The displacement of such peoples by colonists from industrialized societies exemplified the survival of the fittest. With the later rise of genetics, the explanations were recast once again, in genetic terms. Europeans became considered genetically more intelligent than Africans, and especially more so than Aboriginal Australians. (Diamond 18–19)

While no longer unchallenged, such assumptions continue to enjoy wide currency today: "Many (perhaps most!) Westerners continue to accept racist explanations privately or subconsciously. In Japan and many other countries, such explanations are still advanced publicly and without apology. Even educated white Americans, Europeans, and Australians . . . assume that there is something primitive about the Aborigines themselves" (Diamond 19).

Diamond finds, however, that contrary to this assumption, "modern 'Stone-Age' peoples are on the average probably more intelligent, not less intelligent, than industrialized peoples" (Diamond 19), and he goes on to explain that the more advanced technologies and greater social and political complexity of Western societies are a product not of any innate superiority, past or present, of their peoples but rather of various geographical advantages—and the accumulated and cascading effects thereof—enjoyed by the inhabitants of Eurasia. Two of the most fundamental advantages were the presence of domesticatable, herbivorous, herd animals that could be used for food, labor, and transportation, and the absence of insurmountable geographical barriers to transportation and hence to trade and the sharing of inventions across the entire Eurasian land mass (Diamond 31). Domestication of animals enabled food to be produced rather than hunted and gathered, which greatly increased the food supply and led to greater population density and a sedentary rather than nomadic way of life (Diamond 30).

These changes, in turn, both demanded and enabled the emergence of more complex political organization and innovations such as writing and steel tools and weapons—technologies that developed more rapidly because of the dissemination of each technological advance throughout the Eurasian landmass. And these advances made logistically feasible the establishment and sustenance of large armies of conquest armed with guns and other steel weapons. In addition, the cohabitation of dense human populations with dense populations of domesticated animals led to the evolution of virulent diseases that mutated from the domestic animals and to which Eurasians over time developed an immunity that was lacking in the peoples they encountered on their voyages of exploration and conquest. As a result, indigenous peoples fell victim by the millions not only to Europeans' military and logistical advantages but also to their diseases, which played an even greater role than weapons and other technologies in the subjugation and, in many cases, ultimate extermination of non-European peoples (Diamond 29).

Thus, contrary to the assumption that some peoples (e.g., Western Europeans) are "naturally" or "inherently" more intelligent, civilized, or "advanced" than others, the current and historical dominance of certain peoples over others is due not to any inherent superiority of the dominant group but rather to the snowballing or cascading effects of certain geographical differences set in motion in the dimmest reaches of prehistory. As Diamond concludes, "History followed different courses for different peoples because of differences among peoples' environments, not because of biological differences among peoples themselves" (Diamond 25).[3]

Harmful Consequences of the Essentialism Schema

Essentialist beliefs and judgments about people are not only false, they are also in many cases extremely harmful because of the social policies, institutions, and structures they produce and support. Stephan Chorover has noted that, in general, "ideas about human nature will influence judgments about the reasonableness of particular social policy objectives" (Chorover 4). Richard Lerner concurs, noting that

> our views about nature and nurture influence our opinions about why certain people may have problems and about what, if anything, can be done for remediation. . . . How do we treat those less fortunate than we? How do we act toward the poor or the homeless? How do we regard criminals or the mentally disturbed, and what do we believe about the possibility or even the desirability of attempting rehabilitation with them? How do we behave toward those who hold beliefs and engage in behavior we dislike or find reprehensible or believe is immoral? What do we tell our children about such people? How do we explain to our children, and to ourselves, why these people are different? Do we contend, for instance, that these people are inherently bad—that because of their temperament, constitution, or heredity they are intrinsically and inevitably the way they are? Or do we teach our children—through word

and example—that these differences do not constitute differences in basic human value or in fitness in society, that the differences in how these people behave and in what they believe reflect only their distinct experiential history? (Lerner 7, 171)

That the essentialism schema has "consequences not just for how people will be judged, but also for how they are likely to be treated" (Levy, Plaks, and Dweck 186) has been verified by empirical studies. One major negative social consequence of the essentialism schema is the establishment of ineffective and counterproductive policies to address social problems. Research has revealed, for example, that because many Americans embrace the essentialist view that people simply are what they are, across time and situations, Americans are more inclined to meet social problems such as violence, drug abuse, war, and terrorism with (largely ineffective) vindictive and punitive responses and less inclined to pursue (the much more effective) preventive and rehabilitative environmental solutions (see Levy, Plaks, and Dweck 185). Specifically, studies have shown that individuals operating with the essentialism schema, "having rendered a negative moral judgment, are significantly more likely to recommend punishment for the transgressor (or to recommend a significantly greater degree of punishment). These studies have also shown that [people operating with a malleability schema] are significantly more likely to recommend education or rehabilitation for wrongdoers" (Levy and Dweck 163). Similarly, researchers have concluded that people who recognize malleability and thus place "more stock in the role of social forces for perpetuating stereotypes, may be more likely than their [essentialist] counterparts to support policies aimed at remedying disadvantages associated with negatively stereotyped groups" (Levy, Stroessner, and Dweck 1434).

Injustice in the Justice System

American social structures, institutions, and policies bear out these conclusions and thus manifest the powerful effects of the essentialism schema. Like the autonomy schema, the essentialism schema plays a central role in the field of criminal law, which has been adamant in resisting the evidence that character is determined by environment. The result is a serious miscarriage of justice.

A small number of judges and legal theorists, recognizing the causal role of trauma in creating criminal character, have argued that the law needs to take these environmental factors into account and acknowledge that it is wrong to punish individuals for having been malformed by a formative environment over which they had no control. As Chief judge David Bazelon of the U.S. Court of Appeals for the District of Columbia argued half a century ago, an accused person should not be held responsible for an unlawful act if it "was the product of mental disease or mental deficit . . . , [which] includes *any abnormal condition of the mind which substantially affects mental or emotional processes and substantially impairs behavior controls*" (Bazelon 390, 392; emphasis added). Noting that people from disadvantaged backgrounds suffer a disproportionate number and degree of such mental deficits (Bazelon 394), as a result of their disproportionate exposure to social toxins and other risk factors of the sort identified by Garbarino and discussed above, Bazelon argues that this fact must be taken into account in deciding how much responsibility for unlawful acts should be attributed to the perpetrators and how much to the society that formed them. Equal justice demands that criminal proceedings take account of the fact that people's cognitive, emotional, and moral development can be impeded "by many circumstances, including the accident of birth" (Bazelon 399): "it is simply unjust to place people in dehumanizing social conditions, to do nothing about those conditions, and then to command those who suffer, 'Behave—or else!'" (Bazelon 402).

Yet despite eloquent and compelling arguments, including a number of more recent law review articles drawing on some of the psychological research discussed above that demonstrates quite clearly the mentally debilitating effects of trauma and social toxins (see Falk; George Wright), the law continues to assume that individuals are responsible for their own character except in the most extreme cases, such as those involving "insanity" or obvious and severe brain damage. The law ignores the fact that long-term exposure to social toxins can cause mental illness and other psychological dysfunctions in some individuals, even if most other individuals exposed to such toxins may not suffer the same degree of damage (see Falk 737, 802–808). As legal scholar George Wright observes, "The current pattern [is one] of universal judicial denial that extreme deprivation may ever preclude responsibility" (495). This position, as Wright explains, produces severe and systematic injustice for the most deprived individuals in our society:

> Well-established legal principles . . . require punishment only for those who bear responsibility for an act. There is a basic contradiction when the principle of no legal guilt without moral responsibility is applied to . . . the "most deprived," . . . who have most severely and persistently

been deprived, through no fault of their own, of what [are] the requisites of moral responsibility. The criminal law systematically punishes substantial numbers of the most deprived who . . . cannot reasonably be said to bear moral responsibility for their charged conduct. (George Wright 463)

This practice—which, as Wright points out, is contradicted by the practice of admitting evidence concerning developmental deprivations during the sentencing phase of a trial (George Wright 475; 491ff.)—is often rationalized by the argument that not attributing responsibility to perpetrators of unlawful acts would deprive them of human dignity by denying them free will. This rationalization, however, simply compounds the injustice, as Wright explains:

We do not enhance the dignity of those deprived of the capacity for morally responsible choice by simply pretending, through the judicial system, that they do bear such responsibility. It is essentially backwards to imagine that a judicial system promotes dignity by falsely ascribing moral responsibility to any group of persons. The first step in enhancing the dignity of criminal defendants is for the legal system to categorize such persons realistically, without engaging in the same *self-serving metaphysical flattery of defendants that has obscured the effects of long periods of undeserved severe deprivation*. (George Wright 501; emphasis added)

The legal profession as a whole, however, along with most of the general populace, has remained deaf to such logic and continues to cling to the essentialist view that people are responsible for their own character, and hence also for whatever behavior it produces, despite the fact that they did not get to choose either their genes or their formative environment, the only two factors by which anyone's character is produced.

Fatalistic Views of Violence, Inequality, and Domination

In addition to resulting in profound and systematic perversions of justice in the judicial system, the basic conviction produced by the essentialism schema—that what people are is determined by their genes and that environmental factors are inconsequential—also leads to three general mistaken beliefs about people that have extremely destructive consequences.

First is the belief "that human life is biologically constrained to manifest aggression, . . . [and] that xenophobia, militarism, ruthless self-ishness, and other less-than-desirable characteristics are necessary and ubiquitous features of human life" (Lerner 172). This belief leads directly to the conclusion that efforts to eliminate war, crime, and other forms of violence are naïve and futile, and that we should simply accept as inevitable the horrible suffering and injustice that such violence produces. Such a conclusion ignores not only the evidence, presented above, that violent people are made, not born, but also historical evidence that violent societies can become nonviolent and vice versa, when their physical, material, social, economic, and/or cultural circumstances change. Thus, rather than seeking to prevent interpersonal and intergroup violence by providing people with more adequate formative environments, American foreign and domestic policies—and expenditures—are grotesquely skewed toward the development of more effective strategies and technologies for inflicting violence on the (not only actually but also supposedly or even just potentially) violent other, thus perpetuating a vicious circle in which violence begets more violence.

Second, "essentialist beliefs serve a function of rationalizing and legitimating existing social inequalities by portraying them as natural and inevitable" (Haslam et al. 67). As Jayaratne and colleagues observe, "Genetic (or 'hereditary') theories have been employed, historically, to justify social hierarchies, and to imply inferiority to certain social groups. Indeed, these theories were used by Hitler to promote hatred toward Jews and other groups deemed inferior. . . . They have also been used to maintain the status quo, particularly with regard to gender, race, and social class" (Jayaratne et al. 80). By emphasizing nature to the exclusion of nurture, the essentialism schema functions "to justify as inevitable the concentration of social, political, and economic power in the hands of those who are alleged to be inherently deserving" (Chorover 26), convincing people that "disparities in wealth, power, and status, far from being the hallmarks of an unjust society, are the just and natural expression of biological ordering" (Chorover 25–26). In such a view, "our present society is totally 'just and fair,' and consequently the poor, weak, homeless, and unemployed are in their proper, biologically established place" (Lerner 183).

In education, essentialism has functioned, through the apparatus of the IQ test, not only to unfairly limit the opportunities of many individuals but also, as recently as the 1970s, to justify and perpetuate discriminatory policies against African American and working-class students (Lewontin et al. 19). A 1969 article in the *Harvard Educational*

Review argued "that most of the difference between blacks and whites in their performance on IQ tests was genetic. The conclusion for social action was that no program of education could equalize the social status of blacks and whites, and that blacks ought better to be educated for the more mechanical tasks to which their genes predisposed them." This same logic was then applied to working-class individuals (Lewontin et al. 19). When, in each of these instances, the judgment is made that certain people are inherently inferior to others, they are held solely responsible for their character and behavior—which results not in compassion and a quest for justice but rather in the conviction that their status represents the natural and just order of things.

This consequence of the essentialist schema takes its most overt form in the Social Darwinist belief that some individuals are genetically predetermined to be morally, intellectually, economically, and/or socially inferior to others. This belief "relocat[es] the cause of inequality from the structure of society to the nature of individuals" (Lewontin et al. 68) and leads to the conclusion that efforts to help the underprivileged and increase equality are morally unnecessary: "If one accepts biological determination, nothing need be changed, for what falls in the realm of necessity falls outside the realm of justice" (Lewontin et al. 236). This conclusion, as Lewontin et al. note, explains the drawing power of sociobiology and certain strains of evolutionary psychology: "It is precisely because biological determinism is exculpatory that it has such wide appeal. If men dominate women, it is because they must. If employers exploit their workers, it is because evolution has built into us the genes for entrepreneurial activity. If we kill each other in war, it is the force of our genes for territoriality, xenophobia, tribalism, and aggression" (Lewontin et al. 237).

Biological determinism also enables the position that efforts to eliminate inequalities are naïve and futile, and that we have no choice but to accept the inequality and even the degradation of some individuals. "For if human social organization, including the inequalities of status, wealth, and power, are a direct consequence of our biologies, then, except for some gigantic program of genetic engineering, no practice can make a significant alteration of social structure or of the position of individuals or groups within it" (Lewontin et al. 18). Indeed, attempts to remedy these inequalities are claimed to "go against nature" (Lewontin et al. 7). As the original Social Darwinist, Herbert Spencer, argued, if the predatory behavior of tycoons is an indelible part of human nature, it "*must* be undergone, and the sufferings *must* be endured . . . ; no re-forms that men ever did broach or ever will broach, can diminish them one jot" (quoted in Chorover 91). In the view of Spencer, and current Social Darwinists as well, poverty is the consequence of the innate weakness, laziness, and general lack of virtue of the poor, and as such it neither can nor should be eliminated (see Chorover 92).

Finally, the essentialism schema can lead to infrahumanization or dehumanization of entire groups of people and thence to war, terrorism, and genocide. As Lerner states, "casting the differences between groups as biological differences makes the threat the out-group poses not one of mere political advantage, but rather one of absolute survival. . . . The enactment of biological determinism into social policies gives us means to make some of our fellow humans less than us. Such prejudice leads inevitably to injustice. All too often it has enabled murder" (Lerner 196). Keller concurs, stating that "having such essentialist explanatory devices available may over time lead to an increase in the severity of discriminatory behaviors and policies, to the extent that essentialist explanations inhibit or reduce the scruples that people would (probably) have about their discriminatory behavior under conditions in which no such essentialist rationalization and justification is available" (Keller 699).

This process often begins with stereotyping and prejudice, which are facilitated by the essentialism schema. Researchers have noted that "people's failure to understand the impact of social environments can contribute to the preservation of pre-existing stereotypes and the formation of new ones" (Levy and Dweck 166) and that the essentialism schema, which prevents people from recognizing the formative impact of social environments, leads to stereotyping and prejudice (see Haslam et al. 63 and 67; Jayaratne et al. 80 and 86; Levy, Plaks, and Dweck 185; and Levy, Stroessner, and Dweck 1426). Keller reports that research findings "support the assumption that essentialism plays a causal role with regard to prejudice and in-group bias" (697), and research by Levy, Stroessner, and Dweck reveals that people operating with the essentialist schema "endorse stereotypes to a greater degree" than do people operating with the malleability schema and that essentialists "also seem to believe to a greater degree that these stereotypical traits are fixed from birth." People with the malleability schema, in contrast, "not only view these stereotypes as less true but . . . also tend to agree more with a social forces explanation, an explanation suggestive of greater group variability and of how things can change over time" (Levy, Stroessner, and Dweck 1426–1427).

From such prejudice and stereotyping it is but a step to infrahumanization and dehumanization, and an essentialist view of human nature also facilitates this step, as Jayaratne et al. explain: "Genetic explanations for problematic behaviors (e.g., violence) among socially disadvantaged racial groups can suggest their *permanent* inferiority. Genetic explanations for valued behaviors among socially advantaged racial groups (e.g., intelligence) can imply their *permanent* superiority. Genetic lay theories thus imply the essentialist nature of such belief systems, highlighting the perceived immutability of social categories" (Jayaratne et al. 87). The effects of the belief that some groups are inherently inferior to others range from indifference to the suffering of an entire people (evident, for example, in the policies of the United States and Europe toward Africa) to ethnic cleansing, war, and genocide.

This attribution of group traits to innate factors more than to shared environmental forces, which is known as the "ultimate attribution error" (Levy et al. 160), produces, in turn, discriminatory behavior toward members of certain out-groups (Levy et al. 158). Noting that there is empirical support for Gordon Allport's assertion that "belief in group essences is a defining characteristic of the prejudiced personality" and that "ethnic cleansing and ethnic genocide have typically been accompanied by essentialist rhetoric," psychologists have concluded "that essentialized social categories lead to the most severe forms of intergroup hostility" (Keller 687, 689, 698).

Indeed, as Richard Lerner observes in *Final Solutions*, "social policies derived from biological determinism . . . often directly determined whether people survived or not. Some of the greatest inhumanities humans have perpetrated on other human beings have been predicated in great part on the doctrine of biological determinism," which holds "that there are genetically fixed and immutable differences between groups of people . . . [and] that changing the environment cannot alter this connection between genes and behavior" (Lerner xix–xx). Genocide, ethnic cleansing, and other forms of interethnic violence are enabled in no small measure by essentialism. Lerner states,

> The doctrine of "nature over nurture" has been ubiquitous in human society at least since the time of Plato, who believed that a human's soul was innate and eternal, and thus unchangeable. Similarly, persecutions in Spain from the fifteenth through the seventeenth century were based on church laws and civil statutes about the unchangeable purity or impurity of a person's blood. Catholics whose families had converted from Judaism even centuries earlier were persecuted solely because of hereditary

impurities, believed to be immutably present in bloodlines regardless of generations of church membership. And no less an institution than the American cavalry, in campaigns against Native Americans throughout the nineteenth century, took actions predicated on a similar biologically determinist conception, specifically the immutably savage nature of the "Indian population." . . . Thus, for at least two thousand years of recorded history social actions have been implemented based on the belief that certain people had something inherent in them, something in their blood, that made them less than human and consequently deserving of persecution or even death. (Lerner 10–11)

Evidence of the Essentialism Schema's Operation

Entity theorists and incremental theorists—that is, people operating with, respectively, the essentialism and malleability schemas—not only subscribe to different beliefs concerning the nature and origin of human character traits, but also engage in clearly distinguished information-processing strategies: "These two implicit theories generate distinct, coherent, mental models that result in distinct patterns of social information processing and social judgment" (Levy, Plaks, and Dweck 180) and in different social and political actions as well (Levy, Plaks, and Dweck 185–186). Suppression of evidence is one of the key means by which the essentialism schema operates. Susan McKinnon's observation that "it requires a studied suppression of the historical record to persist in the assumption" that sexual roles are genetically determined (McKinnon 146) holds not only for gender essentialism but for other instances of essentialism as well. Studies reveal that individuals with an essentialist person-schema are less diligent and more biased than persons with a malleability schema in processing information about other people (see Choi, Nisbett, and Norenzayan 57; Levy, Plaks, and Dweck 191). Since essentialists assume that fixed traits are the main cause of behavior, their *expectation* is that an individual will exhibit relatively little variability over time and from one situation to another (Levy, Stroessner, and Dweck 1422), and they draw *inferences* of character traits from just about any instance of behavior (Levy, Plaks, and Dweck 182). They are thus quicker to *categorize* and *judge* people on the basis of slight behavioral information than are people operating with a malleability schema (Levy, Plaks, and Dweck 191–192, 187). Entity theorists also appear to "tag incoming information in a more evaluative manner" and *encode* it "in ways that facilitate trait judgments" and in forms that are "more susceptible to biased *retrieval*" (Levy, Plaks, and Dweck 187–188; emphasis added). And they are more resistant to considering new information about people and to revising their judgments about people in light of disconfirming information. One study found that "consistent with their belief that traits cannot be changed, entity theorists did not revise their trait judgments of the target (as a liar, a thief, or a cheat) in light of the new information" (Levy, Plaks, and Dweck 183).

The initial judgments of people operating with a malleability schema display a more cautious and less extreme pattern (Levy, Plaks, and Dweck 193). While the information processing of essentialists tends to be "more superficial, rapid, and cognitively untaxing," malleabilists engage in a more "systematic, . . . thorough, effortful processing of information" (Levy, Plaks, and Dweck 196). In addition, they *expect* that individuals will change over time and even from one situation to another, and that the primary causes of behavior will be "context-sensitive psychological variables" rather than fixed traits (Levy, Plaks, and Dweck 191). The malleability person-schema thus "orients information processing toward more dynamic variables and flexible judgments" (Levy, Plaks, and Dweck 193) and produces "a more comprehensive picture of the target" (Levy, Plaks, and Dweck 187). Evidence also suggests that while essentialists tend to store information about people as abstractions, people operating with a malleability schema "will not abstract on-line trait information as readily but rather will continue to store group information chiefly in the form of [individual] exemplars" (Levy, Stroessner, and Dweck 1434).

These different information-processing strategies of the essentialism and malleability schemas lead, in turn, to significantly different judgments about, and actions toward, other people. For one, since, as research has shown, "people's failure to understand the impact of social environments can contribute to the preservation of pre-existing stereotypes and the formation of new ones" (Levy, Stroessner, and Dweck 1425), and since the essentialism schema diverts *attention* away from environmental forces, essentialists are more prejudiced and quicker to stereotype than are malleabilists. Research has provided "clear evidence that entity theorists endorse stereotypes of ethnic groups such as African Americans to a greater degree than do incremental theorists" and that they "believe to a greater degree that these stereotypical traits are fixed from birth" (Levy, Stroessner, and Dweck, 1426–1427). Malleabilists, in contrast, not only attribute less validity to these stereotypes, but

92 The Cognitive Roots of Injustice

also attribute whatever validity they might have to social rather than innate causes (Levy, Stroessner, and Dweck 1427).

Replacing the Essentialism Schema

Replacing the essentialism schema with a more adequate schema that takes account of the constructed and malleable nature of human character would thus contribute significantly to preventing dehumanization and infrahumanization and their often terrible consequences, as well as leading to much more effective and just social policies. Psychologists have concluded that such replacement is possible and that it is a more effective means of reducing social ills than is the targeting of specific stereotypes (Levy et al. 165).

The most common approach to stereotype reduction, presenting people with counter-stereotypical examples, has "met with mixed results at best" (Levy et al. 165). Research suggests that replacing the essentialism schemas with a malleability schema "may establish a way of thinking that discourages stereotyping across the board (i.e., not only in regard to one particular stereotype)" (Levy et al. 165). Studies have shown that subjects in whom a malleability schema was temporarily induced allotted more attention to information that challenged stereotypes and that they therefore (a) attributed less validity to stereotypes, (b) made less extreme characterizations of groups, and (c) refrained from stereotyping individuals (Levy, Stroessner, and Dweck 1434). Noting that these laboratory inductions of the malleability schema were produced by a single, brief intervention, psychologists have reasoned that "a sustained educational program would achieve even more effective and long-lasting effects" (Plaks et al. 143) and have concluded that replacing the essentialist schema with a malleability schema is a more effective way to reduce prejudice than debunking particular stereotypes (Levy 762; Levy, Stroessner, and Dweck 1434; Levy et al. 165): "Research suggests that stereotyping can be potentially reduced by means of an intervention that does not even mention stereotypes but rather alters people's beliefs about the nature and origin of traits. That is, a more potent, long-term [induction of the malleability schema] may reduce people's reliance on fixed traits as a way of characterizing people and predicting their behavior. In doing so, it may decrease the probability that they will form new stereotypes or place as much faith in existing ones" (Levy, Stroessner, and Dweck 1434).

As with the autonomy schema, there are a number of basic ways to promote the replacement of the essentialism schema with the malleability schema. Most crucial, of course, and most central to the role of literature, is the acquisition of more accurate exemplars and the development of corrective information-processing routines, processes that we will discuss at the end of this chapter. Also significant is the development of metacognition regarding essentialism, which involves making people aware of the sources of the essentialism schema, its distorting effects on social cognition, and the harm that it causes, in order to render people more wary of them and potentially resistant to them. We have already discussed the distortions and harm produced by the essentialism schema, and now we turn to its sources.

Sources of the Essentialism Schema

Like the autonomy schema, the essentialism schema has origins in basic cognitive architecture and the natural world with which it interacts. University of Michigan psychologist Susan Gelman argues that essentialism is "an early cognitive bias . . . [that] has its source in the cognitive requirements of categorization in certain domains" (Gelman 7). According to Gelman, essentializing is "a universal habit of the mind" that evolved "because it is beneficial for interactions with the world," especially with animals and plants. Essentialism is "not a *single* adaptation, but the result of several distinct cognitive biases that emerged for varying purposes . . . but inevitably converge in essentialism" (Gelman 15, 16, 323).

These cognitive capacities include distinguishing appearance from reality, inferring hidden properties from the presence of manifest properties, recognizing the operation of hidden causes, tracking the identity of an object over time, and deferring to experts concerning the name and true nature of a phenomenon (see Gelman 314). Gelman explains that each of these constituents of essentialism is crucial for making sense of the world and surviving in it. "We draw inferences from property clusters and distinguish appearance from reality, in order to make (generally) accurate predictions. We search for causes in order to create more useful tools and technologies. . . . We track identity over time in order to recognize individuals," we defer to experts "in order to benefit from cultural knowledge" (Gelman 325), and "language labels are one of the most efficient ways of passing down to future generations the hard-won knowledge of those who came before" (Gelman 271).

94   The Cognitive Roots of Injustice

But while essentializing may be a universal cognitive process, significant differences exist both among cultures and among individuals within a given culture concerning the domains in which it operates and the degree or intensity with which it is enacted, thus indicating that culture, language, and individual training and socialization play a significant role in any given individual's or culture's essentializing (see Gelman 237–238, 281–283, 324). Concerning cultural differences, Gelman surmises that language differences play a significant role. Two basic ways in which language contributes to essentialism are through (1) "conveying membership in a kind (e.g., by labeling an entity with a common noun, or by referring to kind membership with the word 'kind'), and [2] expressing the broad scope of a proposition (e.g., with logical quantifiers, such as 'all,' 'some,' or 'most,' or with generic noun phrases, such as '*Bears* hibernate in winter')" (Gelman 180).

Some linguists believe that nouns virtually produce essentialism. Carey argues that essentialism "derives from the logical work done by nouns," insofar as "every count noun carries with it the idea that the identity of the entity picked out by the noun is unchanged in the face of surface changes" (quoted in Gelman 181–182). "Hearing a label," Gelman explains, "makes one somewhat more likely to construe the category in essentialist ways, compared to hearing a verb or adjective to refer to the same grouping. . . . Nouns 'invite' children . . . to look for commonalities and, potentially, essences" (Gelman 237). And since some languages (e.g., English) give greater prominence to nouns than others (e.g., Mandarin), and "make generic expressions more salient" in other ways as well, language differences may play a significant role in the degree of essentializing a given culture engages in (Gelman 237–238).

Other ethnographic evidence points to additional cultural determinants of greater essentializing on the part of Americans as compared to East Asians, who "have a strong belief in the power of social situations in shaping . . . personality" (Choi, Nisbett, and Norenzayan 58). Koreans, Nisbett reports, believe that personality is much more malleable than Americans do (Nisbett 120). "The notion that there can be attributes or actions that are not conditioned on social circumstances," Nisbett explains, "is foreign to the Asian mentality" (Nisbett 50). "Confucians have always believed, far more than the intellectual descendants of Aristotle, in the malleability of human nature" (Nisbett 16). This difference is epitomized in the fact that

> people in Eastern cultures often use a "tree" as a metaphor for a person, which emphasizes the endless shaping of internal dispositions by

the external environment. For instance, in Korea, a person is believed to be like a white root that takes on the color of the soil in which it grows. If a white root is planted in red soil, it becomes red. (In China, a person is likened to a white silk cloth. If placed in red dye, it becomes red; if placed in green dye, it becomes green.) (Choi, Nisbett, and Norenzayan 58)

In addition to cultural differences in essentializing, there are also individual differences within a given culture. As we saw above, for many individuals the essentializing impulse is overridden by the malleability schema, and Gelman's empirical research has revealed "vast individual variation" in essentializing among American undergraduates (Gelman 287). One source of this difference may be the "tremendous variation in essentialist talk" in parents' communications with their young children (Gelman 289). There is also evidence that essentializing is a response to certain psychological needs that vary from one individual to another.

Indications are that individuals who essentialize more frequently and/or intensely may do so in response to one or more of three different motives: ideological, existential, and epistemic. Ideological motives lead individuals to embrace essentialism as a means of justifying and legitimizing the dominance of their own group over other groups (Keller 687–688). Mannheim University social psychologist Johannes Keller argues that "attributing an essentialist character to social groups, one that is inherently stable and based on a (biological) group essence (e.g., the belief that Caucasians share a common genetic heritage and are privileged because of their 'better' genes), serves the system-justifying [i.e., ideological] function particularly well" (Keller 688). Existential motives, which aim to maintain one's identity, or sense of self, embrace essentialism to "serve a 'boundary reinforcement' function, sharpening a distinction so as to safeguard the person's identity. . . . Ascribing a categorically distinct ontological status to the devalued other may be a particularly reassuring way to ensure that one does not have the 'wrong' essence." Heterosexual men, for example, "may view gay men as categorically different to distinguish themselves sharply from a despised identity" (Haslam and Levy 483). Lerner observes, similarly, that "biological determinism is the glue that holds the nation/race together and separates it from peoples of different nations or races—that is, those with other genes or 'blood'" (Lerner 18). And epistemic motives, in the form of a high need for closure (definiteness, certainty, lack of ambiguity), are also particularly well served by essentialism, which conveys "stability, order, and uniformity" (Keller 688).

Essentialism is also inculcated and enacted by various apparatuses, technologies, techniques, and disciplines. For example, the prominence given by the U.S. Census, opinion polls, questionnaires, and bureaucratic forms of all sorts to the demographic categories of race and gender, rather than to formative social and economic circumstances of birth and upbringing, not only derives from but also promotes the essentialist schema. The same is true of affirmative action, which is implemented on the basis of race and gender rather than social and economic circumstances of birth and upbringing—which, some have argued, would make better economic, ethical, and political sense. Technologies of health care also express and reinforce the essentialist schema, in, for example, their focus on genetic causes and cures at the expense of environmental ones.

The prominence of IQ testing in education is another apparatus both resulting from and inculcating essentialism. Although Alfred Binet, the French originator of the IQ test, rejected the notion that intelligence is innate and immutable, "the translators and importers of Binet's test, both in the United States and in England, tended to share a common ideology, one dramatically at variance with Binet's. They asserted that the intelligence test measured an innate and unchangeable quantity, fixed by genetic inheritance" (Chorover 85). Consequently, for decades, teachers and parents have used these tests as proof of an innate and unalterable ability and treated children accordingly, establishing their self-images as intelligent or dull and then reinforcing these categorizations by "tracking" students into curricula of varying difficulty, prestige, stimuli, and opportunities to learn—multiple forms of self-fulfilling prophecy. Gelman recalls her assumptions when she took the test, sometime around the third grade: "As I understood it, the IQ score would reveal my intellectual capacity—immutable, fixed, and unchanging. . . . The number would not change—it would stay in our permanent records, but more important, it would tell us who we were, and who we could become" (Gelman 3).

Certain forms of evolutionary psychology constitute a "truth regime" that is also both cause and effect of the essentialism schema. In claiming that traits such as aggressivity, competitiveness, male promiscuity, and possessiveness are genetically determined universal elements of human nature, evolutionary psychology naturalizes and legitimizes such behaviors and delegitimizes all alternatives. As Susan McKinnon observes, "In the face of such a fundamental and enduring 'reality,' it becomes difficult to imagine that other structures of relations might be within the scope of human *possibilities* (or even to recognize that, historically, they have been within the scope of human *actualities*)" (McKinnon 147). Psychotherapists operating within this framework thus may "see their task not so much as one in which we might take the responsibility for 'ameliorating' gender inequities, but rather . . . as one in which we bring our contemporary gendered characteristics back into synch with those postulated attributes of our prehistoric savannah sisters and brothers" (McKinnon 147), and such an approach by psychotherapists will contribute another increment to essentialism.

The powerful apparatus of television also reinforces the essentialism schema in several respects. First, it usually presents characters and newsmakers in isolation from their formative circumstances, thus enabling the assumption that the formative effects of experiences and environments are nonexistent or insignificant and that people simply are what they are. Criminal characters in television crime dramas, for example, are usually presented simply as evil perpetrators—and frequently also as members of racial, ethnic, or class minorities—whose formative, criminogenic environments are not represented or even acknowledged. Second, most television characters do not change as a result of their experiences, thus expressing and further reinforcing the assumption that people simply are what they are and that experiences and circumstances don't alter them. This is particularly true of sitcom characters, but it also holds for action heroes—such as Jack Bauer of the popular Bush-era television drama *24*—who suffer terrible physical and psychological trauma yet remain physically and psychologically intact. Broadcasts of sports events, concerts, and indeed all television shows can also give the impression that athletes, entertainers, and actors, respectively, are simply born with their talent, ignoring the degree to which their talent may have been developed through years of training. Finally, television is not a good apparatus for showing the psychological effects of formative circumstances, or even many of the formative circumstances themselves, which are temporally and spatially dispersed and, in some cases, largely intangible and invisible.

Some works of literature are also expressions of and apparatuses for inculcating the essentialism schema. In *Oliver Twist*, for example, Oliver's genteel manner and speech, despite the degrading conditions of his upbringing, are "a constant affirmation of the power of nature over nurture" and the principle "that individual behaviors are the direct consequences of inborn physical characteristics" (Lewontin et al. 18). Zola's Rougon-Macquart novels function in much the same way, suggesting through characters such as Gervaise in *L'Assommoir* "that an individual's

98 The Cognitive Roots of Injustice

life was a result of the unfolding of a hereditary predisposition, and, although environment might temporarily modify its ontogenetic course, in the end heredity triumphed" (Lewontin et al. 24).

Countering Essentialist Prototypes

The essentialism schema produces its biased information processing not only through routines or scripts that direct each information-processing step, but also through multiple forms of essentialist prototypes, which must be countered with corresponding exemplars of malleability. Following is a brief account of these essentialist prototypes and their malleability counterparts, the awareness and understanding of which can, in addition, constitute a significant element of the metacognition that facilitates their replacement.

- *Concepts* embodying the essentialist assumption include labels for people's gender, sexuality, race, ethnicity, class, nationality, and so on, as well as notions such as "bad seed," "blood," or "bloodline," and "chip off the old block." Clichéd racial, ethnic, gender, and sexuality epithets and slurs are particularly prominent essentialist concepts. Such concepts must be replaced with concepts that acknowledge malleability, such as "formation," "development," "nurture," "transformation," "reform," "epiphany," "rehabilitation," "psychological trauma," "emotional scarring," and so on.
- *Prototypic individuals* embodying the essentialist assumption are quite common and include heroic individuals who are unbroken and unbowed by whatever hardships or horrors life confronts them with, as well as, conversely, "bad" people whose badness appears to be inherent and innate, unchanged by even the most supportive and propitious of environments. Such individuals manifest stereotypical qualities unaffected by environmental forces. Exemplars include real and fictional paragons or caricatures of masculinity (Arnold Schwarzenegger and Sylvester Stallone characters in the movies, numerous sports heroes); femininity (numerous female entertainers); race ("Aunt Jemima," the "welfare queen," the "violent black man"); class ("white trash," "trailer trash," "hillbillies, "rednecks"); and national character ("authoritarian" Germans, "snobbish" French, "proper" English, "hot-blooded" Latins). These exemplars must be countered with individual exemplars of malleability, such as individuals bearing the physical or emotional scars of their formative experiences, exhib-

iting physical, moral, or psychological deficiencies that bear traces of their formative origins (e.g., malnutrition or neglect), or manifesting physical, intellectual, or social capabilities that require significant resources and cultivation in order to develop (such as a strong, healthy body or a wealth of knowledge).

- Essentialist *prototypic images* are often a component of the individual prototypes of essentialism, in the form of exaggerated or caricatured facial features (eyes, nose, lips, hair, etc.), body types, postures, body language, dialects, and accents. These images must be countered with images of malleability, indicating histories of nurture, fulfillment, deprivation, neglect, abuse, trauma, and so on. These varying formative experiences are also evident in the differing facial expressions, bodily forms, body language, and postures, as well as in the prosody of a person's speech, all of which can bear traces of the psychological consequences of formative experiences.

- Essentialist *episode scripts* involve "good" characters encountering harmful environmental forces and passing through them uncorrupted, unbroken, and unbowed; "bad" characters encountering supportive, nourishing opportunities and yet remaining uncorrected and unreformed; and other characters persisting in their stereotypical traits despite countervailing influences from their potentially formative environments. These episode scripts must be replaced with malleability episodes in which people are significantly changed, for good or for ill, by an experience. Such experiences will be one of two types: "epiphanic," in which people achieve sudden enlightenment, or "traumatic," in which individuals are deeply wounded and perhaps scarred for life.

- The essentialist *life script*, or prototypical life story, is that of the hero who is born with special powers and who remains pure and uncompromised no matter what conditions life puts him in. The negative counterpart is the essentialist story of the individual "born under a bad sign," a "bad seed" or a "bad apple" who never amounts to anything despite all the opportunities life presents to him. Such scripts are countered by malleability life scripts that portray a character's formative environment and its formative effects, or that portray incremental changes in personality or character as a result of changes in environment or circumstances.

- Prototypic essentialist *emotions* include indifference, disdain, indignation, contempt, revulsion, anger, and even hatred toward people seen as inherently inferior (e.g., the poor, jobless, homeless, and criminal, as well as members of certain nationalities, ethnicities, or races) and excitement, admiration, adoration, and ecstasy toward individuals seen as inherently superior (e.g., rich people, powerful political and religious leaders, sports heroes, entertainment stars, and other celebrities), and confidence, pride, and arrogance on the part of such individuals and resignation, hopelessness, despair, and shame on the part of individuals who deem themselves inherently inferior. These emotions must be countered by malleability emotions, including humility and gratitude on the part of fortunate people for their formative environments and compassion for those who have been deprived of a nurturing formative environment, and righteous anger and resentment on the part of the unfortunate concerning their misfortune and righteous anger and envy toward those who mistake their good fortune for inherent superiority.

- Essentialist emotions, in turn, entail essentialist *action scripts*, including creating and supporting social policies, institutions, systems, and structures that maintain social hierarchies, privileges, exclusions, and other punishments of the deprived. Malleability action scripts, on the other hand, involve pursuing social policies that nurture individuals by providing them with the most supportive formative environments possible — e.g., programs supporting nutrition, childcare, medical care, education, and so on.

As we will see in Chapters 6 through 8 when we examine the three protest novels, literary texts can provide each of these forms of malleability exemplars. Novels are particularly capable of providing malleability exemplars insofar as they can offer comprehensive and detailed accounts of both formative environments and their experiential, formative impact on characters. These exemplars can begin to function immediately as templates for processing information about people, and can continue to do so as long as, aided by metacognition, they remain more accessible than the essentialist exemplars and prototypes. And when they accrue in sufficient quantity, these malleability exemplars will themselves crystallize into malleability prototypes that can replace the essentialist prototypes as the default information-processing templates.

Training in Malleabilist Information Processing

In addition to providing templates for information processing, the accumulation of malleability exemplars through the process of reading also develops readers' malleability information-processing routines, which include the following:

- *Expectations*: that current character must have its origins in past environments and experiences, including privilege and/or deprivation/trauma.
- *Attention and search*: to/for past determinants of character formation—deprivation and trauma in the case of character deficits, and safety, nurture, and care in the case of character strengths—and also for potentially (trans)formative present factors.
- *Inference and supposition*: that certain past environments and experiences must have played a significant role in establishing a person's character traits—deprivation or trauma in the case of character deficits, and safety, nurture, and care in the case of character strengths.
- *Memory retrieval*: memories of one's own formative experiences, as well as those of personal acquaintances or historical figures.
- *Emotions*: humility and gratitude for the nurturing and care one has received, and compassion and righteous anger for the neglect and abuse that others have been subjected to.
- *Action script retrieval*: actions that provide nurturing formative and transformative environments and opportunities—e.g., child development, education, social reform, prevention, education, rehabilitation, and therapy as opposed to neglect and punishment.

Literature can train readers in these routines in two ways. The first is through providing numerous exemplars of malleability in the various forms just discussed. Through repeatedly encountering multiple instances of malleability in these various forms (concept, image, episode, etc.), readers gradually come to *expect* characters (and hence people as well) to have been formed by significant conditions and experiences of their earlier years. As a result of this expectation, they will take greater *notice* of evidence of such events when it is present and will give it greater *attention*, and when such evidence is not present, readers will be more inclined to *search* for it.

Literature can also induce readers, in various ways, to engage in malleabilist information processing. It can induce malleabilist *attention* by focusing on formative forces and malleabilist *expectation* by foreshadowing formative effects. Literary texts can induce readers to *infer* the existence of such formative events in a character's past by providing hints of them, and prompt readers to *suppose* formative events by providing knowledge (and evidence) of the general principle of malleability. Literary texts will also *evoke memories* of malleability, both of one's own formative experiences and environment and of those of personal acquaintances or historical figures. And through such memories, as well as through the sympathetic presentation of characters who have clearly been molded or scarred by events, literary texts evoke the prototypic *emotions* of malleability—humility, gratitude, compassion, and righteous anger. These emotions themselves include action tendencies to aid unfortunate others, which then trigger the *retrieval of* specific *action scripts* of this sort by readers.

CHAPTER 4

Atomism versus Solidarity: Relation of Self to Others

*Two are better than one; because they have a good reward for their labour.
For if they fall, the one will lift up his fellow: but woe to him that is alone
when he falleth; for he hath not another to help him up.*
ECCLESIASTES 4:9–10

*Inasmuch as ye have done it unto one of the least of these my brethren,
ye have done it unto me.*
MATTHEW 25:40

*In all people I see myself. . . .
Whoever degrades another degrades me;
And whatever is done or said returns at last to me.*
WALT WHITMAN, "SONG OF MYSELF" 20, 24

Nature of the Atomism Schema

A third general person-schema, that of atomism, takes individuals to be
unique, self-enclosed entities analogous to billiard balls, different and
fundamentally separate from other individuals (Wolgast 4–5).

The atomism schema magnifies interindividual and intergroup distinctions and obscures our inherent sameness and solidarity with others, blinding us to the fact that each person is practically, psychologically, and ontologically overlapping and interwoven with others, such
that the welfare of one person directly affects and is affected by the welfare of the others. The atomism schema blocks our awareness of these
facts and causes us to view ourselves and others as creatures of "ruthless egoism and unconcern for others" engaged in a zero-sum competi-

104   The Cognitive Roots of Injustice

tion, a Hobbesian war of each against all (Wolgast 19, 4). According to the atomistic view, competition, opposition, and even violence are fundamental to human nature, while cooperation and altruism are, at most, strategies for achieving dominance over others. In producing this vision of persons, the atomism schema potentiates infrahumanization and dehumanization of the other, which further enables various forms of indifference and aggression, including Social Darwinism (Lukes 30; Singer, *Left* 11, 19).

Atomism is the core of Western individualism. As Brooke Foss Westcott, Bishop of Durham, observed in 1890, "individualism regards humanity as made up of disconnected or warring atoms," in direct contrast with "socialism[, which] regards it as an organic whole, a vital unity formed by the combination of contributing members mutually interdependent" (quoted in Lukes 33). The atomism schema was perhaps most clearly articulated in Thomas Hobbes's view of the state of prehistorical human life as "solitary, poore, nasty, brutish, and short," in which each individual was in a death struggle with all other individuals for scarce resources (quoted in Wolgast 4). This basic view is also present in such prominent and influential thinkers as Jean-Jacques Rousseau, who stated that in their natural state humans had "no need of one another" and that "they met perhaps twice in their lives, without knowing each other and without speaking" (quoted in Singer, *Expanding* 3), and John Locke, who embraced what Robert Bellah and colleagues characterize as "an almost ontological individualism," in which "the individual is prior to society, which comes into existence only through the voluntary contract of individuals trying to maximize their own self-interest" (143; see also Wolgast 5).

In this view, as the political philosopher Elizabeth Wolgast explains,

> people can be likened to molecules of gas bouncing around inside a container. Each molecule proceeds independently, is free to go its own way, although it occasionally bumps into others in its path. As molecules have their energy, people are driven by their passions, and their relations with one another reflect both their "love [of] Liberty, and [love of] Dominion over others." No atom helps or moves aside for another; that wouldn't make sense. They are a collection of unrelated units. This fundamental picture I call "social atomism," for it shows society as a simple collection of independent, self-motivated units. (Wolgast 4–5)

As Wolgast's account reveals, the atomism schema embodies three crucial assumptions about individuals. First, it assumes that individuals are distinct and unique beings, ontologically different from each other. Second, it assumes that, psychologically and emotionally, individuals are naturally and fundamentally indifferent to each other at best and often hostile and vicious toward others. And third, the atomism schema takes it for granted that individuals are practically or pragmatically competitive and violent with each other, rather than cooperative, in their fundamental relations.

The assumption of individual ontological distinctiveness or uniqueness is epitomized in the opening words of Rousseau's *Confessions*, in which the author declares, "I am made unlike anyone I have ever met; I will even venture to say that I am like no one in the whole world. I may be no better, but at least I am different" (quoted in Lukes 67). As Tzvetan Todorov has documented, this ontological atomism has a long and impressive pedigree in the West, appearing in the works of the Stoics, Machiavelli, Hobbes, La Bruyère, Pascal, La Rochefoucauld, Kant, and Nietzsche, among others:

> The social dimension, the very fact of life in common, is not generally conceived of as being *necessary* to human beings. . . . A definition of man as solitary and nonsocial is accepted [as a fact needing no argument]. . . . Human beings are certainly caught in the web of social relations, but out of weakness. . . . Dealing with others is a burden to be discharged; asking approval from others is only an undesirable *vanity* that could never be tolerated by the wise man who aspires only to autarchy and self-sufficiency. . . . Society and morality conflict with human nature; they impose the rules of communal life on an essentially solitary being. (Todorov 1–3)

This assumption of individual uniqueness is also prominent in contemporary Americans' views of themselves. Psychologist Richard Nisbett reports that when surveyed about their individual preferences and attributes, Americans typically judge themselves to be more distinctive and unique than they actually are, while Asians have a much lower, more accurate estimation of their individual uniqueness (Nisbett, *Geography* 53–54). Similarly, Americans and other Westerners tend to believe that individual members of a society "are separate units [that] enter into a social contract with one another," whereas "most peoples, including East Asians, view societies not as aggregates of individuals but as . . . organisms" (Nisbett, *Geography* 198).

Psychological atomism, too, is quite prominent in the West in general and in America in particular, with many individuals feeling no urge to help unfortunate strangers or to engage in any actions not dictated by self-interest. As Todorov notes, "It is this concept of man, the immoralist conception, that has won out over that of the moralists, and it is also the concept found in the most influential political and psychological theories of today" (3). This psychological or emotional atomism has been prominent in America from the nation's beginnings, as evidenced by Emerson's declaration that social union "is only perfect when all the uniters are isolated," and that "each man, if he attempts to join himself to others, is on all sides cramped and diminished" (quoted in Lukes 29).

Supporting, and supported by, this psychological atomism is practical atomism, the view that individuals are practically or pragmatically isolated and opposed, that if one aids someone else, one must be sacrificing oneself, and that if one cares for oneself, one must ignore the other's needs. One prominent form of atomism in the United States today is rational choice theory, which combines psychological and practical atomism in the tenet "that the end of individual rational choice is always the maximization of the satisfaction of individual self-interest" (Nussbaum, *Poetic* 16). One of the most famous expressions of this view is an oft-quoted passage from Adam Smith's *The Wealth of Nations*: "It is not from the benevolence of the butcher, the brewer, or the baker that we expect our dinner, but from their regard of their own interest. We address ourselves not to their humanity, but to their self-love, and never talk to them of our necessities, but of their advantage" (quoted in Frank, *What Price* 121). This Gradgrindian atomism, Martha Nussbaum observes, "is a conception that even now dominates much of our public life, in a form not very different from the form presented in [Dickens's *Hard Times*]. . . . It dominates not only economic thought and practice, but also—given the prestige of economics within the social sciences—a great deal of writing in other social sciences as well" (Nussbaum, *Poetic* 18).

Falseness of the Atomism Schema

The atomistic view of human nature is not only pervasive in the West, but also profoundly false and harmful. "The atomistic person," as Wolgast observes, "is an unfortunate myth" (26). It is a myth because all persons are inherently and profoundly interconnected with others, in three basic ways: practically, ontologically, and emotionally-psychologically-neurologically.[1]

Practical Solidarity

In the first place, individuals are profoundly connected to others at the practical level, since no individual is capable of surviving without the help of others. As Todorov observes, the atomistic view of the self is contradicted by the way in which the self is formed and the ways in which it is sustained, both of which demonstrate that others are a prerequisite for the self's survival (not to mention its very existence) and for the development and maintenance of its identity. In terms of physical survival, no individual is capable of surviving at birth without receiving comprehensive and prolonged nurturance and protection from others. And even as adults, all individuals depend—and in virtually all cases, depend continuously and massively—on the actions of others for their food, water, clothing, shelter, transportation, communication, and safety. This fact—that humans are unable to survive without help—means, as Todorov notes, that "we owe others our very existence" and that "sociability is not an accident or a contingency; it is the very definition of the human condition" (Todorov 13).

Nor is practical solidarity limited to the physical body—it is also true of the individual self. "Sociable man," Rousseau remarked, as opposed to the "natural man" described in his earlier quote, is "always outside himself, is capable of living only in the opinion of others and, so to speak, derives the sentiment of his own existence solely from their judgment" (quoted in Todorov 14). Relations to others thus enhance our self rather than diminish it (Todorov 14), and selves mutually interconstitute each other both developmentally and psychodynamically. Developmentally, the qualities of any particular self are the product of its genetically governed proclivities, capacities, and vulnerabilities interacting with—and internalizing and identifying with, or identifying against and rejecting—the attributes and behaviors of those other selves it comes into contact with. Psychodynamically, maintaining one's identity, or sense of self, requires that others recognize our identity elements, which means that which specific attributes others recognize in us plays a significant role in determining which attributes become and remain part of our identity. Thus Todorov states, "My relationship to others is not the product of my own self-interest; it precedes both the self-interest and the 'I.' . . . The self exists only in and by its relations with others" (Todorov 4, 145).

Evolutionary psychologists point out that practical solidarity in the form of altruism and cooperation is only natural for humans. Indeed, altruism in various forms is not uncommon among animals. Some birds, for instance, give warning calls to the flock to alert it to imminent danger from predators, even though doing so exposes their own location to the predator and thus increases their individual risk. Other animals will attack predators who are threatening a member of their pack or herd, thus subjecting themselves to considerable danger. And in duels with other members of their species, most victorious animals eschew killing or even injuring their opponents, even though in doing so they leave the opponents capable of attacking them in the future (Singer, *Expanding* 6–8).

These and other forms of altruism are also evident in humans, among whom anthropologists have identified three basic types—kin altruism, reciprocal altruism, and group altruism—each of which derives, according to evolutionary theory, from the fact that it enhances the survival and propagation of the altruist's genes. Kin altruism does so by preserving the duplicates of one's own genes that are present in close relatives; reciprocal altruism by preserving the genes present in one's own body, through increasing the likelihood of receiving aid from others when one is in danger and thus enhancing the chances of one's own survival and hence reproduction; and group altruism by enhancing the group's odds of survival and reproduction vis-à-vis other groups (see Singer, *Expanding* 11–22). Concerning reciprocal altruism, which is also at the core of group altruism, Singer observes: "If there are advantages in being a partner in a reciprocal exchange, and if one is more likely to be selected as a partner if one has genuine concern for others, there is an evolutionary advantage in having genuine concern for others" (Singer, *Expanding* 44). The logistics of survival, Singer explains, are such that individual survival is sometimes enhanced if the individual is genuinely altruistic rather than merely self-interested: "Suppose two early humans are attacked by a sabertooth cat. If both flee, one will be picked off by the cat; if both stand their ground, there is a very good chance that they can fight the cat off. . . . So two purely self-interested early humans would flee, and one of them would die. Two early humans who cared for each other, however, would stand and fight, and most likely neither would die" (Singer, *Expanding* 47–48). Evolutionary theory, then, supports the notion that practical solidarity in the form of altruistic actions not only exists but has long been part of human nature.

Thus, as UCLA psychologist Shelley Taylor observes in *The Tending Instinct*, "we are a fundamentally nurturant species. . . . Cooperation is the norm, an art form so commonplace and so expected that we are no longer even aware of it. . . . On the whole, daily life is largely devoted to the cooperative exchange of goods and services that help us to achieve a better life. The most marked characteristics of human daily life are caring and cooperation, not the unbridled selfishness that many describe as 'human nature'" (Shelley E. Taylor 12, 41).

Ontological Solidarity

All humans are also connected with each other ontologically, through sharing a common, universal human nature. This simple fact has been obscured in academic circles by recognition that universalist claims have been used to dehumanize, oppress, and even exterminate people who are perceived to lack some supposedly universal human qualities or practices. In attempting to combat these forms of oppression, some intellectuals have emphasized cultural relativism and difference to the extent of denying that there is any such thing as human nature or human universals (see Pinker viii–x, 1–3, 139, 141). Many humanities teachers and scholars, in particular, have reinforced atomism in recent decades by rejecting the notions of "human nature" and "universality" and focusing exclusively on differences among individuals and groups. Patrick Hogan notes, "There has been a general sense in literary study that attention to or advocacy of universals is somehow politically suspect," and hence "when universalism is mentioned in humanistic writing, it is most often denounced as a tool of oppression" (Hogan, *Mind* 8–9). However, as Hogan observes, citing Kwame Appiah, such objections confuse valid universalism with false universalism: "Typically, humanist criticisms of universalism refer back to those universalist claims that derive from and serve to further colonial, patriarchal, or other ideologies supporting unjust domination. . . . In other words, they are objecting to false and duplicitous claims of universalism, assertions of universality that are untrue" (Hogan, *Mind* 9). In Appiah's words, "antiuniversalists . . . use the term *universalism* as if it meant *pseudouniversalism*, and the fact is that their complaint is not with universalism at all. What they truly object to—and who would not?—is Eurocentric hegemony *posing* as universalism" (Appiah 58, quoted in Hogan, *Mind* 9).

While the impulse behind the denial of human nature is understandable and laudable, the denial itself is both untrue and potentially even more harmful than the evils it attempts to combat. And a growing chorus of prominent thinkers has begun to push back against this denial (see, for example, Garber 20, 41). Perhaps the most detailed and comprehensive critique of anti-universalism is that offered by Steven Pinker in *The Blank Slate: The Modern Denial of Human Nature*, which, despite a tendency to overemphasize the innateness of certain practices and behaviors, nonetheless provides massive and indisputable evidence from the biological and social sciences that all human individuals share the same fundamental human nature, in the form of certain innate vulnerabilities, behavioral tendencies, and capabilities. Anthropologists, Pinker reports, "have found an astonishingly detailed set of aptitudes and tastes that all cultures have in common. . . . Hundreds of traits, from fear of snakes to logical operators, from romantic love to humorous insults, from poetry to food taboos, from exchange of goods to mourning the dead, can be found in every society ever documented" (Pinker 55). Terry Eagleton, in the same vein, notes that "all cultures must include such practices as child-rearing, education, welfare, communication, [and] mutual support, otherwise they would be unable to reproduce themselves" (Eagleton, *Idea* 23–24). The fundamental sameness of all people also manifests itself in the basic values and features shared by virtually all cultures (see Eagleton, *Idea* 105–107), which involve "the simplest, most common-place forms of mutual support, respect, and forbearance necessary for group survival" (Bok 53).

The most basic qualities of human nature result from the common features of the human body. Among the most notable commonalities of all human bodies are the needs for "oxygen, nourishment, water, and shelter from the elements" (Bok 80) that characterize "the suffering, mortal, needy, desiring body which links us fundamentally . . . with our fellow beings from other cultures" (Eagleton, *Idea* 111). In response to "the postmodern insistence that the body is a cultural construct" (Eagleton, *Idea* 88) rather than the common ground of human nature, Eagleton writes:

> Meanings can mould physical responses, but they are constrained by them too. The adrenal glands of the poor are often larger than those of the rich, since the poor suffer more stress, but poverty is not able to create adrenal glands where none exist. . . . People who set themselves on fire may feel no pain, but if they burn themselves badly enough they will perish even so. In this sense, nature has the final victory over culture, customarily known as death. Culturally speaking, death is almost limitlessly interpretable. . . . But we still die, however we make sense of it. (Eagleton, *Idea* 87–88)

As a result of sharing the same fundamental human body and its vulnerabilities, including mortality, humans also share the need for a sense of self and the recognition necessary to support it (Todorov 85, 20). As Eagleton states, "A common culture can be fashioned only because our bodies are of broadly the same kind, so that the one universal rests upon the other. . . . Of course human bodies differ, in their history, gender, ethnicity, physical capacities, and the like. But they do not differ in those capacities—language, labour, sexuality—which enable them to enter into potential universal relationship with one another in the first place" (Eagleton, *Idea* 111).

Mark Johnson makes a similar point. Because "we all have bodies that have at least a core set of universal needs and desires," he observes, "there are certain basic-level experiences we all have—experiences of harm and help—based on our embodiment and the material and social conditions of human existence. . . . Given the nature of our bodies, our brains, and our physical and social interactions, we would expect that certain *basic level experiences* (e.g., of harm, of help, of well-being) would be common across cultures" (Johnson 234, 237).

As Eagleton and Johnson both note, the human body, with its needs, deficiencies, and capabilities, exhibits certain basic psychological and social requirements and abilities common to all people. One of the most basic universal facts about the human body is its "premature" birth, which results in the universal need of the infant for help in surviving in its early years and for learning how to survive in its subsequent years. The universal incapacity of infants to care for themselves results, as we have noted, in a universal need for nurture, and the helpless infants' consequent subjection to the individual others who care for them, as well as to the generalized other of their culture whose expectations they inevitably incorporate, results in another universal human attribute: a constitutive self-division or structural lack common to all humans. This common characteristic of human beings is due in large measure, if not entirely, to our colonization by our culture's language—a fact that is often invoked in support of the claim of difference but that itself embodies another universal of human nature. The fact that different humans speak different languages is certainly responsible for important differences in their experiences, characters, and behaviors. But the fact that humans speak at all—that the human being is a speaking-being, or *parlêtre*, as Lacan put it—not only is an important universal in and of itself but also constitutes the basis for other important universals, including both the universal cognitive capacities embodied in language and the universal consequences that follow from one's entrance into language.

Concerning the capacity for language, Noam Chomsky has argued that it is innate in all humans. More specifically, Johnson points out,

"Recent empirical research in the cognitive sciences has revealed that both our concepts and our reasoning about them are grounded in the nature of our bodily experience and are structured by various kinds of imaginative processes. Consequently, since moral reasoning makes use of these same general cognitive capacities, it, too, is grounded in embodied structures of meaning" (Johnson 1). Johnson goes on to explain that "in general, we understand more abstract and less well structured domains (such as our concepts of reason, knowledge, belief) via mappings from more concrete and highly structured domains of experience (such as our bodily experience of vision, movement, eating, or manipulating objects)" (Johnson 10).

The universal consequences of language for the human self have been articulated most fully by various psychoanalytic theorists. Lacan emphasized the incommensurability between the organic body (the Lacanian "real") and the body's visual perceptual apparatus (Lacan's "imaginary register"), on the one hand, and the social, symbolic order of language, on the other. When people learn language, they translate their bodily states and perceptions into linguistic forms and categories and thus lose an important dimension of their preverbal bodily experience—a process that Lacan dramatically called "symbolic castration" and that child psychologist Daniel Stern described as the "fractur[ing of] amodal global experience" (Stern 176). More recently, Wilma Bucci, a psychoanalytically oriented research psychologist, has found through her own empirical studies of clinical processes as well as through her research on the literature of cognitive science that much intrapsychic conflict is a function of the always incomplete translations between three different registers of experience and memory that are hardwired into the human brain: a subsymbolic, affective-physiological register, characterized by parallel distributed processing; a symbolic register composed of discrete, nonverbal imagistic categories; and a symbolic register composed of language.

Thus the universal lack of self-sufficiency, together with the universal submission to language and to other people, results in a universal self-division. And as Julia Kristeva points out, this universal, self-divided human "nature," or "second nature," is both a profound form of solidarity and, at the same time (ironically), a motive for denying one's sameness with others and seeing them as radically different from oneself. This "difference within us," Kristeva maintains, is "the ultimate condition of our being with others" (Kristeva, *Strangers* 192), a dilemma that we share with everyone else, no matter how different from us they may otherwise be: "that uncanny strangeness . . . is as much theirs as it is ours" (Kristeva, *Strangers* 192). Alternatively stated, "The foreigner is within me"—as those parts of myself that I have rejected in order to assume a particular identity—and "hence we are all foreigners" (Kristeva, *Strangers* 192). This fact that all humans carry a "foreigner," "stranger," or "alien" within themselves thus not only explains their animosity toward some others—onto whom they project their own internal foreignness—it also constitutes a universal condition and thus a common ground, a basis for recognizing a common humanity behind the other's difference. Kristeva sees this universal self-division as the basis of "a cosmopolitanism of a new sort that, cutting across governments, economies, and markets, might work for *a mankind whose solidarity is founded on the consciousness of its unconscious*" (Kristeva, *Strangers* 192; emphasis added).[2]

Human desire, which Kristeva mentions as arising from the self-division that all humans embody, is ultimately, as Todorov observes but Kristeva does not, a desire for recognition and the feeling of existence or sense of identity it provides (Todorov 16). And this need for identity and recognition, which is the ultimate motivation, the root of all other desires (see Bracher, *Social* and Todorov 57, 70, 77–85), is yet another feature that all humans share. As Eagleton notes, "Identity is itself a universal necessity of human existence" (80; see also Hoover 62). And recognition is the primary way in which identity is established and maintained. As Charles Taylor puts it, "Our identity requires recognition by others" (Charles Taylor, *Ethics* 45).

Ethics, concern for the well-being of others, is yet another key element of a common, universal human nature. As Singer notes, "Every human society has some code of behavior for its members. . . . The core of ethics runs deep in our species and is common to human beings everywhere" (Singer, *Expanding* 23, 27). Singer thus concludes that "a readiness to cooperate seems to be part of our nature. . . . This readiness to cooperate is a true universal among humans" (Singer, *Left* 46). This is only to be expected, since, as we have seen, "egoists are at a disadvantage in evolution" and "there is an evolutionary advantage in having a genuine concern for others" (Singer, *Expanding* 128, 44). Moreover, certain specific moral rules also appear to be universal, such as injunctions against incest, rape, and murder (see Pinker 269). In *Common Values*, Sissela Bok argues that in order to survive and reproduce, all cultures must adopt certain minimalist values, including "the positive duties of care and reciprocity," "constraints on violence, deceit, and betrayal," and "norms for procedures and standards of justice" (Bok 41).

Eagleton makes a similar observation and sees these common values as deriving, as does Bok, from the common human body shared by all individuals and cultures: "At the broadest level there are some remarkable consistencies of moral judgment between cultures, which cannot simply be set aside in glib historicist fashion. And this comes as no surprise to the kind of ethical materialist for whom moral values have a relation to our creaturely nature, which has not significantly altered over the ages" (Eagleton, *Idea* 106).

Emotional-Psychological-Neurological Solidarity

The common human body and brain are also the basis of what is perhaps the most significant form of human solidarity, the emotional-psychological-neurological attunement, care, and concern for others that are inherent in the human heart-mind-brain. Cornell economist Robert Frank points out, "On the strength of the evidence, we must say that the self-interest model provides a woefully inadequate description of the way people actually behave" (Frank, *Passions* 256). Instead of acting according to the dictates of narrow self-interest, Frank observes, people often follow their emotions. And as the Scottish moral philosophers noted, emotions such as sympathy and compassion indicate that every individual is inherently concerned with the well-being of others (Wolgast 10, 20–21). In the opening paragraph of *The Theory of Moral Sentiments*, Adam Smith wrote:

> How selfish soever man may be supposed, there are evidently some principles in his nature, which interest him in the fortune of others, and render their happiness necessary to him, though he derives nothing from it, except the pleasure of seeing it. Of this kind is pity or compassion, the emotion which we feel for the misery of others, when we either see it, or are made to conceive it in a very lively manner. That we often derive sorrow from the sorrow of others, is a matter of fact too obvious to require any instances to prove it; for this sentiment, like all the other original passions of human nature, is by no means confined to the virtuous and human, though they perhaps may feel it with the most exquisite sensibility. The greatest ruffian, the most hardened violator of the laws of society, is not altogether without it. (Adam Smith 3)

Smith points out that when we see someone about to be hit on the arm or leg, we naturally retract our own arm or leg, and when we see the blow land, we ourselves suffer a kind of pain. Similarly, he observes, when people are watching a tightrope walker, they naturally adjust their own bodies to maintain balance as if they themselves were on the rope (Adam Smith 4). Any feeling that is being experienced by someone we are attending to, including a character in a story, produces a like emotion in every attentive observer (Adam Smith 5). In some cases, a feeling may be transferred instantaneously from one person to another without the observer's having any knowledge of what caused the other's emotion. "Grief and joy, for example, strongly expressed in the look and gestures of any person, at once affect the spectator with some degree of a like painful or agreeable emotion" (Adam Smith 6). Such experiences of sympathy, Smith maintains, constitute a profound unity between self and other: "By the imagination we place ourselves in his situation, we conceive ourselves enduring all the same torments, we enter as it were into his body, and become in some measure the same person with him" (Adam Smith 4).

Smith's insights have in recent years been elaborated and corroborated by research in cognitive science and social neuroscience. New York University psychologist Martin Hoffman identifies five modes of empathic arousal that he believes are universal, in that "humans in all cultures can be empathically aroused by any of them" (Hoffman 21). Hoffman finds that three of these modes, which he describes as "primitive modes," occur "automatically and involuntarily." One involves a conditioned response, which is produced by multiple experiences in which observation of another person's expressive cues of distress occurs simultaneously with an experience of one's own distress, such as when infants experience distress as a result of their mother's stiffening body and simultaneously experience their mother's facial and verbal expressions of distress. Subsequently, the mother's facial expressions of distress can produce distress in the child even without physical contact (Hoffman 45–46). A second automatic, involuntary mode of empathy arousal is direct association, in which elements of someone else's situation remind one of similar experiences of one's own and thus evoke the feelings that fit the other's situation (Hoffman 47).

The third automatic mode of empathy arousal is mimicry,[3] the process by which individuals duplicate another person's feeling by producing the same facial expressions, postures, muscle movements, and speech patterns of the person they are observing. In their book *Emotional Contagion*, Elaine Hatfield and her colleagues explain the cognitive processes that produce involuntary mimicry. Research has revealed that observers' facial expressions and feelings tend to mimic those of the people they are observing, including changes in the other's expression that are too subtle to be consciously detected, and that these changes in the observers' facial expressions, in turn, produce reactions in their autonomic nervous system (Hatfield et al. 19ff.). A similar process has been discovered in our response to others' voices. Newborns who hear another infant crying begin to cry themselves, and they also synchronize the movements of their head and body with the patterns of the speech they are hearing (Hatfield et al. 27–28).

Adults in conversation have been found to mimic and synchronize their accents, speech rates, vocal intensity, response latency, utterance duration, pause duration, and duration of talkovers (Hatfield et al. 28–29). Muscle mimicry has also been documented: "When we carefully attend to others performing a series of manual activities, we find our own muscles 'helping them out'" (Hatfield et al. 32). In one study, subjects were shown a video tape of an individual stuttering and another tape of two men arm wrestling. Electrodes on the observers' faces and arms revealed that when they watched the stuttering, they produced more EMG activity in their lip area, and when they watched the arm wrestling, they produced more activity in their right forearms (Hatfield et al. 33). Other studies have found significant postural mimicking and mirroring between individuals, and some researchers have concluded that this mimicry sends the message, "I am with you" or "I am like you" (Hatfield et al. 35–36). Such mirroring and mimicking have been found to be particularly subtle and intricate in response to the words, postures, and movements of a speaker (Hatfield et al. 37–38).

Recently, neuroscientists have discovered the neural mechanisms that produce involuntary mimicry and constitute an inherent neurological interconnectedness of all individuals. These key mechanisms are "mirror neurons," which, as we noted in Chapter 1, are a type of brain neuron that, when one person observes another, activates in the observer's brain the same emotional and motor neural networks that operate in the observer's own feelings and actions. UCLA neuroscientist Marco Iacoboni explains, "Our brain produces a *full simulation*—even the motor component—of the observed painful experiences of other people. Although we commonly think of pain as a fundamentally private experience, our brain actually treats it as an experience shared with others" (Iacoboni 124). Such simulation appears to occur in response to any facial expression of emotion we observe in another person: "According to this mirror neuron hypothesis of empathy, our mirror neurons fire when we see others expressing their emotions, as if we were making those facial expressions ourselves" (Iacoboni 119).

The same sort of simulation occurs in response to physical movements: "Neither the monkey nor the human can observe someone else picking up an apple without also invoking in the brain the motor plans necessary to snatch that apple themselves (mirror neuron activation)" (Iacoboni 14). And the mirror neurons also appear to simulate the intentions behind the actions: "Mirror neurons let us understand the intentions of other people: . . . we activate a chain of mirror neurons, such that these cells can simulate a whole sequence of simple actions—reaching for the cup, grasping it, bringing it to the mouth—that is quite simply the simulation in our brain of the intention of the human we are watching" (Iacoboni 34, 77).

Reflecting on the significance of mirror neurons for solidarity, Iacoboni states: "This neural mechanism is essential for building social ties. It is also very likely that these forms of resonance with the painful experiences of others are relatively early mechanisms of empathy, from an evolutionary and developmental point of view" (Iacoboni 124). Psychologist and science writer Daniel Goleman sees mirror neurons as producing an even more profound form of solidarity. When two people meet face to face, he says, their mirror neurons make their "brains 'couple,' with the output of one becoming the input to drive the workings of the other, for the time being forming what amounts to an interbrain circuit" (Goleman, *Social* 39–40). This "coupling" of brains not only produces involuntary empathy with others, but also, through repetition, rewires our brains, altering "the shape, size, and number of neurons and their synaptic connections" (Goleman, *Social* 11). This means that "not just our own moods but our very biology is being driven and molded by the other people in our lives" (Goleman, *Social* 12)—a fact that refutes autonomism and essentialism as well as atomism.

As Iacoboni observes, the discovery of mirror neurons should put the final nail in the coffin of the atomism that has been so prominent in the West:

Western culture is dominated by an individualistic, solipsistic framework that has taken for granted the assumption of a complete separation between self and other. We are entrenched in this idea that any suggestion of an interdependence of self and other may sound not just counterintuitive to us, but difficult, if not impossible, to accept. Against this dominant view, mirror neurons put the self and the other back together again. Their neural activity reminds us of the *primary* intersubjectivity. . . . They show that we are not alone, but are biologically wired and evolutionarily designed to be deeply interconnected with one another. . . . Our neurobiology—our mirror neurons—commits us to others. (Iacoboni 155, 267, 268)

A final form of solidarity that is both psychological and practical is intersubjectivity, or intermental, distributed cognition (Palmer 184): the fact that cognition takes place between individual minds and brains as well as within them. "Mental functioning," Alan Palmer observes, "cannot be understood merely by analyzing what goes on inside the skull but can only be fully comprehended once it has been seen in its social and physical context" (Palmer 184–185). Thus, as David Herman argues, since "minds are spread out among participants in discourse, their speech acts, and the objects in their material environment . . . , cognition should be viewed as a supra- or trans-individual activity distributed across groups functioning in specific contexts rather than as a wholly internal process unfolding within the minds of solitary, autonomous, and desituated cognizers" (Herman 166).

Harmful Consequences of the Atomism Schema

Atomism produces three major harmful consequences. First, by obscuring the commonalities among humans, it prevents or reduces interpersonal, intergroup, and cross-cultural understanding, cooperation, caring, and altruism. Second, by absolutizing self-interest, it validates, celebrates, and even encourages competition and opposition at the expense of cooperation and collaboration. And third, by denying human universals, it deprives us of grounds for criticizing and opposing harmful behaviors, practices, institutions, and systems.

Preventing Care for the Other

First and most directly, the atomism assumption prevents caring for others by causing people to devalue, ignore, discount, suppress, or repress all evidence of their inherent sameness and overlap with others—including their empathy and compassion for others, and that of others for them. As noted above, in recent decades many scholars and teachers in the humanities have inadvertently supported atomism and its harmful consequences by emphasizing differences to the point of denying that any such thing as human nature, or universal human attributes, exists. It is now widely understood how the failure to recognize crucial differences between both individuals and groups can lead to harmful social interactions and oppressive and unjust social policies, institutions, and structures. For example, taking the white, middle-class, Anglo-American, heterosexual male as the prototype of a human being has resulted in serious inequities in law, education, health care, and economic policy, as well as miscalculations in international relations that have produced terrible consequences.

But while recognizing differences is clearly a prerequisite for social justice, denying all sameness is a recipe for disaster. As Iacoboni says, "True cross-cultural encounters are actually made impossible by the influence of massive belief systems—religious and political—that deny continuously the fundamental neurobiology that links us together" (Iacoboni 271). And as Nussbaum observes, "Under the label of 'multiculturalism'—which can refer to the appropriate recognition of human diversity and cultural complexity—a new antihumanist view has sometimes emerged, one that celebrates difference in an uncritical way and denies the very possibility of common interests and understandings" (Nussbaum, *Cultivating* 110). Such a position constitutes a major obstacle to social justice, for if all one sees is the other's differences from oneself, one will be inclined not toward compassion and justice but toward indifference and exploitation or oppression.

If I experience no overlap between my being and that of a suffering other—such as a swatted fly—I will feel no sympathy and take no action to help. If, on the other hand, I apprehend the suffering other as part of my own being—as with a loved one, or simply another human being, or even a beloved pet or a wild animal—then I will feel distress and sympathy and be moved to help. This is because, Cialdini and his colleagues explain, "crucial features of the self exist outside the body of the individual and inside close others. Consequently, what one does to and for these others one does to and for oneself" (Cialdini et al. 492). As Richard Rorty points out, we care about harming others only to the extent that we can identify with them, see them as one of us (Rorty, "Justice" 9). Social justice prevails only insofar as individuals and groups view others as fundamentally like themselves, sharing a common humanity. Crimes against humanity are not seen by their perpetrators as crimes at all, because the perpetrators view their victims as not human, not at all like themselves. Rorty notes that Serbian nationalists, for example, did not see themselves as violating human rights when they raped and murdered Muslim women and children because they did not see Muslims as humans, just as Thomas Jefferson did not see himself as violating human rights in owning slaves because he did not see the slaves as fully human (Rorty, "Human" 67). Thus the way to promote moral progress and social justice, Rorty argues, is to "expand the reference of the terms 'our kind of people' and 'people like us'"—that is, to help people see that others who are different from them are nonetheless like them in fundamental ways (Rorty, "Human" 74). Progress in morality and social justice "consists in an increasing ability to see the similarities between ourselves and people very unlike us as outweighing the differences" (Rorty, "Human" 77).

Atomism impedes moral progress by preventing recognition of overlap between self and other. Empirical studies support this conclusion. Such studies have shown that individuals who perceive overlap or sameness with others—whether in the form of a shared trait or group membership or simply their common humanity—are more perceptive of the others' suffering, respond to this suffering with greater altruism, and have a greater commitment to social justice (see Levy, Freitas, and Salovey 1224; Monroe, "Explicating" and *Heart*). As Stephen Phillips and Robert Ziller observe, "Research suggests that perceived similarity [of self and other] rather than actual similarity is the fundamental link to liking, helping, understanding, and even reduced prejudice. In other words, similarity is in the eye of the beholder" (Phillips and Ziller 421).

Finally, whether people see similarities or differences as more prominent is itself determined largely by whether they are operating with a solidarity schema or an atomism schema. Phillips and Ziller's research reveals that some people operate with a "universal orientation," which leads them to "orien[t] toward, or selectively atten[d] to similarities rather than differences between self and others, . . . [and] that orientation to similarity between the self and other . . . is critical to nonprejudice, whereas a difference orientation between self and other . . . sets the stage for prejudice" (Phillips and Ziller 421). Phillips and Ziller constructed a scale to measure the degree to which individuals are oriented toward similarity and found that individuals who scored high on the scale were more accepting of minority individuals, finding them "equally attractive, equally similar, and equally desirable as a potential work partner," as well as "more representative of humankind" than did individuals with low scores (Phillips and Ziller 427–429). They also found that "universally oriented persons are aware of ethnic differences between diverse targets, but rather than emphasizing and negatively evaluating those differences, they have an overriding or prevailing tendency for selectively attending to and accentuating similarities" (Phillips and Ziller 430). They conclude:

> Universal orientation avoids the first treacherous act in interpersonal relations, that is, the separation of self and other, which tends to be followed by an invidious comparison of the self and the other, to justify the separation. Through the simple act of orienting toward differences between self and others, the foundation is set for conflict rather than accord. . . . Moreover, whereas differentiation of self and other tends to be succeeded by a hierarchical orientation or even an elitist view of the self or one's group (vis-à-vis the other), integration of self and other is succeeded by a more nonprejudiced view. Nonprejudice begins with an orientation toward similarities between self and other, followed by an integration, or the perception of unity between the self and other even to the extent of seeing the self reflected in the other. (Phillips and Ziller 427)

Phillips and Ziller further argue that this universal orientation, or inclination to perceive solidarity with others, is itself the product of a cognitive schema that governs social information processing: "Universal orientation . . . is characterized by a slant, set, perceptual readiness, or habitual orientation to others [i.e., a person-schema] . . . in which there is selective attention to self–other similarities" (422).

Another way in which the atomistic absolutization of difference impedes caring is by supporting our tendency to blame victims for their own suffering. When assessing how much responsibility people bear for their own distress, we assign significantly less blame when we see them as overlapping with ourselves than we do when we regard them as utterly different and separate from ourselves (see Aron and McLaughlin-Volpe 91). The exact reason for this reduction in the fundamental attribution error, which we discussed in Chapter 2, has not yet been determined, but it in all likelihood involves atomism's blinding us to the fact that differences among individuals and peoples are much less significant than our samenesses and are, in fact, largely the result of different circumstances: both different formative environments and different current situations. That is, differences among individuals and groups are the result largely of differences in environment, not differences in their genetic material, or "nature." And because atomism takes differences to be inherent rather than contingent, it prevents recognition of the extent to which people cannot legitimately be blamed for their negative behaviors or character traits (any more than they can legitimately be credited for their positive ones) because these behaviors and traits are largely the product of a difference in environment, not a difference in nature, as we saw in Chapters 2 and 3.

Differences cannot and should not be ignored. But neither should they be absolutized, as they often are in multiculturalism. Rather, they should be understood as subordinate to and derivative from the common capabilities, needs, and vulnerabilities that all humans share. Differences in behaviors must be recognized as the result of differences not only in character but also in circumstances. And differences in character must be recognized as the result of differences not only in genetic endowment but also in formative environment. We must recognize that "the one who murders has experienced more emotional hardships and deprivations than the rest of us, but he is more like us than different" (Strean and Freeman 267). Such recognition enables the insight that if I were that person or "those people," in that situation, with their specific, socially, materially, and culturally produced beliefs, values, hopes, dreams, capabilities, and vulnerabilities, I would be and do exactly as they are being and doing.

A third way in which atomism prevents caring and altruism is by blinding people to the suffering of others. The judgment that the other is suffering and in need is crucial, for if this judgment is not made, one will feel no compassion and no inclination to help the other. By foregrounding differences between people, the atomism assumption allows people to believe that "they" don't have the fully human sensitivity that "we" do and so aren't terribly bothered by circumstances, such as loss of loved ones or squalid living conditions, that would cause "us" great pain (see Levy, Freitas, and Salovey). An example is the commonplace assumption among Americans during the Vietnam War that whereas Americans suffered greatly when they lost loved ones in the war, Asians did not value individuals and thus did not suffer when members of their families or communities were killed. Members of privileged groups have historically been, and continue today to be, profoundly unperceptive of the needs of nonprivileged groups, often believing that the squalor in which the other group lives is the condition that most suits members of such a group and that it has even been chosen or preferred by them. Historically there are the blindnesses of colonizers toward the suffering of the colonized, of whites toward the suffering of blacks, of capitalists toward the suffering of workers, of men toward the suffering of women, and of the rich toward the suffering of the poor.

Perhaps the most complete blindness concerns the needs of that diverse group that we categorize as criminals. Because these individuals have in many cases inflicted some sort of suffering upon others, they are often seen as subhuman creatures capable only of inflicting pain, not feeling it. And since it is often their pain that causes lawbreakers to engage in their harmful behaviors to begin with, our failure to see their pain prevents us from recognizing and addressing key causes of their transgressions. That this is true of addicts incarcerated for possession of illegal substances or impoverished individuals imprisoned for theft can be acknowledged by many people after some reflection. But most people fail to perceive the suffering of those who commit murder, rape, or child molestation. Yet experts who have studied such individuals have found that their crimes are efforts to cope with severe mental anguish and/or dysfunction of one sort or another (see Gilligan; Grand; Katz; Wolf). In cases such as these, perceiving the other's suffering is a prerequisite not only for reducing that suffering but also for preventing the suffering that this individual or group might inflict on another. But this perception is prevented by the atomistic denial of a common human nature.

And finally, the atomism schema impedes caring and helping by prompting people to devalue, ignore, discount, suppress, or repress their own and other people's inherent emotional and neurological solidarity, in the form of empathic attunement with others. If we recognize our own inherent capacity and inclination for empathy and altruism as part of who we are, a key element of our identity or sense of self, we will be much more aware of these impulses when they stir in us, and much more welcoming and supportive of them when we feel them in ourselves, finding enjoyment and pride in feeling, expressing, and enacting them. And if we recognize this same inherent capacity and inclination in other people, we will be much more welcoming and nurturing of empathy in them, fostering it in them by expecting it (the phenomenon of the self-fulfilling prophecy) and meeting it with recognition and approbation when it is expressed and enacted. If, on the contrary, we operate with the atomism schema and neither recognize nor value empathy in ourselves or others, empathy and the care and aid it produces will be minimized in both ourselves and others (see Dale T. Miller).

Validating Indifference, Competition, Aggression, and Rapacity

The myth of the atomistic person as a creature of "ruthless egoism and unconcern for others" (Wolgast 19) engaged in a zero-sum competition, a Hobbesian war of each against all (Wolgast 4), not only inhibits caring and altruism, it actively naturalizes and thus encourages indifference, ruthless competition, aggression, and rapacity. It entails a society in which "the elderly and frail must compete with the young and strong, men compete with their childbearing wives, the handicapped compete with the well endowed. Correspondingly, the economy of the community is seen as an n-person game in which each player plays against all the others to maximize his advantage" (Wolgast 19). This consequence is especially evident in Social Darwinism, which views life as "a struggle in which those who make it shouldn't let themselves be dragged down by those who don't" (de Waal 28) and which supports "an evolving ideology of private enterprise and *laissez-faire*, postulating absolute equality of opportunity and the claim that private accumulation leads to public welfare" (Lukes 30).

The atomism of Social Darwinism was taken to heart and put into practice by ruthless industrialists such as John D. Rockefeller and Andrew Carnegie, who used it to excuse and justify their accumulation of obscene wealth through brutal labor practices and cutthroat competitive tactics. Social Darwinism allowed Rockefeller to blithely and piously assert that "the growth of a large business is merely a survival of the fittest, the working out of a law of nature and a law of God" (quoted in Mills 64–65) and Andrew Carnegie to declare that the "best interests of the race" were served by an economic arrangement that "inevitably gives wealth to the few" (quoted in Mills 72). Later, Ayn Rand preached "that egoism is no vice, but rather a virtue," and "that if we have any obligation at all, it is to ourselves" (de Waal 32).

This form of atomism has not yet disappeared from the corporate world. Nicolaus Mills observes, "A century later the defenders of corporate Darwinism don't come so well known or with such impressive credentials, but the corporate culture they have managed to establish is as coherent and ruthless as that of the 1890s, and it has helped create in America the widest gap between rich and poor of any industrialized nation" (Mills 72–73). Some corporate Darwinists are quite well known and exert great influence on American opinions and economic policies. These include Rand disciples such as Alan Greenspan, the former chairman of the Federal Reserve who on at least one occasion referred to poor people as parasites, and Republican vice presidential nominee Paul Ryan, who proposes fiscal policies that would gut health care for the elderly along with other social programs while further enriching the wealthiest Americans.

Supported by the atomism schema, Social Darwinism has not only survived, but is actually thriving in American today.

Eliminating the Basis for Criticism

A final harmful consequence of the atomism schema is the fact that ontological atomism—the denial that there are such things as universal human traits or human nature—eliminates the firmest foundation available for criticizing beliefs, values, actions, practices, institutions, or systems that are destructive and unjust. As Pinker states, "Human nature provides a yardstick to identify suffering in any member of our species," whereas "the relativist climate in many academic circles does not allow [various] horrors to be criticized" (Pinker 172). Without recourse to a common, universal human nature, who can say that any given individual or group is suffering as the result of any particular circumstances or conditions—such as genital mutilation, stoning, infanticide, amputation, genocide, ethnic cleansing, torture, and racial, gender, and sexual discrimination—much less criticize such circumstances as unjust (see Pinker 172; Bok 24)? Kate Soper points out, "Discourses that would deny any shared structure of cognition, need and affectivity may . . . license a callous political neglect of the sufferings and deprivations of others" (quoted in Eagleton 57). Thus, "far from being conducive to discrimination, a conception of human nature is the reason we oppose it. . . . No one likes being enslaved. No one likes being humiliated. No one likes being treated unfairly, that is, according to traits that the person cannot control. The revulsion we feel toward discrimination and slavery comes from a conviction that however much people vary on some traits, they do not vary on these" (Pinker 145).

Eagleton makes a similar point, noting that if it were true, as cultural relativism would have it, that "nature, sex, and the body are wholly the products of convention," then it would be "hard to know how one is supposed to judge, for example, that one sexual regime is more emancipated than another" (Eagleton, *Idea* 92). The only solid, non-arbitrary basis for judging certain political regimes to be unjust and opposing them, Eagleton reminds us, is our ontological solidarity—our common human nature, or "what the young Marx calls our 'species being'—

126   The Cognitive Roots of Injustice

needs such as food, sleep, shelter, warmth, physical integrity, companionship, sexual fulfillment, a degree of personal dignity and security, freedom from pain, suffering, and oppression, a modest amount of self-determination and the like" (Eagleton, *Idea* 99–100). The universal needs of the human body that we all hold in common provide the ultimate criteria for determining whether a given society or practice is just: "Natural needs—needs which we have just by virtue of the sort of bodies we are, whatever myriad cultural forms they may assume—are criterial of political well-being, in the sense that societies which thwart them should be politically opposed" (Eagleton, *Idea* 100).

The same point holds for ethical judgment more generally. The academic denial of ontological solidarity (sameness, human nature, or universality) results, first, in the reduction of the other to a mere cipher of the theorist's own discourse. Christopher Norris states, "Those vacuous appeals to an ethics or a politics of radical 'difference' . . . always end up by constructing the 'other' as an empty, unthinkably alien position within discourse whose lineaments can only be descried in the image of the theorist's own concerns" (Norris 119). Moreover, the denial of ontological solidarity and absolutization of difference renders unethical any effort to truly help the other (Norris 35–36).

The self-defeating and self-contradictory nature of the denial of sameness becomes starkly evident in the work of the most powerful advocate of the absolute alterity of the other, Emmanuel Levinas, who bases his claim in a nonlinguistic, pre-epistemic, pre-ontological founding apprehension that he claims we all have of the other. As Derrida pointed out in his critique of Levinas, if the other were really absolutely different from oneself, one could not even be aware of the other's existence, much less say anything valid about, or engage in ethical actions toward, this other. Norris draws on Derrida's argument to provide a withering critique of the claim of absolute alterity:

> "It is impossible," Derrida writes, "to encounter the alter ego (in the very form of the encounter described by Levinas), impossible to respect it in experience and in language, if this other, in its alterity, does not *appear* for an ego (in general)." And again: "(o)ne could neither speak, nor have any sense of the totally other, if there was not a phenomenon of the totally other, or evidence of the totally other as such." From which it follows that we must have knowledge of the other—understand him or her by analogy with our own experience—if "otherness" is not

to become just a form of inverted autism, an empty locus upon which to project our ideas of a radical (hence wholly abstract and unknowable) difference. . . . Levinas's notion of "infinite alterity" must remain just that—a notional appeal devoid of ethical substance—unless it acknowledges (which can scarcely be denied) the need to *put oneself in the other's place* in order to recognize that claim. (Norris 48–49)

Replacing the Atomism Schema

Because of the harm it produces, "we need to loosen the hold that the atomistic picture has on our thinking, and recognize the [impact that this] theory has on our judgments and our moral condition" (Wolgast 27). Research has revealed that helping individuals to perceive their sameness with others can reduce animosity and aggression and increase kindness and cooperation. Inducing individuals to take the perspective of another has been found to lead to increased perception of self–other overlap, or symbolic merging of self and other (ontological solidarity) and thence to greater helping (Cialdini et al. 482–483; see also Galinsky, Ku, and Wang 115, 121). Inducing individuals to focus on a common group identity "leads them to allocate resources away from themselves and to other in-group members" (Cialdini et al. 492; Brewer 165ff.; Gaertner and Dovidio 71ff.). Similarly, finding abstract formulations to characterize both one's own and others' goals or actions that had previously been formulated in more concrete, mutually exclusive terms can also improve understanding and cooperation (Cialdini et al. 492; Levy, Freitas, and Salovey 1224–1225). And correcting the faulty atomistic information processing of hyper-aggressive individuals has been found to produce a reduction in their aggressive behavior (Hudley and Graham).

In light of these findings, replacing the atomism schema with the solidarity schema, which will systematically enhance the perception of sameness, should produce similar but more wide-ranging benefits. And such replacement can be promoted by providing numerous exemplars in all forms of each of the three types of solidarity, exposing the flaws of atomistic information processing and training readers to avoid these faulty routines, and helping readers develop metacognition of atomism, solidarity, and their respective sources and consequences. As we have done in the previous chapters, we will first consider the sources of the atomism schema, as a way of contributing to metacognition.

Sources of the Atomism Schema

Although the atomism schema is deeply flawed and harmful, it is based in a kernel of truth that must not (and in most cases cannot) be ignored: every individual body and brain are physically distinct and separate from every other individual body and brain, and as a result, so is every individual person or self. And as a consequence of this separation, each individual inevitably experiences competition, opposition, and even aggression both toward and from other individuals, no matter how much cooperation, caring, and altruism the self or others may also engage in. Furthermore, there are times when standing alone, refusing to conform, is the greatest virtue. In such cases, solidarity can be quite harmful, and it is thus important to distinguish between (a) the solidarity of an in-group loyalty, which may foster intergroup hostilities, and (b) what Richard Rorty calls a "larger loyalty" (see Rorty, "Justice"), a universal solidarity motivating an individualistic nonconformity that eschews more parochial (and potentially harmful) solidarities.

The problem is not that the atomistic view of individual selves as separate and in competition and opposition is utterly false or that solidarity is always best; the problem is that the truth of atomism, like those of autonomism and essentialism, is only half of the story, and that by itself, in the absence of the complementary truth of solidarity, it constitutes a profoundly false and harmful understanding of persons, their relationships, their limitations, and their possibilities. What is needed is thus a rejection not of atomism per se but rather of its absolutization. And in order to make this correction, it is helpful, and perhaps necessary as well, to understand the causes of this absolutization of atomism. That is, how is atomism able, in certain societies, such as ours, to so largely eclipse the fact of human solidarity?

We begin, as with the autonomism and essentialism schemas, with the role of fundamental, largely innate, psychological mechanisms that produce our awareness of separation of self and other. While such separation seems self-evident to most adults, it appears not to be so to infants. Their sense of themselves as a separate, distinct, physically bounded entity is not given at birth; rather, it is developed as the result of certain neural structures interacting with the infant's bodily experiences. Child psychologist Daniel Stern has identified a number of key experiences through which infants construct a sense of themselves as a physically separate entity. One is the experience of proprioceptive feedback, the sense of control one has over one's own movements in contrast to the lack of control one has over the movements of other people, or the different consequences resulting from one's own actions and the same actions of others (e.g., darkness is experienced when one closes one's own eyes but not when others close their eyes) (Stern 71–81). Another source of the sense of separateness is experiences of "being a nonfragmented, physical whole with boundaries and a locus of integrated action, both while moving (behaving) and when still" (Stern 71).

Neurologically, this process of constructing a sense of oneself as separate from others appears to based in significant measure on a class of neurons that Iacoboni has dubbed "super mirror neurons" (Iacoboni 156). Mirror neurons, as we saw above, fire for both our own actions, emotions, and intentions and those of other people. Indeed, empirical studies suggest that we are constantly engaging in subtle (and usually unconscious) imitations of other people (Iacoboni 201–202). But if this is the case—if our mirror neurons are firing whenever we perceive or imagine other people—what prevents us from involuntarily imitating every person we encounter or think about? The answer, according to Iacoboni, appears to lie in the activity of super mirror neurons, a type of neuron that increases its firing during the individual's own actions and decreases its firing or shuts down completely when one observes the actions of other people (Iacoboni 210–211). Iacoboni observes that super mirror neurons together with bodily feedback "allow us to internally represent self and other with some level of independence, even while they are mirroring each other" and concludes that super mirror neurons' "differential coding for action of the self (increased firing rate) and for actions of others (decreased firing rate) may represent a wonderfully simple neural distinction between self and other implemented by these special types of super mirror neurons" (Iacoboni 265, 203).

A third psychological factor that may play a role in the ascendancy of atomism (and the other faulty person-schemas as well) is the penchant of the human mind for simplicity (Todorov 43). As Gordon Allport noted years ago, "Outer reality is in itself chaotic—full of too many potential meanings. We have to *simplify* in order to live" (quoted in Moskowitz 173, emphasis in original). Empirical studies have found numerous instances of what psychologists call "cognitive miserliness," which has variously been attributed to lack of cognitive capacity, mental laziness, and the desire for efficiency (Moskowitz 174ff.). Whatever its cognitive underpinnings, the urge to simplify finds fulfillment in much conservative thinking in general (see Jost et al.) and in atomism in particular (see Scheuer 126, 135–136).

One final psychological force that appears to contribute to atomism is pride or vanity. Todorov argues that "it is out of pride that men profess different variants of the asocial idea, that they heap so many sins and crimes on themselves, so much selfishness, brutality, parricide!" (Todorov 44). Embracing atomism provides people with two sources of pride, Todorov argues. First, it allows them to feel that they have superior intellectual integrity and courage. "Those who resist this simplification [of atomism] are immediately accused of being moralistic and cowardly: They do not dare face the truth. . . . It is flattering for the individual to think of himself as . . . carrying on a solitary search for truth rather than for the approval of his public" (Todorov 44). And second, atomism allows its proponents to view themselves as much more self-sufficient and in control than they actually are: "They can hide their basic incompleteness and present themselves as masters of their destiny. They are ready to admit anything but their dependence, their need of others" (Todorov 45).

Ideology also clearly plays a major role in producing and promoting atomism, and this is particularly true of American ideology. Iacoboni declares that "philosophical and ideological individualistic positions especially dominant in our Western culture have made us blind to the fundamentally intersubjective nature of our own brains" (Iacoboni 152). Tocqueville saw atomism as a product of American democracy. "For Tocqueville," Lukes observes, "individualism [read atomism] was the natural product of democracy . . . , involving the apathetic withdrawal of individuals from public life into a private sphere and their isolation from one another, with a consequent weakening of social bonds" (Lukes 13). American individualism, in Tocqueville's view, is "a deliberate and peaceful sentiment which disposes each citizen to isolate himself from the mass of his fellows and to draw apart with his family and his friends . . . [and which eventually] attacks and destroys all others and is eventually absorbed into pure egoism" (Tocqueville, quoted in Lukes 13). In America, individuals "become accustomed to considering themselves always in isolation [and] freely imagine that their destiny is entirely in their own hands." American democracy "not only makes each man forget his forefathers, but it conceals from him his descendants and separates him from his contemporaries; it carelessly throws him back on himself alone and threatens finally to confine him entirely in the solitude of his own heart" (Tocqueville, quoted in Lukes 13–14).

One specific historically dominant and still quite powerful contributor to atomistic ideology is patriarchy. As Shelley Taylor observes, prominent scientific books—"big, chest-thumping books that touted our selfish, individualistic, aggressive nature" and in which "each person is to others as little more than an opportunity for manipulation or exploitation" (Shelley Taylor 9)—completely ignore the experience of women: "In their myopic focus on the aggressive experience of men, they ignore a very rich aspect of both women's and men's lives, namely the caring, nurturant side of human nature. When we look instead to women's lives for clues about human nature, the significance of nurturance snaps into place with such clarity that you wonder how its centrality could possibly have eluded scientific concern for so long" (Shelley E. Taylor 10).

Another major conduit of atomist ideology is American education. Insofar as education promotes the ideology of American individualism, it is also a significant source of atomism. Princeton psychologist Dale Miller argues convincingly that scientific theories that people are motivated primarily by self-interest have "spawned a norm of self-interest, the consequence of which is that people often act and speak in accordance with their perceived self-interest solely because they believe to do otherwise is to violate a powerful descriptive and prescriptive expectation" (Dale T. Miller 1053). This norm of self-interest is thus a self-fulfilling prophecy, as Miller explains:

> The assumption of self-interest contributes to its own confirmation in at least two ways. First, individualistic cultures structure their social institutions to reflect their belief that people are naturally disposed to pursue their self-interest, which results in these institutions fostering the very behavior their structure presupposes occurs naturally. . . . Second, . . . individualistic cultures spawn social norms that induce people to follow their material self-interest rather than their principles or passions . . . : people act and sound as though they are strongly motivated by their material self-interest because scientific theories and collective representations derived from those theories convince them that it is natural and normal to do so. As Kagan (1989) has observed, "People treat self-interest as a natural law and because they believe they should not violate a natural law, they try to obey it." . . . Interpreting the presence of self-interested behavior to suggest that self-interest is inevitable and universal rather than historically and culturally contingent only serves to strengthen the layperson's belief that pursuing self-interest is normatively appropriate, rational, and enlightened. The result of this is a pos-

itive feedback loop: The more powerful the norm of self-interest, the more evidence there is for the theory of self-interest, which, in turn, increases the power of the self-interest norm. (Dale T. Miller 1059)

The consequences of educating students in the self-interest norm have been empirically demonstrated with regard to economics education. Cornell economist Robert Frank conducted multiple empirical studies to assess whether exposure to the self-interest model of behavior that is dominant in economics courses actually affects students' own behaviors in cooperative activities. One study found that while most students engage in more cooperative behavior as they progress through college, this is not the case with economics majors: "For students in general there is . . . a pronounced tendency toward more cooperative behavior with movement toward graduation, [but this trend] is conspicuously absent for economics majors" (Frank, *What Price* 172). Frank hypothesized that "even a single semester of introductory microeconomics would have a measurable effect both on students' expectations of the level of self-interested behavior in society and on their own propensities to behave self-interestedly" (Frank, *What Price* 175). Testing these tendencies in students in three classes at the beginning and again at the end of the semester, Frank found that students in a traditional introductory economics class, which emphasized the self-interest model of behavior, became both less cooperative themselves and more cynical regarding the likelihood that other people would cooperate. Students in a second economics class, however, which did not emphasize the self-interest model, did not show this tendency and in fact showed a greater tendency to engage in cooperative behavior on some measures. And students in an introductory astronomy course manifested an even greater increase in cooperative behavior (Frank, *What Price* 174–176). Based on these and other studies, Frank concludes "that emphasis on the self-interest model tends to inhibit cooperation," "that economists are more likely to free-ride"—i.e., fail to contribute their fair share in cooperative ventures—and that "the differences in cooperativeness" between economists and noneconomists "are caused in part by training in economics" in general and more specifically by "repeated exposure to [an atomistic] behavioral model whose unequivocal prediction is that people will defect [from cooperation] whenever self-interest dictates" (Frank, *What Price* 176–177).

Even more significant than education in the promotion of atomism is television. In *The Sound Bite Society: Television and the American Mind*, Jeffrey Scheuer notes multiple ways in which the medium and content of television programs promote atomism. As noted above, one source of atomism is the human mind's attraction to simplicity, and television, Scheuer argues, is "a simplifying filter" that "atomizes information, breaking it down into particles" (Scheuer 23, 80–81). The targets of this atomizing include people. Television is "a medium wedded to discrete moments, locations, events, and individuals" (Scheuer 55), and it promotes the atomistic view of people by focusing on individuals, "who typically seem unaffected by broader social forces," and "de-emphasiz[ing] more complicated, abstract, or ephemeral entities such as groups, institutions and associations, social movements, traditions, trends, public taste or opinion, or complex, ambiguous, or growing characters" (Scheuer 75).

Television also emphasizes self-interest over altruism and cooperation. Television advertising is "a relentless invitation to self-indulgence, acquisitiveness, unlimited consumption," and television fiction "tends to celebrate affluence and acquisitiveness as normal, while ignoring voluntarism, community activism, political engagement, or other pursuits or careers that involve self-sacrifice or personal connections to larger groups or causes. . . . TV projects a world dominated by greed, banality, guile, lust, and violence" (Scheuer 40). Television comedies are populated by characters who are little more than bundles of self-interest engaging in egoistic and narcissistic actions that are in real life often the cause of significant distress for others but that are portrayed in comedy as benign and even endearing. A prime example is the top-rated *Two and a Half Men*, in which the regular characters are all in various ways self-indulgent users of other people, primarily women. Television dramas are rife with characters who pursue self-interested actions that are harmful and often violent rather than benign.

Competition is also continuously represented and celebrated on television. Entire genres of television programming, comprising hundreds of individual shows and thousands of episodes, are constituted by fabricated, staged competitions. These include not only game shows, talent competitions, and "reality"-based competitions such as the *Survivor* series, but also the numberless sports competitions supporting and supported by entire channels devoted to broadcasting, reporting on, and analyzing sports competitions. These broadcasts often themselves embody a competitive or confrontational format and often focus on and celebrate the most aggressive and even violent moments in the games, endlessly replaying these moments and lauding the competitive zeal— and sometimes even the meanness and "killer instinct"—of the most aggressive players. The competition paradigm has even come to dominate much of the "news" at both the local and the national level, with political events often being framed as competitions between two individuals or parties and elections being approached as "horse races" rather than reported and analyzed in terms of the costs and benefits of the various different policy proposals that are at stake.

Television dramas and comedies are also based upon interpersonal conflict and struggle rather than cooperation and collaboration. As Scheuer notes, "TV favors conflict and . . . loves violence. . . . TV personalizes human interactions, dramatizes them as conflicts (arguments, courtroom drama, police and military standoffs), and freights them with violence" (Scheuer 85, 75). As has often been noted, many dramas contain episodes of extreme violence. Indeed, violence is so prominent in television programming that it has been estimated that by the time students graduate from high school, they have on average viewed thousands of murders on television (Scheuer 170).

Countering Atomist Exemplars and Prototypes

Awareness of these sources of atomism can enable people to take steps to resist them, whether by avoiding them, decommissioning them, or compensating for their effects. The most important response, of course, is to replace atomist exemplars, prototypes, and information-processing routines with their solidarity counterparts. These multiple, micro forms of knowledge are distributed not only throughout multiple neural networks in the brain but also throughout multiple cultural practices and artifacts and social structures, institutions, and policies that function simultaneously as products, producers, and prostheses of these faulty, harmful cognitive structures. Since atomism exists and operates as multiple forms of exemplars, prototypes, and information-processing routines, replacing it with a solidarity schema requires correcting many, if not all, of these micro forms. This includes, first, decommissioning prototypes and exemplars such as the following.

Prototypic individuals embodying atomism include Homo Economicus, Hobbesian man, the exile, the *isolato* (the isolated individual), the man who fears romantic commitment, the wanderer, the traveling man, the playboy, the hermit, the prospector, the trapper, the hunter, and the staunch individualist. As Bellah and colleagues observe, American literature has produced some iconic exemplars of the atomistic individual: "A deep and continuing theme in American literature is the hero who must leave society, alone or with one or a few others, in order to realize the moral good in the wilderness, at sea, or on the margins of settled society" (Bellah et al. 144).

Two particularly noteworthy prototypes are the cowboy and the hard-boiled detective, who have a unique talent and sense of justice that both alienate them from society and constitute their greatest value (Bellah et al. 145–146). In addition to such figures as the Lone Ranger, Sam Spade, and Serpico, specific exemplars of the atomistic individual also include individuals of a decidedly more selfish bent, such as the late-nineteenth-century robber barons (Rockefeller, Carnegie, Vanderbilt, Mellon, Stanford, Morgan) and current business narcissist Donald Trump. Other current exemplars of the atomistic man include the "survivor man" of several television shows, exemplified by Les Stroud of *Survivorman* and Bear Grylls of *Man vs. Wild*, who are deposited in desolate locations and must procure water, food, shelter, and protection from creatures of the wild using little more than their own wits and courage.

Such atomistic individuals must be countered by exemplars who embody solidarity in one or more of its three forms. Psychological-emotional-neurological solidarity is exemplified by individuals who manifest a strong commitment to other individuals or a group, including those who put the welfare of their family, their team, their group, or their nation ahead of their own individual concerns. Exemplars of practical solidarity include individuals whose interdependence with others is constitutive of their identity, such as the character of George Bailey in *It's a Wonderful Life*. And ontological solidarity finds exemplars in characters whose common humanity shines through despite their differences, as it does between the schoolmaster Daru and his prisoner in Camus's "The Guest."

Prototypic *body images* of the atomistic individual include the powerful, muscular, tough bodies of college and professional athletes (including professional wrestlers with names such as "The Rock"), of which literally thousands of exemplars appear on television each year; powerful action heroes, with exemplars ranging from the traditional Superman to Sylvester Stallone's Rocky to Arnold Schwarzenegger's Conan the Barbarian and the "Terminator," and more recently characters portrayed by former wrestler Dwayne "The Rock" Johnson; and the indestructible bodies of cowboys in saloon brawls who receive multiple blows to head and body from fists, boots, whiskey bottles, and chairs without sustaining any significant damage. Television and movie images of the hero silhouetted against the landscape or facing down antagonists also powerfully reinforce the atomistic ideal. Lonely, desolate figures, such as a homeless man or an abandoned corpse, are exemplars of the negative (as opposed to idealized) aspect of atomism.

These images of atomism can be overridden by images of solidarity. Exemplars of practical solidarity include images of a group of individuals whose bodily movements are synchronized or coordinated in activities such as dancing, military drills, and teamwork in sports or at work (as in the performance of a construction crew or a rescue crew). Ontological solidarity is exemplified by images of bodies and faces of very different appearances responding similarly to a common situation, such as a natural disaster, a political rally, or a sporting event. And exemplars of emotional-psychological-neurological solidarity include the involuntary mimicking by one person of another person's facial expressions, bodily postures or movements, and/or emotions.

The atomistic individual is in many ways defined by atomistic *episode scripts*, actions demonstrating uniqueness (the individualist, the loner), self-sufficiency (e.g., survivor men), imperturbability and impenetrability (tough guys), triumph (winning competitions, making big money on a slick business deal), withdrawal from society (e.g., the lonely hero, the cowboy, the exile), struggle, opposition, and battle (athletic contests, fights, military battles). These same actions, when engaged in continuously or repeatedly, come to constitute *life scripts*, biographical templates for the trajectory of a good, admirable, and honorable life. Atomist life scripts include a life spent accumulating wealth (often by exploiting, oppressing, and brutalizing other people), a life spent developing a certain skill or capability (artistic, athletic, intellectual) to a unique level of perfection, and a life lived in tranquil isolation, above the fray, such as that imagined by Wordsworth in his poem "Peele Castle."

The antidote to such scripts is episodes and life stories in which individuals receive aid from others (practical solidarity), manifest empathy and compassion by giving aid to others (psychological-emotional solidarity), or act and live in light of their common humanity with others. The life of George Bailey in Frank Capra's *It's a Wonderful Life* exemplifies each of these forms of solidarity.

The *prototypic emotions* of an atomistic individual are pride, arrogance, and smugness regarding one's own superior position, and indifference, scorn, disdain, contempt, and hatred toward other individuals, all of which can be seen in competitions of all kinds, including business competition, international relations, and war. These emotions prime and motivate *action scripts* characterized by the pursuit—and the institutionalization—of narrow self-interest, instrumentalism in all relations, unilateral action, and competition. Exemplars of such action scripts include the pursuit of profits with no regard for worker and consumer welfare, athletes and coaches attempting to "just win" by whatever means and at whatever cost, individuals using others simply as instruments for their own sexual satisfaction or social or economic advancement, and, most crucially, international and domestic policies, institutions, and systems based on and dedicated to preserving the narrow economic self-interests of plutocrats, pursued with an arrogant unilateralism, and executed by the prideful employment of unique military might.

These atomist emotions must be countered with compassion and humility, which will in turn motivate actions of assistance and care. Here again, the character George Bailey is exemplary, as both an exponent of compassion and humility and an agent of care and aid.

Correcting Atomistic Information Processing

In addition to decommissioning these atomistic prototypes and exemplars, replacing the atomism schema also involves correcting or replacing the various atomistic information-processing routines. People operating with the atomism schema *expect* that in interhuman encounters, selfishness, difference, isolation, and competition—including deceit, betrayal, treachery, and aggression—will dominate, rather than altruism, sameness, togetherness, collaboration, and cooperation (see Dale T. Miller). As a result, they will *notice* and *attend to* these atomistic qualities and overlook or disregard evidence of solidarity. When there is little or no evidence of atomistic qualities, atomists will *search for* them, and in some cases they will "find" atomism where none exists by *inferring* it from obscure or ambiguous actions or situations. And if they are unable to find any information that they can interpret in this direction, they may simply *suppose* that the atomistic qualities are present anyway.

People operating with the atomism schema will also *encode in memory* individuals, episodes, lives, images, emotions, and action scripts of self-interest, competition, isolation, and aggression but not the corresponding exemplars of altruism, cooperation, community, and reparation and will also be much more likely to *retrieve from memory* examples of atomism than examples of solidarity. As a result, they will be prone to experience the atomistic *emotions* and *retrieve* the atomist *action scripts* identified above.

Such atomistic information processing is present in various types of aggressive behavior. It has been found to underlie the behavior of hyper-aggressive boys, whose aggression is often triggered by perceiving hostile intent where the evidence for hostility is ambiguous or even nonexistent (Dodge and Crick; Hudley and Graham). Such information processing involves *expecting* other people to be hostile, *noticing* and *attending to* hostile cues while ignoring or discounting cues indicating lack of hostility, *inferring* hostility from ambiguous cues, and *supposing* hostility even when there is no evidence of it.

Atomistic information processing is also evident in public policy decisions. During the Cold War, the United States and the Soviet Union interpreted each other's actions as motivated by a hostile intention, but we now know that many of these actions were motivated by vulnerability and fear, rather than hostility. A similar atomistic, dog-eat-dog view of human behavior is now guiding the information processing of both sides of the "War on Terror." Each side is blind to the ontological, emotional, and practical solidarity that binds them together, and each sees the other's actions as motivated solely by aggressive self-interest and the wish to dominate.

When George W. Bush declared that he could not understand why the attackers did what they did, he did not *seek* evidence concerning the hijackers' motives because he did not *expect* there to be any evidence other than their presumed evil nature. Completely blind to ontological solidarity, he simply *supposed* (drawing on atomistically encoded memories such as the attack on Pearl Harbor) the attackers to be utterly different from himself, rejecting a priori any and all evidence to the contrary that had already been produced by experts on terrorism and the Middle East. On those occasions when the Bush administration did consider reasons for the attacks (beyond the attackers' supposed "evil nature"), the reasons offered were focused, in true atomistic manner, on the attackers' supposed differences from us: their cultural and religious indoctrination, their "hatred of our freedoms," and their barbarian self-interest in the form of getting seventy-two virgins in heaven.

We Americans, the Bush administration smugly presumed, are completely different: *we* could never be indoctrinated or brainwashed, *we* love and protect our freedoms, and *we* are much too noble to pursue such base self-interest. Ironically, in his blindly warmongering response to the attacks, Bush, as a number of commentators pointed out, revealed himself to be very like his enemy. Steve Olwean commented that "to an outside observer the rhetoric on both sides sounds remarkably similar, whether it be from a U.S. president or an al-Qaeda leader" (Olweean 121; see also Abdullah 135).

These atomist information-processing routines must be replaced with corrective routines that grasp universal human solidarity and thus lead not only to very different interpersonal behaviors but to dramatically different collective actions as well, including foreign and domestic policies. One way to induce *attention to* solidarity is through the repeated presentation of the sorts of solidarity exemplars sketched out in the previous section. By repeatedly attending to solidarity, people will become more able and inclined to *expect* it and hence to *infer*, *suppose*, and *recall* solidarity as well.

As we will see in later chapters, literature and schema criticism also employ other techniques for inducing people to perform and hence develop the various solidarity information-processing routines.

CHAPTER 5

Homogeneity versus Heterogeneity: The Structure of Character

Do I contradict myself?
Very well then I contradict myself,
(I am large, I contain multitudes.)
WALT WHITMAN, "SONG OF MYSELF" 51

For there is not a just man upon earth, that doeth good, and sinneth not.
ECCLESIASTES 7:20

And why beholdest thou the mote that is in thy brother's eye, but perceivest
not the beam that is in thine own eye?
LUKE 6:41

A fourth general person-schema that is responsible for profound distortions of perception and egregious miscarriages of justice is the homogeneity schema, which produces one-dimensional perceptions of people as either all good or totally bad, purely altruistic or completely egoistic, and so on. The corresponding corrective schema, in contrast, that of heterogeneity, enables people to recognize the intra-individual diversity of character in everyone, both self and other.

People differ considerably concerning the degree to which they are able to recognize the coexistence of positive and negative qualities in the same individual or group, and this difference is determined largely by which of these two contrasting schemas they are operating with. As Else Frenkel-Brunswik observes, these differences are sometimes evident in children: "Some individuals are more apt to see positive as well as negative features in their parents and can accept feelings of love and hate toward the same persons without too much anxiety or conflict. Others seem compelled to dramatize their image of the parents in seeing them either as altogether good or as altogether bad" (Frenkel-Brunswik, "Intolerance" 116). While people operating with a heterogeneity schema (which researchers sometimes refer to as "high-complexity" subjects) expect, search for, attend to, and encode both positive and negative traits in both themselves and others, people employing the homogeneity schema ("low-complexity" subjects) expect homogeneity in both self and other and thus overlook and fail to register contradictory traits (see Mayo and Crockett 336–338; Stein 163–164, 176).

To perceive individuals and groups accurately and fairly, then, rather than as simply good or bad, one must employ a heterogeneity person-schema, which enables one to recognize and accommodate the existence of both positive and negative qualities in both self and others. As Crockett explains, "Most other people . . . are ambiguous stimuli, displaying both favorable and unfavorable characteristics in their behavior. Consequently, if the perceiver is to recognize and to respond to both the favorable and unfavorable aspects of another's behavior, his cognitive system must permit the attribution of both favorable and unfavorable qualities to a single person." Crockett hypothesized "that individuals high in cognitive complexity with respect to other people . . . will more often use both positive and negative attributes in their descriptions of others," and he found that this was indeed the case: "Subjects low in complexity, compared with highs, were more likely to separate people into two groups on the basis of a good–bad dichotomy" (Crockett 65–66).

Costs of the Homogeneity Schema

By preventing people from apprehending the characterological complexity and heterogeneity of both others and themselves, the homogeneity schema has profound effects on social actions, policies, and institutions. Ignoring the internal heterogeneity of other individuals and groups facilitates either demonizing or idolizing them, which then enables either attacking them or following them blindly. And blindness to one's own internal (individual or group) heterogeneity leads one to project one's own negative qualities onto certain subalterns (see Horowitz, *Cognitive* 152; Newman et al. 260).

This dual homogenization of self and other, by enabling one to externalize one's negative attributes onto the putatively evil or inferior other, paves the way to excluding, attacking, and even exterminating the other by engendering beliefs such as Hitler's idea that Jews were "vermin," terrorists' belief that infidels deserve death, and George W. Bush's conviction that "we" Americans are a peaceful, freedom-loving people, while "they," the 9/11 attackers and their sympathizers, are evil people who hate freedom.

In preventing cognizance of the internal multiplicities, complexities, tensions, and self-contradictions that characterize both individuals and groups, the homogeneity schema thus produces a binaristic, dualistic, polarized perception of people that facilitates profoundly harmful public policies, collective actions, and social and economic systems and structures. It does so most fundamentally through prejudice. Prejudiced individuals, Frenkel-Brunswik reports, are more prone to see other people in terms of dichotomous concepts, such as strong/weak, clean/dirty, moral/immoral, and normal/deviant, and they tend to be averse to ambiguities and qualified characterizations (Frenkel-Brunswik, "Tolerance" 268). The degree to which people stigmatize, denigrate, and dehumanize other individuals and groups is thus due in part to whether their person-schema incorporates heterogeneity and complexity. As Crockett explains, "For a number of reasons, individuals with relatively complex cognitive systems with respect to other people should also be relatively ambivalent in their orientations toward others, less likely than those with noncomplex systems to divide mankind into two groups on the basis of a good–bad dichotomy" (Crockett 65).

More specifically, the homogeneity schema motivates the defense of projection, which is central to much prejudice and dehumanization. As Newman and colleagues explain, projection is motivated by an effort to maintain a sense of oneself as purely and unambiguously good: "Projection is . . . driven by efforts to avoid awareness of the possibility that one might possess undesirable personality traits. . . . Active efforts to banish thoughts about one's unwanted attributes . . . have the unanticipated effect of leading those attributes to play an important role in how one construes others' behavior" (Newman et al. 260).

The function of projection in relation to the homogeneity schema is perhaps best described in the accounts that Kleinian psychoanalysis provides of the so-called paranoid-schizoid position. The paranoid-schizoid position (the origins of which will be discussed below) is characterized by a splitting of one's representations of both self and other into good and bad halves, with one half (usually the good self and the bad other) being conscious and acknowledged and the other half (usually the bad self and the good other) being repressed and often projected (the bad self onto the other) and/or introjected (the good other into the self) (see Clarke 129–137). Splitting, as Simon Clarke observes, "is essentially an attempt to create order out of chaos: the product of splitting is the formation of boundaries and a strong sense of 'us' and 'them,' 'good' and 'bad'" (Clarke 123–124). In addition, splitting, together with projection, enables one to maintain a secure (homogeneous) identity, or sense of self, by escaping those behaviors or character traits that contradict that sense of self and thus threaten to destroy it.[1] Robins and Post note, "To reject the other is to disown the flawed aspects of ourselves. . . . All badness is outside, all goodness inside" (Robins and Post 93).

The homogeneity schema thus contributes massively to exclusion, conflict, and violence at both the interpersonal and the intergroup level. Its effects can be seen in the "negative 'frame' of each other" that Aaron Beck finds operating in "chronically feuding couples": "Each partner blot[s] out the favorable attributes of the other as well as the pleasant memories of more tranquil days, or reinterpret[s] them as false. The process of framing le[ads] them to suspect each other's motives and to make biased generalizations about the deficiencies of 'badness' of their mate" (Beck 7). Beck observes that the same sort of thinking is prominent in nonpatients as well and that it extends beyond individuals to intergroup relations: "Even people who [are] not psychiatric patients [are] susceptible to this kind of dysfunctional thinking. They routinely fram[e] out-group members negatively, just as they fram[e] their everyday friends or relatives with whom they [are] in conflict. This kind of negative framing also appear[s] to be at the core of negative social stereotypes, religious prejudice, and intolerance" (Beck 8). Indeed, the homogenizing of self and other through splitting and projection is at the heart of racism and anti-Semitism, in which black people and Jewish people, respectively, are seen as totally bad or debased and are used as receptacles for projected negative or unwanted behaviors and character traits, allowing white racists and anti-Semites to feel pure, innocent, and good (see Clarke 127ff.).

This dynamic has major consequences and does tremendous harm on a massive scale in other intergroup relations as well, including international relations. Beck comments that "a similar sort of biased thinking seem[s] to be a driving force in ideological aggression and warfare" (Beck 8). It is evident in the personification of the enemy as evil; in the conviction that "we must kill enemy soldiers because they are bad, not because they happened to be drafted into the army just as we were"; in "the slaughter of civilians . . . [which] illustrates how soldiers are inclined to see evil in everyone on the other side"; and in the fact that "the individuality, the humanness of the persons on the other side is blotted out [and] they are visualized as representations of all that is bad in the world" (Beck 204).

The homogenizing, dichotomizing dynamic is particularly evident in the attitudes of terrorists. Writing before the 2001 terrorist attacks, Beck observed that "the perpetrators [of various Jewish, Islamic, and Christian terrorist attacks in recent years] demonstrate[d] typical dichotomous thinking—perversely branding the victims as the criminals and glorifying the offenders as the saviors" (Beck 21). Since the 9/11 attacks, many commentators have noted the homogenizing, dualistic representations of self and other that terrorists operate with. Clark McCauley states that "terrorists see the world precariously balanced between good and evil" (McCauley 14), and John Mack explains that terrorists operate with a "dualistic, dichotomizing, or polarizing habit of mind," which "divides the world into conflicting polarities—good and evil, God and the Devil, for or against, friend and enemy, deserving or undeserving." This dualistic mind-set, Mack states, is able to apprehend "separation and difference more easily than unity and connection" (Mack 177).

Nor is this cognitive schema limited to terrorists. It is also prominent in responses to terrorism, which are rife with splitting (Clarke 133). Rubén Ardila notes that while "terrorists divide the world into black and white, good and bad," this tendency is quite widespread and is present also in the targets of terrorist attacks: "In general, the enemy is the devil; it is Satan. This term is used indiscriminately by both Arab leaders and Western leaders to refer to the enemy" (Ardila 12). Fakhry Davids makes a similar observation, noting that the West sees the conflict with terrorism as "a conflict between the enlightened, civilized, tolerant, freedom loving, clean living democrat versus the bearded, robed, Kalashnikov bearing bigoted, intolerant, glint in the eye fundamentalist fanatic," while the terrorists and his supporters see him as "the humble believer with God on his side versus the infidel armed with all the worldly might of the devil" (quoted in Clarke 133).

Mack notes that since the 9/11 attacks, "the proponents of dualistic thinking ('This is a war of good against the evildoers,' or 'We must destroy America, the Great Satan') on both sides have had a lock on public discourse, as committed patriots have heaped scorn upon those who do not fall into line, while cheerleaders of terrorism exhort their followers to commit further acts of violence" (Mack 178). As an example of this homogenizing, polarizing mind-set at the highest levels of the U.S. government, Mack cites the "former national security advisor who rejected the notion that U.S. policy had anything to do with the 9/11 attacks [and adhered to] the linear, straitjacketed thinking that divides people categorically into good and evil ones, and that cannot see, or chooses not to see, the interconnections among various conditions and events" (Mack 178).

Such a view of the other as homogeneously evil and oneself as purely good actually functions to induce the other into acting in ways that confirm the distorted image of himself. This process, known as projective identification in Kleinian psychoanalysis, "continually creates a factual history of proof on all sides of the wrongness of the perpetrating 'other' and the rightness of the victimized 'us.' . . . After a while all sides have a body of concrete grievances that support their correct stance and view of the 'other,' as well as their justification in responding to unjust wrongs" (Olwean 119).

The consequences of this mutual homogenization are dire. Diane Perlman warns that "if we use a paradigm that splits the world into right and wrong, good and evil, us against them, and winning or losing in a zero sum game, everyone will eventually lose. . . . Acting in this right–wrong paradigm will magnify these same attitudes and feelings in our enemies, who will continue to find new ways of using our power against us, deepening the cycle of retaliation" (Perlman 17–18). In fact, the West's homogenization of the East has played a significant role in provoking the terrorist attacks. Mack explains, "It is expressions of dualistic thinking in the form of blindness to diversity, obliviousness to the effects of inequalities of resources, and a lack of concern for the vast suffering that prevails on this planet, that have given rise to the present dangerous crisis," and he warns that this mind-set "must be transcended if we are to survive as a species" (Mack 178).

The influence of the homogeneity schema is particularly prominent and virulent in "the polarized, Manichean worldview—the vision of the righteous engaged in a crusade against the damned and damnable— that is now the mainstream ideology of the Republican Party" (Westen 392). This worldview colonized the Republican Party during the eight years of the George W. Bush administration, as documented by Glenn Greenwald in *A Tragic Legacy: How a Good vs. Evil Mentality Destroyed the Bush Presidency*. Greenwald argues that Bush assessed "all significant matters, personal and public/political" through the homogenist "template of the glorious and all-consuming battle between Good and Evil" (48), and that as a result, "virtually all significant events of the Bush Era are a by-product of his core Manichean mentality" (xii). This schema provided Bush with "a core, unshakable conviction of [his] own rightness" (xii-xiii). For George W. Bush, "there always exist[ed] a clear and identifiable enemy who [was] to be defeated by any means, means justified not only by the pureness of the enemy's Evil but also by the core Goodness that [Bush] believe[d] motivate[d] him and his movement" (48). Because "for the Manichean believer, the battle between Good and Evil . . . subordinates all other considerations and never gives way to any conflicting or inconsistent goals" (48), Bush's homogeneity schema "legitimize[d], and even render[d] inevitable, some of the most amoral and ethically monstrous policies, justified as necessary means to achieve a morally imperative end . . . —from indefinite, lawless detentions, to the use of torture, to bloody preventive wars of choice, the abduction of innocent people literally off the street or from their homes, to radical new theories designed to vest in the president the power to break the law" (Greenwald xii–xiii).

Homogenization also produces less obvious but no less dire consequences outside war, terrorism, and other instances of overt enmity and aggression. As Clarke notes, homogenizing, dichotomous thinking, in the form of the distinction between good and bad, friend and foe, "is basic to the functioning of political systems" (Clarke 130). And as Neil Altman points out, splitting and projection can lead to atrocities, violence, and other forms of profound injustice on the home front. "Guilt can be projected onto the victim, as occurs massively in a lynching when the mob jumps to the conclusion that the person lynched must be guilty of some heinous crime," and can terminate in dehumanization of the other (Altman, "Manic" 336).

Projective identification, in which people are actually induced or coerced by our actions to behave in the negative manner that we are attributing to them, is a key factor, Altman maintains, in the establishment and maintenance of the American underclass. For example, people who are impoverished by an unfair economic system are more likely to engage in crime and to be cynical about the usefulness of education. As a result, they drop out of school or commit crimes, thus reinforcing their negative stereotype in the eyes of privileged groups: "Preconceptions of ghetto residents as criminals and as lazy thus seem to be confirmed, leading to a self-perpetuating cycle" (Altman, "Manic" 333). This cycle is reinforced by negative media images of such individuals, which are internalized by the individuals themselves. The result of this process of projective identification, Altman explains, is that privileged

Americans are able to disown key negative qualities that they themselves possess and attribute them solely to members of the American underclass. For example, politicians see exploitation in welfare cheats but not in their own refusal to pass campaign finance reform bills, and mainstream Americans focus on the violent behavior of ghetto residents while remaining blind to the violent behaviors of police officers. In a process going all the way back to slavery, mainstream America has created and maintained an underclass that is induced by its living conditions to behave in ways that mainstream America then uses as evidence of the homogeneously negative nature of members of this class, which, in turn, is thought to justify its systematic maltreatment of them (Altman, "Manic" 333–334).

Falseness of the Homogeneity Schema

In addition to producing these harmful consequences, the homogeneity schema is also profoundly misleading, supporting a notion of character that, as psychologists David DeSteno and Piercarlo Valdesolo demonstrate in their book *Out of Character*, "is fundamentally wrong" (DeSteno and Valdesolo 5). They argue that the idea that character is homogeneous, "a stable fixture" of either good or bad qualities, which is referred to by moral philosophers as the inseparability thesis (Doris 20–21, 70–71), "is fundamentally incorrect" and that "as a richer understanding of character emerges, the line between 'good' and 'bad' begins to blur" (DeSteno and Valdesolo 10, 61). Thus "when it comes to character, nothing is black or white. . . . [Rather,] character is much like a scale—how a person acts at any moment is determined by how the scale is tipping, or where along the continuum it's balanced at that exact moment. . . . The scale can shift, and shift quickly, in either direction" (DeSteno and Valdesolo 17, 12).

Philosopher John Doris offers a similar view in his book *Lack of Character*, where he observes that even many of the Nazi war criminals were not purely evil persons. On the contrary, as we saw in Chapter 2, "a very substantial percentage of perpetrators in the Holocaust had previously led lives characterized by ordinary levels of compassion" (Doris 54), thus exhibiting what Doris refers to as "a kind of diachronic fragmentation: Their behavior during the Holocaust was inconsistent with antecedently manifested dispositions" (Doris 57). Doris notes that some war criminals also exhibited "synchronic fragmentation," revealing "inconsistent dispositions over temporally limited periods." One such individual, Eduard Wirths, "was described by prisoners in terms such as 'kind,' 'decent,' and 'honest,' but he was also the man who closely administered the camp's system of selections and mass murders" (Doris 57). Similar accounts were given of the infamous Josef Mengele, who was said to be attentive, kind, and generous to the very children whom, days or minutes later, he sent to the crematorium, thus leading one prison doctor to refer to him as "*l'homme double.*" Such cases were quite common, Doris reports. "As [Primo] Levi put it, 'Compassion and brutality can coexist in the same individual in the same moment, despite all logic.'" Thus, Doris concludes, even the worst people are not homogeneously evil (Doris 58).

Perhaps even more disturbing than the fact that supposedly evil people embody good impulses and traits is the fact that all of us supposedly good people contain wicked impulses and other bad traits. As DeSteno and Valdesolo assert, "There lurks in every one of us the potential to lie, cheat, steal, and sin, no matter how good a person we believe ourselves to be" (DeSteno and Valdesolo 7). There is massive evidence of this intrapersonal heterogeneity—that is, of the badness in "good" people. William James invoked evolutionary logic to argue that "we, the lineal representatives of the successful enactors of one scene of slaughter after another, must, whatever more pacific virtues we may also possess, still carry about with us, ready at any moment to burst into flame, the smoldering and sinister traits of character by means of which they lived through so many massacres, harming others, but themselves unharmed" (quoted in Pinker 56).

Herbert Strean and Lucy Freeman agree, only they locate the cause of our murderous impulses in universal features of individual development rather than in evolutionary history. In *Our Wish to Kill: The Murder in All Our Hearts,* they argue that because all humans have experienced, at least in infancy, the sense of abandonment or betrayal by a needed source of love, "we are all potential killers when we are or feel we may be abandoned by someone we hold crucial for our life. . . . All of us to some degree are would-be killers, for none of us can ever be loved all the time by those whose love we crave consistently. . . . We are all potential murderers. . . . The difference is a matter of degree" (Strean and Freeman 31, 33, 37). Although most of us do not directly kill other people, most of us do, in fact, engage in vicarious or indirect murder, Strean and Freeman contend. We do so whenever we desire to see "bad guys" killed: "When we hear about a murderer, rarely do we want to understand what drove him to murder; more often we wish to kill him." Our murderous impulse in such cases is identical to that of the murderer: "The vengefulness we feel toward a murderer, which drives us to champion execution, is identical to the wish for revenge the murderer feels for what he believes to be the horrendous injustices in his life" (Strean and Freeman 244).

Pinker cites similar evidence of "normal," "good" people harboring murderous impulses. Noting that "more than 80 percent of women and 90 percent of men fantasize about killing people they don't like, . . . [and that] people in all cultures take pleasure in thinking about killings, if we are to judge by the popularity of murder mysteries, crime dramas, spy thrillers, Shakespearean tragedies, biblical stories, hero myths, and epic poems," Pinker declares, "I doubt that the brains or genes of most of the lauded protagonists would differ from those of their vilified counterparts" (Pinker 316–317).

While most people do not personally and directly kill other people or inflict other forms of violence on them, every American citizen engages in such acts indirectly, as a result of our government's direct acts of killing—in war and capital punishment, which are often celebrated by ordinary people—as well as its indirect acts of killing, such as "the millions of Germans who starved to death following World War II," or "the hundreds of thousands of Iraqi children who died of starvation and disease following our military aggression" in the First Gulf War (Piven 137), or the thousands of gay men (and others) who died in the early years of the AIDS epidemic as a result of the Reagan administration's inaction.

The indifference, satisfaction, and in some cases even jubilation experienced by many Americans in response to the suffering and death of both real-life and fictional villains indicates that such events satisfy deep, albeit often unconscious, wishes and impulses. And there is evidence that we not only enjoy the suffering or demise of certain others when it occurs, but also act (again, often unconsciously) in ways that provoke others to behave in a manner that will justify in our minds our own violent actions toward them.

Piven suggests, for example, that American policy may have been designed in some degree "to incite bin Laden to envy and rage so that we might have an enemy, so that we might also have an evil demonic threat that would galvanize the American people and enable us to displace our rage and anxiety" (Piven 137). Explaining that such intentions are often unconscious, Piven argues that "we must always ask to what degree we invite enemies to fulfill our fantasies as well. . . . The question is how much we also needed an enemy to scapegoat [in order] to fulfill our fantasies, and how much we invited his reprisal [in order] to maintain the fantasy of our goodness and moral sovereignty" (Piven 137). Lest we think we are above such brutality, Piven reminds us that "we too have our fictions and our murderous propensities, disguised as myths and a propaganda of self-righteousness. We have had our slaves, witch trials, and insidious exploitation of Native America" (Piven 137). Indeed, as McCauley states, "we have to face the fact that normal people can be terrorists, that we are ourselves capable of terrorist acts under some circumstances" (McCauley 6). The fact is that, as Abdullah puts it, "the seeds of terrorism lie within each of us" (Abdullah 135).

In addition to the foregoing evidence, the fact that individuals are heterogeneous, composed of both good and bad traits and impulses, is also demonstrated by the numerous studies cited in Chapter 2 concerning the powerful role that circumstances play in determining whether a person engages in good behavior or bad behavior. The fact that our behavior can be so powerfully influenced by the situation we are in indicates that we harbor quite divergent, and even mutually contradictory impulses. As DeSteno and Valdesolo state, "Subtle changes in environment or context can lead any of us to be both saints and sinners" (DeSteno and Valdesolo 227). Such vices as gambling, jealousy, cowardice, and hypocrisy, they argue, are often more the product of the situation than of a person's character (DeSteno and Valdesolo 191, 82, 234, 31). And the consistency of behavior that is often taken as evidence of a homogeneous character is itself less the result of some presumed homogeneity of character than of the cross-situational consistency of certain key behavior-determining factors (Doris 65).

As a result of this evidence, personality theorists and moral philosophers are increasingly abandoning the notion that character and personality are homogeneous. Doris argues that "personality should be conceived of as *fragmented*—an evaluatively disintegrated association of situation-specific local traits" (Doris 64). Personality is not often homogeneous, he maintains. "For a given person, the dispositions operative in one situation may have an evaluative status very different from those manifested in another situation; evaluatively inconsistent dispositions may 'cohabitate' in a single personality" (Doris 25).

DeSteno and Valdesolo agree, stating that "we can all exhibit a range of 'character types' " because "character, like color, varies along a continuum," and "where people end up at any one moment often depends on the context" (DeSteno and Valdesolo 233–234). They argue that character, far from being homogeneous, is composed of "dueling systems," which they refer to as the grasshopper, which aims for immediate gratification, and the ant, which seeks long-term satisfaction (DeSteno and Valdesolo 15). Whether we behave in a cruel manner or a compassionate manner in any given instance is determined by two factors: the relative strength of the two opposing systems and the nature of the situation (DeSteno and Valdesolo 24).

Each of these systems, moreover, is itself composed of multiple processes, not all of which are conscious (DeSteno and Valdesolo 37). Pinker explains, "The mind is not a homogeneous orb invested with unitary powers or across-the-board traits." Rather, "some faculties may endow us with greed or lust or malice, but others may endow us with sympathy, foresight, self-respect, a desire for respect from others, and an ability to learn from our own experiences and those of our neighbors. . . . Perhaps all of us are capable of being saints or sinners, depending on the temptations and threats at hand" (Pinker 40, 41, 166, 260).

Replacing the Homogeneity Person-Schema

Given the falseness of, as well as the tremendous harm caused by, judgments of homogeneity, replacing the homogeneity schema must be a central goal for anyone who is committed to social justice.

Fortunately, developing a heterogeneity person-schema is not only possible, but is actually the norm—at least to a degree. According to Kleinian psychoanalysis, normal human development involves a progression from the homogenizing, dichotomizing cognition of the paranoid-schizoid position to the more comprehensive and integrated perception of self and others that characterizes what Kleinians refer to as the depressive position. Clarke explains, "The tendency to split good and bad part objects lessens and the perception of persons containing both good and bad develops. . . . There is a recognition of both good and bad within the self which allows a recognition of this in others" (Clarke 137; see also Robins and Post 79).

Unfortunately, most people are quite prone, especially under stress, to revert to the homogenizing cognition of the paranoid-schizoid position, indicating that the heterogeneity schema is not so robust in most people as to maintain its control of information processing in some of the very circumstances in which it is most crucial for it to do so. What is therefore needed is further development and strengthening of the heterogeneity person-schema in most individuals, so that it is more readily accessible, more automatically activated, than the homogeneity schema, and thus continues to function as the default information-processing structure even when the self is under stress and is thus inclined to resort to more simplistic and self-confirming modes of cognition. As with the other three benign person-schemas, development of the heterogeneity schema can be promoted by enhancing metacognition, by providing striking exemplars of heterogeneity, and by engaging people in performing more adequate, heterogeneity-recognizing information-processing routines.

Developing Metacognition

Literature can promote metacognition of homogeneity by helping people recognize their propensity for homogenizing others, understand the falseness of homogenization and the harm that it produces, and thus cue themselves to resist and reverse homogenization. It can do this in two basic ways. First, it can portray characters homogenizing other characters and at the same time depict the faultiness and harm of this homogenization. And second, by engaging readers in perceiving characters, forming judgments of them, and developing feelings toward them, it offers them experiences of their own social cognition that, upon reflection, can reveal to them their own homogenizing tendencies.

To Kill a Mockingbird, for example, performs both of these functions. It provides readers with examples of homogenization, its falseness, and its harmful and unjust consequences in the children's perception of Boo Radley as a deranged monster and Mrs. Dubose as a mean old woman, as well as in the white society's infrahumanization of black people. And insofar as readers participate in any of these homogenizations, they may be prompted to recognize and reflect on their experiences when the novel exposes the falseness and unjustness of the homogenized images of these characters by finally revealing Boo Radley's empathy and love for the children, Mrs. Dubose's heroic struggle with her morphine addiction, and Calpurnia and Tom's intelligence, courage, fortitude, and forbearance.

Sources of the Homogeneity Schema

Metacognition can also be promoted, we have seen, by understanding the sources of a person-schema. The most basic source of the homogeneity schema is the innate mechanism that automatically catego-rizes other animals, including humans, as friend or foe. As evolutionary psychology explains, throughout human history, survival has often de-pended on the ability to instantaneously identify another person as an enemy or an ally: "Encounters with others had to be rapidly categorized as either threat or non-threat with a distinct boundary between them. There was no latitude for ambiguity. . . . A single false negative (mis-identifying an enemy as a friend) would have been fatal" (Beck 38–39; see also Hogan, *Understanding* 179–180).

The homogenizing responses of approach and avoidance appear to be supported by dichotomous neural underpinnings, separate neural sys-tems involving different circuitry and different neurotransmitters. The approach system utilizes the neurotransmitter dopamine and produces pleasure, while the avoidance system utilizes norepinephrine and pro-duces anxiety (Westen 78). Research has revealed that the amygdala makes an initial dichotomous, homogenizing appraisal of other people: "A continual amygdala-driven appraisal goes on outside our awareness, regardless of whether we consciously think about the issue. . . . The amygdala automatically and compulsively scans everyone we encounter for whether they are to be trusted: *Is it safe to approach this guy? Is he dangerous? Can I count on him or not?*" (Goleman, *Social* 22, empha-sis in original; see also Ochsner 249–251). Larsen describes the amygdala as "a specialist in dualistic thinking. It throws the cerebral cortex into a simpler mode . . . ; when the cerebral cortex is beset with urgent signals from the amygdala, it goes into either/or thinking" (Larsen 28, 41).

The homogeneity schema would also appear to derive in part from a more general innate homogenizing, dichotomizing affective process. Research has revealed that the brain's emotion-processing systems tend to turn ambivalent emotional inputs into an unambivalent output. Ito and Cacioppo explain, "The affect system has evolved to produce bi-polar endpoints because they provide both clear bivalent action tenden-cies and harmonious and stable subjective experiences" (quoted in Ho-gan, *Understanding* 176). For example, "The inputs may be partially anger-producing and partially fear-producing, but the output is likely to be anger (with a confrontation response) or fear (with a flight response), not some combination of the two" (Hogan, *Understanding* 176).

Another major source of the homogeneity schema is, ironically, the mind's own heterogeneity, which constitutes a threat to the individual's identity, or sense of self. At the most primitive levels of the brain, this heterogeneity takes the form of "the plexi and ganglia of the autonomic

154   The Cognitive Roots of Injustice

and peripheral systems," which Larsen describes as "a truly schizo-phrenic babble of primitive voices as neural structures, physiological organs, and hormones announce their separate needs" (Larsen 29). Larsen contends that "most human beings are in fact terrified by their own plurality" and that this fear motivates the "inclination to think monolithically" (Larsen 29).

Kleinian psychoanalytic theory, similarly, views the homogenizing produced by the paranoid-schizoid position as a defense against one's own intrapsychic heterogeneity as well as the intrapersonal heterogeneity of other persons. At the beginning of life, the infant experiences the world through two primary categories of feeling: pain and pleasure. The child experiences the mother as the source of both painful and pleasurable experiences, but does not experience both feelings as deriving from the same person. Rather, the child perceives the pain-producing aspect of the mother and the pleasure-producing aspect as two separate persons, one homogeneously good and the other homogeneously bad (see Robins and Post 76; Volkan 28). This is the paranoid-schizoid position. Some people never get beyond it, and most people, as we have noted, revert to it in some degree when their sense of self is threatened (Robins and Post 77), in which case one exhibits "a tendency to exaggerate the 'goodness' or the 'badness' of those one meets" (Robins and Post 79)—that is, a tendency to homogenize the other.

In addition to homogenizing the other, the infant engages in a corresponding homogenizing response toward itself, projecting or otherwise externalizing the aggressive self that hates and fears the bad mother and owning the benign self that loves the good mother. In response to the dawning recognition that the loving mother and the persecuting mother are the same person, and that one thus loves and hates the same person—a recognition that constitutes the basis of what Kleinian theory refers to as the "depressive position"—the infant protects its sense of self by disowning its own hatred and aggression, repressing these feelings and projecting them onto others. As Robins and Post state, "Creating bad others is a necessary part of acquiring a distinct identity in childhood" (Robins and Post 92).

This strategy of establishing identity through the homogenizing, dichotomizing processes of splitting and projection continues in adulthood, as we discussed earlier, where these processes result in the manufacture of enemies. Vamik Volkan argues in *Our Need to Have Enemies and Allies* that people need enemies as a way to construct and maintain an identity, or sense of self. As Robins and Post explain, "To say 'these things are specially good and are specially part of me' is to say 'those other things are specially bad and not part of me but part of others.' . . . We project into strangers what we disown in ourselves. We end where they begin. . . . Enemies, therefore, are to be cherished, cultivated, and preserved, for if we lose them our self-definition is endangered" (Robins and Post 91–92). Thus although it "results in a world populated by groups with varying degrees of animosity, excessive self-regard, and fear of others," Robins and Post maintain that this homogenizing/dichotomizing, splitting/projecting identity-creating and -maintaining process is "a psychological necessity" (Robins and Post 92). This means that the "innate tendency to idealize the in-group and demonize the out-group can never be eradicated. The germs of that more primitive psychology remain within the personality, ready to be activated at times of stress. Thus otherwise psychologically healthy individuals can be infected by paranoid thinking when the group with which they identify is attacked" or otherwise threatened (Robins and Post 93).

Other inherent properties of human nature and the human condition may also contribute to homogenization. It has been noted that homogenizing, dichotomizing categorization has been observed in virtually all cultures, and some authors have taken this fact to be the result of basic cognitive processes such as perception, thinking, and language use (Beck 153; see also Elbow 51–53). Peter Elbow states: "Binary thinking seems to be the path of least resistance for the perceptual system, for thinking, and for linguistic structures. The easiest way to classify complex information is to clump it into two piles. Indeed, the most instinctive and tempting clumps to use for complex data are the old favorites: like/don't like, ours/theirs, right/sinister, sheep/goats. This is why dichotomies tend to come packaged with positive and negative poles" (Elbow 53). Many structuralist thinkers, including Roman Jakobson and Claude Lévi-Strauss, held that dichotomous, binary thinking was fundamental to the production of thought and meanings at all levels (see Mergler and Schleifer 64–71; Dundes 40, 46; Tyson 213, 224–225, 232, 254, 262).

Cultural factors are also a significant source of the homogeneity schema. This fact is evident in the different levels of awareness that have been found between American and Japanese individuals concerning contradictory emotions in themselves and in others. When Americans look at another person's face and perceive the emotion the person is feeling, they tend to see either positive or negative emotions, and not both. Japanese, on the other hand, are "likely to report seeing both positive and negative emotions in the same face" (Nisbett, *Geography* 187). In addition, East Asians appear to be more capable than Americans of accepting contradictory emotions in themselves (Nisbett, *Geography* 187–188). Westerners, furthermore, are more likely to view the actions of others as the product of either altruistic or selfish motives rather than both (Nisbett, *Geography* 205–206), and they tend generally to judge behavior to be either right or wrong, rather than both or neither (Nisbett, *Geography* 199).

Such inability to tolerate ambiguities in people is fostered, according to Frenkel-Brunswik, by the inculcation of dichotomies such as vice/ virtue, badness/goodness, and dirtiness/cleanliness as "natural and eternal, excluding any possibility of individuals trespassing from the one side to the other" (Frenkel-Brunswik, "Intolerance" 117). Religion and nationalism are major sources of this inculcation. Concerning the role of religion, Beck observes that dualistic thinking permeates world religions and that "with their emphasis on absolute (dualistic, overgeneralized) evaluative judgments, many religions often reinforce people's tendencies to judge themselves and other people in biased ways: good versus evil, benevolent versus malicious" (Beck 36).

Mack provides a similar assessment of the role of religion in promoting dichotomous thinking and notes the role played by nationalism as well: "Political and religious institutions have a powerful role in shaping and perpetuating dualistic thinking," and "nationalism . . . is a particularly powerful augmenter of dualistic thinking" (Mack 178). In many cases, nationalism and religion work together to promote such thinking and the violence it enables. As Mark Juergensmeyer explains, "By identifying a temporal social struggle with the cosmic struggle of order and disorder, truth and evil, political actors are able to avail themselves of a way of thinking that justifies the use of violent means. . . . Those who want moral sanction for their use of violence, and who do not have the approval of an officially recognized government, find it helpful to have access to a higher source: the meta-morality that religion provides" (Juergensmeyer 182).

In addition to invoking religion, politicians also promote homogenizing and dichotomizing by evoking fear. As Larsen explains, information that is processed in a state of fear is routed more directly to primitive structures such as the amygdala that "keep people stupid and polarized in their thinking" (Larsen 28). George W. Bush's rhetoric after the 9/11 attacks is a powerful example (see Wessells 59–61).

As with the other three faulty schemas, television also appears to play a significant role in establishing and reinforcing the homogeneity schema. First, television blinds us to the intrapsychic heterogeneity of ourselves and others by largely excluding certain traits, activities, and modes of being from representation and thus sending the tacit message that they don't exist or at least aren't worth noticing. Kristen Harrison argues that "media representations, and television representations in particular, depict a constricted and simplified view of human attributes and endeavors" and that such constricted portrayals "imply that only a small collection of attributes, roles, and endeavors are valid aspects of personhood" (Harrison 266, 269). In addition, Harrison argues that the restricted range of human attributes presented on television produces "a tendency for a certain narrow range of self-aspects—those most frequently depicted by television characters—to become chronically accessible or easily activated within memory . . . to the exclusion of less frequently depicted roles and aspects of character" (Harrison 269). And this chronic restriction of accessibility, we can surmise, affects not just one's perception of self but also one's perception of others.

Furthermore, many of the characters portrayed on television are one-dimensional, either virtuous or vicious. While some dramatic protagonists (e.g., police officers in crime dramas) are clearly flawed, few of their antagonists are correspondingly endowed with virtues, and in any event, the protagonists are generally presented as possessing considerably more virtues than the antagonists. The same dynamic is present in many news stories, where certain types of individuals (law enforcement officers, American military personnel, successful entrepreneurs) tend to be depicted without flaws while their antagonists (law-breakers, military enemies, unsuccessful competing entrepreneurs) are typically shown with their flaws foregrounded and their virtues invisible. Such portrayals, repeated from one program to another as well as from one episode to another in a given program, reinforce the homogeneity schema by presenting multiple exemplars of individuals who are fundamentally either good or bad.

In addition to being a prominent feature of television fiction, promoting homogeneity may be inherent in the very nature of the televisual medium. In comparison with literature, television would seem not to be a very good apparatus for showing heterogeneity. Television foregrounds behavior, and while behavior can reveal heterogeneities of character, it usually does so only to the trained observer—i.e., one possessing the heterogeneity cognitive schema—and even then in only a limited manner. It is much more difficult for television to portray motives of any sort, much less intrapsychic complexities, tensions, divisions, and conflicts, especially when these are unconscious. This deficiency occasionally becomes apparent, when, for example, a prominent TV personality or public figure with a carefully scripted or managed positive persona is revealed to have a "dark" side that was totally hidden from the public. Examples include televangelists who are discovered to have been engaging in behaviors that are antithetical to their professed and, to all previous appearances, lived values, or when an admired sports figure is revealed to have engaged in disreputable actions. But the great majority of TV personalities preserve their appearance of homogeneity, because television, unlike literature, cannot easily communicate off-screen behaviors or unexpressed feelings, impulses, and motives that run counter to the screen persona.

Replacing Homogenist Prototypes and Exemplars

As we have seen with the other schemas, while understanding the sources of a schema can aid in efforts to replace it—for example, by decommissioning some of the sources or motivating greater resistance to them—the crucial activity in replacing a harmful person-schema is to provide and rehearse corrective, counter-exemplars and information-processing routines. This means flagging and correcting or countering each of the various forms of the homogeneity judgment.

The *propositional* form of homogeneity is found in statements such as George W. Bush's declarations that the 9/11 attackers were evil people who hated our freedoms and that we are "good, freedom-loving people," as well as in his declaration that Iran, Iraq, and North Korea were the "Axis of Evil." More mundane but frequent statements concerning ordinary individuals enact the same homogenizing distortion, often through the simple use of homogenizing, dichotomizing categories, such as "good" and "bad": any time we describe someone as a "good person" or a "bad person," we both reveal and further reinforce a significant blindness to their full humanity. Such homogenist propositions must be countered with propositions articulating the heterogeneity principle. Some of the most striking and memorable—and hence effective—counterpropositions are literary, such as Faust's anguished cry, "Zwei Seelen wohnen, ach! in meiner Brust!" ("Two souls, alas, do dwell within my breast!") and the Roman poet Catullus's utterance, "Odi et amo . . . et excrucior!" ("I hate and I love, . . . and it crucifies me!").

The homogeneity schema is also promulgated through the use of positive *concepts* such as "honor," "integrity," "character," and "purity," as well as negative concepts such as "wickedness," "evil," "badness," and "shamefulness"—and also by negative names for heterogeneity, such as "impurity." Whenever such a term is applied to people, it surreptitiously imports the supposition that homogeneity of character is possible, that it is admirable, that it should be striven for in oneself and expected and policed in others, that its presence should be rewarded (through loyalty or obeisance), and that its absence should be corrected or punished (through social and moral censure or worse). Such homogeneity concepts must be countered with concepts embodying recognition of heterogeneity, such as "ambivalence," "hybridity," "hesitation," "misgiving," "remorse," "guilt," and "shame."

Homogeneity *episode scripts* also exert significant force in enacting this view of self and others. Such scripts are enacted and reinforced whenever a character or person behaves true to type—by, for example, resisting temptation (or yielding to it), maintaining "integrity" (or consistently failing to do so), behaving "honorably" (or dishonorably)—and especially when they do so while manifesting no ambivalence (in the form of hesitation or second thoughts). These episode scripts must be overwritten by episodes involving inconsistent, hesitant, reluctant, remorseful, and reparative actions. *Uncle Tom's Cabin*, for example, provides an episode of heterogeneity when it tells of the wicked slave owner Simon Legree's wavering between a life of sin and a life of virtue as his mother pleaded with him to choose the latter.

The clearest example of a homogeneity *life script* is the melodrama, in which protagonist and antagonist single-mindedly pursue agendas of good and evil, respectively. Other examples include the uncompromisingly virtuous youth of Horatio Alger stories, who doggedly adhere to the straight and narrow path, as well as their more overtly mythical prototypes in which the hero resists temptations, perseveres, and remains pure. Negative counterparts of this virtuous homogeneity life script include narratives of real and fictional lives in which persons such as Jeffrey Dahmer and countless other violent figures engage in harmful behaviors beginning at an early age and then proceed unwaveringly on this path through their entire lives, giving the impression that they are pure evil and incapable of a more benign life course.

The homogeneity life script must be countered with life stories in which characters enact opposing traits from one episode or period to another, as in the movement of the slave Topsy in *Uncle Tom's Cabin* from the self-described wickedest creature that ever lived to an altruistic missionary in Africa.

The *prototypic individuals* most exemplary of homogeneity are the heroes and villains of the homogeneity episode scripts and life scripts. These include saints and other religious figures (Jesus, Mohammed) who resist temptation and overcome all external obstacles to remain pure and true to themselves, as well as national leaders (Aeneas, Odysseus, Penelope, and George "I cannot tell a lie" Washington) and military heroes (Patton, MacArthur, Eisenhower) who never blink, doubt, hesitate, or falter. Tough, powerful athletes are also significant prototypes of homogeneity, teaching young boys, for example, that real men are homogeneously masculine, completely devoid of "feminine" qualities.

Our memories are also populated with prominent exemplars of negative homogeneity, in the form of numerous real and fictional individuals who appear purely wicked or evil. These include historical figures such as Hitler and Stalin, contemporary figures such as Saddam Hussein, Osama bin Laden, and Muammar Gaddafi, and most of the fictional criminals who inhabit television crime dramas and the evil megalomaniacs at the center of many crime, suspense, and action movies. The prototypic homogeneous individual must be countered by exemplars of heterogeneous individuals, such as Okonkwo, the hyper-masculine protagonist of Chinua Achebe's *Things Fall Apart*, who is motivated in everything he does by fear, specifically the fear of being thought weak and feminine.

Homogeneity is also enacted and inculcated in *body images*, particularly in facial expressions, body postures, and dress, as well as gestures, movements, and actions, that are devoid of any hints of ambiguity, ambivalence, moral conflict, hesitation, wavering, waffling, or flip-flopping. Expressions of homogeneous meanness, cruelty, cowardice, and dishonesty can be found in the scowls, sneers, grimaces, and shifty gaze of the villains of melodramas, Westerns, and horror films, as well as in their wicked laughs, black costumes, and often frenetic gestures and body movements. Homogeneous honor, honesty, fairness, and courage are likewise exhibited in the steadfast gaze, upright posture, straightforward gestures and movements of the honorable heroine or hero, as well as in her white dress and his white hat.

To counter homogeneity body images, some of the same qualities that demonstrate heterogeneity in episodes—inconsistency, hesitancy, reluctance, remorse—can also be portrayed in characters' facial expressions, vocalizations, postures, and movements. Bigger Thomas's sobbing and stammering when talking with Max at the end of *Native Son*, for example, provides a graphic visual and auditory image of the tender side of an individual who is also a brutal killer.

In producing the perception of self and others as all good or all bad, the homogeneity schema promotes *emotions* of love and admiration for supposedly good others, pride for one's supposedly good self, feelings of fear, contempt, and hatred for supposedly bad others, and shame and depression in response to the perception of oneself as totally bad or worthless. Examples of the positive emotions can be seen in the jubilation and adulation with which people respond to their religious, political, military, and athletic heroes; the pride that many of these heroes themselves manifest when they are experiencing their presumed purity or invincibility; the fear, contempt, and hatred expressed toward religious, political, military, and athletic opponents who are perceived to be completely unworthy; and the shame and depression experienced by individuals who have fallen from public grace, jobless or homeless people who perceive themselves as complete losers, or athletes who experience themselves as worthless after a loss.

These homogenist emotions must be replaced by ambivalent emotions. Instead of hatred (toward supposedly totally bad characters) or love and adoration (toward characters presumed to be purely good), ambivalent emotions—anger tempered with compassion, and qualified admiration, respectively—embody the recognition that a "bad" person is not pure evil and a "good" person is not without flaws.

Homogenist emotions lead to the *retrieval of* corresponding *action scripts.* People who feel adulation for supposedly all-good individuals will often emulate them, follow them blindly, subjugate themselves to these individuals, do homage to them, perform all sorts of services for them, and overlook or ignore harmful and unjust behavior on their part—whether in a romantic relationship or in a business, political, military, or sports context. Conversely, individuals who feel pride at their own supposed unadulterated worth will expect this sort of service from others. And on the negative side, people who feel fear, contempt, or hatred toward an apparently irredeemably bad other will exhibit various forms of aggression toward this other, supporting harsh punishment for criminals, war against dictators, and brutal battle against sports or business opponents.

Such action scripts must be replaced with heterogeneity action scripts, which involve not doing violence to "bad" people and blindly following or subjecting oneself to "good" people, but rather containing

162 The Cognitive Roots of Injustice

the "bad" people to prevent them from doing further harm—through, for example, imprisoning Bigger Thomas rather that executing him—and respecting "good" people, emulating them, and learning from them without worshiping them and doing obeisance to them, a balance that Jurgis Rudkus, for example, strikes with regard to his mentor at the end of *The Jungle*.

Replacing Homogenist Information-Processing Routines

Homogenist information processing involves, first of all, the *expectation* that other people will embody either positive or negative traits rather than both (see Mayo and Crockett 336). When both positive and negative traits are evident, individuals operating with a homogeneity schema will *attend* to only one set of traits, positive or negative, rather than both (Stein 164). The restricted expectation and attention result not only in perception being dominated by "relatively unessential aspects" of other people but also in "glaring omissions of fact" concerning them (Frenkel-Brunswik, "Intolerance" 134). As Frenkel-Brunswik states, "A desperate effort is made to *shut out* uncertainties the prejudiced individual is unable to face. . . . In order to reduce conflict and anxiety and to maintain stereotyped patterns, certain aspects of experience have to be *kept out of awareness.* Assumptions once made, no matter how faulty and out of keeping with reality because of a neglect of relevant aspects, are repeated over and over again and not corrected in the face of new evidence" (Frenkel-Brunswik, "Intolerance" 119; emphasis added).

Disconfirming facts about people are further excluded by *information-search* routines that systematically seek only information that will confirm the homogeneous perception of the other and that systematically avoid disconfirming information (Frenkel-Brunswik 115). In addition, *inference* and *supposition* sometimes fabricate confirming information on the basis of little or no evidence. Frenkel-Brunswik tells of prejudiced white children listening to a story about a black boy and then ascribing to him negative characteristics that were never mentioned in the story (Frenkel-Brunswik 124). In other instances, people operating under the homogeneity schema will take a single, minor detail about someone and *interpret* and elaborate that detail into a major revelation concerning the person's character (Frenkel-Brunswik 122, 126).

The same deficiencies occur in processing information about oneself, limiting one's self-awareness and self-integration and thus increasing projection and projective identification, which further distort one's perceptions and judgments of other people. Stein notes, "Low-complexity subjects tend to *focus on* and react to a single perspective of the self while apparently losing sight of the other available self-conceptions" (Stein 163). Research has revealed that "the lack of a rich and differentiated [self-schema] limit[s] the individual's ability to *attend to* and *encode* the new information" in memory (Stein 175; emphasis added). Thus "when a schema is less complex, the individual has a smaller and less diverse array of information available in *memory* that can be brought to bear in processing the new and contradictory information. In this case the individual has less flexibility in thinking about the self, and, consequently may have more difficulty *attending to* and *utilizing* the new and contradictory information" (Stein 164; emphasis added).

As we discussed earlier, when an individual fails to recognize and own his or her own impulses and qualities, these elements of self will often be projected onto others, thus further distorting one's information processing about other people. Failure to own certain emotions and action tendencies of one's own will also distort one's perception and judgment of others, by depriving one of certain information-processing tools and options (see Frenkel-Brunswik, "Intolerance" 118–119).

These faulty, homogenist information-processing routines must be replaced by routines capable of apprehending heterogeneity. Literary texts promote the development of heterogeneity routines in several ways. The simplest, most straightforward means is by explicitly describing characters as heterogeneous, composed of mutually contradictory or conflicting qualities, thus engaging readers in attending simultaneously to two contrary aspects of a single individual. A slightly less direct way is through portraying manifestly heterogeneous characters without explicitly remarking upon their heterogeneity. And a more challenging technique is to provide hints in the form of behavioral clues or the narrator's intimations that qualities contrary to the overt ones are also present in a character. The more explicit indications of heterogeneity serve to prime heterogeneity in readers' minds, thus increasing their *expectation* of encountering it, as well as their *attending* to it when it is encountered, and *searching* for it, *inferring* it, and/or *supposing* it when it is not manifest. These latter activities—searching, inferring, and supposing heterogeneity—are further induced by the more subtle suggestions of heterogeneity.

Other, nonliterary means of developing information-processing routines for apprehending human situatedness, malleability, and autonomy, as well as intrapersonal heterogeneity, will be discussed in the final chapter. But first, having described the nature of the four faulty general person-schemas, explained the flaws in their functioning, mapped the kinds of harm they cause, identified their key sources, and sketched out the means for replacing them with more adequate schemas, we turn to an examination of three prominent American protest novels for a more systematic and detailed demonstration of how literary texts can facilitate this replacement and, in doing so, enact a radical cognitive politics that promotes social justice by addressing the psychological roots of injustice.

PART III

HOW PROTEST NOVELS WORK TO REPLACE FAULTY PERSON-SCHEMAS

CHAPTER 6

The Jungle

Art is a representation of life, modified by the personality of the artist, for the purpose of modifying other personalities, inciting them to changes of feeling, belief and action.
UPTON SINCLAIR, "ART" 356

Upton Sinclair was adamant that the purpose of literature should be to promote social justice. "The true purpose of art is to alter reality," he declared. "All art is propaganda. It is universally and inescapably propaganda; sometimes unconsciously, but often deliberately, propaganda" (Sinclair, "Art" 355). As this chapter's epigraph indicates, Sinclair believed that literature is capable of altering reality and rescuing suffering people from their misery because it can change people's feelings, beliefs, and actions.

The key beliefs and feelings that Sinclair wanted *The Jungle* to change were those of empowered people toward working-class people. Writing shortly after the novel was published, Sinclair indicated that he was especially concerned with correcting two faulty beliefs: (1) "that the individual was to blame for failure" and (2) that individuals were responsible for their own character flaws—their "degeneration . . . in body, mind and soul"—beliefs that coincide with what I have described as autonomism and essentialism. As Sinclair explains, he was concerned with the fact that the educated, empowered classes—

> those who had voices—they did not know! They were sitting at ease and speculating about it; they had been born to success themselves, and were prattling that the individual was to blame for failure. I, alone of all men who had education and a voice, had been down into the social pit,

and had lived the life of the proletarian; so that I . . . knew, of my own experience, things of which all the doctors and wise men, the scholars and statesmen of the world, were ignorant. I had tested upon my own person the effects of cold and hunger, of misery and disease and despair. I had tried to the full the power of the individual will, and found its impotence; I had watched the beginning and the swift progress of degeneration—in body and mind and soul—in myself, and, more horrible yet, in those I loved. . . . And so I knew, with a knowledge that no man could impeach, the cause and the meaning of all the evils that are raging in modern society—of neurasthenia, melancholia, and hysteria; of drunkenness, insanity, and suicide; of prostitution, war, and crime. (Sinclair, "What" 349–350)

The purpose of *The Jungle* was to correct these faulty beliefs and the unjust feelings and actions that follow from them in order to rescue masses of individuals from misery and injustice: "The proletarian writer is a writer with a purpose; he thinks no more of 'art for art's sake' than a man on a sinking ship thinks of painting a beautiful picture in the cabin; he thinks of getting ashore, and of getting his brothers and comrades ashore" (Sinclair, "What" 352).

Developing the Situationism Schema

Nobody rose in Packingtown by doing good work. (60)

In accord with Sinclair's stated intention, *The Jungle* engages all the elements of the autonomy schema and reworks them into the contrary elements of the situationism schema, which recognizes the powerful impact of circumstances on behavior and life outcomes. The central technique through which the novel promotes this schema change is by establishing Jurgis Rudkus as an exemplar of autonomy and then systematically and relentlessly confronting him with insurmountable circumstances, thereby turning him into an exemplar of situatedness. Each insurmountable circumstance involves an episode in which Jurgis's will is confronted by an obstacle that even the greatest effort is unable to overcome. This repeated sequence develops for readers a new episode script that challenges the autonomy schema's effort-produces-success script for the default position in processing situations of struggle. In the process, the dominance of the autonomy life script, the rags-to-riches story, is eroded by multiple life stories of rags-to-suffering, and the hard-working, self-reliant Jurgis is transformed.

At the beginning of the novel, Jurgis is an *individual* exemplar of autonomy and a vehicle for the other prototypes of autonomy. His very presence in America is the result of his industriousness and self-reliance: in order to earn the money for his emigration from Lithuania, he hiked almost four hundred miles to work on a railroad in Poland, endured "a fearful experience, with filth and bad food and cruelty and overwork," worked hard, abstained from drinking and fighting, escaped from gamblers who tried to rob and kill him, and worked his way the four hundred miles back home (25). Each of these episodes adds an increment to the autonomy *episode script* in which an individual overcomes circumstances to maintain virtue and/or achieve a goal, and together these autonomy episodes constitute a brief autonomy *life story* of virtue and hard work leading to success.

The autonomy assumption is also embodied in Jurgis's physical *image* at the beginning of the novel (he is a huge, powerful man who towers above the other workers [6, 32]); in his *emotions* of confidence concerning his abilities (32), his pride, joy, and arrogance concerning his accomplishments (32, 33, 43), and his indifference and contempt for those who fail to find work (23, 58); in the *proposition* that he has the "ability to get work for himself, unassisted by anyone" (32; see also 49); and in his *conceptualization* of men who fail to get work as "unfit" and "broken-down tramps and good-for-nothings" (58, 23). Jurgis also enacts the dominant *action script* of the autonomy schema: whenever he encounters difficulties, he considers only one remedy, working harder (20, 22, 70); it never occurs to him that the solution to his difficulties is only to be found in changing the circumstances of his existence.

Propositional Knowledge and Metacognition

The Jungle systematically counters each of these elements of the autonomy schema with corresponding elements of situationism. Propositional refutations of the autonomy assumption occur throughout the novel. We are told fairly early in the novel that, far from being autonomous and self-reliant, Jurgis and his family were "utterly lost" and "pitiable in their helplessness" when they landed in America (26). Later we are told that Jurgis's belief in his ability to rise above his circumstances through hard work is false: "Jurgis . . . thought he was going to . . . rise and become a skilled man; but he would soon find out his error—for nobody rose in Packingtown by doing good work" (60). When Jurgis survives a brutal blizzard, he is exultant, believing that "he had met the enemy and conquered, and felt himself the master of his fate," but readers are warned that he is about to fall "into some cowardly trap in the nighttime" (111), which he soon does when he is injured in "an accident . . . that no man can help" and begins to realize "that the best powers of a man might not be equal to" the circumstances that he is confronted with: "that here, in this ghastly home of all horror, he and all those who were dear to him might lie and perish of starvation and cold, and there would be no ear to hear their cry, no hand to help them!" (113).

After he is imprisoned for attacking his wife's rapist, he realizes that far from being autonomous and self-reliant, he is helpless against his circumstances, that "he was of no consequence—he was flung aside, like a bit of trash, the carcass of some animal. . . . They had ground him beneath their heel, they had devoured all his substance; they had murdered his old father, they had broken and wrecked his wife, they had crushed and cowed his whole family; and now they were through with him, they had no further use for him" (154). Jurgis is unable to identify the ultimate cause of his fate; he knows only that it lies beyond himself, in others. But Sinclair makes the circumstances and their causes explicit for readers: "it was the thing men have called the system that was crushing him to the earth" (155). Later the socialist orator reiterates the point that it is not the workers themselves but rather "the iron hand of circumstances" constituted by the "accursed system" that is to blame for the workers' misery (286), and that conversely their masters, who "do nothing to earn what they receive," are not to be credited for their wealth (289). And finally, at the socialist dinner, Dr. Schliemann articulates the utter lack of autonomy of the Jeffersonian "independent" farmer that has long served as the American ideal, describing him as "a stunted, haggard, ignorant man, . . . toiling from four o'clock in the morning until nine at night, . . . scratching the soil with his primitive tools, and shut out from all knowledge and hope, from all the benefits of science and invention, and all the joys of the spirit—held to a bare existence by competition in labor, and boasting of his freedom because he is too blind to see his chains!" (325).

While these propositional statements play an important role in the decommissioning of the autonomy schema, most of *The Jungle*'s schema-changing work is done not by explicit, propositional refutation of the autonomy assumption but rather by the enactment of nonpropositional forms of the knowledge that circumstances largely determine behaviors and life outcomes. Each of these various forms of exemplars embodies recognition of the fact that circumstances over which one has no control can always override character in determining behavior, and can also override behavior in determining life outcomes. To the extent that any of these exemplars become encoded in readers' memory, they can help to correct the faulty information processing of the autonomy schema as explained above. And if and when the number and intensity of exemplars for any form of knowledge reach critical mass, they will form a new, situationist prototype for that form of knowledge.

Situationist Episodes

One of the primary means by which *The Jungle* undermines the harmful and deficient autonomy schema is by correcting the faulty *character→behavior→ success/failure* episode script (one's character determines one's behavior, and one's behavior determines whether one succeeds or fails) that is at the heart of this schema. This episode script is deeply flawed—and profoundly unjust—because it leads one to focus, in episodes of success or failure, on behavior and character and ignore the powerful role that circumstances play in determining a person's life outcomes and thus to blame people for failures or bad behaviors, as well as to credit people for successes and good behaviors, that were determined more by circumstances than by character. This flawed and unjust episode script thus needs to be corrected by incorporating into it the role of circumstances. (See Diagram 3, next page.)

The Jungle promotes the development of this more adequate, situationist episode script by repeatedly representing the power of circumstances in two types of episodes: (1) episodes in which circumstances determine behavior in spite of countervailing character traits (*circumstances→character→behavior*) and (2) episodes in which circumstances determine outcome in spite of countervailing behavior (*circumstances→ behavior→success/failure*). Such episodes function incrementally to add the role of circumstances to the incomplete script, *character→ behavior→success/failure*, and promote the establishment of the situationism script as the prototype for appraising people's good and bad behaviors and their successes or failures.

The *circumstances→behavior→failure* script is ubiquitous in the novel. For example, despite faultless behavior (i.e., their best efforts to protect themselves against fraud) in the purchase of their house, Jurgis's extended family finds itself with an old (rather than the adver-

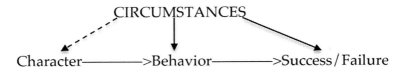

Diagram 3. How circumstances affect life outcomes

tised new), tuberculosis-infected structure for which their contract requires them to pay over half again as much as they were led to believe it would cost them (68–69). Despite working hard at their jobs (another instance of faultless behavior), Jurgis and Marija—and countless other workers—find themselves in dire straits when they fall victim to accident, their hours are reduced, or their factories close (69, 112, 87). And when their jobs do survive, the workers themselves are worn down by their work and tossed aside like worn-out parts (121). Episodes such as these—in which the best efforts of the ablest individuals are thwarted by insurmountable obstacles, and failure and suffering are the result of circumstances, not weak character or lack of effort—provide readers with numerous exemplars of situatedness that they can use as templates for processing information about unsuccessful people, and these exemplars will contribute to the development in readers of a more adequate alternative to the autonomy schema's *effort→success* episode script for deciding on the causes of success and failure.

The same is true of *circumstances→character→behavior* episodes, in which bad behavior is shown to be a product more of circumstances than of character. Jurgis's drinking, for example, is presented as an exemplar not of weak character but rather of circumstances: he first begins to drink because ordering a drink is required where he eats and cashes his paycheck (80–81). Similarly, his beating of young Stanislovas is the result not of wickedness on Jurgis's part but rather of the family's desperate situation: the boy must be forced to go to work despite his fear of the cold (after suffering severe, agonizing frostbite), or the family will starve. Jurgis's beating of his wife's boss is also presented as the product of circumstances: the boss has raped Ona, which has understandably enraged Jurgis (147–148).

Prostitution, often viewed as the result of low morals on the part of prostitutes, is also transformed into an exemplar of situatedness. Most of the prostitutes in Packingtown, we learn, were coerced into prostitution in order to get or keep a job and thus avoid starvation: "Here was a population, low-class and mostly foreign, hanging always on the verge of starvation, and dependent for its opportunities of life upon the whim of men every bit as brutal and unscrupulous as the old-time slave-drivers; under such circumstances immorality was exactly as inevitable, and as prevalent, as it was under the system of chattel slavery" (104). In some cases, women were literally enslaved: "Thousands of them came to Chicago answering advertisements for 'servants' and 'factory hands,' and found themselves trapped by fake employment agencies, and locked up in a bawdy-house," where their clothes were taken away or they were drugged and kept prisoner (243).

Other immoral and/or criminal acts are also presented as the result of circumstances rather than character, and hence function as exemplars of situatedness rather than autonomy. *The Jungle* offers a powerful explanation of the situatedness of criminal behavior in general, which turns all criminals and all criminal actions into exemplars of situatedness. We are told that the other individuals in jail with Jurgis are the product of

> a city in which justice and honor, women's bodies and men's souls, were for sale in the market place, and human beings writhed and fought and fell upon each other like wolves in a pit; in which lusts were raging fires, and men were fuel, and humanity was festering and stewing and wallowing in its own corruption. *Into this wild-beast tangle these men had been born without their consent; they had taken part in it because they could not help it*; that they were in jail was no disgrace to them, for the game had never been fair, the dice were loaded. They were swindlers and thieves of pennies and dimes, and they had been trapped and put out of the way by the swindlers and thieves of millions of dollars. (160; emphasis added)

The Jungle also presents the various acts of corruption and systemic violence perpetrated by "the swindlers and thieves of millions of dollars," as well as the acts of brutality, including those of the traffickers in slave-prostitutes, as exemplars of situatedness, making it clear that these acts are the product not primarily of wicked character but rather of the larger circumstances constituted by the system of laissez-faire capitalism. Sinclair points out early on that, in the capitalist system, competing businesses are "required to be deadly rivals by the law of the land, and ordered to try to ruin each other under penalty of fine and imprisonment!" (42). This system produces ruthlessness and exploitation all the way down the chain of command, pitting individuals within a given business against each other:

Here was Durham's, for instance, owned by a man who was trying to make as much money out of it as he could, and did not care in the least how he did it; and underneath him, ranged in ranks and grades like an army, were managers and superintendents and foremen, each one driving the man next below him and trying to squeeze out of him as much work as possible. And all the men of the same rank were pitted against each other; the accounts of each were kept separately, and every man lived in terror of losing his job, if another made a better record than he. So from top to bottom the place was simply a seething cauldron of jealousies and hatreds; there was no loyalty or decency anywhere about it, there was no place in it where a man counted for anything against a dollar. (59)

Such a system "was a war of each against all, and the devil take the hindmost . . . ; you understood that you were environed by hostile powers that were trying to get your money, and who used all the virtues to bait their traps with" (74). Sinclair makes even the exploiters into exemplars of situatedness, making it clear that they are not really to blame for their behavior and are ultimately themselves victims of the circumstances constituted by laissez-faire capitalism: although Jurgis blamed the bosses for his dreadful working conditions, "the truth to be told was it was not always their fault; for the packers kept them frightened for their lives" (87). That the ultimate blame for workers' misery lies in the system is made apparent when the humane International Harvester plant suddenly closes because "they had made all the harvesting machines that the world needed": "It was nobody's fault" (193). By encoding multiple such *circumstances→character→behavior* episodes in their episodic memory, readers become more capable of apprehending the circumstantial determinants even of inhumane behavior rather than automatically attributing it to the agent's character.

Situationist Life Stories

The novel offers multiple situationist life stories to challenge and erode the dominance of the rags-to-riches autonomy script with a life trajectory leading from rags to death—or worse: to injury, illness, unemployment, starvation, addiction, and/or prostitution before death. Jurgis's father, Old Antanas, who comes to America expecting to see his family thrive and prosper, works in a pickle room that produces sores on his feet until he collapses and is carried home, where he lies "wasting away to a mere skeleton" and choking on his own blood until finally he mercifully expires (77). Ona realizes her hopes of marrying Jurgis and starting a family, only to be made chronically ill by her work, raped by her supervisor, and deprived of the support of her imprisoned husband before dying an agonizing, gruesome death at the end of a horrific labor: "Dead! *dead!* And she was only a girl, she was barely eighteen. Her life had hardly begun—and here she lay murdered—mangled, tortured to death!" (182). Equally ghastly is the short life of Stanislovas, who, after being forced to become an appendage of a machine in order to survive, one day falls asleep at work after drinking too much beer and is killed and eaten by rats (275). Marija survives, but her dreams of marrying Tamoszius have been dashed by her family's poverty, and she becomes a cynical prostitute and morphine addict (273–277).

In addition to these more detailed stories, the novel also provides numerous condensed exemplars of the rags-to-death-or-worse life script of situationism. There is, for example, the brief account of Mary Dennis, the consumptive single mother of a crippled and epileptic little boy who was fired from her job in order to make a place for the more able Marija (61). And there is the brief explanation that Jonas's predecessor had been "crushed in a horrible and nameless manner" by a heavy iron cart loaded with hams (62).

By experiencing the long narrative through which Jurgis and his family are gradually defeated by circumstances over which they have no control, as well as shorter life stories of the same sort regarding other characters, readers acquire a more valid alternative to the rags-to-riches life script of the autonomy schema. By getting readers to encode multiple stories of this sort in their episodic memory, *The Jungle* provides them with multiple rags-to-rags-or-death exemplars, which can both guide their future information processing and also contribute to the formation of a rags-to-rags-or-death life script to counter the myopic autonomy life script as the prototype for framing and evaluating people's lives.

Individual Exemplars of Situatedness

The Jungle is also replete with individual exemplars of situatedness, characters overwhelmed by circumstances they cannot control. In addition to the protagonists of the episodes and life stories just discussed, all of whom are individual exemplars of situatedness, readers encounter multiple additional exemplars throughout the novel. At the wedding celebration there is Jadvyga Marcinkus, who supports her invalid mother and three younger sisters by painting cans; Mikolas, her fiancé of five years, who has to support his large family and has lost his job because of an accident in which he contracted blood poisoning (14); the old man Jokubas Szedvilas, who is struggling to pay overdue rent on his delicatessen; and the rheumatoid old widow Aniel, who supports her three children by doing washing for almost nothing (19).

Children are particularly powerful exemplars of situationism, since they are clearly seldom responsible for their life circumstances. In *The Jungle* such exemplars include children scavenging for food in the garbage dump (30–31); the anonymous little boy whose ears freeze on his way to work and then break off when a man tries to warm them by rubbing them (79); Elzbieta's young sons Vilimas and Nikalojus, who have to sell newspapers by day and sleep in doorways at night to help support the family (118); her two crippled sons, Juozapas, who lost a leg when he was run over, and the three-year-old Kristoforas, who lives a wretched life crawling about with a congenitally dislocated hip and then dies a horrible death after eating contaminated food (123); and her oldest son Stanislovas, who is put to work on the production line as a cog in the giant machine and thus has his fate determined: "and so was decided the place in the universe of little Stanislovas, and his destiny till the end of his days. Hour after hour, day after day, year after year, it was fated that he should stand upon a certain square foot of floor from seven in the morning until noon, and again from half-past twelve till half-past five, making never a motion and thinking never a thought, save for the setting of lard-cans" (71). By encoding these exemplars, as well as the prototypes they help to form, in readers' memories, the novel helps readers apprehend the power of circumstances over human behavior and destiny when they evaluate the behaviors and life outcomes of real people.

Images of Situatedness

The autonomy bias is also powerfully supported by prototypic images of the human body, and at the beginning of *The Jungle* Jurgis embodies this image perfectly: he is a powerful, exuberant, striking figure who towers above the other workers clamoring for a job and has no difficulty in attracting the attention of the hiring boss (6, 32). By the end of the novel, however, this image has been transformed into that of a gaunt, haggard specter who lacks the strength necessary to complete a single day's work. Similar exemplary images abound of bodies that have been worn down, worn out, wounded, emaciated, or literally crushed by their circumstances of life and work, and these images, when encoded in episodic memory and/or consolidated into prototypical images, help people recognize such circumstances behind the failures they encounter in real people outside the text.

Situationist Concepts

The Jungle also works to replace concepts embodying the assumption of autonomy with signifiers that deemphasize the role of character and underscore instead the role of circumstances in determining behavior and life outcomes. For example, desolate workers, instead of being labeled failures or losers—or "unfit" and "broken-down tramps and good-for-nothings," as Jurgis initially calls them (58, 23)—are conceptualized as "victims" of the system (171, 299). And the packers, categorized as "captains of industry" in the autonomy schema, are reconceptualized in the novel as "pirates of industry," "foul monsters of sensuality and cruelty" (317), "ravenous vultures," "tyrants," "oppressors" (171), "exploiters" (296), and "parasites" (320), while "capitalist production" is similarly recast as destruction, waste (320), and corruption (325), and "success" is conceptualized as pride, luxury, and tyranny (316). By arming readers with such alternative concepts embodying tacit recognition of the role of circumstances in both success and failure, the novel provides them with yet another tool for escaping the myopia of the autonomy schema when assessing and categorizing real people outside the novel.

Situationist Emotions

Readers also repeatedly experience, through empathy, the emotions embodying the realization that circumstance, not character, is the primary determinant of behavior and life outcomes. Each time readers encounter one of the many instances discussed in the preceding paragraphs of characters being victimized by forces beyond their control, they experience the emotions of fear, anguish, despair, sympathy, and/or righteous anger, and the repeated experiencing of such emotions associates them with their respective objects (workers, poor people, capitalists), such that future perception or thought of the exemplary individuals, episodes, life stories, concepts, images, or propositions of situationism will likely be colored by the respective emotion. And as explained in Chapter 1, these emotions will not only prime readers to make the correspondent situationist appraisals, they will also motivate specific, situationist actions.

Situationist Actions

Sympathy will incline one to help the object of one's sympathy, and outrage will potentiate acts of aggression against a perceived source of harm. *The Jungle* promotes the further association of these emotions with specific forms of helping and aggression by linking them with particular actions on the part of Jurgis and other characters, and this process promotes readers' development of action scripts that counter those of the autonomy schema.

When one is operating with the autonomy schema, the solution to every problem is for the individual to "work harder." People impose this action script on others and they embrace it for themselves. As noted above, Jurgis lives by this action script for the first part of the novel. Whenever he encounters difficulties, he considers only one remedy: working harder (20, 22, 70). It never occurs to him that the solution to his difficulties is only to be found in changing the circumstances of his existence. Pursuing such change in circumstances is the dominant action script of the situationism schema. And in *The Jungle*, the fundamental circumstance that needs to be changed is the system of laissez-faire capitalism. The novel thus directs readers' sympathy for victimized workers and their anger at the capitalist victimizers toward the capitalist system itself, rather than at the individual victimizers—who, as discussed above, are themselves presented as pawns in the same game as the workers.

Thus the general action script promoted by *The Jungle* is to build, by educating and organizing (300, 318), a society that provides for everyone rather than meting out further harm to the unfortunate and additional power and wealth to the already fortunate. In addition to altering readers' knowledge and emotions concerning success and failure, and winners and losers, within the capitalist system, the novel thus also facilitates a link in readers' minds connecting anger at the oppressive system and sympathy for its victims to activities of educating and organizing to change the system, thus increasing the inclination toward such action on the part of readers when they put the novel down.

Situationist Information-Processing Routines

As these new knowledge components are internalized by readers, they begin to change the faulty information-processing routines that continually produce and reproduce the harmful appraisals, emotions, and actions regarding others. They incline readers to expect, notice, attend to, search for, infer, suppose, and commit to memory the circumstances influencing characters' behavior and destiny.

The novel also trains its readers more directly in such processing routines. It does so early on by telling us quite explicitly to *expect* circumstances to derail Jurgis and his family: "Jurgis . . . thought he was going to . . . rise and become a skilled man; but he would soon find out his error—for nobody rose in Packingtown by doing good work" (60). And a bit later, when Jurgis believes that "he had met the enemy and conquered, and felt himself the master of his fate," the novel warns readers that he is about to fall "into some cowardly trap in the night-time" (111), which he soon does when he is injured in "an accident . . . that no man can help" (113).

Situationist information-processing routines are also developed by repeatedly presenting readers with—and thus giving us no choice but to attend to—situational constraints and affordances and their role in determining characters' behaviors and life outcomes. Thus after reading several chapters of the novel, we begin to *expect* circumstances to determine the success or failure of any effort that struggling individuals may make to escape from their misery, and whenever we encounter a new character, we are able safely to *infer* on the basis of inconclusive evidence—and to *suppose* in the absence of all evidence—that the character's life condition is largely if not totally the result of circumstances (either fortunate or unfortunate).

Reading *The Jungle* may also remind readers of the time they lost a job through no fault of their own, or of a job that left them physically or emotionally exhausted and hence not on their best behavior. Repeated *rememberings* of experiences in which one's own behaviors or outcomes were determined more by one's circumstances than by one's character will increase the ease and frequency with which such memories will come to mind in the future and serve as templates for processing information about others in similar circumstances (see Schank). And experiencing the *feelings* of sadness and anger that may accompany such memories, along with the feelings of sympathy for characters victimized by the system and righteous anger at the system and its supporters, accustoms readers to these emotional states and thus makes these emotions more accessible to them when they confront similar situations outside the novel.

Developing the Malleability Schema

[T]he best dog will turn cross if he be kept chained all the time. (117)

Novels are perhaps the most effective means of replacing the essentialism schema. Such texts powerfully demonstrate, and induce readers to expect, seek, attend to, infer, suppose, and encode in memory the formative and transformative effects of material, social, and cultural environments on character, thus promoting the establishment of a malleability schema in place of the essentialism schema.

The Jungle promotes alternatives for each element of the essentialism schema. For the static, permanent character, the novel substitutes the malleable character that manifests profound physical, psychological, social, intellectual, and moral transformations in response to environmental forces. In place of episodes and life stories of inherently good or bad, successful or unsuccessful individuals, the novel provides episodes and narratives of individuals formed, re-formed, and de-formed by the Social Darwinist system of laissez-faire capitalism and the rule of luck and chance. And in place of feelings of admiration for the successful and indifference or scorn for the unsuccessful, *The Jungle* induces the emotions of moral anger and compassion, respectively. These new emotions, in turn, activate action scripts of changing this body- and soul-destroying system instead of defending and celebrating it as the apogee of freedom.

Propositional Knowledge and Metacognition

The proposition that environment forms, de-forms, and re-forms character is articulated multiple times in the novel, in varying degrees of explicitness and specificity. At the opening scene of the wedding celebration, for example, readers are told that the practice of killing animals hour after hour and day after day makes men more violent: "men who have to crack the heads of animals all day seem to get into the habit, and to practice on their friends, and even on their families" (21). Later, when Jurgis's temperament turns dark as a result of his incapacitating leg injury, the narrator comments: "They say that the best dog will turn cross if he be kept chained all the time, and it was the same with the man" (117), and "a man can get used to anything in the course of time" (119).

If lack of activity can harm character, work can be just as damaging. We are also told quite explicitly that the work in Packingtown destroys people's human faculties and transforms them into dumb beasts. When Elzbieta is forced to do "stupefying, brutalizing work," she is left with "no time to think, no strength for anything. She was part of the machine she tended, and every faculty that was not needed for the machine was doomed to be crushed out of existence" (133). That living conditions determine moral character is also made explicit in the condemnation of evangelists who urge the oppressed workers to repent for their sins: "They were trying to save their souls—and who but a fool could fail to see that all that was the matter with their souls was that they had not been able to get decent existence for their bodies?" (218). The most severe statement of human malleability is uttered by the socialist Dr. Schliemann, who asserts that the living conditions of most people keep them from attaining full humanity: "the majority of human beings are not yet human beings at all, but simply machines for the creating of wealth for others. They are penned up in filthy houses and left to rot and stew in misery" (325).

Individual Exemplars of Malleability

Virtually all the workers in the novel are individual exemplars of malleability, for most of them have been permanently damaged both physically and psychologically in significant ways by their living and working conditions. Most workers in the pickle-rooms have, like old Antanas, terrible sores on their bodies, and some are incapacitated by the acid eating through the joints of their fingers. Most of the butchers have cut their thumbs so often that they are no longer functional. Skinners have worn their fingernails off by pulling the hides, and the beef-luggers are broken down after just a few years of carrying two-hundred-pound quarters into the railroad cars. The men working in the cooking rooms contract the tuberculosis that is incubated there, and the workers in the chilling-rooms are frequently plagued by rheumatism and only last about five years. The wool-pluckers have their fingers eaten off by the acid the wool is treated with. And so on (see 96–97).

The women in Packingtown are also deformed by their living and working conditions. We have already noted the stupefying, dehumanizing effects that Elzbieta's job has on her. At the end of the novel we are told, "Her soul had been baked hard in the fire of adversity, and there was no altering it now" (301), indicating that some deformations are not reversible. Ona, as a result of being forced to return to work too soon after her pregnancy, "was never again a well person as long as she lived," suffering from "headaches and pains in the back, and depression and heartsickness, and neuralgia," and we are told that "the great majority of the women who worked in Packingtown suffered in the same way, and from the same cause" (106).

Criminals, too, become exemplars of malleability in *The Jungle*, which presents them as products of a harmful environment instead of inherently bad individuals. Jack Duane, "a college-bred man [who] had been studying electrical engineering," is transformed into a criminal by a series of misfortunes and injustices (159), and criminals in general are presented not as individuals who were born evil but as people who are the products of a toxic environment, "the drainage of the great festering ulcer of society," a "wild-beast tangle" into which "these men had been born without their consent" (160). Likewise, most of the tramps whom Jurgis encounters in the countryside were originally working men who had been transformed by "the losing fight" of working (208). Prostitutes are also powerful exemplars of human malleability, as demonstrated by the figure of Marija, an initially ebullient and hardworking woman who has, by the end of the novel, been so completely transformed that Jurgis "could hardly believe that she was the same woman he had known in the old days; she was so quiet—so hard!" (276). Nor are poverty and oppression the only factors that deform people, as demonstrated by the example of the drunken, demoralized, and abandoned eighteen-year-old packer's son, Freddie Jones (222ff.).

Many of these characters also embody images of malleability. The workers' bodies have usually been mutilated, broken down, or worn out by the environment in which they have been forced to live and work. Jurgis's fellow prisoners also provide exemplary images of malleability: they are described as "hideous to look upon" (160), embodying visual evidence, like the workers, of the deforming effects of the environment upon body and soul.

Life Stories of Malleability

Jurgis's life provides the primary malleability life story in the novel, revealing how environmental forces can transform a life, body and soul, for good and for ill. He soon "grow[s] more matter-of-fact, under the endless pressure of penury" (119–120) and shortly thereafter becomes alcoholic (134–135). His wife's rape and his subsequent imprisonment for attacking her rapist eviscerate him ("they had devoured all his substance") and transform him into an enraged avenger: "every hour his soul grew blacker, every hour he dreamed new dreams of vengeance, of defiance, of raging, frenzied hate" (155). Upon his release from prison, after he finds his family evicted from their house and his wife in the throes of an agonizing labor that soon proves fatal to both her and the baby, he has become "hardened and embittered" (185). And after his son Antanas drowns in the street, he tries to protect himself by extirpating the tender feelings that make him vulnerable, "tearing up all the flowers from the garden of his soul, and setting his heel upon them" (203).

His body and soul are restored by the different environment of the countryside during his brief life as a tramp (207), but soon after his return to the city a few months later, another accident renders him a beggar (219), and soon thereafter he becomes a robber, out of desperation and through the influence of Jack Duane (238), and then a scab and an agent of the corrupt establishment (262) before a chance encounter with his wife's rapist triggers his violence, which lands him once again in jail. Though he buys his release from jail, he soon finds himself homeless, penniless, starving, and reduced to stealing cabbage to survive (268–269).

At this point, when his very humanity is almost extinguished—"Jurgis was a man whose soul had been murdered, who had ceased to hope and to struggle—who had made terms with degradation and despair" (292; see also 279)—he happens upon the socialist meeting, where the orator's speech transforms him yet again ("a new man had been born") by explaining the causes of his condition in a way that gives his life meaning and provides him with a reason to go on living (293).

Malleability Emotions and Actions

Like the situationism schema, the malleability schema shifts the blame for bad behavior or failure from the individual to the environment and in doing so elicits the emotions of sympathy for the individual and anger toward the external forces that harm the individual. Each episode and exemplar of the physically and mentally harmful effects of the environment elicits one or both of these emotions in readers, and these emotions then become directly associated with such individuals and events, such that when one subsequently encounters such an individual or event, one is likely to automatically experience the feeling. And as discussed with autonomy, the feelings of anger at the system and sympathy for its victims incline one toward actions of helping the victims and harming the system; such inclinations, as we discussed in the previous sections, are encouraged by the novel's representation of educating and organizing as the prime actions through which the system can be overthrown and its victims transformed.

Also, through relentlessly engaging readers in attending to, identifying, and recalling the various changes that environmental conditions and events produce in characters' bodies and souls, the novel enhances readers' capabilities and habits of expecting, attending to, searching for, inferring, supposing, encoding, and recalling such formative, transformative, re-formative, and de-formative effects when processing information about real people outside the novel. Instead of seeing people as simply who and what they are, readers will be more likely to see them, more adequately, as individuals who are what they are because of their past, formative experiences and environments, who may have been nurtured or damaged in certain ways by these forces, and who remain susceptible to further nurturance or damage by their experiences and environments in the present and future. And as a result of seeing people in this fuller, more comprehensive manner, readers will be more likely to take actions, including educating, organizing, and voting in ways that reduce the harmful effects of the environment and increase its nurturing effects.

Developing the Heterogeneity Schema

[H]e fought a battle with his soul. (203)

The Jungle does not foreground heterogeneity. There are virtually no propositional or conceptual articulations of the principle, and episodes, exemplars, and narratives embodying heterogeneity are much less numerous and substantial than they are (as we shall see) in *The Grapes of Wrath* and *Native Son*. Nonetheless, wherever situatedness and/or malleability is represented, heterogeneity is implicit, because a fundamental heterogeneity of character—the potential to behave and to be in different, mutually contradictory ways—is a prerequisite for both situatedness (behaving differently in different situations) and malleability (change in character over time).

The most substantial individual exemplar of heterogeneity is Jurgis. In addition to manifesting mutually contrary attributes over time, Jurgis also experiences his heterogeneity quite intensely at times, struggling with contrary impulses. His first such struggle is over alcohol: "there came a time when nearly all the conscious life of Jurgis consisted of a struggle with the craving for liquor. He would have ugly moods, when he hated Ona and the whole family, because they stood in his way. . . . This was not always his mood, of course; he still loved his family" (134–135). When his young son Antanas dies, Jurgis is torn between feelings of tenderness and anguish for his loss, on the one hand, and feelings of rage at his fate, on the other: "he fought a battle with his soul. He gripped his hands and set his teeth together—he had not wept, and he would not—not a tear! It was past and over, and he was done with it. . . . And every time that a thought of it assailed him—a tender memory, a trace of a tear—he rose up, cursing with rage, and pounded it down" (203).

Jurgis subsequently experiences struggles with his conscience after he hires a prostitute (209–210) and when he becomes a scab during a strike (262), but by the time he meets Marija again and hears of her life in the brothel, he has largely succeeded in repressing his tender feelings and memories. His encounter with Marija, however, revives this dormant part: "The depths of him were troubled and shaken, memories were stirred in him that had been sleeping so long he had counted them dead! . . . It had been the task of his recent life to fight them down, to crush them out of him; never in his life would he have suffered from them again, save that they had caught him unawares, and overwhelmed him before he could protect himself" (278–279).

Developing the Solidarity Schema

I speak with the voice of the millions who are voiceless. . . . With the voice of humanity, calling for deliverance! (286–287)

The Jungle is in many ways an extended documentary of the harm caused by atomism, the assumption that individuals are fundamentally separate and isolated from each other, and ultimately opposed to each other. But while the novel documents the harm caused by the Hobbesian war of each against all, its refutation of the faulty atomistic assumption that is partially responsible for this reality is much less explicit and thoroughgoing.

The atomistic assumption is prominent in *The Jungle*. It is articulated in explicit, propositional form by Tamoszius when he describes Packingtown as "a seething cauldron of jealousies and hatreds . . . [with] no loyalty or decency anywhere about it" (59).

Jurgis learns this lesson well, and soon he is seeing his life through the lens of atomism: "He had learned the ways of things about him now. *It was a war of each against all,* and the devil take the hindmost. You did not give feasts to other people, you waited for them to give feasts to you. You went about with your soul full of suspicion and hatred; you understood that you were environed by hostile powers that were trying to get your money, and who used all the virtues to bait their traps with" (74; emphasis added). Jurgis's atomistic vision is corroborated by the omniscient narrator's description of life in Packingtown, where people were "as busy *as ants—all hurrying breathlessly, never stopping to look at any thing nor at each other,*" and "the *solitary* trampish-looking foreigner . . . was as much *alone* as he hurried past them, as much *unheeded* and as *lost,* as if he had been a thousand miles deep in a wilderness" (168; emphasis added).

Eventually, everything in Jurgis's experience appears to confirm the atomistic notion that humans are basically separate from and at war with each other. Jurgis's desolate condition in a land of plenty, the general division of humanity into the haves and the have-nots, the hostility of the haves toward the have-nots, and the rampant greed and brutality of his fellow humans are evident to him not only in the gazes and actions of the people he encounters but also in the laws, institutions, and even the built environment of this society. The world appears to him "a world in which nothing counted but *brutal might,* an order devised by those who possessed it for the *subjugation* of those who did not." Life appears to him as a "fierce *battle of greed*" that he has lost. Everywhere he goes he feels "hostile eyes following him" and people "who were *deaf* to his entreaties, *oblivious* of his very existence—and *savage* and *contemptuous* when he forced himself upon them." He sees no place for himself anywhere: "every direction he turned his gaze, this fact was forced upon him" (221; emphasis added). Given such a view of human nature, the logical response is that of Jack Duane, who justifies the robberies he and Jurgis engage in with the rationale, "It's a case of us or the other fellow, and I say the other fellow every time" (240).

Propositional Knowledge and Metacognition

This atomistic view of humans appears more valid in *The Jungle* than the vision of socialism that the novel advocates. Indeed, neither the novel itself nor its major proponents of socialism explicitly refute the atomistic vision with arguments for ontological or psychological solidarity. Instead, they simply point out how terrible the atomistic reality is and then propose practical solidarity in the form of socialism as a strategy for mitigating or transcending this awful reality.

The millionaire socialist magazine editor, for example, explicitly subscribes to Social Darwinism and merely tries to counter it with solidarity at a practical level: "Life was a struggle for existence, and the strong overcame the weak, and in turn were overcome by the strongest. Those who lost in the struggle were generally exterminated; but now and then they had been known to save themselves by combination—which was a new and higher kind of strength" (309–310). Even the most extensive and systematic exposition of socialism—that given by Professor Schliemann, "a 'philosophic anarchist'"—ignores ontological and psychological solidarity and embraces an atomistic ontology and ethics, arguing "that the end of human existence was the free development of every personality, unrestricted by laws save those of its own inner being" (319). Schliemann's argument for the solidarity of socialism, like the editor's, is purely pragmatic rather than epistemological or ontological: it is a means of minimizing the terrible waste of human time, energy, and resources that occurs in the competitive capitalist system and maximizing "the positive economies of cooperation" (323).

Individual Exemplars of Solidarity

But while *The Jungle*'s propositional representations of solidarity emphasize its practicality for survival and flourishing without refuting the basic assumption of atomism, the novel presents characters, episodes, and life stories that embody a significant, if only implicit, refutation of atomism in providing a glimpse of the profound sameness and intrinsic interwovenness of all individuals. Emotional solidarity is evident in the novel's episodes, life stories, and individual exemplars of perspective taking, sympathy, generosity, belonging, and self-sacrifice.

Several individual exemplars of this sort are presented in the novel's opening scene of the wedding celebration, where we encounter a number of characters who are sacrificing their desire to marry (a desire that can itself be taken as evidence against atomism) in order to provide for relatives who depend upon them for their survival. Marija later sacrifices her hopes to marry Tamoszius and eventually subjects herself to prostitution in order to provide for Elzbieta and her family. These episodes exemplify practical solidarity, of course, but the generous response of the benefactors to this practical solidarity is motivated by emotional solidarity.

Solidarity Episodes

The novel also offers several significant episodes of solidarity in the experiences of empathy that characters have for each other. After he is imprisoned for attacking Ona's rapist, for example, Jurgis suffers much more severely from imagining what Ona is and will be going through than he does from his own imprisonment: "he saw the thing in its details; he lived it all, as if he were there" (150–151).

There are also episodes of empathy between strangers, such as that of the young settlement worker for Elzbieta and that of the woman at the socialist meeting for Jurgis. In the former instance, "as she listened [to Elzbieta's tale of Ona's death and the family's plight] the pretty young lady's eyes filled with tears, and in the midst of it she burst into weeping" (151), and in the second instance the young, beautiful, well-dressed "lady" addresses Jurgis as comrade and urges him to listen to the socialist orator (284–285).

The orator's speech is itself the most powerful episode of empathy in the novel, both expressing the orator's empathy for his audience and urging them to empathize with all suffering and oppressed people. He manifests empathy for the oppressed workers in his audience when he proclaims, "I have been in your place, I have lived your life, and there is no man before me here to-night who knows it better. I have known what it is to be a street-waif, a boot-black, living upon a crust of bread and sleeping in cellar stairways and under empty wagons. I have known what it is to dare and to aspire, to dream mighty dreams and to see them perish—to see all the fair flowers of my spirit trampled into the mire by the wild-beast powers of life" (287).

The speaker's empathy serves as a model for readers, and the prosodics of his speech induce readers, through the activation of their mirror neurons (see Iacoboni), to feel the same compassion and moral outrage that he does. Readers' empathic mirroring of the speaker's empathy is reinforced by their mirroring of the responses of the young lady and Jurgis, which are themselves the result of mirror-neuron responses to the speaker. This emotional contagion is evident first in the face of the lady, who is transfixed by the speaker: "She sat as one turned to stone, her hands clenched tightly in her lap, so tightly that he could see the cords standing out in her wrists. There was a look of excitement upon her face, of tense effort, as of one struggling mightily, or witnessing a struggle" (285). Jurgis is himself transfixed by the lady's face: "all his thoughts were for this woman's face. A feeling of alarm stole over him as he stared at her. It made his flesh creep. What was the matter with her, what could be going on, to affect any one like that?" (285). Jurgis's fixation on the woman directs his attention to the object of her attention, the speaker, whose powerful emotion then spreads to Jurgis through the prosodics of his speech: "and so Jurgis became suddenly aware of the voice trembling, vibrant with emotion, with pain and longing, with a burden of things unutterable, not to be compassed by words. To hear it was to be suddenly arrested, to be gripped, transfixed" (285). This is the state of the entire audience, for when the speaker paused, "there was an instant of silence, while men caught their breaths, and then like a single sound there came a cry from a thousand people" (287). And this audience includes attentive readers, who are also infected with these same emotions.

Solidarity Emotions

These emotions are reinforced when the speaker pleads with his audience to share his empathy for wounded and dying soldiers on the other side of the world as well as for the thousands of hungry, homeless, and desolate men, women, and children in Chicago. And the speaker's presentation of these individuals' situation and his vivid *images* of their wounded and suffering bodies constitute two additional powerful means of evoking these same emotions in his audience and in the novel's readers.

Here is his description of the soldiers being wounded and killed in battle, with vivid images of their bodily experiences that produce simulations of the same experiences in readers via their mirror neurons: "See the bodies of men pierced by bullets, blown into pieces by bursting shells! Hear the crunching of the bayonet, plunged into human flesh; hear the groans and shrieks of agony, see the faces of men crazed by pain, turned into fiends by fury and hate! Put your hand upon that piece of flesh—it is hot and quivering—just now it was a part of a man!" (289).

The speech proceeds to stoke the audience's and readers' feelings of anguish and outrage by providing descriptions of the living conditions of working people in Chicago, which engage readers in further simulations of their plight:

> Here in this city to-night ten thousand women are shut up in foul pens, and driven by hunger to sell their bodies to live. . . . And these women

are made in the image of your mothers, they may be your sisters, your daughters; the child whom you left at home to-night, whose laughing eyes will greet you in the morning—that fate may be waiting for her! To-night in Chicago there are ten thousand men, homeless and wretched, willing to work and begging for a chance, yet starving, and fronting in terror the awful winter cold! To-night in Chicago there are a hundred thousand children wearing out their strength and blasting their lives in the effort to earn their bread! There are a hundred thousand mothers who are living in misery and squalor, struggling to earn enough to feed their little ones! There are a hundred thousand old people, cast off and helpless, waiting for death to take them from their torments! There are a million people, men and women and children, who share the curse of the wage-slave, who toil every hour they can stand and see, for just enough to keep them alive; who are condemned till the end of their days to monotony and weariness, to hunger and misery, to heat and cold, to dirt and disease, to ignorance and drunkenness and vice! (289)

In addition to providing appraisals on the basis of which readers simulate the emotions of individuals actually experiencing these situations, this description evokes emotion through affect-laden concepts ("hunger," "misery," "struggle," "homeless," "wretched") and through triggering readers' memories of mothers, sisters, daughters, children, and familiars who may be similarly vulnerable, as well as of one's own past and current vulnerability, that intensify the emotions of distress, sympathy, and moral outrage.

This emotional contagion reaches its culminating point at the end of the speech, and the description of the audience's reaction evokes similar emotions in readers by working once again through simulations produced via their mirror neurons:

The audience came to its feet with a yell; men waved their arms, laughing aloud in their excitement. And Jurgis was with them, he was shouting to tear his throat; shouting because he could not help it, because the stress of his feeling was more than he could bear. It was his presence, it was his voice; a voice with strange intonations that rang through the chambers of the soul like the clanging of a bell—that gripped the listener like a mighty hand about his body, that shook him and startled him with sudden fright, with a sense of things not of earth, of mysteries never spoken before, of presences of awe and terror! There was an unfolding of vistas before him, a breaking of the ground beneath him, an upheaving, a stirring, a trembling; he felt himself suddenly a mere man no longer—there were powers within him undreamed of, there were demon forces contending, age-long wonders struggling to be born; and he sat oppressed with pain and joy, while a tingling stole down into his finger-tips, and his breath came hard and fast. The sentences of this man were to Jurgis like the crashing of thunder in his soul; a flood of emotion surged up in him—all his old hopes and longings, his old griefs and rages and despairs. All that he had ever felt in his whole life seemed to come back to him at once, and with one new emotion, hardly to be described. (291–292)

Readers' emotions are evoked here by Jurgis's physical prosodics—his shouting, his waving, his breathing—which are automatically mirrored by readers' brains.

These emotions experienced through reading the novel can have several long-term effects for readers. First, each experience of an emotion accustoms and habituates the reader to it, and renders it more accessible in the future, both in reading and in experiences outside the text. This increase in experiencing distress, sympathy, and moral anger will, in turn, alter readers' information processing in the direction of greater awareness of the factors that cause these emotions—specifically, the suffering of others, the sources of their suffering, and their sameness with oneself—which will then reinforce these emotions.

Solidarity Action Scripts

These emotions will also incline readers toward *actions* embodying the action tendencies inherent in the emotions—in this case, actions of assisting others in need and opposing the conditions and people that are responsible for their suffering.

In addition to constructing this action script, the novel also recruits the figure of Jesus to serve as the prime enactor of this script. The ex-preacher Comrade Lucas describes Jesus as "the man of sorrow and pain, the outcast, despised of the world, who had nowhere to lay his head" (316) and declares that he "was the world's first revolutionist, the true founder of the Socialist movement; a man whose whole being was one flame of hatred for wealth, and all that wealth stands for,—for the pride of wealth, and the luxury of wealth, and the tyranny of wealth; . . . who again and again, in the most explicit language, denounced wealth and the holding of wealth" (316–317). This assimilation of Jesus to the socialism action script provides a model and an inspiration for pursuing the overthrow of plutocracy and the establishment of a government of the people.

The Jungle operates further to establish in readers two primary subscripts for initiating this general action: educating and organizing (300, 318). Educating here means helping people "realize," as the socialist orator puts it, the ultimate causes of the profound and ubiquitous human suffering that engulfs the planet. And organizing means getting people to elect candidates who recognize these causes and are committed to eliminating them. The novel itself is a model for the type of educating that needs to occur to help people realize the ultimate causes of human suffering: replacing the autonomy, essentialism, and atomism schemas that constitute the heart of Social Darwinism and that keep people from apprehending the root causes of their suffering and uniting to eliminate these causes.

The outlines of this education are sketched in the awareness that Jurgis gradually accumulates throughout the novel of the systemic determinants and shared nature of his fate, an awareness that reaches full maturation in the socialist tutorial he receives near the end of the novel, which "set him upon a mountain-top, from which he could survey it all,—could see the paths from which he had wandered, the morasses into which he had stumbled, the hiding-places of the beasts of prey that had fallen upon him" (299). He now realizes that his misery and that of the other workers is caused not by the immutable laws of nature, or fate, but rather by the beef industry, which was "a gigantic combination of capital [that] had crushed all opposition, and overthrown the laws of the land, and was preying upon the people" (299).

Once Jurgis recognizes these root causes of his and others' misery and grasps his solidarity with the rest of humanity, the logical next step is to unite with his fellow human beings to eliminate these causes. This action is the second subscript promoted by *The Jungle*: to organize the workers into a socialist party that will elect government officials who will change the brutal and oppressive economic system. The novel ends with the action of voting as the means by which this new, more just social order can be brought into existence. In ending on this note, it offers readers a simple but far-reaching action script: educate and organize the people to elect a government of the people, by the people, and for the people. This action script is the logical outcome of the situationist, malleabilist, and solidary understanding of human misery that the entire novel has worked to make possible by promoting the development of the corresponding person-schemas.

CHAPTER 7

The Grapes of Wrath

My whole work drive has been aimed at making people understand each other.

JOHN STEINBECK

As he was composing *The Grapes of Wrath*, John Steinbeck wrote to his publisher, "My whole work drive has been aimed at making people understand each other" (quoted in DeMott xl). Although Steinbeck didn't specify what in particular he wanted to make people understand, critics have found that *The Grapes of Wrath* works to correct three widespread and harmful misunderstandings that people have about each other. First is their failure to recognize their profound interconnection with other people.[1] Second is the failure to see that other people are often less responsible for their successes and failures than is their situation (see Kirby 246–247; Lisca, *Wide* 165; and Owens, *Trouble* 101). And third is the denial that people's formative environment plays a major role in determining their character or personality (see Lisca, *Wide* 167–168; Railsback 225–229; Lancaster 436; Hicks 400–402; French 98–99, 106–107; Britch and Lewis 104ff.; Owens, *Re-Vision* 23; and Salter 138–152).

These misunderstandings are the product of the four faulty person-schemas: the first results from the atomism and homogeneity schemas, while the second and third are products, respectively, of the autonomy and essentialism schemas. Like *The Jungle, The Grapes of Wrath* contains features that can work to replace each of these faulty schemas with their more adequate counterparts, the schemas of situationism, malleability, solidarity, and heterogeneity.

Correcting the Autonomy Schema

It ain't the people's fault.
JIM CASY (128)

Propositional Knowledge and Metacognition

Propositional expressions of the principle that circumstances, not people, are responsible for bad actions or outcomes are frequent in *The Grapes of Wrath*, usually uttered by characters rejecting blame for their own or, more frequently, someone else's action. The man who tells Muley Graves he must abandon his farm says, "It ain't my fault. . . . It's the Shawnee Lan' an' Cattle Company. I just got orders" (50–51). Concerning the homicide Tom committed, Muley says, "ever'body knowed it wasn't no fault of yours" (56), and "Judge says he give you a light sentence 'cause it wasn't all your fault" (57). Jim Casy responds to the gas station owner's complaints about the migrants and the state of the country with the declaration, "it ain't the people's fault" (128). The manager of the government camp reassures Rose of Sharon that, contrary to the accusations of the fanatical religious woman, the two girls who miscarried in the camp were not to blame. "It wasn't their fault," he tells her. "I knew them too. They were too hungry and too tired. And they worked too hard. And they rode on a truck over bumps. They were sick" (310).

Most frequently it is Ma who utters the situationism principle. When she learns that Tom has killed Casy's murderer in self-defense, thus putting himself and the entire family in jeopardy, Ma reassures him: "It's awright. I wisht you didn' do it. I wisht you wasn't there. But you done what you had to do. I can't read no fault on you" (392). Similarly, when Rose of Sharon, growing ever more anxious over the fate of her unborn baby, risks exposing Tom by wailing hysterically and blaming him for the plight of herself and the baby, Ma tells her, "I know you can't he'p it, but you jus' keep your mouth shut" and says to Tom, "She can't he'p it. It's jus' the way she feels" (395). And when Rose of Sharon's worst fears are realized a few days later and her baby is stillborn, Ma reassures her, "You couldn' he'p it" (448), and tells Pa, "Don't take no blame" (443).

The fullest propositional articulation of the role of circumstances in producing behavior occurs in passages insisting that the cause of the present unrest in the country is not any supposed flawed character of the dispossessed farmers but rather economic conditions that fail to meet the farmers' quite ordinary and universal human needs, both material and psychological.

One emphatic passage makes this point explicitly and also exposes the failure of the great owners to realize it: "The great owners, striking at the immediate thing, the widening government, the growing labor unity; striking at new taxes, at plans; *not knowing* these things are *results, not causes. Results, not causes; results, not causes.* The causes lie deep and simply—the causes are a hunger in a stomach, multiplied a million times; a hunger in a single soul, hunger for joy and some security, multiplied a million times; muscles and mind aching to grow, to work, to create multiplied a million times" (151; emphasis added). In addition to providing explicit propositional knowledge of the true, situational causes of the present social disruption, this passage also engages readers in metacognition, directing their attention to the owners' "not knowing" the true causes of the disruption and prompting readers to recognize that this not knowing is itself actually the ultimate cause of the problem, since if the owners recognized the situational causes they could and would address them, if only to save themselves.

Readers are given a second experience of this metacognition several chapters later, in a passage that also reiterates, even more explicitly, that it is situation, not character, that produces revolution and that ignorance of this fact—that when certain circumstances prevail, certain behaviors of the masses are inevitable—is the ultimate cause of revolution:

And the great owners, who must lose their land in an upheaval, the great owners with access to history, with eyes to read history and to know the great fact, when property accumulates in too few hands it is taken away. And that companion fact: when a majority of the people are hungry and cold they will take by force what they need. And the little screaming fact that sounds through all of history: repression works only to strengthen and knit the repressed. The great owners *ignored* the three cries of history. The land fell into fewer hands, the number of the dispossessed increased, and every effort of the great owners was directed at repression. . . . The changing economy was *ignored*, plans for the change *ignored*, and *only means to destroy revolt were considered, while the causes of revolt went on*. (237–238; emphasis added)

These two passages not only provide readers with propositional knowledge of the ultimate causes, both material and cognitive, of social

How Protest Novels Work to Replace Faulty Person-Schemas

upheavals, but also engage them in a metacognition that they can use to detect the ultimate, situational, and cognitive causes of such problems when they encounter them outside the text.

Concepts Embodying Situationist Knowledge

The Grapes of Wrath also develops and promotes a number of concepts that tacitly acknowledge the power of circumstances to dictate behavior. For one, the novel invents a new concept in the notion of "got to," which refers to circumstances requiring that one deviate from norms of behavior and perhaps even break the law. The Joads first articulate this concept when Grandpa dies en route to California and they are forced to bury him illegally on the side of the road because they have neither the time nor the money to provide a proper, legal burial for him. Pa remarks that sometimes doing the right thing requires breaking the law, and Casy agrees: "'Law changes,' he said, 'but *got to's* go on. You got the right to do what you *got to* do'" (141; emphasis added).

Casy reiterates this point when Uncle John says he fears he is bringing bad luck to the family and should leave them. "I know this," Casy responds, "—a man *got to* do what he *got to* do. I can't tell you" (224; emphasis added). Later, when Uncle John is overcome with guilt for not acting like Casy and taking the fall for Tom's tripping of the deputy, he asks Pa for two dollars so he can get drunk to escape his feelings. Pa gives him the money, saying, "A fella *got to* do what he *got to* do. Nobody don' know enough to tell 'im. . . . You know what you *got to* do" (269; emphasis added). Casy also invokes the category of the "got to," just before he is killed, when he is lamenting the fact that so many people concern themselves only with short-term benefits and ignore the long-term benefits of collective action. Speaking of Al Joad, whose only concern is to find girls to have sex with, Casy says, "He's jus' doin' what he's *got to* do," and then he generalizes the category to apply to everyone, declaring, "All of us is like that" (385; emphasis added). Near the end of the novel, after Rose of Sharon's baby is stillborn and the floodwaters are rising, Ma invokes the category to reassure Pa: "Don't take no blame. Hush! It'll be awright. They's changes—all over. . . . We'll do what we *got to* do" (443; emphasis added). And in the novel's final, culminating scene, Rose of Sharon offers her breast to the starving man and insists, over his mute protestations of decency, "You *got to*" (453; emphasis added).

Episodes of Situatedness

In addition to such propositional and conceptual situationist knowledge, *The Grapes of Wrath* provides readers with numerous episodes of circumstances overriding character to determine behavior (*circumstances→~~character~~→behavior*) and of circumstances overwhelming behavior to determine life outcomes (*circumstances→ ~~behavior~~→outcomes*).

The novel begins with the episode of the dust storm, an overwhelming situation that both prevents and produces certain behaviors no matter what a person's character might be, and both prevents and produces certain outcomes no matter what behaviors the people might engage in. The narrative goes on to conduct readers through numerous episodes in which individuals' behaviors and destinies are determined by other physical circumstances that are less immune to human intervention but no less inexorable in determining the behaviors and destinies of the affected individuals. Such circumstances include lack of food, lack of transportation, and accidents. Lack of food forces people variously to sell or abandon their possessions, leave their homes, and seek work in California; to work for meager wages, and sometimes at predatory or destructive jobs, if they can find work; to steal, if they cannot find work; and in some cases to perish, when they can find no food to steal. Lacking transportation, Tom and Casy are forced to beg rides from the trucker and the Joads, respectively, and the Wilsons are stranded in a ditch until the Joads arrive and Tom diagnoses and fixes their plugged fuel line.

Particularly noteworthy instances of harmful behavior being instigated by economic circumstances are the banks' foreclosures of the farms and the bulldozer drivers' destruction of the farmhouses. The farmers are told that the owners and the representatives executing the foreclosures are simply doing what they have to in order to survive themselves: "all of them were caught in something larger than themselves" (34; see also 36). The same set of economic constraints reduces the bulldozer driver to a robotic appendage of the capitalist enterprise, controlling his consciousness and hence his behavior as well: "The man sitting in the iron seat did not look like a man; gloved, goggled, rubber dust mask over nose and mouth, he was a part of the monster, a robot in the seat. . . . The driver could not control it, . . . because the monster that built the tractor, the monster that sent the tractor out had somehow got into the driver's hands, into his brain and muscle, had goggled him and muzzled him—goggled his mind, muzzled his speech, goggled his perception, muzzled his protest" (38). These episodes reveal how capitalism establishes a set of social roles and relations that perpetuate the system and its attendant suffering and injustice by restricting and transforming the consciousness of individuals in ways that convince them—and function in other ways to guarantee—that there is no other course of action available to them and render them incapable of reflecting on or conceiving of an alternative system.

Episodes abound in which individuals are subject to catastrophic events that, like the hand of fate, strike them with no warning. There is the westbound land turtle, a clear metaphor for the migrants and for humans in general, which narrowly escapes being smashed when a woman swerves her car to miss it, then barely avoids destruction when a man narrowly fails in his effort to run it over with his truck, and is subsequently picked up, carried away, and finally released by Tom (19–20). Other brief episodes of individuals being struck down with no warning include Muley Graves's father being gored to death by a bull (54), the Jacobs' baby being eaten by a pig (44), the Joads' dog being run over and killed by a car on Route 66 (131), a child being killed in an accident on the same highway (159), and a woman's fingers being shot off by the errant bullet that the deputy fires at Floyd Knowles (264).

In addition to such episodes of inexorable material circumstances and events determining behavior and destiny, the novel takes readers early and often through episodes in which individuals' behaviors and destinies are determined, or at least constrained or triggered, by the actions of other individuals. Most notable are aggressive behaviors by other individuals that provoke, and at times appear to require, aggressive and even violent response. Examples include Tom's tripping the deputy who is shooting at Floyd Knowles and his killing of Casy's murderer in vengeance and self-defense.

In other cases, development of the *circumstances→behavior* episode script is promoted by incidents in which one person's behavior is the result of his or her autonomist bias concerning another person's behavior, which is itself the product of compelling circumstances that the first person initially fails to recognize, but finally does, and then alters his or her behavior as a result of this new, situationist understanding of the other person. In one such episode, Al, the owner of the hamburger joint, has a general attitude of disregard and even hostility toward his customers, as demonstrated by his manipulating the slot machines so that his customers rarely if ever win. However, when an impoverished traveler humbly begs the waitress Mae to sell him half a loaf of bread so that he, his wife, and their two young sons can have something to eat, Al is grudgingly moved by their plight and the man's "humility which was insistent" to overrule Mae's refusal to sell them half a loaf (which she claims would deprive the business of the bread it needs to make sandwiches for its customers), snarling, "Goddam it, Mae. Give 'em the loaf!" (161). Al's simultaneous upbraiding of Mae and generosity toward the family constitutes a significant alteration of Mae's situation, his upbraiding angering her and his generosity shaming her for her own lack of generosity. Mae responds to this new situation by not only giving the man the bread but also selling him ten cents' worth of candy for a penny, an act that is at once generous to the family and aggressive toward Al. Mae's act of generosity, in turn, alters the situation for two truckers who witness it, and this new situation causes them to rethink their initial tip and leave her one three times as large (162).

Additional episodes of this sort include the Joads' encounter with the truculent gas station owner and Ma's encounter with the snide company store clerk. In these episodes (which will be discussed in more detail later), when the first person does recognize that it is the second person's circumstances rather than his character that is the primary cause of his hostile attitude and aggressive behavior, the first person's behavior changes dramatically from anger to compassion. And this change constitutes a significant alteration of the situation of the second person, whose own aggressive behavior consequently is dramatically reduced as well, thus demonstrating how the vicious circle of social conflict can be broken if one party can recognize that it is the other's situation and not his character that is primarily responsible for his aggressive behavior and respond to him in light of this understanding.

Situationist Life Stories

The Grapes of Wrath is also replete with situationist life stories, biographies taking the form of *rags→rags, rags→rags→death*, or *hope→ rags(→death)*, which work to correct the *rags→hard work→riches* situationist life script at the core of American ideology.

The Joads' lives are the most salient and powerful exemplars of these situationist life scripts. Their life up to the beginning of the novel has been one of *subsistence→ hard work→rags*. The novel itself charts their movement from hope for a better life in California to disillusionment, death, desperation, and uncertainty: by the end of the novel, Noah and Rose's husband, Connie, have abandoned the family; Grampa, Granma, and Rose's baby are dead; Tom has been forced to flee for his life; and the rest of the family is without food, taking refuge in an abandoned barn—all as a result of circumstances beyond their control. Each of these lives contributes to the formation of the situationist life script of ~~rags→hard work→~~*bad luck→rags→death*, which, when fully developed, will enable readers to recognize the degree to which failure in life is due not to lack of effort, ability, or virtue but to lack of viable circumstances.

Individual Exemplars of Situatedness

The novel also provides readers with numerous other individual exemplars of situatedness, in the form of minor characters who, like the Joads, either have perished, are perishing, or are struggling to survive in dire circumstances that they did not produce, cannot control, and could not have foreseen.

Muley Graves, Ivy and Sairy Wilson, Floyd Knowles, Tim and Wilkie Wallace, and the Wainwrights are among the named characters whose life histories and current conditions illustrate the overwhelming impact of circumstances. And there are also memorable anonymous exemplars, such as the man at the campground who is returning from California after watching his children starve there, the anonymous man on the highway staring mutely at the body of his dead child, the famished children gathered around Ma Joad's pot of stew hoping for a handout, the two boys staring in awe at the candy behind the glass of Mae's counter, briefly glimpsed trudging men looking for work, and so on. Readers who commit to memory these walking demonstrations of the power of circumstances in determining behavior and destiny will be more likely to take into account the situational determinants of the behaviors and life conditions of people in the world outside the text.

Situationist Images and Emotions

As in *The Jungle*, *The Grapes of Wrath*'s foregrounding of the circumstantial causes of characters' behaviors and life outcomes evokes sympathy for the characters and anger at the system that produces these circumstances, and readers' repeated experience of these emotions in relation to their respective objects increases their inclination to experience the same emotions toward similar extra-textual objects.

In addition to evoking these emotions through its appraisals of the characters as exculpated by their situations, the novel also does so through engaging readers in two types of empathy: involuntary mimicry and perspective taking. Involuntary mimicry is elicited by the images of damaged, suffering, and struggling bodies, both human and animal, which evoke simulations in readers' brains by activating their mirror neurons. The image of the land turtle's being hit by the truck and then struggling to right itself is one such instance: "Lying on its back, the turtle was tight in its shell for a long time. But at last its legs waved in the air, reaching for something to pull it over. Its front foot caught a piece of quartz and little by little the shell pulled over and flopped upright" (19). A similar but more painful empathy is evoked by the image of the Joads' dog being hit by a car: "A big swift car whisked near, tires squealed. The dog dodged helplessly, and with a shriek, cut off in the middle, went under the wheels. The big car slowed for a moment and faces looked back, and then it gathered speed and disappeared. And the dog, a blot of blood and tangled, burst intestines, kicked slowly in the road" (131). The visceral simulation elicited by this image is modeled by the response of young Winfield, who tries unsuccessfully to mask his distress with bravado and then vomits (132).

Empathic mimicry is also elicited in readers by images of suffering human bodies, such as that of Sairy Wilson: "The tent flaps opened and a wizened woman came out—a face wrinkled as a dried leaf and eyes that seemed to flame in her face, black eyes that seemed to look out of a well of horror. She was small and shuddering. She held herself upright by a tent flap, and the hand holding onto the canvas was a skeleton covered with wrinkled skin" (135). Other distressing images of human bodies include the dying Grampa, muttering incoherently with his arms and legs twitching (136–137); the one-eyed man at the wrecking yard, whose "uncovered socket squirmed with eye muscles when his good eye moved," whose clothes were filthy and whose hands were cracked and cut (178); the dying children of the man returning from California, "little fellas layin' in the tent with their bellies puffed out an' jus' skin on their bones, an' shiverin' an' whinin' like pups" (191); the woman at the Hooverville whose knuckles are blown off by the deputy's stray bullet, staring in horror at her fingers, which "hung on a string against her palm" (264); the murderous clubbing of Casy's head, "the heavy club crash[ing] into the side of his head with a dull crunch of bone" (386); Tom's crushed and bleeding nose (387); and Rose of Sharon's dead baby, "a blue shriveled little mummy" lying on a newspaper (442).

The body postures and facial expressions of people in distress also evoke empathic mimicry via readers' mirror neurons. Instances include the brief snapshot of the desolate father staring mutely at the body of a child just killed in an auto accident (159), the description of the impoverished boys staring in awe at the candy behind Mae's counter (161), the circle of fifteen hungry children lusting after the stew Ma is cooking (252), and the "hard smothered sobbing" of Tom after he has been humiliated by the vigilantes (280). In addition to evoking sympathy, and in some cases anger, in readers, these images embody powerful evidence of situatedness. Readers who commit to memory these striking visual exemplars of the power of circumstances in determining behavior and destiny, together with the powerful emotions they evoke, will be more able and more likely to take into account, and respond with similar emotions to, the situational determinants of the behaviors and life conditions of people in the world outside the text.

In addition to being evoked by such images, sympathy is also elicited by the novel's provision of three types of empathy-inducing information: (1) portrayals of the Joads' and other migrants' difficult and desperate situations, (2) descriptions of their subjective experiences of (thoughts and feelings about) these situations, and (3) presentations of their behavioral responses to these situations. The following passage describing the trip to California in unreliable cars and on a very tight budget includes all three types of information, thus eliciting empathy in readers and, through the empathy, sympathy for the travelers:

'F we can on'y get to California where the oranges grow before this here ol' jug blows up. 'F we on'y can . . .

In the day ancient leaky radiators sent up columns of steam, loose connecting rods hammered and pounded. And the men driving the trucks and the overloaded cars listened apprehensively. . . . If something breaks—well, if something breaks we camp right here while Jim walks to town and gets a part and walks back and—how much food we got?

Listen to the motor. Listen to the wheels. Listen with your ears and with your hands on the steering wheel; listen with the palm of your hand on the gear-shift lever; . . . for a change of tone, a variation of rhythm may mean—a week here. . . . Jesus, if it's a bearing, what'll we do? Money's goin' fast. (120)

Throughout the novel, accounts of the migrants being swindled as they sell their possessions and buy cars and parts; leaving behind the families, friends, homes, farms, tools, animals, and other things that give them a sense of self; running out of food and money; desperately seeking work without success; obtaining work only to find that it doesn't pay a living wage; being threatened, evicted, and beaten by deputies and vigilantes; seeing loved ones die or desert them; and other difficult experiences repeatedly engage readers in acts of perspective taking that produce sympathy for the migrants and, in some cases, anger toward their oppressors.

These repeated experiences of empathy and sympathy also function to train readers in the sorts of attention, recollection, inference, and other information-processing routines that lead to empathy and the resultant sympathy, thus enhancing the capability and inclination of readers to experience sympathy for individuals who are overwhelmed by their circumstances.

Situationist Actions

Finally, the action tendency of helping, which is an integral part of the emotion of sympathy and of the situationism schema as a whole, is reinforced and given direction in *The Grapes of Wrath* by the portrayal of numerous episodes of helping in response to the helper's perception of the recipient's difficult situation.

The most notable instances of helping involve providing a hungry person with food or drink. Examples include Tom giving Casy a drink from his whiskey bottle, Muley Graves sharing his rabbits with Tom and Casy, the Joads inviting Casy to breakfast, Mae and Al giving the family bread and candy, Ma letting the hungry children have a taste of her stew, the Wallaces feeding Tom breakfast, the company store clerk lending Ma a dime for sugar, and Rose of Sharon nursing the old man.

There are also other instances of generosity motivated by sympathy for the plight of the aid recipient: the trucker giving Tom a ride in spite of the risk, Casy helping Ma with her chores even though they are considered "woman's work," the gas station owner burying the Joads' dog, the Wilsons and Joads helping each other, Floyd Knowles and the Joads helping each other, Casy helping Floyd escape, and the Wallaces giving Tom part of their work.

Such episodes construct a helping script by repeatedly inducing readers' brains to simulate the intentions and actions they are reading about (see Iacoboni 94–95), and this helping script is linked to the feeling of sympathy and embedded in the situationism schema, thus increasing the likelihood that when readers perceive the difficult situations of people outside the text and feel sympathy for them, they will also take action to assist them.

But in addition to the action of helping others cope with their difficult situations, the situationism schema entails the more fundamental action of altering their difficult situations. And this means changing the unjust economic system that is responsible for most of the difficult situations people encounter in the novel. Being attuned to the situational determinants of human behavior leads to the realization that, at least in the case of the injustices perpetrated by the agents of capitalism, "there's nobody to shoot" (41)—that is, no individual is to blame for the eviction of the tenants and the destruction of their homes.

Preventing these injustices requires changing the system that variously allows, enables, entices, and coerces individuals to perform unjust and harmful actions. To the extent that individuals' consciousness and behavior are the result of circumstances beyond their control, they cannot ultimately be held responsible for the harm and injustice of which their actions are the immediate cause. And to the extent that these circumstances are a product of human institutions and systems rather than a force of nature, efforts to prevent harm and injustice should be directed toward changing the institutions and systems rather than the individual human slave-operators of the institutions and systems. As one farmer puts it, "There's some way to stop this. It's not like lightning or earthquakes. We've got a bad thing made by men, and by God that's something we can change" (41).

The imperative to change the economic system is presented most emphatically in chapter 25, in which Steinbeck emphasizes that it is not simply heartless owners who are depriving starving migrants of food; it is rather the situation the owners are placed in by the current system of commerce, in which "[t]he works of the roots of the vines, of the trees, must be destroyed to keep up the price." The novel elicits moral outrage in readers over the failure of a nation that has been able to produce such amazing crops to create a system whereby this agricultural bounty can be distributed to hungry children instead of destroyed to maintain prices: "the failure hangs over the State like a great sorrow. . . . There is a crime here that goes beyond denunciation. There is a sorrow here that weeping cannot symbolize. There is a failure here that topples all our success" (348–349).

This and other passages in *The Grapes of Wrath* work to induce in readers the development of an action script of system change as the ultimate end of their understanding of situationism and their feelings of moral outrage and sympathy for the victims of the current system. Prerequisite to such change, however, is another basic action: informing and educating the general public about (a) the harm and injustice caused by the present system and (b) the faulty ideological assumptions about human nature and behavior that naturalize, legitimize, and sustain the present system. This action of educating is modeled by the novel itself, and its particulars are exemplified by the features discussed in this chapter.

Training in Situationist Information Processing

The Grapes of Wrath trains readers in situationist information processing first and foremost by focusing their *attention* on, rather than allowing them to continue to ignore, both the circumstances influencing characters' behavior and the characters' experience of the compelling force of those circumstances.

The novel directs readers' attention to the unjust conditions and treatment out of which financial ruin and crime often arise, while most media accounts of (real or fictional) ruin or crime, in contrast, engage their audience in attending primarily to the financial failure or crime itself, ignoring both the situational forces operating on the actor and the actor's experience of these forces. This media focus not only leads the audience to commit the fundamental attribution error (seeing the agent's disposition as the sole cause of the action), but also reinforces the deficient attention script of the autonomy schema underlying this error.

The Grapes of Wrath, in contrast, fosters the more adequate attention script of the situationism schema by focusing readers' attention on the powerful physical, material, social, and cultural forces bearing down on people (as in the two cases in which Tom kills another man, as well as other instances in which the Joads and others break the law), and the resulting physical and psychological desperation they experience, which may leave them destitute, with virtually no options other than ruin and/or crime.

These same detailed enumerations of circumstantial determinants of behavior and conditions of existence also train readers' *expectations* and their *inference* and gap-filling processing routines, so that after reading several chapters of *The Grapes of Wrath*, we begin to *expect* circumstances to determine the success or failure of any effort that struggling individuals make to escape from their misery, and whenever we encounter a new character, we are able safely to *infer* on the basis of inconclusive evidence—and *suppose* in the absence of all evidence—that the character's life condition is largely if not totally the result of circumstances (either fortunate or unfortunate).

The Grapes of Wrath also works to alter routines of *memory search and retrieval*—for example, by prompting readers to recall certain specific types of memories when processing a particular type of situation. When reading of characters being harassed by police, being hungry, being separated from their families, or having little money and no job, readers may remember similar experiences of their own. The repeated recollections of such instances in which one's own behaviors or outcomes were determined more by one's circumstances than by one's character increase the ease and frequency with which such memories will come to mind in the future and serve as templates for processing the other's situation (see Schank).

The Grapes of Wrath also operates to replace *emotions* such as indifference, disdain, and contempt for victims of bad fortune (and confidence, pride, and self-satisfaction in response to one's own good fortune), which embody, activate, and reinforce the judgments of the autonomy schema, with emotions that incline readers to recognize and respond to the powerful role of circumstances in determining people's behavior and destiny. Such emotions, including sympathy, fear, sadness, anguish, and anger at fate and injustice, prompt readers to seek and find situational causes for characters' distress. For example, the novel's opening scenes of the Dust Bowl, with destitute families being driven from their land, evoke compassion and outrage by portraying the pain, anguish, and fear of the dispossessed families; picturing the expressions, postures, or actions that indicate these emotions; and describing, often in vivid, concrete detail, the bleak and dire circumstances that have produced their misery and desperation.

Each of these techniques works to produce corresponding emotions of fear, anguish, despair, sympathy, and/or moral anger in readers. The repeated experiencing of these emotions in association with their respective objects (workers and other poor people; big owners and capitalists) establishes associations between the emotions and types of people, such that future perceptions and thoughts of other instances of these types will be more likely to arouse, and be processed through, these respective emotions (see Bower and Forgas). In addition, the fact that each of these emotions embodies the assumption of external, circumstantial causes of distress, rather than internal, dispositional causes, inclines readers who are experiencing them to seek and find external, circumstantial causes concerning the particular character or characters to which the novel directs their attention.

With enough repetition, this emotional response, and the ensuing appraisal, can become the default, or prototypic, emotion governing the assessment of all people in distress.

Metacognition and the Correcting of Faulty Processing

In addition to providing readers with situationist exemplars with which to more adequately process information about other people, numerous scenes in the novel train readers to recognize and correct faulty information processing—not by explicitly pointing out the faulty processing but by representing it and prompting readers to recognize it and its harmful consequences.

One such instance occurs when, early in the novel, readers learn that Tom has been convicted of homicide but are not informed of the circumstances of the killing. As a result, readers operating with the autonomy schema may infer that Tom is a dangerous and violent man. When the circumstances of the killing are revealed in a later chapter, however, readers recognize that the situation, rather than Tom's character, was the primary cause of his action, and this information marks the inadequacy of their autonomy schema while also promoting the establishment of the more adequate situationism schema in its place and sowing the seeds of metacognition, through which readers can begin to attend critically to their own cognitive processing.

The novel portrays other acts of aggression in a similar manner, first presenting the act and allowing readers to attribute hostile intention and character to the agent, and then adding information about compelling or constraining circumstances that reveals the action to have been caused less by the actor's character than by the circumstances, many of which are economic or legal. Thus the bulldozer operators who drive the sharecroppers off their land appear malevolent until we learn that this work is the only way they can feed their families. Similarly, the bank officials who foreclose on the farms and the law enforcement officers who serve the eviction notices appear to readers, as to the farmers, to be villains until they inform us that they under orders from the holding companies back East who control the local banks. The deputies who harass the migrants in their roadside Hoovervilles also elicit anger until it is revealed that they are required to make a certain number of arrests each day in order to earn their wages. Readers likewise discover that the agitators who try to start a fight at the government camp are operating under similar economic duress, as is the farmer who reduces the wages of Tom and the Wallaces under orders from the Farmers Association.

Other scenes engage readers in sharing one character's faulty assessment of another character and then discerning the crucial omitted information concerning the second character's situation and revising the faulty judgment. In one of these episodes, mentioned earlier, the owner of a dilapidated gas station at which the Joads have stopped approaches them "looking truculent and stern" and unleashes a stream of complaints about the travelers who stop, those who don't, and the country in general, asking peevishly "what the country's coming to" (126). Tom attributes the man's complaining to his character and irritably upbraids him as a whiner, until he notices for the first time the man's desperate situation, as manifested in the physical details of the establishment and the owner himself:

> He looked at the gas pump, rusted and old, and at the shack behind it, built of old lumber. . . . And inside the open door of the shack Tom saw the oil barrels, only two of them, and the candy counter with stale candies and licorice whips turning brown with age, and cigarettes. He saw the broken chair and the fly screen with a rusted hole in it. And the littered yard that should have been graveled, and behind, the corn field drying and dying in the sun. Beside the house the little stock of used tires and retreaded tires. And he saw for the first time the fat man's cheap washed pants and his cheap polo shirt and his paper hat. He said, "I didn't mean to sound off at ya, Mister. It's the heat. You ain't got nothin'. Pretty soon you'll be on the road yourself. And it ain't tractors'll put you there. It's them pretty yella stations in town. Folks is movin'," he said ashamedly. "An' you'll be movin', mister." (129)

Tom's information processing in this scene provides readers with a metacognitive understanding, first, of the nature and consequences of flawed, autonomist information processing, exemplified by Tom's initial oblivion to the evidence all around him of the owner's desperate situation, and second, of the kind of attention, focus, information search, and inference required by a more adequate, situationist processing of information about other people, exemplified in Tom's subsequent cognitions. The scene's presentation of the concrete details of the owner's situation, together with Tom's final, situationist processing of them, and his shame at not having done so to begin with, provide readers both with a metacognitive perspective and a model of situationist information processing that they can use beyond the novel.

The scene further promotes metacognition by demonstrating the power of the situation in action. First, Tom's recognition that it is the owner's situation and not his character that is responsible for his attitude changes Tom's (perceived) situation: instead of being confronted by an irritating complainer, Tom realizes that he is actually in the presence of an anxious, suffering victim of circumstances. This alteration of Tom's (perceived) situation, resulting from Tom's more adequate cognition, changes his emotion and hence his behavior toward the owner: instead of chastising him, he commiserates with him.

And this change in Tom's behavior constitutes an actual change in the owner's situation: instead of being confronted by a testy customer, he is now being offered sympathy by a fellow human being. As a result of this altered situation, the owner's behavior toward the Joads changes from confrontation to kindness, such that when the Joads' dog is hit and killed by a car moments later, he generously offers to undertake the onerous task of digging a hole in the hard, baked soil of the blistering cornfield and bury the dog for the Joads (131). This scene fosters readers' metacognition by dramatically demonstrating (1) the power of (perceived) situation to determine behavior, (2) the importance of recognizing people's situations before passing judgment on them and responding to them, and (3) the efficacy of changing people's behavior by changing elements of their situations that one can control, such as one's own attitudes and behaviors toward them.

This exercise in metacognition and corrective information processing is repeated later in the novel, in Ma's encounter with the snide clerk in the company store at the peach orchard (375–376). Ma is initially angered by the man's rude behavior (374), because she has not considered that his situation may be the cause. But when she learns that he doesn't own the store but only works there, she draws the situationist inference that his rudeness is due not to some meanness of character but rather to his shame at his need for the job and his consequent complicity in the company's price gouging. This inference changes Ma's (perceived) situation from a confrontation with a rude man to an encounter with a clerk who is ashamed, and this new (perceived) situation produces a change in Ma's tone, demonstrating the situationist principle.

This principle is demonstrated again by a change in the clerk's behavior: the change in Ma's tone constitutes a sufficient change in the man's actual situation so that he no longer needs to be defensive and rude, and when Ma asks if she can have ten cents' worth of sugar on credit and he informs her that he is under strict orders not to extend credit to anyone, he proceeds to lend her a dime of his own money so she can get the sugar (376).

In a third scene, readers are induced to identify the faulty, autonomist information processing in the absence of its recognition by those engaged in it. Here one gas station attendant, watching the Joads pull onto the highway toward the Mojave desert, comments to another attendant that the Joads must be senseless and subhuman to attempt such a trip in their old wreck, completely ignoring the fact that the Joads' situation affords them no alternative (221). Readers, however, are acutely aware of the Joads' lack of options (a point that Tom himself had just made to the attendant's partner [220]) and are thus able to recognize how completely flawed—and profoundly unjust—the attendant's social information processing is.

Through such repeated observations and experiences of the inadequacy of autonomist information processing, readers develop the capability and habit of attending to their own processing and including in it the situational factors that the autonomist schema excludes.

Correcting the Essentialism Schema

[T]hey . . . changed as in the whole universe only man can change. (196)

Propositional Knowledge and Metacognition

The knowledge that people are the product of their environment more than of some supposed inherent essence or personal choice is presented in propositional form on several occasions by *The Grapes of Wrath*. Early on readers hear from a tenant farmer that owning "a little property" makes one bigger in a certain way, while owning more property than one can see or work with one's hands diminishes one and turns one into a servant. Such an owner "can't do what he wants, he can't think what he wants. The property is the man, stronger than he is. And he is small, not big. Only his possessions are big—and he's the servant of his property" (40). Later, readers are told that "the quality of owning freezes ['the great owners'] forever into an 'I,' and cuts [them] off forever from the 'we'" (153).

Readers are also informed that being on the road changes the farmers into migrants and are given detailed knowledge of how such transformation occurs—namely, it is the result of the different sensations, challenges, and threats the farmers encounter on the road, which require different cognitive activities and physical actions in order to cope with them: "The movement changed them; the highways, the camps along the road, the fear of hunger and the hunger itself, changed them. The children without dinner changed them, the endless moving changed them. . . . And the hostility changed them, welded them, united them" (282).

The novel also states quite explicitly that those who are generally thought to be bad people—criminals and revolutionaries—are a product of their living conditions. Casy reports to Tom that he realized when he was in jail that "what made [the other prisoners] bad was they needed stuff. An' I begin to see, then. It's need that makes all the trouble" (382). The novel makes a similar point about revolutionaries, explaining that they are not born revolutionaries but are made such by need. "Paine, Marx, Jefferson, Lenin were results, not causes," the narrator explains (153). The causes of such men and their actions are unfulfilled human needs: "a hunger in a stomach, multiplied a million times; a hunger in a single soul, hunger for joy and some security, multiplied a million times; muscles and mind aching to grow, to work, to create, multiplied a million times" (151).

Malleability Episodes

In addition to providing such propositional articulations of human malleability, *The Grapes of Wrath* also provides readers with exemplars of the formative and transformative effects of three types of experience—traumatic, epiphanic, and quotidian—that will henceforth enable readers to more readily and adequately expect, search for, remember, and focus on malleability in human events that they witness or think about.

Episodes of transformation by traumatic experiences include the dispossession of their land suffered by Pa, Grampa, Muley Graves, and countless other farmers. Muley Graves tells Tom and Casy that Pa has not been the same since he saw the bulldozer run into his house (49), and when Grampa dies on the road to California, Casy tells the Joads, "Grampa didn' die tonight. He died the minute you took 'im off the place" (147). Uncle John, we are informed, changed profoundly years ago when his wife and unborn baby died as a result of a ruptured appendix that John dismissed as a stomach ache until it was too late. "The death of his wife," we are told, "followed by months of being alone, had marked him with guilt and shame and had left an unbreaking loneliness on him" (98; see also 70). Milly Jacobs was similarly traumatized when a pig ate her unattended baby: "Never did get over it. Touched ever since," Tom reports (44). Pa Joad was also changed by guilt, his over his belief that he mishandled the birth of his oldest son, Noah, who has a misshapen head and suffers from what today would probably be diagnosed as some form of autism (80).

There is also the case of Pretty Boy Floyd (to which Ma keeps referring), whose treatment by law-enforcement officers transformed him from a high-spirited youth into a vicious criminal, as Ma describes: "He done a little bad thing an' they hurt 'im, caught 'im an' hurt him so he was mad, an' the nex' bad thing he done was mad, an' they hurt 'im again. An' purty soon he was mean-mad. They shot at him like a varmint, an' he shot back, an' then they run him like a coyote, an' him a-snappin' an' a-snarlin', mean as a lobo. An' he was mad. He wasn't no boy or no man no more, he was jus' a walkin' chunk a mean-mad" (78).

Other transformative experiences are epiphanic rather than traumatic. Two such instances involve the ex-preacher Jim Casy, whose first epiphany, which took place when he went into the wilderness to sort through his confusions about sin, transformed him from a preacher into a listener, and whose second epiphany, which occurs when he is in jail after confessing (falsely) to tripping the deputy, transforms him from a listener into a labor organizer. A third instance of epiphanic malleability is Tom's transformation into a labor organizer as a result of thinking about Casy and remembering his words (419).

Just as the accumulated influence of a powerful personality can result in a transformative epiphany, so can the influence of a powerful story. Steinbeck makes this point concerning stories the migrants share in their camps: "The story tellers, gathering attention into their tales, spoke in great rhythms, spoke in great words because the tales were great, *and the listeners became great through them*" (325; emphasis added). Steinbeck proceeds to demonstrate this point through a story about an epiphany regarding a trauma that itself evokes epiphanies in both the migrant listeners and the novel's readers concerning similar traumas. The story, told by a former soldier who fought against Geronimo, is of an Indian warrior who is shot by the storyteller and his comrades:

> They was a brave on a ridge, against the sun. Knowed he stood out.
> Spread his arms an' stood. Naked as morning, an' against the sun.

The Grapes of Wrath   **213**

Maybe he was crazy. I don' know. Stood there, arms spread out; like a cross, he looked. Four hundred yards. An' the men—well, they raised their sights an' they felt the wind with their fingers; an' then they jus' lay there an' couldn't shoot. Maybe the Injun knowed somepin. Knowed we couldn' shoot. Jes' laid there with rifles cocked, an' didn' even put 'em to our shoulders. Lookin' at him. Head-band, one feather. Could see it, an' naked as the sun. Long time we laid there an' looked, an' he never moved. An' then the captain got mad. "Shoot, you crazy bastards, shoot!" he yells. An' we jus' laid there. "I'll give you to a five-count, an' then mark you down," the captain says. Well, sir—we put up our rifles slow, an' ever' man hoped somebody'd shoot first. I ain't never been so sad in my life. An' I laid my sights on his belly, 'cause you can't stop a Injun no other place—an'—then. Well, he jest plunked down an' rolled. An' we went up. An' he wasn' big—he'd looked so grand—up there. All tore to pieces an' little. Ever see a cock pheasant, stiff and beauti-ful, ever' feather drawed an' painted, an' even his eyes drawed in pretty? An' bang! You pick him up—bloody an' twisted, an' you spoiled him—you spoiled him—you spoiled somepin better'n you; an eatin' him don't never make it up to you, 'cause you spoiled somepin in yaself, an' you can't never fix it up.

And the people nodded, and perhaps the fire spurted a little light and showed their eyes looking in on themselves. (325–326)

The storyteller has been permanently damaged—traumatized—by his epiphany that he has killed something better than himself, and the story, along with his question, invites his listeners and Steinbeck's readers to search their memories for a similar experience of having killed something better than themselves, thus promoting the development of metacogni-tion concerning such transformations as well as the possible produc-tion by readers of new, memory-based personal exemplars of traumatic-epiphanic transformation.

Malleability Life Scripts

People are also changed by experiences that are neither traumatic nor epiphanic but that produce no less profound transformations. Such experiences result from an alteration in living or working conditions, which requires transformations in consciousness, behavior, and person-ality in order to thrive or, in some cases, even survive, in the new con-ditions. Such malleability episodes have the structure: *Change in Situa-*

tion→Change in Behaviors→Cognitive-Emotional Changes→Change in Character. Thus when farmers lose their farms and become bulldozer drivers, fugitives, or migrants, their new working or living conditions change them into a different type of person. Such changes reveal the truth of the Marxist principle that one's forms of consciousness are the consequences of one's mode of production: different material environments and conditions of existence require people to engage in different modes of information processing—expectation, attention, and so on—in order to perform the sorts of labor necessary for them to survive.

One richly developed exemplar of this sort of malleability is the transformation of the bulldozer operator:

> He could not see the land as it was, he could not smell the land as it smelled; his feet did not stamp the clods or feel the warmth and power of the earth. He sat in an iron seat and stepped on iron pedals. . . .
> He did not know or own or trust or beseech the land. If a seed dropped did not germinate, it was no skin off his ass. If the young thrusting plant withered in drought or drowned in a flood of rain, it was no more to the driver than to the tractor. (38)

Another such exemplar is Muley Graves, who, when driven from his farm, turns to fugitive hunting and scavenging and is transformed by this altered mode of production. Tom observes that Muley, who remains on the land when he is evicted from his farm and his family leaves for California, has changed, when he advises hiding from rather than standing up to the deputies who come to investigate their cooking fire. Muley responds: "Yeah! . . . I was mean like a wolf. Now I'm mean like a weasel. When you're huntin' somepin you're a hunter, and you're strong. Can't nobody beat a hunter. But when you get hunted—that's different. Somepin happens to you. You ain't strong; maybe you're fierce, but you ain't strong. I been hunted now for a long time. I ain't a hunter no more" (60).

Other exemplars of such malleability are the farmers who become migrants. The novel describes in great detail the transformations in cognition, behavior, and eventually identity that occur as a result of their change in living conditions. The first change occurs as a result of the farmers' reliance on their automobiles to get them to California. This reliance demands a profound alteration in their information-processing routines of attention, categorization, inference, emotion, and action:

And the men driving the trucks and the overloaded cars listened apprehensively [*=attention*]. How far between towns. If something breaks—well, if something breaks we camp right here while Jim walks to town and gets a part and walks back [*=action script*] and—how much food we got?

Listen to the motor. Listen to the wheels. Listen with your ears and with your hands on the steering wheel; listen with the palm of your hand on the gear-shift lever; listen with your feet on the floor boards. Listen to the pounding of the old jalopy with all your senses: for a change of tone [*=attention*], a variation of rhythm may mean—a week here? That rattle [*=categorization*]—that's tappets [*=inference*]. Don't hurt a bit. But that thudding [*=categorization*] as the car moves along—can't hear that—just kind of feel it. Maybe oil isn't gettin' someplace [*=inference*]. Maybe a bearing's startin' to go [*=inference*]. Jesus, if it's a bearing, what'll we do [*=emotion*]? Money's goin' fast.

And why's the son of a bitch heat up so hot today? This ain't no climb. Le's look. God Almighty, the fan belt's gone [*=perception, emotion*]! Here, make a belt outa this little piece a rope [*=action script*]. (120)

The novel describes the transformation that this new mode of information processing produces in Al: "Al, at the wheel, his face purposeful, his whole body listening to the car, his restless eye jumping from the road to the instrument panel. Al was one with his engine, every nerve listening for weaknesses, for the thumps or squeals, hums and chattering that indicate a change that may cause a breakdown. *He had become the soul of the car*" (124; emphasis added). Getting to California requires directing all one's senses to the sounds, sights, smells, and feel of the car, and these changed modes of attention, concern, perception, emotion, and action eventually change one's personality or character:

And the thought, the planning, the long staring silence that had gone out to the fields, went now to the roads, to the distance, to the West. That man whose mind had been bound with acres lived with narrow concrete miles. And his thought and his worry were not any more with rainfall, with wind and dust, with the thrust of the crops. Eyes watched the tires, ears listened to the clattering motors, and minds struggled with oil, with gasoline, with the thinning rubber between air and road. Then a broken gear was tragedy. Then water in the evening was the yearning, and food over the fire. Then health to go on was the need and strength to go on, and spirit to go on. The wills thrust westward ahead of them, and fears that had once apprehended drought or flood now lingered with anything that might stop the westward crawling. (196–197)

The novel further describes how the changed material circumstances of the migrants produces a transformation in their social relations, behaviors, and values. As the migrants constructed campsites every night and dismantled them the next morning, they developed new practices, laws, and codes demanded by their new circumstances: "Then leaders emerged, then laws were made, then codes came into being. . . . The families learned what rights must be observed, . . . and the families learned, although no one told them, what rights are monstrous and must be destroyed, . . . because the little worlds could not exist for even a night with such rights alive" (194–195). These changes culminate in an alteration of the very nature, the identity, of the farmers: "Thus they changed their social life—changed as in the whole universe only man can change. *They were not farm men any more, but migrant men.* . . . The movement changed them, the highways, the camps along the road, the fear of hunger and the hunger itself, changed them. The children without dinner changed them, the endless moving changed them. *They were migrants*" (196, 282; emphasis added).

Another group of exemplars of this sort of incremental malleability is the parents and grandparents of the current California landowners, who are presented as having undergone an even more extensive series of transformations, from frantic thieves, to squatting farmers, to shopkeeping farmers, to slaveholding agricultural industrialists, when survival demanded changes in their mode of production. The ancestors of the current owners were originally "a horde of tattered feverish . . . frantic, hungry men" when they invaded California. Then they stole the land from the Mexicans and became squatters, "put[ting] up houses and barns . . . [and] turn[ing] the earth and plant[ing] crops" (231). As they became established, and their material conditions and modes of production changed, they themselves underwent further transformations in order to survive. Supplying the material, social, and emotional needs of family and community gives way to making the most money possible, which means ceasing to grow certain crops and raise certain livestock and beginning to grow others. These new crops, in turn, require new forms of labor (behavior) in planting, cultivating, and harvesting, and these new forms of labor require new types of laborers—slaves/serfs—

in order to maximize profit. As a result, the owners themselves become soft and out of touch, like the Mexican owners their grandparents stole the land from (231–233).

Developing the Heterogeneity Schema

I figured . . . I was a damned ol' hypocrite. But I didn't mean to be.
JIM CASY (24)

Episode Scripts

The Grapes of Wrath works to develop the heterogeneity schema in readers by presenting them with multiple episodes in which a character manifests two mutually contradictory attitudes or behaviors.

One noteworthy episode of simultaneous egoism and altruism occurs when Tom and Casy encounter Muley Graves at the abandoned Joad homestead. When Muley reveals the rabbits he has trapped, Casy asks him if he is going to share them. Muley fidgets in embarrassment and finally says he has no choice but to share, since Casy and Tom are hungry, indicating that, on the one hand, he is understandably reluctant to part with food that has been hard for him to come by, but that at the same time he can't not share his food with others when they too are hungry.

This same heterogeneity is evident in Al, the owner of a hamburger joint. When Mae the waitress initially refuses to sell bread to the migrant, Al growls, "God Almighty, Mae, give 'em bread" (160), his growling indicating his egoistic opposition to his own altruistic act. And lest Al's egoism be overlooked, the end of the scene shows him cheating his customers by cashing in one of his slot machines, which are rigged to deliver the jackpot at regular intervals that Al secretly charts. Mae's behavior also evinces heterogeneity. After Al shows her up by countermanding her refusal to sell the man the bread, she sells the entire loaf for ten cents and then, on top of that, sells the man ten cents' worth of candy for only one cent. These acts of generosity are simultaneously acts of aggression against Al for showing her up: her generosity costs Al money. Finally, when two truckers, one of whom has been a regular customer, observe Mae's generosity, they leave her seventy cents in tips rather than their usual twenty cents. When Mae sees that they have each left half a dollar rather than the customary quarter and calls after them that they have change coming, one of them responds, "You go to hell," as they walk out the door, the harsh response indicating the presence of a gruff toughness that is in conflict with their tenderhearted generosity (162). A similar instance of heterogeneity is found in the company store clerk, who, as we saw above, is initially coldhearted and rude to Ma but then reveals his compassionate and generous side by lending her money from his own pocket (375).

The most profound episode of heterogeneity, which engages readers in a metacognitive recognition of their own mutually contradictory qualities, involves the story of the killing of the magnificent Indian warrior, quoted above. The storyteller recalls how, after seeing the mutilated body of the brave he and his comrades had shot, he felt that he had spoiled something better than himself and that as a result he has also spoiled something in himself beyond repair. He is aware that his act of killing triumphed over his more human and humane side, which had prevented him from firing on the brave, and that, having committed the act of killing, he has done irreparable damage to his humane side. This act of recognition manifests both sides: his inhumane side, which he recognizes as the agent of his act of killing, and his humane side, which is reflecting on and feeling guilty about the inhumane side and its killing. Readers are prompted to engage in a similar act of self-reflection, when the storyteller asks his audience if they have ever felt this way after, for example, killing a beautiful cock pheasant. The text suggests that they have indeed had such an experience: "And the people nodded, and perhaps the fire spurted a little light and showed their eyes looking in on themselves" (326). This introspection on the part of the storyteller's audience, itself induced by the storyteller's own introspection, here functions as a model for the novel's readers to emulate and search their memories for instances in which they, too, felt that they had spoiled something better than themselves and hence something in themselves as well. This prompt engages readers in expecting, attending to, searching for, recalling, or perhaps inferring such negative qualities in themselves, and exercising these information-processing activities develops their ability to apprehend such heterogeneity in others as well as in themselves.

The language in this scene also works to promote metacognition of collective heterogeneity in respect to Euro-American civilization more generally. It suggests that the killing of the brave is like the crucifixion of Jesus—that is, the killing of a divine being by ignorant, frightened people. The brave is presented as a Christ figure, standing "naked as morning, an' against the sun . . . arms spread out; like a cross, . . . [a]gainst

The Grapes of Wrath 219

the sun, with his arms out. An' he looked big—as God" (325, 326). The killing of the brave recalls, furthermore, the Oklahoma homesteaders' killing of Indians when they claimed the Indians' land, and as such it prompts readers to recognize that in perpetrating the genocide of Native Americans, Euro-Americans killed something better than themselves and, in so doing, the best part of themselves as well.

Such a recognition can constitute the first increment in the development of a heterogeneity schema through which (Euro-)American readers can recognize their own immoral and murderous actions and impulses and the morally superior aspects of peoples they continue to denigrate and destroy. Something like this was perhaps what Steinbeck had in mind when he wrote, concerning the stories told at the camps, that "the listeners became great through them" (325): readers are enlarged by using such episodes of heterogeneity as templates that enable them to recognize heretofore unacknowledged parts of themselves and others—specifically, the savage parts of themselves and the noble parts of others they have dismissed as savages.

Heterogeneity Life Scripts

The Grapes of Wrath also reveals heterogeneity diachronically, by having a given character manifest one quality in one situation and the opposite quality in another set of circumstances. In so doing, it shows situatedness and malleability to be functions of heterogeneity. That is, a person can manifest mutually contradictory qualities in two different situations only if he or she possesses both qualities, and a person can be transformed into a different sort of person only if these new qualities were already present in the person in nascent form.

Lives that reveal diachronic heterogeneity include those of Tom, Casy, Uncle John, Ma, Pa, and Rose of Sharon. Tom is, at different times, both a killer and a Christ figure, both confrontational (e.g., to the truck driver, the gas station owner [at first], and the one-eyed man in the wrecking yard) and conciliatory (e.g., to the gas station owner [later], to the vigilantes, and to the guard at the peach camp). Casy reveals himself to be spiritual at one moment and carnal the next. Uncle John similarly lives a life of ascetic restraint, guilt, and reparation, punctuated by episodes of extreme self-indulgence (trying to eat an entire hog by himself, hiring prostitutes, getting drunk). Ma becomes increasingly self-assertive and at times even mean as the family's situation becomes more dire, but she continues to exhibit gentleness and compassion from time to time. Pa becomes increasingly passive, submissive, and despondent as the novel progresses, yet he responds to the flood with vigorous assertiveness. And Rose of Sharon begins the novel completely self-involved and ends it with an act of profound generosity as she suckles the starving man.

Each of these characters, like the protagonists of the preceding episodes, serves as an exemplar of the complexity and self-contradictions that characterize every person, and by encoding these characters in their memory as exemplars of heterogeneity, readers become more able and more inclined to recognize the heterogeneity of real people they encounter or think about.

Prototypic Emotions and Action Scripts

Recognition of a person's heterogeneity replaces the emotions of hatred and adoration with more tempered and ambivalent feelings and leads to action scripts involving forbearance, mercy, and generosity rather than punishment or subservience. The forbearance script is enacted, for example, by Pa's giving Uncle John money so he can get drunk, by Ma's recognition that Tom couldn't help killing Casy's murderer and that Rose of Sharon couldn't help blaming Tom for her lack of adequate nourishment, and by the Joads' and Wainwrights' not condemning Al and Aggie for being sexually active before marriage.

Other examples of actions that contribute to the construction of a forbearance script based on recognition of heterogeneity include the government camp manager's treatment of Ma and the religious fanatic (and apparent epileptic) Mrs. Sandry. Recognizing that she is ill and can't help herself, the manager works to contain Mrs. Sandry's actions and mitigate the harm she has done, rather than condemning and punishing her for upsetting Rose of Sharon and others with her vicious and harmful words. And instead of *ordering* Ma not to hit Mrs. Sandry, he asks her to *try* not to hit her, recognizing that Ma may not be able to keep from hitting Mrs. Sandry but trying to help her refrain from doing so by offering her encouragement and understanding.

A similar forbearance is enacted at the camp with the outside agitators who try to start a fight so the deputies can come in and shut down the camp. The security committee recognizes that the agitators are not entirely bad individuals and so, rather than beating them, tries to help them understand the consequences of their actions, including the harm they will ultimately be doing to themselves if they succeed in getting the camp shut down.

The most thoroughgoing enactments of forbearance motivated by recognition of heterogeneity are those of Jim Casy. The first such act involves Casy's rejection of the very notions of sin and virtue, asserting that "some of the things folks do is nice, and some ain't nice, but that's as far as a man got a right to say" (26). Casy also recognizes that while "got to's" sometimes come from circumstances, at other times they result from negative character traits over which people have no control but which do not totally define the people. He thus recognizes that the fact that Uncle John can't keep from getting drunk at times and that Pa and many others can't forego meat today in order to support the strike does not make them homogeneously bad people, and so he refrains from condemning them. And he even eschews violence against his killers, realizing at his final moment, like Jesus, that his killers aren't simply evil but rather that they don't know what they're doing—that they are acting out of fear and ignorance in trying to destroy the union of striking workers.

Correcting the Atomism Schema

Maybe all men got one big soul ever'body's a part of.
JIM CASY (27)

Propositional Statements

The Grapes of Wrath includes multiple propositional statements concerning each form of solidarity: practical, psychological, and ontological.

The fact that everyone is interconnected at a *practical, economic* level is made explicit numerous times in the novel. It is expressed in several statements indicating that one person's gain is another's loss, such as when the tenant tells the bulldozer driver that his actions are rendering nearly a hundred people homeless (40), and when Tom tells the campground owner that he wishes there were some way for him to make a living without taking it away from someone else by charging exorbitant camping fees (188). The point is also clear, if somewhat less explicit, in the migrant's statement that "Grampa took his lan' from the Injuns" (236) and in Ma's statement to the hungry children that she "can't rob the family" to feed them (257).

Solidarity at the practical level is also articulated in statements on the importance of mutual aid. Tom makes this point when he suggests that the Joads and Wilsons travel together (149). A man at the government camp observes that the solidarity of the migrants in the camp protects them from the police harassment suffered by migrants outside the camp and suggests that establishing a similar solidarity outside the camp through unionizing would solve the problem of low wages (357). Casy makes the same point at the strikers' camp outside the peach orchard (383). And in his last conversation with Ma, Tom recalls a similar point that Casy had made by quoting Ecclesiastes: "'Two are better than one, because they have a good reward for their labor. For if they fall, the one will lif' up his fellow, but woe to him that is alone when he falleth, for he hath not another to help him up'" (418). Solidarity constitutes "a kind of insurance," the novel suggests: "A man with food fed a hungry man, and thus insured himself against hunger" (195–196). Conversely, the rejection of solidarity, it is suggested on several occasions, puts one at risk. As Huston tells the would-be agitators at the government camp, "You're jes' harmin' yourself" (344). Casy makes the same point to Tom about the scabs: "Tell 'em they're starvin' us an' stabbin' theirself in the back," he says (383).

Psychological solidarity also receives propositional articulation. Sairy Wilson experiences psychological solidarity in the form of the need she feels to help others. "We're proud to help," she tells Ma. "People needs—to help" (142). The ruthless automobile merchants recognize psychological solidarity in the experience of obligation: "Get 'em [i.e., potential customers] under obligation. Make 'em take up your time. Don't let 'em forget they're takin' your time. People are nice, mostly. They hate to put you out" (64). Casy experiences psychological solidarity in the form of love, stating that his love for people makes him want to make them happy: "I love people so much I'm fit to bust, sometimes . . . , an' I want to make 'em happy" (26).

It is Casy who also provides the most direct statements concerning *ontological solidarity*, which he conceptualizes as a transcendentalist union of all people and, indeed, of all things. He suggests to Tom early on that "all men got one big soul ever'body's a part of" (27), and in the grace he says at the Joads' breakfast the next morning he describes the vision of ontological solidarity he experienced during his epiphany in the wilderness: "There was the hills, an' there was me, an' we wasn't separate no more. We was one thing. An' there was me an' the hills an' there was the stars an' the black sky, an' we was all one thing. An' that one thing was holy" (83).

Another form of ontological solidarity is articulated by Tom in his final conversation with Ma. When Ma asks him how she'll be able to know what's happened to him after he leaves, Tom muses:

Well, maybe like Casy says, a fella ain't got a soul of his own, but on'y a piece of a big one—an' then—. . . Then it don' matter. Then I'll be all aroun' in the dark. I'll be ever'where—wherever you look. Wherever they's a fight so hungry people can eat, I'll be there. Wherever they's a cop beatin' up a guy, I'll be there. If Casy knowed, why, I'll be in the way guys yell when they're mad an'—I'll be in the way kids laugh when they're hungry an' they know supper's ready. An' when our folks eat the stuff they raise an' live in the houses they build—why, I'll be there. See? God I'm talking like Casy. Comes of thinkin' about him so much. Seems like I can see him sometimes. (419)

The ontological solidarity Tom articulates here reflects the same mystical, transcendentalist oneness described by Casy: his essence, his soul, his spirit, exists not just in his body but in everyone else who thinks, feels, and acts as he does. But Tom's words also suggest another form of ontological solidarity, one that is a function of the formative impact that one person (in this instance Casy) can have on another (here, Tom): as Tom himself acknowledges, his listening to Casy and subsequently thinking about him and remembering his words, has significantly changed Tom, to the point that he is now speaking and acting like Casy. And his statement to Ma that "[w]herever they's a fight so hungry people can eat, [he'll] be there" and that he'll "be in the way kids laugh when they're hungry an' they know supper's ready" suggests that his spirit or soul— his essential being—is to be found in whatever human activities and enjoyments may result from his actions or from the same principles.

Solidarity Episodes

In addition to such propositional articulations, solidarity is also exemplified in numerous episodes in *The Grapes of Wrath*. Early on, the novel presents *practical solidarity* in the form of the ecological system of nature. Chapter 3 begins with a description of how even plant life is dependent on the wind and on other forms of life: "the grass heads were heavy with oat beards to catch on a dog's coat, and foxtails to tangle in a horse's fetlocks, and clover burrs to fasten in sheep's wool; sleeping life waiting to be spread and dispersed, every seed armed with an appliance of dispersal, twisting darts and parachutes for the wind, little spears and balls of tiny thorns, and all waiting for animals and for the wind, for a man's trouser cuff or the hem of a woman's skirt, all passive but armed with appliances of activity" (18).

Later, the novel presents practical solidarity at the human level through a generic episode of two families pooling their resources: "One man, one family driven from the land; this rusty car creaking along the highway to the west. I lost my land, a single tractor took my land. I am alone and I am bewildered. And in the night one family camps in a ditch and another family pulls in and the tents come out. . . . [T]wo men are not as lonely and perplexed as one" (152). This practical solidarity among humans finds its culmination in the extended episode of the Joads' stay at the government camp, where the residents share responsibilities, risks, and benefits and as a result achieve a secure, humane way of life that is disrupted only by the absence of sufficient work for everyone.

The novel also presents a number of other episodes demonstrating the economic and security benefits of practical solidarity. Black Hat, one of the residents of the government camp, relates the story of the Akron turkey shoot, in which union members foiled the union-busting efforts of the establishment by marching with their rifles five thousand strong through Akron out to their "turkey shoot" and back again, thereby demonstrating to the establishment their solidarity and their potential to respond with a substantial force of their own to any forceful attempts to disrupt their union (344–345). The jailhouse protest, recounted by Casy (382), which succeeds in procuring decent food for the prisoners, also demonstrates the efficacy of collective action, and the strike led by Casy at the peach orchard (378ff.) demonstrates both the potential of practical solidarity and the dire consequences when such solidarity is not achieved. And near the end of the novel, the collective action of building a dike, organized by Pa, succeeds in preventing the boxcar camp from flooding until a tree uprooted by the stream tears a hole in the dike (440–441).

The multiple episodes in which owners band together to fix wages and prices and intimidate the workers also demonstrate the efficacy of practical solidarity, albeit in a negative way. And even the episodes of tension and conflict between the owners and the migrants demonstrate the practical solidarity of these two groups, the fact that each group needs the other: the migrants need the owners to give them work, and the owners need the migrants to harvest their crops, as one of the migrants points out when he says, "how'd your goddamn crops get picked if it wasn't for us?" (333).

There are also numerous episodes demonstrating to readers the various forms of *psychological solidarity*. One form is the need for, and pleasure taken in, closeness, togetherness with other people. Sairy Wilson demonstrates this need when she asks Casy to pray for her. She explains

The Grapes of Wrath 225

that it is not prayer per se that she needs but rather "somebody close enough—to pray" (218), and she recalls the closeness she felt as a girl when she sang to people: "Folks use' ta come an' listen when I sung. An'—when they stood—an' me a-singin', why, me an' them was together more'n you could ever know. . . . They wasn't nothin' got in between me an' them. An'—that's why I wanted you to pray. I wanted to feel that clostness, oncet more" (218–219). Episodes of singing and dancing among the migrants, as well as preaching, drunkenness, and sex, are presented as other means of achieving such closeness (see 327–330). Casy manifests this need in his preaching, in his sexual encounters, in his desire to lead people, and in his desire to listen to them and live with them (96). The normality of this need for closeness is demonstrated by how strange we find its absence, in Noah and also in John during his ascetic periods (98).

Other episodes of psychological solidarity take the form of involuntary emotional attunement. After the devastating dust storm, the women attune to the men's mood and the children to their parents': "And the women came out of the houses to stand beside their men—to feel whether this time the men would break. The women studied the men's faces secretly, . . . and the children sent exploring senses out to see whether men and women would break. The children peeked at the faces of the men and women" (7). Later, the novel describes "the children listening with their souls to words their minds do not understand" (152).

In the Joad family, such emotional attunement is what enables the family to function. Ma serves as the emotional fortress, "the citadel of the family, the strong place that could not be taken." Her husband and children "could not know hurt or fear unless she acknowledged hurt and fear," and therefore "she had practiced denying them in herself. . . . She seemed to know that if she swayed the family shook, and if she ever really deeply wavered or despaired the family would fall, the family will to function would be gone" (76).

Psychological solidarity also manifests itself in mimicry, which is sometimes deliberate and conscious and other times involuntary and unconscious. When the pig is slaughtered, Winfield mimics it: "He stuck his finger against his throat, made a horrible face, and wobbled about, weakly shrilling, 'I'm a ol' pig. Look! I'm a ol' pig. Look at the blood, Ruthie!' And he staggered and sank to the ground, and waved arms and legs weakly" (105). Al's involuntary mimicry of Tom is more profound: "Al saw the dark brooding eyes of his brother, and the prison calm, the smooth hard face trained to indicate nothing to a prison guard, neither resistance nor slavishness. And instantly Al changed. Unconsciously he became like his brother" (87).

A bit later in the novel, there is a fleeting and easily overlooked episode that exemplifies the multitude of involuntary and unconscious acts of mimicry that psychologists have found people engage in whenever they are together and that are an important means of communication and mutual understanding. The gas station owner, who has been complaining to Tom and Casy about the state of the country, in which people are unable to make a living any longer, stops speaking. "He took off his silver hat and wiped his forehead with his palm. And Tom took off his cap and wiped his forehead with it" (128).

Psychological solidarity is also present in the previously discussed episodes of compassion and aversion to inflicting or acquiescing in another's suffering, including the episodes of Muley Graves sharing his rabbits with Tom and Casy, the Joads feeding Casy, the gas station owner burying the Joad's dog, the truckers leaving Mae a big tip, the Joads sharing food with the Wilsons, Ma giving the hungry children a taste of her stew, Al and Mae selling food at a discount to the hungry family, Floyd Knowles sharing dangerous information with Tom, the Wallaces sharing their breakfast and their work with Tom, the soldiers being unable to fire upon the brave, the store clerk lending Ma money to buy sugar, Ma and Tom arguing over who should take the seven dollars Ma has saved, the father starving himself so his son can have food, and Rose of Sharon breastfeeding the starving father.

The final encounter between Ma and Tom provides readers with two of the novel's most powerful episodes of practical, psychological, and ontological solidarity, demonstrating just how profoundly interwoven two individuals can be and the degree of self-sacrifice that such solidarity can entail. The first episode occurs when Ma tries to persuade Tom to take her last seven dollars so that he can flee the area to avoid capture for killing Casy's murderer:

"Hol' out your han', Tom. I got seven dollars here."

"I ain't gonna take ya money," he said. "I'll get 'long all right."

"Hol' out ya han', Tom. I ain't gonna sleep none if you got no money. Maybe you got to take a bus, or somepin. I wan you should go a long ways off, three–four hundred miles."

"I ain't gonna take it."

"Tom," she said sternly. "You take this money. You hear me? You got no right to cause me pain."

"You ain't playin' it fair," he said. (417)

As this interchange demonstrates, the self–other overlap between two people can at times be so thoroughgoing that one actually cares more for the other's safety and well-being than for one's own. Thus Ma makes the point to Tom that his vulnerability will cause her more pain than her own famine, and his reply, "You ain't playin' it fair," makes the paradoxical and ironic point that she is in a sense being unfair and even selfish by looking out for him at her own expense—because her suffering would cause him more grief than his own suffering would.

Their profound psychological and ontological solidarity here thus confronts Ma and Tom with a paradox: each wants above all to protect the other, but since each is himself/herself the other's most valued element of self, the best way to protect the other is to protect oneself. But since one's own most valued element of self is the other, the best way to protect oneself is to protect the other. This paradox demonstrates how profoundly interconstituted self and other can be. To the extent that one's self is interconstituted with other selves, it is impossible to separate one's own interests from the interests of these other selves. Since I need these other selves in order that I might continue to be who I am, I also need to care for these other selves. Moreover, the very act of caring for another provides me with a tacit, identity-supporting recognition: the other's needing or benefiting from my care demonstrates my value and significance. Thus in caring for the other, I am profoundly caring for myself as well. The converse is also true: since the other needs me, I am acting in an uncaring manner toward the other if I fail to care for myself.

The final encounter between Tom and Ma demonstrates to readers how both of these logics operate in the most intense and crucial of relationships, which include those between parents and children as well as those between romantic partners. Readers may be prompted by this episode to reflect on their own most intimate relationships and experience quite vividly and immediately how helping the intimate other benefits themselves and how their being benefited by this other provides the other with fulfillment. And such reflection enhances both one's habitual awareness of and hence one's enactment of one's emotional solidarity with all other humans.

Exemplary Individuals

Tom's musings following this interchange with Ma manifest an equally profound solidarity with Casy, who is now dead. His statement to Ma, "God I'm talking like Casy. Comes of thinkin' about him so much. Seems like I can see him sometimes" (419)—recalls the experience of the Apostle Thomas ("doubting Thomas"), who was skeptical of Jesus's promise of posthumous solidarity with his followers ("Lo, I am with you always") until Jesus actually appeared to him after the crucifixion. Tom's solidarity with Casy is thus assimilated to the solidarity Jesus promised his followers. The same is true of Tom's promise of solidarity with Ma even after he leaves. His assurance that he will "be all aroun' in the dark . . . , ever'where—wherever you look" (419) echoes Jesus's promise to his disciples that "where two or three are gathered together in my name, there am I in the midst of them" (Matthew 18:20). And Tom's declaration to Ma that he'll be wherever people are struggling, or enjoying the fruits of their struggle, recalls Jesus's solidarity with the oppressed, articulated in his commendation of those who help the suffering— "Inasmuch as ye have done it unto one of the least of these my brethren, ye have done it unto me" (Matthew 25:40)—as well as in his condemnation of people who fail to help those in need: "Inasmuch as ye did it not to one of the least of these, ye did it not to me" (Matthew 25:45). This episode's presentation of both Casy and Tom as Christ-figures in the context of Jesus' avowed ontological and psychological solidarity with all humans simultaneously establishes Tom and Casy as powerful exemplars of such solidarity and rescues the figure of Jesus from supernaturalist delusions in order for it to perform a similar function for readers.

This same technique of recruiting Jesus as an exemplar, or template, for processing the actions of a character is employed in the novel's final episode and most famous (and infamous) scene: Rose of Sharon's suckling the old man. This act, which invokes the Christian communion and the Pietà, along with iconographic images of Mary suckling Jesus, is also a supremely Christ-like act, in which Rose of Sharon—whose name, from Song of Solomon, is taken by Christians to be another name for Jesus—becomes, like Casy and Tom before her, an exemplar of solidarity that itself invokes the ultimate Christian exemplar of solidarity.[2] Here, too, the profound solidarity of Jesus is recovered from its theological sequestration as a supernatural act performed by a supernatural being and offered to readers—in itself as well as through the Christ-figures of Casy, Tom, and Rose of Sharon—as a powerful exemplar to use as a template for understanding and responding to other people.

Life Scripts

These scenes also punctuate exemplary life stories of solidarity, in which the lives of Casy, Tom, Rose of Sharon, and Ma move toward and culminate in an expansion of self to include all other selves and a sacrificing of one's atomistic self for this larger, solidary self. These exemplary lives offer a striking alternative to the atomistic life script, in which the aim of life is to achieve vertical separation from others—domination over them—through ruthless competition.

Tom's achievement of solidarity with others, and ultimately with all who are struggling and suffering, is presented as the culmination of his life story, the bringing to fruition of a potential that has been present in him all along, as indicated by Ma's earlier remark to him: "They's some folks that's just theirself an' nothin' more. . . . You wasn't never like that, Tom. . . . Ever'thing you do is more'n you" (353). Other characters in the novel share a similar trajectory. In addition to Casy, there is also Ma, who achieves a similar sense of universal solidarity when she states near the end, "Use' ta be the fambly was fust. It ain't so now. It's anybody" (444). And of course Rose of Sharon manifests what is perhaps the most dramatic movement from atomism to solidarity, at the end of the novel giving of her own body so that a stranger may live. Her solidarity, too, has been an inherent possibility from the beginning, as indicated by Ma's earlier statement to her as Granma is dying, "When you're young, Rosasharn, ever'thing that happens is a thing all by itself. It's a lonely thing. I 'member, Rosasharn. . . . They's a time of change, an' when that comes, dyin' is a piece of all dyin', and bearin' is a piece of all bearin', an' bearin an dyin' is two pieces of the same thing. An' then things ain't lonely any more. An' then a hurt don't hurt so bad, 'cause it ain't a lonely hurt no more" (209).

The common trajectory of these lives establishes a life script in which solidarity is the telos of human development, the culmination of maturity. And it is presented as a secular version of the exemplary Christian life, the goal of which is to imitate the generativity and self-sacrifice— the solidarity—enacted by Jesus.

Prototypic Emotions and Action Scripts

The primary emotions of the solidarity schema are love and compassion, which are both exemplified by key characters and evoked in readers through their recognition of their sameness with these characters. The primary exemplar of love and compassion is Casy, whose great love for people—"I love people so much I'm fit to bust, sometimes," he says (26)—is consubstantial with his sense of unity with everyone: "What's this call, this spirit?" he asks. "It's love" (26). Ma manifests a similarly

230   How Protest Novels Work to Replace Faulty Person-Schemas

powerful love when she lies alone with the dead Granma all night as the family crosses the Mojave desert. "Casy said in wonder, 'All night long, and she was alone.' And he said, 'John, there's a woman so great with love—she scares me'" (229). And Tom and Ma, in their final encounter, and Rose of Sharon in the novel's final scene, also manifest profound love and compassion for the needy other.

Love and compassion both include action tendencies of care and aid, including, when necessary, sacrifice for others, as in the final conversation between Tom and Ma, where each is prepared to sacrifice greatly in order to protect the other. Since others are neurologically and psychologically part of one's extended self, such sacrifice is only logical: it makes sense to sacrifice part of one's immediate, personal self in order to protect and sustain a crucial part of one's larger self. When one apprehends one's solidarity with the other, this self-sacrifice comes naturally, as when parents and romantic partners (like the couple in O. Henry's "The Gift of the Magi") sacrifice for their children and lovers.

The Grapes of Wrath presents multiple instances of sacrifice for family members, including Ma's silently holding Granma's dead body across the Mojave desert, her giving the seven dollars to Tom, and, in the novel's final scene, the father's starving himself so his son can eat. But the novel also shows this altruistic script operating between non-intimates and even strangers, in episodes such as Muley Graves sacrificing two of his three rabbits for Tom and Casy, the Joads sacrificing part of their breakfast and transportation for Casy, the Joads and Wilsons sacrificing food, money, and a comforter for each other, Casy sacrificing his freedom by taking the fall for Tom, the Wallaces sacrificing part of their breakfast and their work for Tom, and Casy and (quite possibly) Tom sacrificing their lives so that others, complete strangers, might have a chance to live a decent life. The novel emphasizes that this altruistic script follows naturally from the apprehension of one's solidarity with all humans. As a labor organizer told Casy, "You ain't doin' it for fun, no way. Doin' it cause you have to. Cause it's you" (384).

The novel insists that this script of helping others in need trumps scripts of law, custom, and decorum. When his publisher requested that he eliminate the final scene of Rose of Sharon's suckling the old man— a scene that many readers even today find "creepy," "weird," and even "sick"—Steinbeck refused, stating that the point of the novel depended on that scene. The point is that helping people in need must take precedence over everything else. While in normal circumstances a dirty old man sucking on the breast of a young girl, and the girl receiving a mysterious—possibly sexual—pleasure from this act, would be disturbing, to say the least, Steinbeck's iconographic framing of this scene as a version of the Pietà and his use of the name Rose of Sharon, which is both a symbol of and a name for Christ, indicate that this act has ultimate, transcendent value, because, whatever else it may be, it is a life-saving act.

In addition to helping others in need, solidarity also entails collective action. Since people are neurologically attuned to each other, fundamentally dependent on each other, and composed of the same basic needs and vulnerabilities, it is only logical that when they become more needy they should unite and organize. Exemplars of this action include, first, the roadside encounters, such as that between the Joads and the Wilsons, then the Hoovervilles and the government camp, and finally the Akron turkey shoot, the strike at the peach orchard, and Tom's decision to carry on Casy's work.

Such ad hoc acts of solidarity, however, whether in the form of self-sacrifice or union and organization, will not by themselves bring about social justice. Rather, they remain preliminary to the more substantial action of social change, serving to sustain vulnerable individuals and groups until change that incorporates solidarity into the very structures and institutions of a society can be effected, as well as functioning to bring about such institutional and structural changes. This is the ultimate action script promoted by *The Grapes of Wrath*: changing the system from one that assumes, rewards, and requires atomistic actions that leave the general populace vulnerable to displacement, exploitation, and exclusion for the benefit of the few, to a system in which solidarity is assumed, enabled, and rewarded, and the earth's bounty is shared by everyone (see 347–349). This was the primary goal of the organizing action of *The Jungle*, and it is the action script that Tom is formulating at the end of *The Grapes of Wrath*, when he says to Ma: "I been thinkin' how it was in that gov'ment camp, how our folks took care a theirselves, an' if they was a fight they fixed it theirself, an' they wasn't no cops wagglin' their guns, but they was better order than them cops ever give. I been a-wonderin' why we can't do that all over. Throw out the cops that ain't our people. All work together for our own thing—all farm our own lan'" (418). Such a system constitutes both the practical goal and the culmination of solidarity.

A fourth action is necessary, however, in order to enable the organizing and system-changing actions. That action is educating. The need to educate people is made explicit in *The Jungle*, and it is also the primary action performed by that novel. In *The Grapes of Wrath*, the importance of educating is not articulated explicitly. Rather, it is demonstrated by the ways in which people's ignorance of and failure to understand solidarity, as well as situatedness, malleability, and heterogeneity, not only prevent them from organizing but also lead them to harm themselves and others by opposing those who do recognize solidarity in its various forms and are attempting to promote its more complete actualization. Casy makes this general point when he is saying grace at the Joads' breakfast: "I got thinkin' how we was holy when we was one thing, an' mankin' was holy when it was one thing. An' it on'y got unholy when one mis'able little fella got the bit in his teeth an' run off his own way, kickin' an' draggin' an' fightin'. Fella like that bust the holiness. But when they're all working together, not one fella for another fella, but one fella kind of harnessed to the whole shebang—that's right, that's holy" (83).

The Grapes of Wrath demonstrates in a number of ways that operating with indifference, or in opposition, to one's solidarity with other human beings is a result of failing to recognize and understand oneself. Thus when the outside agitators at the government camp are apprehended, Huston says to his comrades, "Awright, boys, put 'em over the back fence. An' don't hurt 'em. They don't know what they're doin'" (344). This allusion to the words of Jesus on the cross—"Father, forgive them, for they know not what they do" (Luke 23:34)—is repeated by Casy when he twice says to his crucifiers right before they club him to death, "You fellas don' know what you're doin'" (386). Shortly before his death, Casy made a similar observation about the strike-breakers: "I wisht they could see it," he says. "I wisht they could see the on'y way they can depen' on their meat" is to join in the strike (384).

Tom repeats Casy's last words when he is telling Ma of Casy's death, and then he says about his own reflexive killing of Casy's murderer, "Ma, I didn' know what I was a-doin'" (392). And later, when Ruthie betrays Tom by threatening to have him kill the girl who stole her crackerjacks, Ma says, "[S]he didn' know what she was a-doin'" (413). By explaining these failures of solidarity as the result of ignorance of solidarity, the novel indicates just how important the act of educating people about solidarity is and implicitly establishes the action script of education as a key component of the solidarity schema.

The Grapes of Wrath develops this education script in readers by engaging them in registering multiple facets and instances of it. And this demonstration is itself part of the novel's multifaceted working to educate its readers on precisely this point. These various instances demonstrate that educating people about solidarity comprises several steps.

First, it involves helping people recognize and understand the three basic types of solidarity, as discussed above. Understanding practical solidarity is crucial because without grasping the multiple and complex ways in which they depend on others and others on them, individuals will unwittingly act in ways that harm not only others but also themselves, as we have just discussed regarding the actions of those who "don't know what they're doing." Understanding emotional or psychological solidarity is important so that people recognize, welcome, and nurture their own and others' need to be needed—their need to help, as Sairy Wilson puts it—rather than seeing that need as a weakness and repressing or rejecting it. And understanding ontological solidarity—i.e., recognizing the fundamental ways in which we are the same as every other human being—is crucial for preventing dehumanization and other forms of othering, such as those enacted against the Okies, which pave the way for doing violence and injustice to the other.

Second, people need to understand how the existence of each form of solidarity logically entails the pursuit of social actions, institutions, and structures that provide for the well-being of everyone, and that failing to help others is actually acting against one's own self-interest, both practical and psychological, and is possible only when one fails to apprehend one's practical, psychological, and ontological solidarity with others.

And third, people need to be educated concerning the specific types of action that will be necessary in order to realize a social and economic system in which everyone can flourish—starting with the action of educating. The schema change promoted by *The Grapes of Wrath* is the fundamental action script associated with the solidarity schema. Helping readers replace their atomism schema with a solidarity schema will enable them to apprehend solidarity where now they see only difference, separateness, and opposition with others, and this apprehension of solidarity will in turn enable the other three action scripts—self-sacrifice, uniting and organizing, and system change—that are necessary and sufficient for the realization of social justice.

Any of the novel's exemplars of solidarity that we have been discussing can, when committed to memory, prime readers to recognize that, contrary to the dominant American ideology of individual independence, self-reliance, and atomism, they are profoundly united—practically, psychologically, and ontologically—with every other human being they encounter or imagine. And the encounter with all of these and other exemplars of solidarity throughout the novel also increases readers' capabilities of experiencing solidarity and acting accordingly. As we discussed in Chapter 1, recent neurological findings suggest that when we read about the actions or feelings of fictional characters, "we literally experience the same feelings" and action tendencies ourselves, because reading about characters' expressions and actions activates the same neurons in our brains that are operating when we ourselves engage in similar feelings or actions (Iacoboni 4–7, 94–95). Thus reading about characters feeling sympathy and being generous toward others activates the same neural pathways and networks that produce our own sympathetic feelings and altruistic actions outside the reading experience, and the repeated activation of these neural networks by our reading increases their capability of being activated by events we encounter outside the novel. Reading episodes of solidarity thus not only enhances our understanding of solidarity, but also directly increases our capability and likelihood of experiencing it and acting on it.

Metacognition and Correction of Faulty Processing

The most important education, of course, is not that which provides propositional knowledge but rather that which produces "deep learning," the development of more adequate information-processing structures, including metacognition.

Many of the multiple, powerful episodes of feeling sympathy and helping others through which readers are conducted by *The Grapes of Wrath* also work to enhance their metacognition. One particularly noteworthy instance is Muley Graves's reflections on sharing his rabbits with Casy and Tom. When Casy asks Muley if he's going to share,

> Muley fidgeted in embarrassment. "I ain't got no choice in the matter." He stopped on the ungracious sound of his own words. "That ain't like I mean it. That ain't. I mean"—he stumbled—"what I mean, if a fella's got somepin to eat an' another fella's hungry—why, the first fella ain't got no choice. I mean, s'pose I pick up my rabbits an' go off somewheres an' eat 'em. See?"
>
> "I see," said Casy. "I can see that. Muley sees somepin there, Tom. Muley's got a-holt of somepin, an' it's too big for him, an' it's too big for me." (51–52)

In addition to demonstrating the nature and power of automatic empathy, this passage, through Casy's final musing, prompts readers to ask themselves what big idea Muley is on to, thus initiating metacognition concerning their own inescapable emotional solidarity with others.

Other episodes demonstrating emotional solidarity work similarly to develop metacognition in readers. The anguish of Ma and Uncle John over the famished children surrounding Ma's pot of stew induces similar feelings in readers and may prompt memories of, and reflection on, their own involuntary empathy. Al and Mae's generosity in selling food at a loss to the hungry family, despite their reluctance to do so, together with the truckers' spontaneous generosity in leaving a large tip for Mae, induces readers to reflect on reasons for the generosity and thereby to recognize and better understand the nature of involuntary empathy and emotional contagion, including their own. The deep sadness and shame that the soldier feels over having shot the Indian brave, together with his prompting his audience to search their memories for a comparable experience of their own (326), elicits a similar metacognition in Steinbeck's audience. And Rose of Sharon's mysterious smile prompts readers to wonder what type of satisfaction she is receiving and thereby to recognize and reflect on what Erik Erikson called "generativity," the basic human need to be of use to others, which Sairy Wilson had earlier articulated as the need to help.

By inducing readers, in these various ways, to replace their atomism schema with a solidarity schema, the novel works to enhance their ability to apprehend solidarity where until now they have seen only difference, separateness, and opposition with others. This apprehension of solidarity will, in turn, enable and motivate the other three action scripts of solidarity—self-sacrifice, uniting and organizing, and system change—that are together necessary and sufficient for the realization of social justice.

The Grapes of Wrath thus repeatedly engages readers in a set of cognitive activities that, *with enough repetition,* can replace the faulty person schemas that govern most Americans' social information processing with more adequate schemas that will enable readers to achieve the following understandings concerning any and all other people:

1. All good or bad behaviors that people engage in, and whatever successes or failures they experience, are ultimately caused more by external circumstances over which they have no control than by their own character and actions.
2. Whatever good or bad character traits people have are ultimately not their own doing but are rather the result of their having had either an adequate or an inadequate formative environment and experiences.

3. However different or alien other people may appear to be, I am fundamentally united with them through our common needs, our mutual interdependence, and our inherent emotional attunement with each other's emotions and actions.

As we have seen in earlier chapters, research in social cognition has shown that when people achieve these understandings of others, their action toward these others changes from neglect, discipline, and punishment to assistance, including political and social actions leading to the amelioration or replacement of harmful and unjust economic, social, and cultural policies, institutions, and structures, which are based on the corresponding misunderstandings.

CHAPTER 8

Native Son

I didn't see them and they didn't see me.
BIGGER THOMAS (425)

Challenging autonomist and essentialist assumptions concerning the causes of violent behavior was Wright's stated goal in *Native Son*. And demonstrating people's heterogeneity and universal solidarity is clearly also central to the novel. The essentialist assumption that people are born good or bad rather than made that way by their environment is rejected by the novel's title: "native son" indicates that the novel's protagonist, Bigger Thomas, is a product not of some supposed racial heritage but rather of the white supremacist society into which he was born, without his consent or even foreknowledge.

In "How 'Bigger' Was Born," Wright emphasizes that the five violent, "bad" black men who served as models for Bigger Thomas, and whom he knew personally, were not born bad but were products of the oppressive, racist society in which they grew up and lived. Wright notes that he needed to indicate quite clearly "the nature of the environment that produced these men . . . , or the reader [would] be left with the impression that they were essentially and organically bad" (437). Wright proceeds to explain how the white society has conditioned the "millions" of Bigger Thomases, black and white, who he says exist everywhere (441), and how Bigger is "an American *product*, a *native son* of this land . . . , a *product* of a dislocated society," which has "*conditioned* . . . his organism" (446, 447; emphasis added). "[W]hen the time came for writing," Wright states, "*what had made him and what he meant* constituted my plot" (454; emphasis in original). And his aim, he says, was to present Bigger's life in "terms which would, in the course of the

238 How Protest Novels Work to Replace Faulty Person-Schemas

story, *manipulate the deepest held notions and convictions of [readers']
lives"*(454–455; emphasis added). That is, he wanted to present Bigger
in a way that would alter readers' fundamental and faulty assumptions
about all the Biggers in the world, specifically, and about human nature
generally. Hence the novel's systematic attack on the schema of essentialism, along with those of autonomy, atomism, and homogeneity.

Correcting the Autonomy Schema

You can't win.
STATE'S ATTORNEY BUCKLEY (13)

Propositional Knowledge of Situationism

The proposition that bad circumstances are the (or at least *a*) major
cause of bad actions is found in several places in the novel, in various degrees of explicitness.

Its most direct articulation comes from Bigger himself as he is trying to escape the haunting image of Mary's bloody head by rationalizing what he has done. "Hell," he says, "she *made* me do it! *I couldn't
help it!*" (113; second emphasis added). Less categorical but more credible is Jan's exculpation of Bigger when he visits him in jail and tells him,
"[I]t's your right to hate me, Bigger. I see now that *you couldn't do anything else* but that; it [killing Mary] was all you had. . . . I've been thinking this thing over and I felt that I'm the one who ought to be in jail for
murder instead of you" (288; emphasis added).

The most systematic articulation of the situationism principle occurs
in Max's defense of Bigger (though it is interwoven with the articulation of the malleability principle, which we will discuss in the next section). Max asserts that "the background of this boy must be shown, a
background which has acted powerfully and importantly upon his conduct. . . . [W]e have denied the personality of this boy. . . . Hemmed in,
limited, circumscribed, he sees and feels no way of acting except to hate
and kill that which he thinks is crushing him" (388–390). "[T]he way
we have treated this boy," Max concludes, "*made him do* the *very* thing
we did not want" (395; first emphasis added). These repeated claims
that Bigger couldn't help what he did, because forces beyond his control made him do it, establish in readers' minds the situationism proposition in explicit form, and whether or not they accept its application to

Bigger, it can work to inform their future perceptions of real-life Biggers and other individuals as well.

Situationist Concepts

The novel also provides readers with a number of situationist concepts with which to counter the assumption of autonomy. One is the concept of luck. The only difference between Bigger and the venerated white forebears, Max says, is that they were "lucky" and Bigger was not (393). In acknowledging the central role that circumstances play in determining people's behavior and life outcomes, the situationist concept of luck counters the autonomy schema's conceptual denial of situatedness through demonizing concepts that locate responsibility solely in the actor—concepts such as those found in Bigger's characterization by the newspapers, which call him "an irreformable sneak thief and liar" who "comes of a poor darky family of a shiftless and immoral variety" and compare him to an ape, a "jungle beast," and "the missing link" (279–280).

The novel also furnishes a situationist substitute for the autonomist concept of crime, which is seen as an autonomous act of a wicked person (a "criminal"). In his defense of Bigger, Max both questions the validity of the very notion of crime and asserts an alternative concept to replace it. The attempt to execute Bigger, he declares, is "*oppression*, an attempt to throttle or stamp out *a new form of life* . . . that expresses itself, like a weed growing from under a stone, in terms *we call crime*. Unless we grasp this problem in the light of this new reality, we cannot do more than salve our feelings of guilt and rage with more murder when a man, *living under these conditions*, commits *an act which we call a crime*" (391; final three emphases added). By highlighting the motivated and disputable labeling of Bigger's action as crime, and offering an alternative concept for this action ("new form of life"), the novel arms readers with a situationist concept to counter and replace the autonomist individual-blaming concept of "crime."

The most prominent situationist concept offered by the novel is "fate," which, as the title of book 3, presides over and characterizes not only Bigger's fatality at the end but also his entire life. Fate embodies the recognition that all human life is subject to multiple and sometimes massive crucial contingencies beyond the ken and control of any individual, and the use and currency of this concept primes people to recognize this fact concerning others' lives as well as their own.

Situationism Episode Scripts

As *The Jungle* and *The Grapes of Wrath* demonstrate, one of the most effective means of correcting the autonomy schema is to provide multiple episodes in which behavior and life outcomes are caused primarily by circumstances that individuals can't control. But while the coercive force of the circumstances represented in these two novels is fairly obvious once the circumstances are pointed out, many of the situations that determine behavior are, as we noted in Chapter 2, invisible to observers. This invisibility may be due to any one of three different causes.

First, people for whom a given set of circumstances is not determinative of behavior often have difficulty recognizing the impact of a similar set of circumstances on the behavior of others. Circumstances that may strike readers as relatively benign or lacking in coercive, seductive, or prohibitive force for behavior can nonetheless be overwhelming for certain people, and unless we recognize this fact, we will often fall victim to the autonomy assumption and judge situationally induced behaviors to be the result of free choice instead. For example, people who are not afraid of heights, open spaces, or closed spaces often have difficulty understanding the responses of acrophobic, agoraphobic, and claustrophobic individuals. And many men (and some women) have had difficulty believing that women who are abused by their husbands are sometimes utterly convinced that their lives or those of their children are in imminent danger, such that their only recourse is to kill the abusive man (see Westervelt).

Second, people also often have difficulty recognizing the powerful emotions evoked by a situation and/or the behaviorally determinative force these emotions have for the actor. This difficulty is due to one or more of several factors, including (a) the fact that these emotions are not always expressed; (b) the fact that when they are expressed, they are sometimes disguised or distorted; and (c) the fact that many individuals are quite inept at reading even the expressed, undisguised emotions of others.

And third, many people fail to recognize the meaning or purpose that certain actions have for the actor. Specifically, most observers fail to recognize that most acts of aggression are intended and perceived by their actors to be defensive—that is, responses to perceived threats or harm—and/or justifiably retributive. Examples of this failure can be found in virtually every intergroup conflict, including wars, where most individuals on each side believe their aggression and violence to be defensive or retributive and hence justified.

Native Son addresses the problem of the invisibility of situations by confronting readers with repeated episodes portraying the emotional impact of circumstances on an individual and making evident the motivational force of these emotions on the individual's behavior.

Instead of the repeated *circumstances→behavior* and *circumstances→life outcomes* episode scripts of *The Jungle* and *The Grapes of Wrath*, in *Native Son* we have a *circumstances→emotion→behavior* script. More specifically, the novel's representation of Bigger Thomas repeatedly presents his aggressive actions as episodes of *circumstances→fear→fight/flight*. By repeatedly directing readers' attention to how circumstances evoke fear in Bigger, which compels him to fight or flee, the novel not only helps readers understand the force of circumstances on behavior but also helps them develop a *circumstances→fear→fight/flight* script as the default mechanism for processing and explaining aggressive behaviors.

Much of the novel's work in establishing the *circumstances →fear→ fight/flight* episode script involves portraying, explaining, and emphasizing the specific fears evoked in Bigger by his circumstances. Wright's calling book 1 of the novel "Fear" emphasizes that virtually all of Bigger's actions—most of which involve some form of either fight or flight—are motivated by this emotion. The title "Fear" prompts readers to recognize this fact and primes them to identify the numerous instances of fear that are present in Bigger and to recognize their twofold source (in Bigger's circumstances and his character) and their impact on his behavior—thus rehearsing situationist information-processing routines.

More specifically, the novel's multiple repetitions of the *threatening circumstances→fear→fight/flight* episode script train readers to—when they see someone fighting or fleeing—expect, notice, search for, remember, infer, and/or suppose the existence of fear and a fear-inducing perception of threat on the part of the fighter/fleer, as opposed to supposing the cause of the behavior to be simply a bad or weak character (the supposition generated by the autonomy schema). The repetition of multiple episodes of *threatening circumstances→ fear→ fight/flight* also provides readers with multiple exemplars of threatening situations (including nonphysical threats), of fear (including physiological responses and other forms of fear), and of behavioral responses to fear (including psychological defenses), thus making readers better equipped to recognize, infer, and suppose the presence of threats, fear, and fight/flight in their multiple and often disguised forms.

Threat→Fear

Native Son conducts readers through multiple episodes in which they (a) recognize one or more of three basic types of threat—physical, economic, or psychosocial; (b) apprehend the threat as the cause of one form or another of fear; and (c) identify each instance of fear as the prime motivator of either fight or flight, aggression or avoidance, on Bigger's part.

In the opening scene, in which Bigger is attacked by a huge rat with long yellow fangs that tear his pants leg, readers not only witness but in most cases also empathically experience Bigger's terror at the threat of severe physical injury and perhaps even death (from rabies or infection). Readers have no difficulty understanding and sharing Bigger's combined fight/flight response to the rat—or the fight/flight response of the rat itself, which is in many ways simply a mirror image, and a symbol, of Bigger.

As the novel progresses, this basic *threat→fear→ fight/flight* script is repeated again and again with variations in the form and the degree of obviousness of each element, with each repetition contributing incrementally to the formation of readers' situationist information-processing routines as well as their prototypes of threat, fear, and fight/flight.

Other physical threats that confront Bigger include the danger of being shot during or after the planned robbery of Blum's Delicatessen (25), being arrested on his way to the Daltons' house (44), being arrested or perhaps even lynched if he accidentally brushes against the white woman who answers the Daltons' door (45), being executed if he is discovered alone with Mary Dalton in her room, and of course being executed if he is arrested for Mary's killing and presumed rape.

Bigger is also continuously fearful of economic harm. Specifically, he is afraid that if he does not get the job with the Daltons, his family will be removed from public assistance and may find themselves homeless and even starving (12), and more generally, he is afraid that white society will never allow him to have a decent job (12).

The most frequent, pervasive, and powerful threats, however, are psychosocial—threats to Bigger's identity, or sense of self. Such threats are often the most difficult for observers to perceive, and this is particularly true when the observers themselves have little or no experience of the threats or the situations that cause them, which is the case for many white readers in this instance. The novel thus goes to some lengths to make such threats explicit, and in providing readers with multiple new exemplars, it expands the repertoire of threats that can be recognized by readers' situationism schema.

The first exemplars of psychosocial threats to Bigger's sense of self are put-downs from his mother, who, in her desperate and understandable efforts to divert Bigger from the self-destruction to which she fears he is headed, is trying to shame him into becoming more responsible toward himself and his family. In the opening scene, she tells Bigger that she wonders why she ever gave birth to him, questions his manhood, warns him that he's heading for the gallows, and calls him a "boy," a "fool," a "tramp," "just plain dumb black crazy," and "the most no-countest man I ever seen in all my life" (8–11).

The most substantial threat to Bigger's sense of self, of course, comes from the white supremacist society, which in numerous ways sends him the same message as his mother. This fact is signaled and symbolized by the billboard that Bigger sees being put up across the street as he leaves his apartment. The sign shows the white face of the state's attorney looking straight at the viewer—Bigger, in this case—and saying, in "tall red letters: YOU CAN'T WIN!" (13). Soon thereafter Bigger notices a plane skywriting and wistfully remarks to his friend Gus that he would like to fly but knows he, unlike white men, will never get the chance. Bigger observes to Gus, "They [white people] got things and we ain't. They do things and we can't. It's just like living in jail. Half the time I feel like I'm on the outside of the world peeping in through a knothole in the fence. . . . Why they make us live in one corner of the city? Why don't they let us fly planes and run ships? . . . I reckon we the only things in this city that can't go where we want to go and do what we want to do" (20–21).

Movies constitute another exemplar of psychosocial threats. When Bigger goes to the movie, the newsreel confronts him with images of women, wealth, and luxury that he knows will never be his: "smiling, dark-haired white girls lolling on the gleaming sands of a beach," who are described by the voiceover as "the daughters of the rich . . . , represent[ing] over four billion dollars of America's wealth and over fifty of America's leading families" (31). And in the feature film, he is confronted with white society's racist vision of black people as nothing but wild savages: "pictures of naked black men and women whirling in wild dances" to the beating of drums (33).

The white world in general, including that of well-meaning but naively paternalistic whites such as the Daltons, also constitutes a significant threat to Bigger's sense of self. As he enters the "cold and distant world" of the rich, white community in which the Daltons live, Bigger is acutely aware, and fearful, of the white gaze, and by the time he arrives at the Dalton house "only fear and emptiness filled him" (44). He first fears that he has committed an egregious *faux pas* by going to the front door (he was unable to find a path to the back), and when he rings the doorbell, the unfamiliar sound of the gong makes him fear that he has broken it (44). When the white housekeeper answers the door and invites him in, he is fearful that he will not be able to enter without brushing against her (an absolute taboo for a black man in the 1930s), and after he enters, he fears that virtually every move he makes will be judged wanting by the white gaze: he is afraid that he has broken the easy chair when he sinks down into its plush cushion, that he had stared too long at the blind Mrs. Dalton as she passed him in the hall, and that he is not directing his gaze appropriately, exhibiting correct body language, or responding properly in his conversation with Mr. Dalton (45–48).

Bigger is also threatened by Mary (65), as she herself perceives ("I scare you?" she asks him [63]). He is threatened by a number of things Mary does, not the least of which are her attempts to recruit him as an ally and co-conspirator against her father, upon whom Bigger is now dependent for his livelihood. But his sense of self is most threatened by the mixed signals she sends him about who and what he is. On the one hand she and her boyfriend Jan treat Bigger as an equal: they shake his hand, sit close to him (literally rubbing shoulders—and thighs—with him), drive the car, and eat and drink with him. Yet at the same time they also behave in ways that indicate that they view him as inferior to themselves: Mary orders him to drive to Jan's apartment rather than to the university; Jan does not just offer Bigger his hand, he insists that Bigger shake it; they both coerce Bigger to take them to a black diner and to eat and drink with them there, despite his obvious reluctance and discomfort; they speak of "Negroes" as sources of emotion to energize the communist revolution; and finally they order him to drive around while they proceed to have sex in the back seat as though Bigger were not present. Hence "the guarded feeling of freedom he had while listening to her was tangled with the hard fact that she was white and rich, a part of the world of people who told him what he could and could not do" (65).

By conducting readers through these multiple *threat→fear* episodes, foregrounding the different types of threat and fear and detailing fear's various manifestations or symptoms, *Native Son* is simultaneously promoting the development in readers of a more adequate, situationist episode script and training them in more adequate information-processing routines that will enable them to expect, recognize, focus on, search for, infer, recall, and/or suppose such threats and fear when they encounter or consider any of the millions of real-life Biggers that, as Wright points out, exist in our society (see Wright, "How" 441). Being able to do this is crucial, for most people are oblivious to the fear (including shame and depression) that motivate most violent behavior. Wright's representation of the various situational causes, types, and symptoms of Bigger's fear helps readers develop a situationism schema that includes these various forms of threat and fear as prominent causes of the various forms of violence that the millions of real-life Biggers perpetrate.

Fear→Fight/Flight

In addition to detailing the threatening circumstances that Bigger experiences and the symptoms of fear that these circumstances produce in him, *Native Son* also lays out the repeated fight and flight responses that this fear triggers in him, thus providing readers with multiple exemplars of, and engaging them in multiple rehearsals of, the *threatening situation→fear→fight/flight* episode script.

Bigger's first impulse in response to his fear is usually flight, which is the title of the novel's second book. Psychologically wounded by his mother's harsh criticism in the first scene, he flees the apartment to seek the comfort of his friends at Doc's poolroom. But he is unable truly to flee the larger circumstances that are causing his fear, so his most common move is to flee fear itself. Before he leaves his apartment, he withdraws emotionally from his family and represses his fear and despair:

> Vera went behind the curtain and Bigger heard her trying to comfort his mother. He shut their voices out of his mind. He hated his family because he knew that they were suffering and that he was powerless to help them. He knew that the moment he allowed himself to feel to its fullness how they lived, the shame and misery of their lives, he would be

swept out of himself with fear and despair. So he held toward them an attitude of iron reserve; he lived with them, but behind a wall, a curtain. And toward himself he was even more exacting. He knew that the moment he allowed what his life meant to enter fully into his consciousness, he would either kill himself or someone else. So he denied himself and acted tough . . . ; his courage to live depended upon how successfully his fear was hidden from his consciousness. (10, 42; see also 37)

Indeed, all of Bigger's fight responses—his acts of aggression—are themselves revealed to be instances of flight, not from his psychologically threatening circumstances, from which there is no escape, but from the emotions (primarily fear) that these circumstances evoke in him. This response is evident in the opening scene, when Bigger sadistically torments his sister, Vera, by dangling in her face the giant dead rat that he has just killed, "enjoying his sister's fear" (7). One reason he enjoys his sister's fear is that it frees him from his own fear: his terrorizing his sister is an act of projective identification that induces terror in another as a way of blocking his awareness of his own terror. A similar externalizing defense against his own fear is operating when he accuses Gus of being afraid to rob Blum: "Bigger was afraid of robbing a white man and he knew that Gus was afraid, too. . . . He had argued all of his pals but one into consenting to the robbery, and toward the lone man who held out he felt a hot hate and fear; he had transferred his fear of the whites to Gus. He hated Gus because he knew that Gus was afraid, as even he was; and he feared Gus because he felt that Gus would consent and then he would be compelled to go through with the robbery" (25).

By framing Bigger's aggression and violence as the result of his fear, the novel prompts readers to encode them in memory as exemplars of *fear→flight* episodes, rather than simply attributing them to an inherently vicious character. And these exemplars will make readers more able to recognize the flight and fear that are at the core of real-life episodes of aggression.

Such externalization is not always an effective or feasible defense against fear, however, and often the only way Bigger can escape from his fear is through sex or violence. The novel provides various episodes exemplifying the defensive function of violence. In one episode, Bigger and Gus attempt to stare each other down. As the tension mounts, "Bigger's stomach tightened as though he were expecting a blow and were getting ready for it. His fists clenched harder. In a split second he felt how his fist and arm and body would feel if he hit Gus squarely in the mouth, drawing blood; Gus would fall and he would walk out and the whole thing would be over and the robbery would not take place. And his thinking and feeling in this way made the choking tightness rising from the pit of his stomach to his throat slacken a little" (26). As the face-off continues, the images of violence proliferate and intensify in Bigger's mind: "Bigger's stomach burned and a hazy black cloud hovered a moment before his eyes, and left. Mixed images of violence ran like sand through his mind, dry and fast, vanishing. He could stab Gus with his knife; he could slap him; he could kick him; he could trip him up and send him sprawling on his face" (27).

The novel reproduces this same basic episode script, in which threatening circumstances are the ultimate cause of violence, in the most egregious acts of violence Bigger commits: his killing and beheading of Mary and his rape and murder of Bessie. Mary's death is the result not of any conscious intention on his part to do her harm but rather of his efforts to keep her quiet, for fear that her mother will discover his presence in her bedroom—a discovery that Bigger fears could get him lynched. And his gruesome decapitation of her dead body is similarly the product not primarily of his hatred of her, which is certainly real and powerful, but rather of his need to dispose of her body for fear of being executed for her death. His brutal murder of Bessie, though quite deliberate, is similarly the product not of any brute instincts Bigger might have but of the same terror of being caught and executed.

Bigger's raping Bessie right before he kills her is also the product of his terror rather than of some bestial or oversexed character. It is simply the most violent instance of a method that Wright has shown Bigger using from the beginning to calm himself when he is fearful. When Bigger contemplates the likelihood that his friends will agree to rob Blum, sexual release is one of the ways he seeks to calm himself: "Bigger felt an urgent need to hide his growing and deepening feeling of hysteria; he had to get rid of it or else he would succumb to it. He longed for a stimulus powerful enough to focus his attention and drain off his energies. He wanted to run. Or listen to some swing music. Or laugh or joke. Or read a *Real Detective Story Magazine*. Or go to a movie. Or visit Bessie" (28). He and Jack promptly leave Doc's and go to a movie theater, where they masturbate (30). That afternoon, back at Doc's shortly before they are to commit the robbery, Bigger's fear again becomes intense, and "his entire body hungered for keen sensation, something exciting and violent to relieve the tautness" (36). A few pages later we are told explicitly that Bigger "passed his days trying to defeat or gratify powerful impulses in a world he feared" (42), once again rehearsing the episode script in which Bigger's sexual acts and violent behaviors are recognized as products of his fear, which is itself a consequence of his threatening situation: *threatening situation→fear→violence/sex (fight/flight)*.

Situationist Life Script

The establishment of this episode script is *Native Son*'s major contribution to the development of a situationism schema in readers. The novel does, however, develop the other schema elements as well. The life script developed by the novel is, like the episode script, composed of the themes of the novel's three books—*(threatening situation)→fear→ (fight)/flight →fate*—only extended over Bigger's entire lifetime.

Wright emphasizes that understanding the behaviors and consequent destiny of a person like Bigger requires apprehending these connections, and also recognizing that such apprehensions are often hard to come by—a metacognitive appeal to readers to make a concerted effort to achieve precisely this recognition:

> [Bigger] knew as he stood there that he could never tell why he had killed. It was not that he did not really want to tell, but the telling of it would have involved an explanation of his entire life. The actual killing of Mary and Bessie was not what concerned him most; it was knowing and feeling that he could never make anybody know what had driven him to it. His crimes were known, but what he had felt before he committed them would never be known. (308)

Much of the time, the deepest causes of human behavior and the life outcomes it produces remain hidden from others, because they are not privy to the (often invisible) situation to which the behavior is responding or to the precise emotional response that the situation produces in the actor and that then motivates the behavior, the purposes of which are often also themselves opaque or misconstrued. By promoting the development in readers of the situationist life script—*(threatening situation)→ fear→ (fight)/flight→fate*—the novel helps equip them to take these situational factors into account as central to any valid explanation of a person's life outcome. Armed with this situationist life script, readers may then *expect* every violent behavior and life to be a consequence of threats and fear and will *attend to* these threats and fear when they are discernible. When they are not in evidence, readers will *search for* them or *infer* them, or, in the absence of all evidence, they will *suppose* or posit them. And they will *encode* such lives in their *memory* as exemplars of situated lives, which will thus reinforce the situationist life script and make subsequent recognitions of situatedness more likely.

Individual Exemplars of Situatedness

Native Son depicts multiple individuals who are exemplars of situationism. Bigger is, of course, the most obvious, but there are others as well. Like Bigger, each member of his family is also a victim of circumstances beyond their control. The same is true of Bigger's girlfriend, Bessie, and his friends Jack, Gus, and G. H. Mary is a powerful exemplar of circumstances determining destiny, as are her parents: in Mary's death, each suffers a serious loss for which they themselves are not immediately responsible.

An additional significant set of exemplars is the slaveholding forefathers, whom Max speaks of in his defense of Bigger. Max emphasizes that their brutal actions (e.g., slavery and genocide), like Bigger's, were largely the result of their threatening circumstances: "they were faced with a difficult choice: they had either to subdue this wild land or be subdued by it. . . . [I]n conquering they *used* others, used their lives . . . , [because they] were engaged in a struggle for life and their choice in the matter was small indeed" (388–389). By stating that the slaveholders "were engaged in a struggle for life" and that "their choice in the matter was small indeed," Max provides a situationist explanation for some of the most brutal collective actions in human history and in doing so constructs a powerful exemplar of situatedness that can serve readers as a template for assessing not only Bigger's actions but other acts of brutality as well.

Images of Situationism

Native Son also occasionally provides images embodying the situationist understanding of Bigger and other characters. The most significant of these involve people's bodies being moved, injured, captured, or destroyed by forces in the situations in which they find themselves.

The most graphic images are those in which Bigger is himself the major circumstantial force to which others are subjected—particularly Mary and Bessie, whose bodies are fondled, manipulated, raped (in Bessie's case), and finally killed (and in the case of Mary, decapitated) by Bigger. Mrs. Dalton's blindness, and Bigger's mother's physical fatigue (both acute and chronic) are less gruesome but nonetheless significant imagistic evidence of the power of circumstances over individuals. Bigger's body also manifests his lack of autonomy in graphic ways on a number of occasions. His involuntary physiological reactions to threatening circumstances, cited above, are one instance. Others occur in the descriptions of his hungry and cold body when he is on the run and his being knocked off the water tower with the freezing water from the fire hose and being dragged down the stairs, with his head bumping against the steps.

Two particularly significant situationist images are experienced by Bigger in jail. The first is the image of Jesus on the cross, which Rev. Hammond describes: "Look, son. Ah'm holdin' in mah hands a wooden cross taken from a tree. A tree is the worl', son. 'N' nailed to this tree is a sufferin' man. Tha's whut life is, son. Sufferin'" (286). Bigger rejects the preacher's assertion that the crucifix also offers a solution to human suffering (in the form of faith in Jesus) but embraces the situationist understanding embodied in the image of the human condition as subjection to overwhelming external forces: "He was feeling the words of the preacher, feeling that life was flesh nailed to the world, a longing spirit imprisoned in the days of the earth" (286).

Later, after Bigger's talk with Max, another image of the limiting and constraining power of circumstances (along with atomism and solidarity, to be discussed in the final section), which people can neither escape nor understand, arises in his mind: "he saw a black sprawling prison full of tiny black cells in which people lived; each cell had its stone jar of water and a crust of bread and no one could go from cell to cell, and there were screams and curses and yells of suffering and nobody heard them, for the walls were thick and darkness was everywhere" (361).

These passages prompt attentive readers to view their own and others' lives through the template of these images, searching for common denominators in the images and the human condition, a search that culminates in an intensified recognition and understanding of the situatedness of all human lives, one's own and others'. And this experience, in turn, will increase the accessibility of these situationist images and the situationism schema generally for processing information about self and others outside the text.

Situationist Emotions

Through such images as well as the other forms of knowledge of situatedness, *Native Son* operates to replace the default emotions of the autonomy schema—pride, arrogance, contempt, and hatred—with compassion for the Biggers of the world.

Eliciting empathy for Bigger from his readers was central to Wright's purposes in the novel (see "How" 456–462), and this empathy produces sympathy for him. Although some readers apparently feel little more than anger and hatred toward Bigger, many are empathically moved to compassion by the descriptions of Bigger's physiological symptoms of fear in books 1 and 2; by sharing, through Wright's use of point of view, the uncertainty and danger of Bigger's efforts to escape detection as Mary's killer in "Flight"; and by his helplessness and hopelessness in face of his inevitable doom in "Fate." This emotional mimicry and perspective taking that the novel engages them in regarding Bigger Thomas trains readers to empathize with real-life Biggers, which in turn makes them more attuned to the situational determinants of these individuals' behavior.

Action Scripts of Situationism

The action tendency of helping, which is part of the emotion of compassion, is channeled by *Native Son* into two specific action scripts, primarily through the statements of Max. The first script is to alter the situations of young men like Bigger so as to provide opportunities for them to achieve a meaningful life through means other than violence, rather than ignoring their needs for such opportunities or providing them, as Mr. Dalton does, only with opportunities for inane diversion (see 295). The second action scripted by the novel is to refrain from killing murderers like Bigger and instead put them in a situation, in the form of a humane, respectful prison, that drastically reduces their opportunity to do violence while at the same time providing them with a modicum of the recognition and identity that they have never had and that they have been seeking through violence (see 398–399, 401, 404–405). In this way, the novel works to establish the situationist action scripts of

Correcting the Essentialism Schema

I beg you to recognize human life draped in a form and guise alien to ours, but springing from a soil plowed and sown by all our hands.
BORIS MAX (388)

Propositional Knowledge of Malleability

Native Son offers powerful propositional knowledge of human malleability in Max's articulation of the exculpating (or at least mitigating) environmental forces that are responsible for Bigger's bad character.

"I plead with you," Max says to the judge, "to see a mode of *life* in our midst, a mode of life stunted and distorted, but possessing its own laws and claims, an existence of men growing out of the soil prepared by the collective but blind will of a hundred million [white] people. I beg you to recognize human life draped in a form and guise alien to ours, but springing from a soil plowed and sown by all our hands" (388). Max further argues that both Bigger and the lynch mob are products of their respective environments, "powerless pawns in a blind play of social forces" (390). He also states that "warping influences . . . have played . . . hard upon Bigger Thomas," that "the way we have treated this boy made him do the *very* thing we did not want" (395; emphasis in original), that Bigger's killing "was *living* only as he knew how, and as we have forced him to live," and was the manifestation of a "longing to gratify impulses akin to our own but denied the object and channels evolved through long centuries for their socialized expression" (400; emphasis in original).

Malleability Concepts

These statements by Max include numerous anti-essentialist concepts as well. Buckley and the newspapers characterize Bigger through the use of essentialist concepts, words embodying the assumption that his criminal character is the result not of his formative environment but of an essentially different, non-human nature. The newspaper employs multiple essentialist terms to refer to Bigger, including "an ape," "a jungle beast"

(279), the "missing link," an "irreformable sneak thief and liar" (280), and "a criminal and intractable nature" (281), and Buckley does as well, calling him a "human fiend" (407), "bestial monstrosity" (408), "black lizard," "black mad dog," "subhuman killer" (409), "hardened black thing" (410), "beast," "piece of human scum" (411), "black cur," "infernal monster" (412), "ghoul," "worthless ape," "cunning beast" (413), and "demented savage" (414).

Countering such essentialist concepts, which embody the supposition that Bigger has not been formed and cannot be re-formed, are phrases in Max's speech indicating that Bigger's character has been formed by his environment, not preconstituted by his race. These concepts include "deform" (67), "stunted," "distorted," "growing out of," "springing from" (388), "warping influences" (395), "developed" (394), "conditioned" (384, 397), "evolved" (400), and, particularly, "mode (or form) of life" (388). This latter concept is used by Max to argue that Bigger's differences from his accusers constitute not a difference in substance (i.e., a different species) but simply a difference in form that has resulted from the different environment in which Bigger was forced to live.

Individual Exemplars of Malleability

Native Son provides multiple individual exemplars of malleability, which enhance readers' ability to recognize the experiential and environmental sources of the character traits of real people.

Significant individual exemplars include Bigger's mother, his sister, his brother, and Bessie. The novel emphasizes that Bigger's mother's entire being has been beaten down by years of grueling labor and stress, and the early signs of the same exhaustion and defeat in his sister, Vera, and the lack of energy, purpose, and meaning in his brother, Buddy, are clearly the result of their hard lives and limited opportunities (108–109).

These exemplars embody powerful images of malleability, manifesting the impact of the formative environment in their bodily form. Buddy's gaze and body language, which are explicitly contrasted with Jan's, evince the effects of his environment: "Buddy was soft and vague; his eyes were defenseless and their glance went only to the surface of things. . . . Buddy's clothes seemed aimless, lost, with no sharp or hard edges, like a chubby puppy. Looking at Buddy and thinking of Jan and Mr. Dalton, [Bigger] saw in Buddy a certain stillness, an isolation, meaningless" (108). Bigger's mother's eyes, face, and body language manifest the more intense effects of a much longer oppression: "he saw how soft and shapeless she was. Her eyes were tired and sunken and darkly ringed from a long lack of rest. She moved about slowly, touching objects with her fingers as she passed them, using them for support. Her feet dragged over the wooden floor and her face held an expression of tense effort" (108). As for Bigger's sister, Vera, "even though her face was smaller and smoother than his mother's, the beginning of the same tiredness was already there. How different Vera was from Mary. He could see it in the very way Vera moved her hand when she carried the fork to her mouth; she seemed to be shrinking from life in every gesture she made. The very manner in which she sat showed a fear so deep as to be an organic part of her" (108–109).

These images of bodies oppressed, depressed, defeated by their conditions of existence contrast starkly with—thus demonstrating the profoundly different formative environment of—the bodies of Jan, Mr. Dalton, and Mary, as well as with the images Bigger sees in the newsreel "of smiling, dark-haired white girls lolling on the gleaming sands of a beach" (31).

Bessie's pleasure-oriented character is likewise shown to be a product of "the narrow orbit of her life," when Bigger realizes that "from her room to the kitchen of the white folks was the farthest she ever moved. She worked long hours, hard and hot hours seven days a week, with only Sunday afternoons off; and when she did get off she wanted fun, hard and fast fun, something to make her feel that she was making up for the starved life she led" (139). Although we are given no details about their background, Bigger's friends Jack, Gus, and G.H. are also exemplars of malleability, having apparently been formed by much the same environmental forces as Bigger has (see 357).

Nor are exemplars of malleability limited to oppressed black characters. Mary's deep, unconscious racism is explicitly attributed to her environment by Max when he states, "[W]e conditioned [her] so that she would regard Bigger Thomas as a kind of beast" (397). By extension, it is clear that the same is true of Mary's parents, of Jan, of Max, and even of Buckley and the rest of the white racists clamoring for Bigger's execution. Indeed, everyone is an exemplar of malleability, because everyone's character is formed by their environment, as Max suggests when he argues that the difference between successful white people and people like Bigger is that the former have had an environment that actualized their best potentials while the latter have not: "*We were lucky. They are not.* We found a land whose tasks called forth the deepest and best we had. . . . We poured and are still pouring our soul into it. . . . They are yet looking for a land whose tasks can call forth their deepest and best" (393; emphasis added).

The novel's most powerful individual exemplar of malleability is, of course, Bigger himself. Wright first reveals Bigger to be a highly deficient and negative character and then leads readers, partly through Max's defense of him, to reconstruct, infer, and postulate how these negative qualities were produced by the toxic, racist environment in which Bigger has been forced to live his entire life. In addition, the novel also shows, in "real time," as it were, Bigger's character being transformed into a much more positive form by the recognition and empathy he receives in jail from Max and Jan, coupled with the intense pressure to make sense of his life in the face of his imminent execution.

Bigger's moral flaws are numerous and profound. He is mean—sadistic, even—as we see in the opening scene when he dangles the giant dead rat in Vera's face until she faints from terror. He is irresponsible, selfish, self-indulgent, and self-involved, as demonstrated by his reluctance to help his family economically (11), his masturbation in the movie theater (30), and his exploitation of Bessie as a sex object. He is violent, as we see when he knocks Gus down, strangles him, holds a knife to his throat, and forces him to lick the knife (38–39). He is also rapacious, as his fondling of Mary and his rape of Bessie reveal, and murderous, as demonstrated by his killing of Bessie and of Mary as well (if we follow Bigger's own reasoning regarding the latter incident).

But *Native Son* establishes Bigger as a powerful exemplar of malleability by making it clear that he is not himself the cause of these profound moral flaws—that his flawed character is due to developmental deficits in emotional intelligence, which are themselves caused by the toxic, white supremacist environment in which he grew up. As Wright himself explicitly states in "How 'Bigger' Was Born," Bigger is "emotionally unstable, depressed, and unaccountably elated at times, and unable even, *because of his own lack of inner organization which American oppression has fostered in him*, to unite with members of his own race" (448; emphasis added).

Bigger's hostility and violence are clearly shown to derive from a severe deficit in what has been called "the keystone of emotional intelligence": an ongoing awareness of one's internal states such that one notices and accurately identifies one's feelings as they are occurring (Goleman, *Emotional* 43, 4). Such awareness, as Daniel Goleman explains, "is the difference between, for example, being murderously enraged at someone and having the self-reflexive thought 'This is anger

I'm feeling' even as you are enraged. . . . This awareness of emotions is the fundamental emotional competence on which others, such as emotional self-control, build" (Goleman, *Emotional* 47). People who lack awareness of their emotions, a state known as alexithymia, have "difficulty describing feelings—their own or anyone else's—and a sharply limited emotional vocabulary. What's more, they have trouble discriminating among emotions as well as between emotion and bodily sensation, so that they might tell of having butterflies in the stomach, palpitations, sweating, and dizziness—but they would not know they are feeling anxious" (Goleman, *Emotional* 50–51).

This is precisely Bigger's fundamental emotional problem. One of the most significant features of the fear experienced by Bigger Thomas, and by Biggers in general, is its alexithymic quality: instead of being experienced as an emotion—that is, as a set of visceral, motor, imagistic, and ideational elements that Bigger recognizes and labels as "fear"—his fear, and the rest of his emotions as well, are experienced primarily as isolated physiological states, motor impulses, or (occasionally) visual images, which means that Bigger is largely incapable of moderating and directing his emotions and is instead controlled by them. The result is often violence.

The connection of Bigger's alexithymia and lack of emotional control with his violent behavior is made clear on a number of occasions. One instance occurs early in the novel when Bigger describes to Gus the feelings he has whenever he thinks about how white people have limited what he can aspire to. "Every time I think about it," he says, "I feel like somebody's poking a red-hot iron down my throat" (20). Bigger continues, telling Gus that white folks live in his stomach, and Gus indicates that he has a similar experience. "It's like fire," Bigger says. "And sometimes you can't hardly breathe," Gus responds (22). Bigger also indicates his inability to control this emotion, his feeling of helplessness when it engulfs him: "'That's when I feel like something awful's going to happen to me . . .' Bigger paused, narrowed his eyes. 'Naw; it ain't like something going to happen to me. It's . . . It's like I was going to *do something I can't help*'" (22; emphasis added).

This alexithymia, lack of control, and resulting violence are also dramatized in the episode in Doc's pool hall when Bigger's fear of robbing Blum's Delicatessen manifests itself as a physiological force that will run its course without Bigger's control or consent or even his full awareness: "the fear that Gus would really go made the muscles of Bigger's stomach tighten; he was hot all over. He felt as if he wanted to sneeze and could not; only it was more nervous than wanting to sneeze. He grew hotter, tighter; his nerves were taut and his teeth were on edge. He felt that something would soon snap within him" (25; see also 26).

The same developmental deficiency manifests itself in the second episode at the pool hall, when Bigger actually assaults Gus as the moment to embark upon the robbery approaches and he is overcome with anxiety. The narration of this assault directs readers' attention to its defensive and largely automatic, involuntary nature, emphasizing the powerful role played in Bigger's violent action by emotions that are outside his awareness and hence beyond his control. As Bigger is waiting with Jack and G.H. for Gus to arrive, "[h]e felt impelled to say something to ease the swelling in his chest. . . . He spoke without looking. His entire body hungered for sensation, something exciting and violent to relieve the tautness" (36). When Bigger sees Gus approaching, his anxiety intensifies to the point that he feels sick, and he is overcome with an impulse, of which he is only vaguely aware, to do something to Gus. When Gus arrives, Bigger kicks him hard, without warning, knocking him to the floor, and then begins laughing in a way that soon becomes hysterical, "feeling something like hot water bubbling inside of him and trying to come out" (37). Gus threatens retaliation but walks away, and Bigger grabs him from behind, choking him and bringing him to his knees. Then, all of a sudden, "the muscles of [Bigger's] body gave a tightening lunge and he saw his fist come down on the side of Gus's head; *he had struck him really before he was conscious of doing so*" (38; emphasis added).

Bigger manifests a similar lack of emotional awareness and control when he is with Jan and Mary: "His heart was beating fast and he struggled to control his breath. This thing was getting the better of him; he felt that he should not give way to his feelings like this. *But he could not help it*" (70). By the time they arrive at Ernie's Kitchen Shack, Bigger's physiological functions have been so affected by his anxiety that he is unable to eat: "When he tried to chew he found his mouth dry. It seemed that the very organic functions of his body had altered" (73). Here too, the tension is relieved only by violence: after he has killed Mary, "he felt a lessening of tension in his muscles" (114).

The novel further indicates that Bigger's fear and lack of emotional control are exacerbated by another developmental deficiency, his inability to empathize and read others' minds—that is, to understand their intentions or feelings. His deficits in empathy are quite evident in his relations with his family and his friends. He is unmoved by Vera's terror at the rat (7), by his mother's pleas for him to take on more responsibility

(8–10), or by Gus's begging him to cease tormenting him with the knife (38–40), and he is oblivious to even the most basic need of Mary—her need for oxygen—as he suffocates her while attempting to prevent her from speaking (85–86). His lack of mind-reading ability is even more evident in his reactions to the Daltons' efforts to befriend him. He is uncertain about Peggy's intentions: "Peggy seemed kind enough, but maybe she was being kind in order to shove her part of the work on him" (54). He is similarly uncertain about Mrs. Dalton: "He did not know just how to take her" (61). He is particularly confused by Mary: "She worried him. . . . She puzzled him" (59).

What he finds most threatening, however, is the effort by Jan and Mary to befriend him. When Jan offers him his hand in friendship, "Bigger's entire body tightened with suspense and dread" (66). Mary's efforts to reassure Bigger of Jan's sincerity merely compound his confusion and anger:

> "It's all right, Bigger," she said. "Jan *means* it."
> He flushed warm with anger. Goddam her soul to hell! Was she laughing at him? Were they making fun of him? What was it that they wanted? Why didn't they leave him alone? . . . He was trying desperately to understand. He felt foolish. . . . He felt naked, transparent; he felt that *this white man*, having helped to put him down, *having helped to deform him*, held him up now to look at him and be amused. At that moment he felt toward Mary and Jan a dumb, cold, and inarticulate hate. (67; emphasis added; see also 71–72)

Virtually every instance of anxiety, fear, and/or anger experienced by Bigger makes manifest these developmental deficits. And these deficits, in turn, point directly to the deficiencies of his formative environment. The novel's descriptions of Bigger's overwhelming feelings and violent actions as uncontrollable and even largely unintended prompt readers to recognize and encode Bigger's violence not as his own actions but rather as the product of forces beyond his control that are victimizing him. And the recognition that these forces are alien to Bigger and beyond his control induces readers to wonder about their provenance and thus to search for, infer, and/or suppose what kinds of formative factors might have produced them.

A quick search of the text reveals poverty, lack of a father, and an exhausted and depressed mother as likely factors. Contemporary readers with some knowledge of developmental psychology may infer that his chronically exhausted and depressed mother would not have been able to supply the young Bigger with the emotional attunement a child needs in order to develop emotional intelligence, and they may also suppose that his treatment by white supremacist society triggered the release of excessive stress hormones in Bigger that have been shown to result in reduction in the neurological capacity to regulate emotions.

In this way, by repeatedly directing readers' attention to the deficits in Bigger's emotional intelligence and their causal role in his violent behavior, and prompting readers to reflect on the formative origins of these deficits, *Native Son* develops and encodes in readers' memories a powerful exemplar of malleability that will enhance their ability to recognize human malleability and the effects of a deficient formative environment beneath every deficiency of emotion and behavior they encounter in others outside the text.

Episodes of Malleability

In addition to intimating malleability behind Bigger's developmental deficiencies, *Native Son* also presents episodes in which his malleability of character is immediately present, rather than merely implied. There are four episodes in which Bigger manifests emotional, characterological, and behavioral changes in response to an epiphanic, transformative experience.

First, killing Mary gives Bigger a sense of agency, and hence a sense of self, that he has never had before. He feels "like a man reborn" (111), "a lessening of tension in his muscles" (114), and "a kind of eagerness . . . , a confidence, a fullness, a freedom" (116). His newfound sense of self makes him less subject to the burden of fear that he had carried his entire life, and this reduction in fear also enables him to begin to empathize with other people. While eating breakfast with his family the morning after killing Mary, he notices for the first time their fear, hopelessness, and despair and the way their formative environment has left them de-formed, or formless, as discussed above (108). When he met Gus, G.H., and Jack in the drugstore later that morning, "[i]t was the first time he had ever been in their presence without feeling fearful" (113). Because he does not fear them, he is not aggressive; instead, he is generous to them, buying them beer and cigarettes (111–112). And later that same day, he (also for the first time) begins to see Bessie as something more than a means of satisfying his sexual urges: "His mind tried to grasp and encompass as much of her life as it could, tried to understand and weigh it in relation to his own . . . , [and] he felt the narrow orbit of her life" (138–139).

A second episode of malleability occurs when Jan visits Bigger in jail. Jan tells Bigger that while he initially felt anger and hatred toward him for killing Mary, his own time in jail allowed him to reflect on Bigger's situation and brought him to empathize with Bigger and feel compassion toward him: "I was in jail grieving for Mary and then I thought of all the black men who've been killed, the black men who had to grieve when their people were snatched from them in slavery and since slavery. I thought that if they could stand it, then I ought to. . . . I felt that I'm the one who ought to be in jail for murder instead of you" (288). Jan's empathy activates Bigger's own still largely undeveloped empathic capabilities, and he responds in kind: "The word had become flesh. For the first time in his life a white man became a human being to him; and the reality of Jan's humanity came in a stab of remorse: he had killed what this man loved and had hurt him. He saw Jan as though someone had performed an operation upon his eyes, or as though someone had snatched a deforming mask from Jan's face" (289).

Bigger's emerging empathy also results in a further alteration of his perception of and behavior toward his family. He realizes for the first time the suffering that his actions have caused them (298), and when his mother begs him to turn to Jesus so that she can see him again in heaven, he promises that he will, even though he knows there is no afterlife, because he realizes what such an assurance will mean to her (300).

This transformation of Bigger's character—from violent, rapacious murderer into empathic, compassionate figure—is completed by two additional episodes of malleability: his two jailhouse conversations with Max. In the process of telling Max how he felt and why he killed, Bigger comes to understand himself as he never has before, and also to feel understood and accepted as never before. After Max expresses compassion for Bigger and implicitly absolves him of a large portion of his guilt by telling him that the white people who want to kill him are "mad because deep down in them they believe that they made you do it" (358), Bigger "felt that Max was kind, and he felt sorry for him" (359). And after Max leaves, Bigger feels more relaxed and at peace than he ever has before (359). He realizes that "in Max's asking of those questions he had felt a recognition of his life, of his feelings, of his person that he had never encountered before" (360), and he begins to feel a deep connection with all the rest of humanity and to experience a profound, though

Native Son 261

as yet tenuous and fleeting, empathy for the white people who hate him and want to kill him:

> With this new sense of the value of himself gained from Max's talk, a sense fleeting and obscure, he tried to feel that if Max had been able to see the man in him beneath those wild and cruel acts of his, acts of fear and hate and murder and flight and despair, then he *too* would hate, if *he* were *they*, just as now *he* was hating *them* and *they* were hating *him*. (361)

This remarkable act of taking the perspective of those who hate him, which Bigger was incapable of before his killing of Mary, his imprisonment, and his talks with Jan and Max, demonstrates human malleability and the profound transformative impact that certain experiences and/or a change in environment can have on a person, and it establishes Bigger as a powerful exemplar of malleability that readers can draw on for processing information about other apparently irredeemable individuals beyond the text.

The final episode of malleability occurs as a result of Bigger's conversation with Max just hours before his execution. In this final scene in the novel, the formerly unreflective, emotionally illiterate, self-involved, and hateful Bigger completes his transformation into a paragon of self-awareness, empathy, and spirituality. "I sort of saw myself after that night," Bigger tells Max, recalling the night he killed Mary. "And I sort of saw other people too." And then, in an act performing his newly developed ability to see other people, "[h]e saw amazement and horror on Max's face, [and he] knew Max would rather not have him talk like this" (425). Max's amazement and horror signal the profound difference between this emotionally literate Bigger and the previous Bigger, the emotionally illiterate rapist and murderer, whose full humanity had been prevented from developing by his oppressive environment.

Max's amazement at Bigger's transformation also indicates that even though he had made the malleability argument at Bigger's trial, he himself had not realized the full extent of Bigger's previously stymied potential or the full formative and transformative power of the environment. Now that he does so he is horrified by his own complicity in the dehumanization of Bigger that this failure of realization indicates, as well as by the fact that the amazing human being that Bigger has just become is now going to be exterminated like the vermin the essentializing white racist society still believes him to be.

262 How Protest Novels Work to Replace Faulty Person-Schemas

The depth of Bigger's humanity and the profundity of his transformation are reinforced when, in an act of incredibly generous but sadly inaccurate empathy, Bigger asks Max if he thinks the people who hate him will arrive at a similar insight. Max knows they will not, but doesn't want to disillusion Bigger, so he instead tries to support Bigger by encouraging him to believe in himself, despite the fact that his killings were wrong (427). At the end of Max's peroration, Bigger expresses a final insight that elicits despair and terror in Max and constitutes the final increment of Bigger's transformation:

> Mr. Max, you go home. I'm all right. . . . Sounds funny, Mr. Max, but when I think about what you say, I kind of feel what I wanted. It makes me feel I was kind of right. . . . They wouldn't let me live and I killed. Maybe it ain't fair to kill, and I reckon I really didn't want to kill. But when I think of why all the killing was, I begin to feel what I wanted, what I am. . . . What I killed for must have been good! . . . It must have been good! When a man kills, it's for something. . . . I didn't know I was really alive in this world until I felt things hard enough to kill for 'em . . . (429)

The novel once again marks the transformation this insight represents in Bigger by emphasizing, through Max's response, how far beyond normal self-awareness it lies: when Bigger finishes, Max's eyes are full of terror, which indicates that Max realizes the truth of what Bigger is saying and that Bigger's killing, like killing in war, is therefore morally justified as self-defense (a point Max himself had made at the trial [396] but apparently didn't realize the full implications of), and that this means that killings such as those that Bigger committed are justified and won't stop until the selves of all the Biggers in the world are secure enough so as not to require such a terrible defense.

What Max's recognition of Bigger's malleability entails is the conclusion that people like Bigger, who kill other people, do so because their formative environment has produced emotional deficits and character flaws that leave them so vulnerable that the only way they can see to defend themselves, when they encounter certain threats in their current environment, is to do as Bigger did. And this understanding leads to the further understanding (a) that it is their formative environments and not the individuals themselves that are thus ultimately responsible for such violence and (b) that such violence won't stop until formative environments are altered so that they no longer produce individuals such as Bigger. Readers who understand and share Max's insight here will be more capable of using the exemplar of Bigger to recognize the malleability of even the apparently most depraved of individuals.

Each of these scenes portraying Bigger's transformation contributes to readers' development of a malleability episode script and person-prototype according to which events and circumstances elicit or enable people to change to a significant degree, in contrast to the episode script of essentialism, according to which events and circumstances simply constitute the background or context in which people manifest their immutable character. With its culminating scene, *Native Son* has completed its construction of Bigger Thomas as a powerful exemplar of malleability, first negative and then positive. Readers who recognize the deforming consequences of Bigger's original formative experiences and environment and the re-forming and transforming effects of his final experiences and environment now have, in the figure of Bigger etched in their memories, an individual exemplar of malleability that can aid them in recognizing the undeveloped human potential of whatever real-life Biggers they may encounter or consider, as well as the formative forces that have made them what they are and the (re)formative forces that might help them become more than they currently are.

Malleability Life Script

The foregoing episodes also contribute to readers' development of the malleability life script, *formative environment→character→behavior→ life outcomes*, which recognizes the formative impact of environment on character and hence its determinative role in behavior and life outcomes. Rather than reinforcing the dominant life script of essentialism, *bad character→violent behavior*, the novel promotes the development of a malleability life script: *developmental deficits→bad character→violent behavior*. *Native Son* also develops the crucial final component of this malleability life script, the role of the formative environment in producing developmental deficits and the character flaws that follow from them, thus promoting the development in readers of the complete life script of the malleability schema: *inadequate formative environment→emotional deficits→bad character→violent behavior→bad life outcomes*.

As noted above, readers are prompted to recognize from the beginning of the novel that Bigger's lack of emotional intelligence is the result not of some inherent incapacity but rather of an inadequate formative environment. And such recognition may trigger malleabilist memories, information searches, inferences, or suppositions concerning the specifics of the formation not only of Bigger Thomas but of Biggers in general. That is, these malleabilist information-processing acts induced by the novel may result in readers' recalling, discovering, inferring, or supposing a number of facts about human development in general and the development of violent individuals in particular such as the following:

1. That in order to develop emotional intelligence, children need their feelings to be *recognized*: attended to, attuned with, mirrored, and verbalized by their caregivers. It is these "countless small, nourishing exchanges between parent and child that build emotional competences" (Goleman, *Emotional* 234).
2. That one characteristic of the early lives of some of the most violent criminals is the absence of such experiences (Goleman, *Emotional* 102).
3. That being male constitutes a significant risk factor in emotional development: "Boys, for whom the verbalization of affects is deemphasized, may become largely unconscious of their emotional states, both in themselves and in others" (Brody and Hall, quoted in Goleman, *Emotional* 131).

For readers who already possess this knowledge, *Native Son* provides confirmation and vivid and memorable exemplars to reinforce it and activate it when they assess real-life Biggers. And for readers who do not yet possess it, the novel provides multiple instances and varying degrees of suggestion pointing toward it. The account of Bigger's background, for example, is entirely consistent with an environment in which Bigger did not receive adequate emotional sustenance of this sort. In addition to losing his father to violence when he was a child (74), itself a traumatic event of the sort that can harm emotional development, Bigger has been raised in poverty, in a neighborhood suffused with despair, crime, and gangs, by an overworked, exhausted, depressed mother who, as we noted above, was in all likelihood unable to provide him with optimal emotional care—precisely the risk factors that are usually found in the backgrounds of violent criminals.

If readers have not registered the impact of Bigger's formative environment on his character from such hints in the novel's first two books, Wright makes sure that they do in book 3. He does so by having Max repeatedly argue that Bigger's bad character is the result of his living conditions and by having Bigger transformed in jail, as we have just discussed, into a reflective, empathic, compassionate person. Max asserts at the outset that white racist society is responsible for Bigger's bad character. He tells Buckley when they meet in jail, "I'm defending this boy because I'm convinced that *men like you made him what he is*" (292; emphasis added).

Throughout the remainder of the novel, Wright provides multiple indications of specific factors of Bigger's environment that have made him the type of person he is. When the Daltons visit Bigger's cell, Max indicates that Bigger's "com[ing] from an oppressed people" (294) and being deprived of "a meaningful life" are key to understanding his bad character and actions, and at the coroner's inquest he poses the rhetorical question, "Mr. Dalton, do you think that the terrible conditions under which the Thomas family lived in one of your houses may in some way be related to the death of your daughter?" (328), thus inducing in readers the malleabilist life script: *inadequate formative environment→emotional deficits→bad character→violent behavior.*

When Max is questioning him about his feelings toward Mary, Bigger describes another toxic factor in his formation: "Mr. Max, you know what some white men say we black men do? They say we rape white women when we got the clap and they say we do that because we believe that if we rape white women then we'll get rid of the clap. That's what some white men *say*. They *believe* that. Jesus, Mr. Max, when folks says things like that about you, you whipped before you born" (351; emphasis in original). And concerning being deprived of opportunities, Bigger states:

> "Mr. Max, a guy gets tired of being told what he can do and can't do. You get a little job here and a little job there. You shine shoes, sweep streets; anything. . . . You don't make enough to live on. You don't know when you going to get fired. Pretty soon you get so you can't hope for nothing. You just keep moving all the time, doing what other folks say. You ain't a man no more. You just work day in and day out so the world can roll on and other people can live. . . . They don't even let you feel what you want to feel. They after you so hot and hard you can only feel what they doing to you. They kill you before you die." (353)

That Bigger's rapacious, murderous character is the responsibility not of Bigger himself but of those who control his environment is emphasized repeatedly by Max in his trial defense of Bigger. Bigger's bad character, he tells the judge, has sprung "from a soil plowed and sown by all our hands" (388). "[T]he background of this boy must be shown," he declares, "a background which has acted powerfully and importantly upon his conduct" (388). More specifically, Max argues, "School stimulated and developed in him those impulses which all of us have, and then he was made to realize that he could not act upon them" (394). The most important impulses are those of self-realization, which requires doing meaningful work, and Bigger is deprived of this opportunity: "Your Honor, remember that men can starve from a lack of self-realization as much as they can from a lack of bread! And they can *murder* for it, too!" (399; emphasis in original).

Bigger killed, Max argues, because of "[t]he hate and fear which we have inspired in him, woven by our civilization into the very structure of his consciousness, into his blood and bones, into the hourly functioning of his personality." His killing was thus "a physiological and psychological reaction, embedded in his being" by the white establishment (400). Max therefore concludes, "We planned the murder of Mary Dalton. . . . [T]he way we have treated this boy made him do the *very* thing we did not want. . . . Or, am I wrong? Maybe we *wanted* him to do it! Maybe we would have had no chance or justification to stage attacks against hundreds of thousands of people if he had acted sanely and normally!" (394–395; emphasis in original).

Through such characterizations of Bigger's background, Max constructs a life story of malleability that counters the essentialism life script, in which people's behavior and destiny are the result of their inborn, inherent characteristics and lays the responsibility for bad character not on the shoulders of those who possess it but rather at the feet of those who are responsible for the formative experiences and environment that produced it. And readers who commit this life story, with its toxic formative environment, to memory are better able to resist the cognitive inclinations and cultural forces of essentialism and more accurately attribute responsibility for the characters of the real-life Biggers and other stigmatized people as well.

Emotions Resulting from the Recognition of Malleability

The emotions of contempt, anger, and hatred expressed in the discourse of Buckley, the newspaper, and the mob concerning the essentialized rapist-murderer Bigger Thomas are typical of the feelings fostered by the essentialist schema. *Native Son* counters these emotions with sympathy and moral outrage. The novel's detailing of Bigger's psychological conditioning and resultant emotional helplessness by a toxic environment elicits profound sympathy from readers for this atheist-rapist-murderer. As Martha Nussbaum observes, *Native Son*

> avoids evoking an easy sympathy that would say, despite differences in circumstance, we are all brothers under the skin. The white reader has difficulty identifying with Bigger; not only his external circumstances, but also his emotions and desires, are the products of social and historical factors. But beneath the facile kind of sympathy lies the possibility of a deeper sympathy, one that says: This is a human being, with the basic equipment to lead a productive life; see how not only the external circumstances of action, but also anger, fear, and desire have been deformed by racial hatred and its institutional expression. The unlikeness that repels identification becomes the chief object of our concern. . . . We cannot follow the novel without trying to see the world through Bigger's eyes. As we do so, we take on, to at least some extent, his emotions of rage and shame. . . . This leads us as spectators to feel a further range of emotions—a deep sympathy . . . for Bigger's predicament, a principled anger at the structures of racism that have made him as he is. (*Poetic* 94)

By eliciting sympathy for Bigger in response to his deprived and oppressive formative environment, and "a principled anger" toward the forces that produce and maintain this unfair environment, *Native Son* promotes the integration of these emotions as default emotions of the malleability schema. In addition, by interweaving our sympathy with a continuous recognition that Bigger's plight, including his character and behavior, is the result of a racist system that for his entire life has brutalized him, tantalized him, and deprived him of the opportunity to develop a sense of self that could be sustained without fear and violence, the novel promotes the development in white readers of guilt over their responsibility for all the Biggers (white and black) and their horrific and brutal actions. Max's tears at the end model for readers this response to Bigger's story, insofar as they are tears of anguish and guilt and definitely not tears of consolation.

Scripts for Action in Light of Malleability

Readers' sympathy and guilt regarding Bigger's rotten social background incline them to help, rather than punish, all the Biggers of the world and motivate them to make reparation for the harm they have caused the Biggers and the rest of the world.

Native Son channels these general action tendencies into a specific action script, articulated by Max in his statement to the judge, in which he exhorts white society to endeavor to understand the social causes that have produced Bigger's character and behaviors and then work to change these causes: "I ask you to recognize the laws and processes flowing from such a condition, understand them, seek to change them. If we do none of these, then we should not pretend horror or surprise when thwarted life expresses itself in fear and hate and crime. . . . Men are men and life is life, and we must deal with them as they are; and if we want to change them, we must deal with them in the form in which they exist and have their being" (388).

It is clear from Max's earlier chastisement of Mr. Dalton that what is needed is not philanthropy, the futility and self-serving nature of which is epitomized in the gift of ping-pong tables through which Dalton tries to assuage his guilt for the condition of black people. As Max tells Dalton, "This boy and millions like him want a meaningful life, not ping-pong" (295), which means that the only truly helpful action would involve change "of a more fundamental nature" (295)—that is, the restructuring of society to ensure equal rights and equal opportunities for the millions of Biggers to live a meaningful life. The action script promoted by *Native Son* in conjunction with the recognition of malleability is thus the pursuit of fundamental social change, and its prerequisite, the understanding of how a person's living conditions determine his or her character and behavior.

Training in Malleabilist Information Processing

In addition to providing readers with multiple malleability templates in the form of these various exemplars, *Native Son* also trains readers more directly in malleabilist information processing. When most people contemplate a real-life rapist or murderer, they focus on the individual's evil deed and thus arrive at the same general response as the newspapers and lynch mob do about Bigger: he is an evil person who should be killed or incarcerated for life.

Native Son trains readers in more adequate and just information processing. It does so, first, by showing readers that Bigger's moral failings are actually the result of undeveloped and malformed cognitive-emotional capacities. Second, the novel provides enough information early on about Bigger's background for readers to realize that these developmental deficits were caused by his toxic formative environment. And third, to solidify these causal connections in readers' minds, the novel presents explicit and powerful arguments from Max and statements from Bigger himself showing how Bigger's character deficiencies were produced by the toxic white-supremacist society in which he grew up.

In these ways, *Native Son* promotes the development of information-processing routines that *expect, seek, infer, suppose,* and *attend to* cognitive and emotional deficiencies as motivating forces underlying every observed act of violence, and then *expect, seek, infer, suppose,* and *attend to* toxic environmental factors as the root causes of these cognitive and emotional deficits. That is, by repeatedly prompting readers to consider how Bigger came be a bad person, and hence to recognize how the white establishment made him the flawed character that he is, *Native Son* not only reduces readers' hostile judgments, emotions, and action tendencies regarding the novel's protagonist, but also fosters the development of information-processing routines that *expect* environmental forces to have a formative impact on people; that *attend to* those forces when they are evident and *infer* them, *search for* them, or *suppose* them when they are not evident; and that *categorize* people and environmental factors and *encode* them *in memory* with malleabilist rather than essentialist concepts.

In real life, we never really get to watch someone being formed; even if we know the person and observe him or her continually from birth, it is very difficult to see the influence of environment on character formation; rather, we have to reconstruct, infer, or postulate most of the formative processes. *Native Son* helps readers develop these malleabilist information-processing routines by repeatedly engaging readers in making the causal connections between specific elements of the formative environment and specific character traits in Bigger.

Developing the Heterogeneity Schema

I acted hard. . . . But I ain't hard. . . . I ain't hard even a little bit.
BIGGER THOMAS (425)

On the face of it, Bigger Thomas seems to be the prototypical evil person. As noted above, he is self-centered, self-indulgent, hostile, aggressive, and violent to the point of being a rapist and a murderer. If ever an individual deserved to be written off as simply evil with no redeeming qualities, Bigger would be a strong candidate. But *Native Son* demonstrates in multiple ways, large and small, that Bigger is not homogeneously evil, and in doing so, it contributes significantly to the development of a heterogeneity person-schema in readers.

Bigger's heterogeneity is shown in two forms: synchronic and diachronic. The diachronic demonstration of Bigger's heterogeneity coincides with the story of his transformation into a reflective, empathic, compassionate man, examined in the previous section on malleability and elaborated on in the following section on solidarity. Such transformation reveals that while Bigger's negative qualities may be more evident and actualized, especially at the beginning of the novel, he nonetheless has always possessed the positive qualities *in potentia*. All that is necessary to actualize the positive qualities is an environment that will elicit their expression and nurture their development, as Max indicates in his plea to the judge (393).

Propositional Knowledge of Heterogeneity

In addition to demonstrating Bigger's diachronically actualized heterogeneity, the novel presents readers with multiple forms of knowledge of Bigger's synchronic heterogeneity, and that of other characters as well.

The novel offers propositional knowledge of this point on several occasions. Early on, for example, we are told that underneath Bigger's tough demeanor lies a profound vulnerability: "He knew that the moment he allowed himself to feel to its fullness how they lived, the shame and misery of their lives, he would be swept out of himself with fear and despair. . . . So he denied himself and acted tough" (10). We are also informed early in the novel of Bigger's heterogeneity along another axis—violence and indifference: "These were the rhythms of his life: indifference and violence; periods of abstract brooding and periods of intense desire; moments of silence and moments of anger. . . . He was like a strange plant blooming in the day and wilting at night; but the sun that made it bloom and the cold darkness that made it wilt were never seen. It was his own sun and darkness, a private and personal sun and darkness" (29). The most powerful statement of Bigger's heterogeneity comes when he tells Max shortly before his execution, "I thought they [white people, who prevented him from pursing his ambitions] was hard and I acted hard. . . . But I ain't hard, Mr. Max. I ain't hard even a little bit" (425).

Heterogeneity Episodes

One of the most prominent and powerful forms of heterogeneity knowledge in *Native Son* is the episodic, in which a character's heterogeneity is revealed by manifesting two opposed qualities in the same moment, scene, or time period. Bigger's heterogeneity is evident in the opening scene, where his violent qualities, evident in his killing of the rat and in his taunting of Vera with it, coexist with his vulnerability in face of the rat and his kindness and sympathy toward his brother, Buddy. Later, he manifests a similar heterogeneity in his treatment of Gus, whom he first commiserates, banters, and conspires with, then kicks, strangles, and humiliates, and finally the next day treats to beer and cigarettes. And in the jail cell, he feels both hatred and compassion for his mother and the rest of his family.

The most dramatic and compelling episodes of heterogeneity, however, are the two killing scenes. In the scene with Mary, Bigger's gruesome decapitation of her with his knife and a hatchet is conjoined with his horror and revulsion at his own action, demonstrating that in addition to the cold, calculating, brutal side of him there is also a more humane side. After he chopped off Mary's head, "[h]e was not crying, but his lips were trembling and his chest was heaving, [and] [h]e wanted to lie down upon the floor and sleep off the horror of this thing" (92). And later, despite the feeling of agency, empowerment, and identity that he derives from Mary's killing, he is continually haunted by the recurring intrusion into his consciousness of the bloody image of her severed head (see 99, 113, 116, 118, 207, 132).

A similar revulsion indicating the presence of a profound, visceral reluctance to harm another human being haunts him as he is raping and killing Bessie. During the rape, he feels repulsions of remorse for his violence alternating with his sexual pulsion: "Yes. Bessie. Now. He had to now. *don't Bigger don't.* He was sorry, but he had to. He. He could not help it. Help it. Sorry. Help it. Sorry. Help it. Sorry" (234). Likewise, a powerful inhibition intrudes momentarily into his killing of Bessie as he is about to smash her skull with a brick: "He straightened and lifted the brick, but just at that moment the reality of it all slipped from him. . . . No! Not this! His breath swelled deep in his lungs and he flexed his muscles, trying to impose his will over his body. He had to do better than this. Then, as suddenly as the panic had come, it left. But he had to stand here until that picture came back, that motive, that driving desire to escape the law" (236; emphasis in original). After he has smashed her head repeatedly with the brick, his more human impulses express themselves once again:

> Then a dreadful thought rendered him incapable of action. Suppose Bessie was not as she had sounded when the brick hit her? Suppose, when he turned on the flashlight, he would see her lying there staring at him with those round large black eyes, her bloody mouth open in awe and wonder and pain and accusation. A cold chill, colder than the air of the room, closed about his shoulders like a shawl whose strands were woven of ice. It became unbearable and something within him cried out in silent agony. (237–238)

And a few moments later, after Bigger has dumped Bessie's body down the air shaft and then realizes that all his money is in her dress pocket, his revulsion at the consequences of his action prevent him from retrieving the money: "Should he go down and get [the money]? Anguish gripped him. *Naw*! He did not want to see her again. He felt that if he should ever see her face again he would be overcome with a sense of guilt so deep as to be unbearable" (239; emphasis in original). The novel's insertion of such moments of revulsion, inhibition, and remorse in the midst of revolting actions establishes these episodes and Bigger himself as exemplars of the internal heterogeneity that characterizes all humans, even those who may appear to be homogeneously bad.

There are also episodes involving the actions of other characters that contribute to the development of the heterogeneity schema in readers. Most notable are Jan and Mary's treatment of Bigger, and the Daltons' financial practices. In their interactions with Bigger, Jan and Mary reveal themselves to be simultaneously egalitarian and authoritarian. Offering Bigger one's hand, driving the car, sitting beside Bigger in the front seat, and sharing a meal with Bigger, as Jan and Mary do, are all manifestations of their egalitarian values and their sincere desire to treat Bigger as an equal. Yet they enact these egalitarian gestures in a manner that betrays a profoundly unegalitarian position: they *order* Bigger (albeit in a friendly manner) to shake Jan's hand, yield the wheel to Jan, sit between them in the front seat, eat with them in Ernie's Kitchen Shack, get drunk with them, drive around while they make love in the back seat, and finally drive a helplessly drunk Mary home by himself late at night.

Mr. and Mrs. Dalton are similarly self-contradictory in their treatment of black people. Offering Bigger a job with a generous salary, supporting the Boys Club, encouraging Bigger to get an education, participating in the NAACP, and (especially) donating over $5 million to "colored schools" (56), as the Daltons do, demonstrate a real commitment to helping black people. But these acts of generosity are outweighed by the racist business practices of Mr. Dalton, such as his charging exorbitant rent for the Thomases' one-room rat-infested apartment and his refusing to rent apartments outside the Black Belt to African Americans.

Other, less obvious exemplars of heterogeneity include Bigger's mother, Max, Reverend Hammond, and State's Attorney Buckley. Bigger's mother obviously loves Bigger desperately and worries and works herself to exhaustion to support him, yet her attempt to keep him out of trouble involves calling him names that wound him and have probably caused him significant harm over time. Rev. Hammond clearly wants to help Bigger, but actually just further alienates him, in admonishing him to be like Jesus. Conversely, Buckley, who wants to kill Bigger, actually shows him a degree of empathy. And Max, who castigates the racist society that, he argues, is ultimately responsible for Bigger's killings, and who vehemently contests this society's dehumanization of Bigger, nonetheless manifests a trace of racism in the very terms he uses to defend Bigger: while his characterization of Bigger as a different "form of life" is intended as an assertion of his humanity, it is ambiguous and also connotes, at best, a kind of subspeciation (see Erikson) or even infrahumanization. Through such episodes, these characters become, along with Bigger, exemplars of intrapersonal heterogeneity, embodying and enacting both good and bad qualities.

Emotions Evoked by Recognition of Heterogeneity

The recognition that rapist-murderers like Bigger are not pure evil and that, conversely, law-abiding people are not homogeneously good leads to more ambivalent emotions toward both types of people.

Specifically, cognizance of Bigger's vulnerable, reflective, empathic, remorseful, and compassionate qualities elicits a sympathy for him that tempers, if not totally displaces, feelings of anger, animosity, and hatred toward him. When, in the final scene, Max realizes the depth of Bigger's humanity, his compassion for him increases and he appears overwhelmed with anguish at the thought of Bigger's imminent execution. Readers who recognize Bigger's humanity feel the same, and this experience of compassion for Bigger associates compassion with heterogeneity, such that in the future, readers who apprehend real-life Biggers through their (perhaps newly developed) heterogeneity schema rather than their homogeneity schema will be more able, and more likely, to feel compassion for them as well.

Similarly, recognition of the Daltons' negative qualities tempers the admiration that is often felt toward wealthy people (especially kind, philanthropic ones) with a feeling of moral disapprobation and perhaps anger and resentment as well. These emotions are also evoked (or reinforced) by Max's expressions of anger and moral outrage at Mr. Dalton's racist business practices and his obtuseness regarding the humanity of Bigger and other black people. These negative emotions, when associated with the Daltons in readers' memories, will be activated to one degree or another in response to other apparently benign rich people whenever the Daltons are accessed as an exemplar of that category.

Action Scripts Responding to Heterogeneity

The appraisals and consequent compassion elicited by the heterogeneity schema also entail a particular type of action: inhibiting the expression, and promoting the atrophy, of people's negative qualities, and promoting the expression and development of their positive qualities. In *Native Son* this action script is represented in the more specific form of incarcerating Bigger, which is the action Max urges the judge to take instead of execution. Max's argument to the judge also emphasizes the more general action of supporting the expression and development of the benign side of the heterogeneous Bigger: "What would prison mean to Bigger Thomas? It holds advantages for him that a life of freedom never had. To send him to prison would be more than an act of mercy. You would be for the first time conferring *life* upon him. . . . He would have an identity, even though it be but a number. . . . Sending him to prison would be the first recognition of his personality he has ever had" (404–405). In this plea, Max is arguing that anyone with a shred of humanity deserves the opportunity to enact that humanity and develop it.

The action script entailed by a recognition of the heterogeneity of all individuals is to provide all individuals—who are all heterogeneous, composed of both positive and negative qualities—with limits on and obstacles to the enactment and strengthening of their negative qualities and opportunities for and assistance in enacting and developing their positive attributes.

Metacognition and the Correction of Faulty Information Processing

By portraying Bigger's benign qualities against the background of his malignant traits, the novel engages readers in recognizing positive characteristics in negative individuals, as well as the profound falseness of homogenizing characterizations, such as those that Buckley and the newspapers produce of Bigger.

In addition, readers' repeated and sustained experience of recognition of the phenomenon of positive traits in negative people alters their information-processing routines. The cognitive habituation to the perception of the positive within the negative gradually leads readers to *expect* to find good qualities in "bad" people, to *attend to* such qualities when they are present and to *encode* them in memory as exemplars of heterogeneity, and to *search for, infer, or suppose* such qualities when they are not manifest, so that when they consider criminals and other stigmatized individuals in real life, they will be more capable of, and more inclined to, take their benign, human qualities into account as well.

Developing the Solidarity Schema

. . . and the sun's rays melted away the many differences, the colors, the clothes, and drew what was common and good upward toward the sun. (362)

Native Son confronts white, middle-class readers with a character who is as different from them as can be imagined and then works to help them recognize that this other overlaps and coincides with them in much more profound ways than he differs from them.

The novel employs multiple schema elements, or forms of knowledge, to demonstrate that Bigger Thomas and hence Biggers in general share ontological, psychological-emotional, and practical solidarity with white readers. That is, it shows Bigger to have the same deep human needs, vulnerabilities, and capabilities as white readers do (ontological solidarity), to have a life interwoven with those of white readers, such that his fate has profound ramifications for theirs and vice versa

How Protest Novels Work to Replace Faulty Person-Schemas

(practical solidarity), and to be capable of eliciting empathy and sympathy from white readers (emotional solidarity).

Propositional Knowledge and Concepts of Solidarity

The ontological form of solidarity receives strong propositional articulation from both Bigger and Max in book 3. After his conversation with Max, in which he experiences recognition for the first time, Bigger begins to apprehend his profound sameness with all other humans: "He wondered if it were possible that after all everybody in the world felt alike? . . . If that white looming mountain of hate were not a mountain at all, but people, people like himself, and like Jan" (360–362).

Bigger's final visit with Max, just hours before his execution, provides another powerful propositional articulation of ontological solidarity, as Bigger wonders to Max if the hatred and violence of the white prosecutor, judge, lynch mob, and society in general who are responsible for his execution are the same as his own hatred and violence, in that they are the result of a deep human need that is not being satisfied. "Mr. Max," he says, "I know the folks who sent me here to die hated me; I know that. B-b-but you reckon th-they was like m-me, trying to g-get something like I was, and when I'm dead and gone they'll be saying like I'm saying now that they didn't mean to hurt nobody . . . th-that they was t-trying to get something, too . . . ?" (425).

Native Son provides a further propositional articulation of sameness beneath differences by explaining the differences between the Biggers and the law-abiding citizens as the result of different formative environments. In his plea to the judge, Max emphasizes, in a statement also articulating malleability, that contrary to the assumptions of the mob, the newspapers, and the prosecutor, Bigger is a human being, that his differences from his white counterparts are the result not of a different, non-human nature but of different formative circumstances producing different effects on the same common human nature. "I plead with you," he says to the judge, "to see a mode of *life* in our midst, a mode of life stunted and distorted, but possessing its own laws and claims, *an existence of men* growing out of the soil prepared by the collective but blind will of a hundred million people. I beg you to *recognize human life* draped in a form and guise alien to ours, but springing from a soil plowed and sown by all our hands" (388; emphasis added). This statement of solidarity also advances knowledge of solidarity in the form of a *concept*—"a *mode of life* stunted and distorted . . . , human life draped in a *form* and *guise* alien to ours" (emphasis added). Here human difference is presented as more superficial than sameness: it is only the "mode," "guise," and "form" of life that are different, "alien," rather than life itself, as is assumed by the dehumanizing, othering terms disseminated by Buckley ("silly alien," "bestial monstrosity," "black lizard," "black mad dog," "subhuman killer," "hardened black thing," etc. [407–410]), which deny Bigger's humanity and hence his ontological sameness with white people.

Max goes on to indicate two additional dimensions of sameness, affirming Bigger's own intuitions. Bigger and the white mob, he observes, have the same feelings, and they have them for the same basic reason: "Today Bigger Thomas and that mob are strangers, yet they hate. They hate because they fear, and they fear because they feel that the deepest feelings of their lives are being assaulted and outraged. And they do not know why; they are powerless pawns in a blind play of social forces" (390). Max also points out that in his core, Bigger is like the white people's own revered forefathers, and that the differences between them are secondary and contingent, a matter of luck rather that essence. "In [Bigger] and men like him," he says, "is what was in our forefathers when they first came to these strange shores hundreds of years ago. We were lucky. They are not. We found a land whose tasks called forth the deepest and best we had. . . . They are yet looking for a land whose tasks can call forth their deepest and best" (393).

Max explains further a few pages later that the twelve million black people in America have been "conditioned broadly by our own notions as we were by European ones when we first came here, [and] are struggling within unbelievably narrow limits to achieve that feeling of at-home-ness for which we once strove so ardently. . . . If anybody can, surely we ought to be able to understand what these people are after. This vast stream of life, dammed and muddied, is trying to sweep toward that fulfillment which all of us seek so fondly" (398).

Max also gives propositional form to *practical solidarity*, the interwovenness of the lives of Bigger and his haters, by arguing that Bigger's fate is the result of actions taken by white people and warning that Bigger's execution, if allowed to occur, will have harmful consequences for white people. In his defense of Bigger, he asserts: "[I]f we can understand how subtly and yet strongly his life and fate are linked to ours—if we can do this, perhaps we shall find the key to our future, that rare vantage point upon which every man and woman in this nation can stand and view how inextricably our hopes and fears of today create the exultation and doom of tomorrow" (382). He warns the judge of "the two possible courses of action open to us and the inevitable consequences flowing from each" (383) and urges "that this boy's life be spared for reasons which I believe affect the foundations of our civilization" (384). In a passage that further indicates how malleability entails practical interwovenness, Max also points out how the actions of white people are woven into Bigger's personality, noting "[t]he hate and fear which we have inspired in him, woven by our civilization into the very structure of his consciousness, into his blood and bones, into the hourly functioning of his personality" (400). "Through the instrument of fear," Max declares, "we determined the mode and the quality of [Bigger's] consciousness" (402).

The novel also directly states the practical, psychological, and ontological solidarity of Bigger with his family: "He had lived and acted on the assumption that he was alone, and now he saw that he had not been. What he had done made others suffer [=*practical solidarity*]. No matter how much he would long for them to forget him, they would not be able to. His family was a part of him, not only in blood [=*ontological solidarity*], but in spirit [=*psychological solidarity*]" (298). This statement establishes all the people who visit Bigger in his cell as *individual exemplars* of psychological solidarity, insofar as they come to visit Bigger because they empathize and sympathize with him and care about him. Their acts of visitation, in turn, are so many *episodes* of solidarity.

Episodes of Solidarity

Indeed, the novel is replete with episodes of solidarity. There are multiple episodes in which Bigger himself displays psychological solidarity, in the form of empathy or sympathy, with other characters. As noted earlier, Bigger experiences brief moments of involuntary empathy for Bessie and Mary immediately before and after he kills them, respectively, for his mother when she visits him in jail, for the deranged man who is briefly his cellmate, for Max when Max first speaks with him and also during his final visit with Max, for his white oppressors during the final scene, and for Max as he is bidding him farewell for the final time.

Similarly, there are multiple episodes portraying other characters demonstrating empathy and sympathy for Bigger, however inadequate, inaccurate, or misguided their feelings of solidarity may be. Such episodes include Mr. Dalton's hiring Bigger, Mrs. Dalton suggesting to him that he pursue his education, Jan and Mary's attempt to be his friends, Jan's forgiving Bigger and recruiting Max to help him, Max's efforts to save Bigger's life, Rev. Hammond's efforts to save Bigger's soul, and even Buckley's apparent intellectual empathy (though not sympathy) for Bigger when he interviews him in jail.

Native Son also presents readers with multiple episodes portraying the practical solidarity of different individuals and groups. The most significant of these is Bigger's killing of Mary, which, as the narrative emphasizes, has a profound effect not only on Mary but also on Mary's parents, on Jan, on Bessie, and on Bigger's family—and, indeed, in the manhunt that follows, on the entire city of Chicago, both black and white. The practical solidarity that Bigger experiences through the effect his action has had on Mary's parents manifests itself in his newfound sense of self (105–107) and his sense of equality with white people: "The knowledge that he had killed a white girl they loved and regarded as their symbol of beauty made him feel the equal of them, like a man who had been somehow cheated, but had now evened the score" (164). The narrative emphasizes his recruitment of Bessie as an accessory after the fact as another instance of harmful practical solidarity: "She would be bound to him by ties deeper than marriage. She would be his; her fear of capture and death would bind her to him with all the strength of her life" (150). His practical (and also psychological) solidarity with Jan is foregrounded by the "stab of remorse" that hits Bigger when Jan visits him in jail and he realizes that "he had killed what this man loved and had hurt him" (289).

Ontological solidarity, too, is presented through multiple episodes revealing Bigger to have the same basic needs, vulnerabilities, and potential as others, including his white accusers, their ancestors, and most importantly, white readers. Bigger's need for agency and identity is demonstrated by the change that killing Mary produces in him, and his need for recognition in his wish to tell his story and his feelings (130, 222, 308, 348, 360ff.), as well as by the change produced in him by the recognition he derives from his first conversation with Max. His common need for solidarity is manifested in his fantasizing about a leader like Hitler or Mussolini who could unite all black people: "There were rare moments when a feeling and longing for solidarity with other black people would take hold of him" (114).

Moreover, despite being an atheist, he is shown to have the same spiritual yearnings for solidarity that Christians find satisfied by their religion. After rejecting religion as an escape and a delusion, he reflects, in a passage echoing the language of the Christian doctrine of redemption and atonement (at-one-ment), on "what he wanted: to merge himself with others and be part of the world, to lose himself in it so he could find himself, to be allowed to live like others, even though he was black. . . . If only someone had gone before and lived or suffered or died—made it so that it could be understood! It was too stark, not redeemed, not made real with the reality that was the warm blood of life" (240–241).

Images of Solidarity

The novel also presents several powerful images of solidarity, which come to Bigger as he is trying to understand the reason for all the hatred and fear. The first image is of atomism, each individual's separation and isolation from every other individual—a separation and isolation which, however, also constitutes a profound sameness, insofar as it is an experience shared by everyone: "he saw a black sprawling prison full of tiny black cells in which people lived . . . , and no one could go from cell to cell and there were screams and curses and yells of suffering and nobody heard them, for the walls were thick and darkness was everywhere. . . . But was this true? He wanted to believe, but was afraid. Dare he flatter himself that much? Would he be struck dead if he made himself the equal of others, even in fancy?" (361–362).

This image of solidarity is followed by a second one, which comes to Bigger as he is struggling to decide whether his first vision of sameness is valid: "Another impulse rose in him, born of desperate need, and his mind clothed it in an image of a strong blinding sun sending hot rays down and he was standing in the midst of a vast crowd of men, white men and black men and all men, and the sun's rays melted away the many differences, the colors, the clothes, and drew what was common and good upward toward the sun" (362). Two pages later he has a third vision in which another atomistic image emphasizing his isolation from the rest of humanity is superseded by an image of solidarity: "He looked out upon the world and the people about him with a double vision: one vision pictured death, an image of him, alone, sitting strapped in the electric chair and waiting for the hot current to leap through his body; and the other vision pictured life, an image of himself standing amid a throng of men, lost in the welter of their lives with the hope of emerging again, different, unafraid" (364).

Two other images embody solidarity in a somewhat different manner. First, there is the recurring "terrible image of Mary's head lying on the bloody newspaper" (132), mentioned earlier, which intrudes into Bigger's awareness half a dozen times during his flight (see also 99, 113, 116, 118, 165). This recurrent intrusion itself embodies a profound, if terrible, practical solidarity with Mary, with whom Bigger is now integrally and inextricably connected. But the image also embodies a more profound, psychological and ontological solidarity, a solidarity grounded in the involuntary empathy and even identification Bigger experiences for Mary, signaled by Bigger's dream, in which he opens a big, heavy, wet, slippery package and finds his own bloody head (165), suggesting his deep, unconscious identification with Mary.

A final image of solidarity is that of Max's wet eyes as he bids Bigger a final farewell. Max's tears demonstrate his empathy, his emotional solidarity with Bigger, as he mourns Bigger's imminent extinction (429). Each of these images provides readers with a concrete, perceptual apprehension of solidarity that, when committed to memory, can prime them to recognize their solidarity with all other humans, including the Biggers of the world.

Solidarity Emotions

Readers directly enact emotional-psychological solidarity with Bigger insofar as they empathize with him and experience sympathy for him. As indicated above, this sympathy is due in part to our recognition of the harmful and painful effects that his situation and his formative environment have had on him. Descriptions of the situations of other people, as we have seen, can elicit the same responses in readers' neural, autonomic, and muscle systems that they would have if they were actually in the situations themselves. Such simulations are elicited, for example, by the various scenes in which Bigger is trying to prevent Mary's body from being discovered and, later, attempting to escape the dragnet that the authorities have deployed to capture him.

Reader sympathy for Bigger is also elicited by the graphic accounts of his physical and physiological reactions, such as when "the fear that Gus would really go [through with the robbery of Blum's] made the muscles of Bigger's stomach tighten; he was hot all over. He felt as if he wanted to sneeze and could not; only it was more nervous than wanting to sneeze. He grew hotter, tighter; his nerves were taught and his teeth were on edge. He felt that something would soon snap within him" (25; see also 26, 36–38, 41, 47, 48, 70, 73, 86–87, 92). As discussed in Chapter 1, such descriptions elicit emotion in readers by evoking, via their mirror neurons, micro-simulations of the actions in their brains and even in their muscles. The same is true of Bigger's vocal prosodics in his final conversation with Max (425, 428–430). We also mirror the sympathy that Jan and Max feel for Bigger, with Max's weeping and physical prosodics in the final scene (425–430) being particularly powerful elicitors of such responses. Each such micro-simulation contributes incrementally to making our sympathy more accessible, and the fact that we find our feeling mirrored by another person (i.e., Max or Wright) validates the feeling and makes it more acceptable, thus making us more capable and more predisposed to experience it in response to real-life Biggers outside the novel.

Finally, our sympathy for Bigger is also the result, in part, of our recognition of our ontological solidarity with him, a recognition that derives from the emergence of his profound capacity for empathy, which culminates in the final scene, where he is revealed to be the most human, humane, and spiritual character in the book. As noted above, Bigger initially experiences empathy for his family, friends, and Bessie after his killing of Mary provides a significant enhancement of his self-esteem. Then, in jail, he responds empathically to Jan's empathy for him, and later, with his execution only hours away, he experiences empathy even for his lynchers (425) and manifests less concern for himself than for his mother, Max, and Jan (428–430). This universal empathy establishes Bigger as a kind of Christ figure, a connection that is also indicated by the fact that Bigger, like Jesus, suggests that his killers don't know what they're doing and his asking Max (again like Jesus) to look after his mother (425).

Solidarity Action Scripts

The solicitude that Bigger exhibits for Max, Jan, and his mother also exemplifies the basic action script of solidarity: taking care of others who are in need. As in *The Jungle* and *The Grapes of Wrath*, Bigger's care for others, as just noted, has echoes of the central message of Christianity contained in Jesus's declaration in the Sermon on the Mount that people should take care of anyone who is suffering, including "the least of these my brethren" (Matthew 25:40).

In *Native Son*, however, Wright clearly distinguishes Bigger's Christlike, universal empathy from the self-serving delusions (e.g., belief in an afterlife) and exclusions (e.g., the belief that some people—like Bigger—deserve to suffer in this life and beyond) that characterize much of Christianity. Bigger's rejection of the idea of an afterlife because there is no evidence to support it and because there is copious evidence that it is embraced because it dulls the pain of existence (he recognizes that religion serves the same function for his mother that alcohol serves for Bessie) establishes universal care as a natural and intrinsically rewarding enactment of the fundamental nature of all humans, including rapists and murderers, rather than as the product of some external threat (e.g., the threat of hell) or enticement (e.g., the promise of heaven).

Like *The Grapes of Wrath* (and in contrast to *The Jungle*), *Native Son* doesn't spell out the socialist implications of this particular action script, but they are clear enough to any attentive reader—as indicated by the fact that Buckley sees these implications quite clearly in the comments Max makes to Mr. Dalton (295). The novel suggests that the fact of human solidarity ultimately entails, and can only be fully realized in, an anti-racist socialism or communism, which is the only viable alternative to the exclusionary and delusional forms of solidarity offered by fascism (to which Bigger is vaguely attracted) and religion (which he firmly and explicitly rejects because of its delusional and oppressive nature).

Native Son contributes significantly to the realization of human solidarity in social policies, institutions, systems, and structures by promoting the development of information-processing structures in people's brains that enable them to apprehend, consistently and fully, their ontological, psychological-emotional, and practical solidarity with all other humans, along with the situatedness, malleability, and heterogeneity that characterize every individual.

PART IV

A RADICAL COGNITIVE SOCIAL CRITICISM

CHAPTER 9

Schema Criticism: Radical Cognitive Politics

Can we in good conscience enjoy the privilege of being able to read and write and know where our next meal will come from and not use our words to advocate for social and planetary justice?
ELIZABETH AMMONS 47

The preceding chapters have made the case that literature is capable of promoting crucial alterations in the multiple forms of knowledge and information-processing routines that govern our individual and collective understanding, emotions, and actions concerning other people.

As noted in the first chapter, however, simply reading literature will not usually suffice to produce the thoroughgoing and enduring schema changes necessary to underwrite significant social change, for three reasons. First, most people do not read the types of texts that are most effective in promoting the necessary schema changes. Second, many who do read such texts do not, without direction or instruction, attend to and *encode in memory*, as such, the corrective exemplars, prototypes, and information-processing routines that we have been discussing. The historical reception of *The Jungle* clearly demonstrates this point: despite the novel's systematic undermining of the four faulty person-schemas, as explained in Chapter 6, and Sinclair's express desire to promote concern and outrage over the plight of workers, many of the novel's initial readers, at least, experienced more concern and outrage over the contamination of food than over the exploitation of workers. Third, even on those relatively rare occasions when readers do read the types of texts that promote such changes with the attention and memory-encoding that produce these changes, the schema alteration that may occur as a result of reading a single novel will usually not be thorough or substantial

288 A Radical Cognitive Social Criticism

enough to contribute significantly to the desired social change. This is because changing cognitive schemas, as discussed in Chapter 1, depends on a person's repeatedly using the new schema in a variety of contexts—that is, activating its prototypes and exemplars and enacting its information-processing routines, ideally with a metacognitive awareness of the nature and importance of the specific alterations in schema elements and information-processing routines that are necessary for producing adequate perceptions and judgments of other people.

Hence the need for schema criticism. Schema criticism is a method for activating, maximizing, and extending the schema-altering processes that certain literary texts are capable of initiating but are rarely able, by themselves, to bring to completion. While it is probably most effective when employed in conjunction with the study of literary texts that promote the development of new exemplars, prototypes, and information-processing routines, schema criticism can also be effectively employed in the study of other types of literary texts, as well as in conjunction with the study of other humanities and social science disciplines. And it can also be effective simply as a mode of social and political discourse in the public sphere.

Whatever the context of its use, schema criticism employs the basic techniques listed below.

1. *Decommissioning harmful, faulty schemas, by helping people develop metacognition* of their own individual and collective use of them. This metacognition can be developed by
   — educating people about the nature, functioning, and consequences of cognitive schemas in general, and faulty, harmful schemas in particular;
   — demonstrating the deficiencies of the faulty schemas—that is, pointing out what crucial information about other people the schemas omit, obscure, distort, discount, or fabricate; and
   — helping people recognize repeatedly, in different contexts, the operation and harmful effects of these faulty schemas, in their own cognition, in discourse, and in social policies, institutions, and systems.
2. Helping people *construct new, more adequate schemas*, through
   — correcting faulty exemplars by pointing out what crucial information about the other they omit, obscure, distort, discount, or fabricate;

—providing more typical, three-dimensional exemplars (and hence also, eventually, more accurate prototypes deriving from these exemplars); and

—developing more adequate information-processing routines (of attention, memory search, information-seeking, inference, etc.), which take account of crucial information about other people that the faulty routines ignore, discount, distort, or fabricate.

3. Continually repeating steps 1 and 2, and engaging people in *employing the more adequate schemas repeatedly* in multiple and diverse contexts, in order to firmly establish them as the default structures for processing information about other people. This activity includes

—repeatedly activating one's metacognition concerning the operations and consequences of the various schema elements;

—repeatedly retrieving the more adequate exemplars and prototypes and employing them as templates in processing information about others; and

—repeatedly enacting the more adequate information-processing routines.

The specifics of these three steps will differ somewhat depending on the context. When working with literary texts that themselves initiate these steps, such as the protest novels discussed in the previous three chapters, the schema critic's first task is to make the text's schema-altering operations explicit to readers, as these three chapters have done. This "positive" form of schema criticism centers on (1) highlighting the adequate exemplars, prototypes, and information-processing acts embodied in the text; (2) explaining how they, in contrast to their inadequate counterparts, work to take account of all the information necessary for arriving at accurate and fair judgments of other persons; and (3) *promoting their encoding in memory as corrective information-processing structures.* This practice can be supplemented by extending the text's operations to extra-textual, real-life persons, events, policies, institutions, and systems, and by contrasting the adequate schema elements with inadequate counterparts in actual social policies, institutions, systems, and structures.

When applied to literary texts that embody the faulty, harmful schemas, schema criticism will first need to explain what crucial information is being systematically omitted and/or unjustifiably fabricated by the text and how these omissions and fabrications lead to judgments, emotions, and actions—including social policies, institutions, and systems—that are flawed, unjust, and harmful. In addition, this "negative" form of schema criticism involves pointing out all the text's faulty exemplars, prototypes, and information-processing acts that are responsible for the fabrications and omissions, explaining how they are deficient (i.e., what crucial information they exclude or make up), and demonstrating their negative consequences.

This metacognition can be enhanced by helping one's audience recognize similar flaws in their own processing of information concerning not only real people and events but also social policies, institutions, and systems. Of particular value is helping people recognize how various cultural texts engage them in—and/or perform for them—autonomist, essentialist, atomist, and homogenist information processing. This involves practices such as pointing out how certain TV programs, films, and works of literature, as well as various social and economic policies (e.g., the tax code), institutions (e.g., courts), and systems (e.g., the economic system) enact—and thus engage their audiences in performing—the exclusion, marginalization, or minimization of the evidence of individuals' situations, formative environments, positive qualities, and human solidarity. By exposing such information-processing flaws and the harm and injustice that result from them, schema criticism not only enhances people's metacognition, but also establishes a solid foundation for rejecting, replacing, or revising such texts, policies, institutions, and systems.

Addressing Harmful Social Policies, Institutions, and Systems

Schema criticism can thus be effectively employed in relation to not only literary texts but also other forms of discourse, including news reports, commentaries, and analyses and political speeches and debates. And schema criticism can also produce a powerful direct response to unjust social policies, institutions, systems, and structures, virtually all of which are based on fundamental assumptions about the relation between the individual and the group and between in-group and out-group. The former include tax policies as well as government programs and systems of welfare, education, health care, personal security, infrastructure, and employment—in short, any policy in which the respective roles of government and the individual, or public and private responsibility, are in question. And how one answers this basic question in each case depends to a significant degree on whether one is operating with the faulty autonomy, essentialism, or atomism schemas or with the more adequate situationism, malleability, and solidarity schemas. If one views the world via the schemas of autonomy, essentialism, and atomism, one will see individuals as being solely responsible for their own character (essentialism), their own welfare and life outcomes (autonomism), and themselves alone (atomism), which means that the role of government should be relatively small if not totally nonexistent (the position of some libertarians).

If one is employing the more adequate schemas of situationism, malleability, and solidarity, on the other hand, one will see individual welfare and life outcomes as inextricably interwoven with those of others (solidarity) and resulting from circumstances and formative environments produced by others (situationism and malleability, respectively), which means that we are all responsible for each other and to each other and must exercise this responsibility through collective actions in the form of policies, institutions, systems, and structures that take our situatedness, malleability, and solidarity into account.

The question of the relation between one's in-group and various out-groups is also involved in the preceding issues, insofar as each of these issues involves class divisions—the divide between the haves and the have-nots. In addition, the relation of in-group to out-group is central to numerous other public policies, institutions, systems, and structures, including those involving war, terrorism, genocide, immigration, commerce, criminality, race relations, gender relations, sexuality, and other intergroup distinctions and relations. Here the faulty essentialism, atomism, and homogeneity schemas will result in positions and actions emphasizing intergroup differences over commonalities, and competition and opposition over cooperation and alliance, while the more adequate schemas of malleability, solidarity, and heterogeneity will enable one to recognize the profound interconnectedness and sameness that subtend all differences among groups and individuals.

When dealing with social policies, institutions, systems, and structures, schema criticism will first examine whether the position in question embodies one or more of the four faulty schemas, or whether it is based instead on their more adequate counterparts. If the position is based on one or more of the faulty schemas, the schema critic will explain what crucial information about certain types of people is being suppressed, discounted, or fabricated in order to justify (explicitly or implicitly) the policy, institution, system, or structure in question. When confronted, for example with regressive tax policies (e.g., historically low tax rates for the rich or tax breaks for prosperous corporations, capital gains, and hedge-fund earnings), or claims that taxation per se is unjust (as in George W. Bush's assertion that "It's your money; you earned it, and the government has no right to take it from you"), schema critics will emphasize crucial information that this position ignores, and that is excluded from the awareness of most people by the autonomism and atomism schemas—namely, that successful people owe their success not just to their own virtues and talents and hard work but also to circumstances over which they have little or no control (situationism) and to their formative environment (malleability), both of which prerequisites for an individual's success are produced by other people (practical solidarity).

Schema critics will provide similar reminders in response to efforts to cut or privatize various government programs, policies, institutions, or systems, such as public education, transportation, and communication systems, and publicly owned, funded, and/or regulated utilities and infrastructure, including water, sewer, gas, electric, and waste-management systems. Here schema critics will point out that fairness requires individuals who are capable of paying more to do so in order to support a commonwealth that is itself a major contributor to, and the necessary condition of, their own private wealth—the preservation of which, moreover, may well be dependent in multiple ways on redistributing a goodly portion of this wealth to people less fortunate than themselves.

Such autonomism-, essentialism-, and atomism-refuting information was eloquently articulated in an extemporaneous response by Massachusetts Senate candidate Elizabeth Warren to the commonplace Republican charge that raising the income-tax rates of the wealthy would constitute (unjust and unprovoked) class warfare:

> I hear [people say,] "This is class warfare . . ." No. There is nobody in this country who got rich on his own—nobody. You built a factory out there? Good for you. But I want to be clear: you moved your goods to market on the roads the rest of us paid for; you hired workers the rest of us paid to educate; you were safe in your factory because of police forces and fire forces that the rest of us paid for. You didn't have to worry that marauding bands would come and seize everything at your factory, and hire someone to protect against this, because of the work the rest of us did. Now look, you built a factory and it turned into something terrific, or a great idea? God bless. Keep a big hunk of it. But part of the under-

Schema Criticism   293

lying social contract is you take a hunk of that and pay forward for the
next kid who comes along.

This statement is an exemplary schema-critical intervention: it reminds
people of the situatedness and the practical solidarity that are fundamental truths about all human accomplishments and that render invalid the
assumption that no one else has any moral claim on the money rich people have accumulated (in a system that rich people have rigged to their
own advantage), or that redistribution of wealth and publicly funded
programs, institutions, and systems are somehow morally or practically
objectionable.

Schema critics will make similar interventions with regard to various
elements of the criminal justice system. Concerning the system's emphasis on punishment over prevention and rehabilitation, schema critics will make the situationist point that criminal acts are determined to
a large degree by circumstances (see Chapter 2 for a fuller argument), as
well as the malleabilist point that criminal character is largely determined
by a formative environment and experiences over which the individual
has little or no control (see Chapter 3), and that all the rest of us are ultimately responsible for the better part of both of these factors (practical
solidarity). And they may also point out that lawbreakers are not at bottom all that different from law-enforcers and law-abiders (ontological
solidarity), because members of all three groups possess the same basic
virtues and vices (heterogeneity), only in different degrees of development, activation, and/or visibility. Each of these points works to undermine both the practical rationale and the emotional motivation for punishment and to produce a practical rationale and emotional motivation
for prevention and rehabilitation.

And when it comes to actions and policies involving indifference,
domination, aggression, or unilateralism in relation to other nations—
which are explicitly or implicitly justified on the basis of supposed "national interests" and of supposed differences between "them" and
"us"—schema critics expose facts obscured by these assumptions, including the fact of universal human solidarity (ontological, psychological, and practical) and heterogeneity ("they" are not all bad, and "we"
are not all good), as well as situatedness and malleability (to the extent
that "their" behavior appears to "us" irrational, immoral, or uncivilized,
it is the result of the different situations in which it occurs, or the different formative environments in which "they" were raised). And these situations and formative environments, schema critics will point out, are

in many cases "our" doing, insofar as our use of even the most common products implicates us in the lives of the other people around the world who contribute to their production. Schema critics will therefore emphasize, with Martha Nussbaum, that "we need to think about our responsibilities to these people, as agents in the creation of their daily circumstances," and ask: "How has the international network in which we consumers are a crucial part shaped their labor conditions? What opportunities do they have? Should we agree to be part of the causal network that produces their situation, or should we demand changes?" (Nussbaum, *Not for Profit* 82).

Each of these interventions can also include instruction in metacognition. Such instruction can be as simple as pointing out that the information one is providing is systematically excluded or fabricated by dominant mindsets operating in certain discourse domains and/or communities. It can also include identifying particular schema elements (i.e., processing routines, exemplars, or prototypes) that produce such distortions, which can be followed by describing, as well as providing, alternative, more adequate schema elements with which to displace the faulty ones.

Conclusion

Through interventions of this sort, schema criticism will be considerably more effective in promoting social justice than other methods of criticism are. The traditional mode of social criticism, in which the critic speaks the truth about power, often accomplishes little in and of itself. Shooting holes in faulty and harmful beliefs, stereotypes, or power-knowledge formations is less than optimally effective in promoting social justice because it fails to sufficiently correct the faulty cognitive schemas that are responsible for the flawed judgments about others that underlie social injustice. The key truth about power that we need to understand and address is the way it operates in, on, and through people's person-schemas, by getting them to (mis)perceive and (mis)judge other people in ways that lead them to experience unjustified emotions and engage in unjust actions toward them. Such understanding is valuable not as an end in itself but rather as a basis for constructing strategies and practices for correcting faulty and unjust information processing.

The key intervention is the fostering of person-schemas that enable people to achieve more adequate understanding of other people, which in turn inspires more appropriate emotions and more just actions toward them. This central aim distinguishes schema criticism from current forms of social criticism, in four crucial ways:

1. Rather than trying to refute false and harmful beliefs, schema criticism focuses on correcting the deficient information-processing structures that are responsible for the production and reproduction of these false and harmful beliefs as well as faulty perceptions, judgments, emotions, and actions concerning other people.
2. Rather than concentrating on the propositional form of faulty knowledge and beliefs, schema criticism focuses on the multiple non-propositional forms, including exemplars, prototypes, and information-processing routines.
3. Recognizing that these forms of knowledge—and hence the cognitive schemas that they constitute—cannot be changed simply through logical, propositional discourse informing people of the truth about other people, schema criticism engages in interventions that correct or replace the key faulty knowledge structures that misguide people's social information processing.
4. These interventions include developing people's metacognition concerning the nature, operation, and consequences of their social information processing and engaging people in repeatedly enacting the more adequate alternative forms of knowledge (exemplars, prototypes, and processing routines) that govern this information processing.

The cognitive retraining at the heart of this development of more adequate person-schemas thus centers on two basic repetitions: repeated encounters with, and encoding in memory of, corrective exemplars, and repeated rehearsals of corrective information-processing routines. The latter alters the procedural memories constituting the various information-processing routines, thus directly altering the way information is processed. The former alters the composition of episodic memory, increasing the population, and hence the accessibility and likely activation, of more adequate exemplars, which themselves lead to the formation of more adequate prototypes in semantic memory. When activated, these more adequate exemplars and prototypes produce more just emotions and actions and/or serve as more reliable templates for information processing.

By repeatedly engaging students, media audiences, and the general public in these cognitive retraining activities, schema criticism can foster the development of more adequate person-schemas in a critical mass of individuals. When, after sufficient repetitions, the more adequate schemas become the default mechanisms for processing information about people, they will automatically be employed whenever these individuals assess other persons. The result will be greater social justice, achieved through the more just social structures, institutions, and policies that one comes to support when guided by the more accurate and comprehensive understanding of other people that the more adequate person-schemas produce.

In sum, by fostering more adequate person-schemas as the default information-processing mechanisms governing people's social cognition, schema criticism improves people's perceptions and judgments of others. These improved perceptions and judgments, in turn, reduce people's support for unjust and counterproductive social policies, institutions, systems, and structures—characterized by neglect and punishment of the unfortunate and further excessive rewards for the fortunate—and lead people instead to support more just and effective policies, institutions, systems, and structures, based on compassion and solidarity, which follow directly from recognizing people's inherent solidarity with each other as well as their situatedness, malleability, and heterogeneity. The more adequate person-schemas thus constitute a psychological basis—and quite likely a prerequisite—for the development of a more just world. Schema criticism, as a critical practice that promotes the development of these more adequate schemas, can make a significant contribution to that end.

Notes

Chapter 1

1. Concerning the influence of Foucault on New Historicists, see Greenblatt; Lentricchia; and Harpham, "Foucault."

2. Balkin finds the fact that it is "actively hostile to offering accounts of the internal processes of the human mind" to be "the most serious failing of the theory of discourse that has come to replace the theory of ideology" (Balkin 186).

3. Some readers may object to my claim that certain knowledge is faulty and that the cognitive mechanisms and processes that produce it are flawed, arguing that the validity of all knowledge is culturally relative and subjective, and rejecting all claims to any sort of objective, evidentiary basis for knowledge. My response is that these arguments are untenable even by those who make them, as can be seen by the fact that the enunciation of such objections enacts the very assumption that it is attacking: critics of my epistemological position must assume that they have valid, objective knowledge of both my argument and of the reality (or lack thereof) to which it presumes to refer. If all knowledge were arbitrary and ungrounded in any reality beyond the mind that constructs it, then there would be no grounds for knowing this fact or for my critics' claims that their "knowledge" concerning knowledge is superior to mine. Furthermore, few epistemological or cultural relativists take the position that the "knowledge" held by racists, sexists, heterosexists, or colonialists—not to mention murderers, rapists, and child-molesters—concerning their respective stigmatized others is just as valid as the knowledge held by their critics concerning these others. Nor do such critics argue for the validity of the "knowledge" that the Holocaust never happened, that global warming is a hoax, that AIDS and Hurricane Katrina were a god's punishment of homosexuality, and so on. For a recent quick, but largely serviceable, critique of the facile dismissal of notions such as truth and objectivity, see Fish 120–134 (see also Pinker 197ff.). Knowledge claims are ultimately adjudicated by experience. If one person claims that a pile of white powder is aspirin and another asserts that it is arsenic, the experience of ingesting the powder will determine who is right. And while the highly structured and controlled experiences known as scientific experiments rarely yield results this unambiguous and definitive, the knowledge they establish also proves

298 Notes to Pages 10–16

itself in real—as the theory of relativity has demonstrated in numerous—and sometimes catastrophic—ways. As Frederick Luis Aldama observes, "While science is not perfect in its measurements, it has allowed us to understand more clearly how certain aspects of reality work. We would not get on a plane and fly across the country if this were not so. Not all our ideas about the world are fictions" (Aldama xii). Thus in what follows, I base my claim that some knowledge and cognitive schemas are faulty and inferior to others on empirical scientific evidence.

4. On various different forms of knowledge, see, for example, Teasdale and Barnard; Smith; Smith and DeCoster; Monk; Huesmann; Fiske; Bucci; and White. A number of theorists, including Foucault and Jameson, have recognized that knowledge takes multiple forms, but they have not addressed how these various forms operate in cognition or how they could be altered. See Foucault, *Archaeology* 181ff. and Jameson, *Political* 13, 87–88.

5. For a detailed and empirically based explanation of the relative roles of knowledge and emotion as determinants of behavior, see Weiner; Fiske; Lazarus; and Westen.

6. See Rubin for an account of how episodic memories are constructed from interactions among multiple basic systems.

7. Whether prototypes are enduring knowledge structures or simply epiphenomena resulting from the simultaneous activation and "averaging" of multiple exemplars on any given occasion is a matter of some dispute, but one that does not, however, bear significantly on the account I give of how they operate or how they can be altered (see Moskowitz 165–166).

8. "Cognitive schema" is sometimes employed virtually synonymously with "concept," which in my usage is just one of the multiple types of knowledge comprised by cognitive schemas. Other writers, including Patrick Hogan and Adrian Wells, use "schema" to refer to the most abstract and general forms of declarative knowledge, to be contrasted with both prototypes (standard or typical cases of a category) and exemplars (specific instances of a category). I follow Taylor and Crocker, Moskowitz, Singer and Salovey, and others in using "schema" to refer to all forms of knowledge, including information-processing routines, concerning a given category, such that abstract knowledge, prototypes, exemplars (or, in Hogan's usage, "exempla"), and information-processing routines are all components of schemas. My account of cognitive schemas, prototypes, exemplars, and information processing is drawn from numerous sources, including Taylor and Crocker; Moskowitz; Schneider; Huesmann; Bless et al.; Singer and Salovey; Hogan *Culture*; *Cognitive*; and *Understanding*; and Anderson and Lindsay.

9. When I say that cognitive schemas are "functional constructs," I mean that they, and the multiple forms and types of knowledge they comprise, do not necessarily have a one-to-one correspondence to any anatomical structures of the brain. On the ontological status of representations and their relation to other levels of analysis in cognitive science, see Hogan, *Cognitive* 30ff. and *Understanding* 27, n. 4; and Davis et al.

10. As with the four assumptions, the forms of knowledge I discuss here are not identified as a group by any cognitive scientists so far as I know. Rather, I have compiled this list by integrating research in cognitive science and in literary

theory with my analyses of literary texts concerned with social justice. Regarding the various specific forms of knowledge, see, above all, the discussion of interactive cognitive subsystem theory (ICS) in Teasdale and Barnard and the discussion of associated systems theory (AST) in Carlston. For literature's contribution to various forms of nonpropositional knowledge, see Gibson et al. On prototypical and exemplary individuals, see Hogan, "Stories." For accounts of knowledge in narrative form, see Hogan, *Understanding*; Wertsch; Monk; and White.

11. Although most prototypes are not stereotypes, most (though not all) stereotypes are prototypes. For an explanation, see Hogan, *Conformism* 126.

12. Hogan uses the term "exemplum/exempla" rather than "exemplar/exemplars" in an effort to avoid the conflation of particular instances with ideal instances (see his "Stories" 39). I follow the more common practice of using "exemplar" to denote any particular instance of a category, whether or not it is "exemplary" in the sense of "ideal."

13. The following account of schema change is drawn largely from Young, Klosko, and Weishaar; Beck; Russell and van den Broek; Horowitz; Monk; Singer and Salovey; Wells; Padesky; Teasdale and Barnard; and Sookman and Pinard.

14. Mirror neurons fire not only when we perform an action ourselves but also when we view someone else performing that action and even when we *read* about a character performing the action (Oatley 19–20; Iacoboni 12). As Marco Iacoboni, a leading researcher of mirror neurons, reports, empirical studies indicate that "mirror neurons help us understand what we read by internally simulating the action we just read in [a] sentence . . . , [and] that when we read a novel, our mirror neurons simulate the actions described in the novel, as if we were doing those actions ourselves" (Iacoboni 93–94).

15. On how emotion controls various specific information-processing steps, see Frijda and Mesquita; Forgas; Clore and Gasper; Ekman; and Bower and Forgas.

16. Such accounts of a character's physical, material, social, political, and/or psychological circumstances can produce emotions in readers in at least two ways: they can contain images that function as perceptual triggers of emotion, as Patrick Hogan notes (Hogan, *What* 54), and they can engage readers in simulating the responses they themselves would have in similar circumstances. In his recent work, Hogan has argued that all emotional experiences are ultimately triggered by perceptions, either actual, imagined, or remembered, and that cognitive appraisals have emotional consequences not by their logic, but only by recruiting such perceptions through attentional orientation, imagination, memory, or related processes (Hogan, *What*).

17. Empirical studies have shown that reading literature frequently elicits explicit personal memories, most of which are emotional in character (see Oatley 60ff., 120–125), and it is probably the case that implicit memories are frequently evoked as well.

Chapter 2

1. Psychologists often refer to "naïve" or "lay" theories, the implicit and usually unconscious assumptions that people have about how the world works. In

300 Notes to Pages 55–82

such usages "theory" is equivalent to my usage of "schema." See Tesser 290: "A schema is a naïve theory."

2. For additional discussion of the negative consequences of autonomism, see Lewis vii–xvi, 16–24, and 29–48 and Bellah et al. viii–xii.

Chapter 3

1. Haslam, Bastian, and Bisset identify six factors of essentialism: immutability, inherence, biological basis, informativeness, consistency, and discreteness (1664). They argue that these are all factors of essentialism because they found them to co-vary in their studies. That is, individuals they tested who subscribed to one of these beliefs tended to hold the others as well. However, I take the position that two of these factors (consistency and informativeness) are more accurately described as elements of the autonomy schema and a third (discreteness) as a feature of the homogeneity schema, discussed in the following chapter. Informativeness and consistency refer to behavioral consistency across time and context and thus, in my view, reflect autonomism more than essentialism (this conflation of autonomism and essentialism is found in the work of other researchers as well). Discreteness, the belief that people either have a certain characteristic or they don't, appears to be more allied with the homogeneity schema.

The fact that these six factors co-vary does not mean that they are necessarily part of the same construct. Co-variation can result from factors all being products of another, as yet unidentified factor, such as conservatism, social dominance orientation, self-affirmation needs, etc. Indeed, the four faulty schemas I discuss tend to co-vary with conservatism and are mutually supportive in various ways (some of which will be discussed in the homogeneity chapter), but they also have a relative independence from each other, which makes it necessary to address each of them. That is, one can't disable all of them by disabling just one.

2. Like Haslam et al., Levy, Plaks, and Dweck also conflate essentialism with autonomism, when they include as part of entity theory the belief that "traits are the primary cause of behavior," and that "people's traits are reliably expressed in behavior"—two beliefs that are at the core of the autonomy schema (Levy, Plaks, and Dweck 191).

3. None of this should be taken to mean that humans are infinitely malleable, however. As Steven Pinker, Terry Eagleton (*Idea*), Peter Singer (*Left*), and others have argued, such a position is itself both false and potentially quite harmful. As Pinker points out, ignoring the limits of human malleability enables the pursuit of false hopes and the establishment of social programs that are not only doomed to fail but can also produce profound suffering and injustice in the process. I find Pinker's account of genetic determinism somewhat misleading, however. While he notes that genetic factors account for only about half of the *variation* among compared individuals (Pinker 374), and while he acknowledges that the individuals in many of the studies he cites come from restricted demographic groups that exclude individuals from deprived backgrounds and thus are not representative of the diversity of human beings (Pinker 375), his account can nonetheless give the impression that humans are much less malleable than

Notes to Pages 106–228   301

they in fact are. In addition, his claims are based on studies of limited disciplinary scope. For example, they do not include studies, such as those cited by Garbarino, that demonstrate the impact that risk factors in the environment have on character, or the studies reported on by Begley demonstrating neuroplasticity.

Chapter 4

1. Aron notes three types of self–other merging: merging of resources (which I am calling "practical solidarity"), merging of perspectives (which I am calling "emotional" or "psychological solidarity"), and merging of characteristics ("ontological solidarity").

2. See Norris 88–94 for an illuminating elaboration of Kristeva's position. Eagleton, citing the work of Slavoj Zizek, makes a similar point (*Idea* 96–97).

3. In addition to these three automatic, involuntary forms of empathic arousal, Hoffman notes that empathy can also be evoked by communicating another's distress through language and by engaging in role-taking, imagining that one is in another person's situation and then imaginatively experiencing what the other feels (Hoffman 49–52).

Chapter 5

1. As I have explained elsewhere, the need to maintain a strong identity, or secure sense of self, is the most fundamental human motivation (see Bracher, *Social*).

Chapter 7

1. Perhaps the most obvious of the novel's targets, this misunderstanding is at any rate the one most discussed by critics. See, for example, Owens, *Trouble* 54, 72–73, 101; Lisca, "Dynamics" 87–97; Reed 609; Shaw; Conder; Britch and Lewis; French 101; Griesbach 582; and Hicks 414.

2. For discussions of the Christian symbolism of this scene as well as other elements of the novel, see Shockley; H. Kelley Crockett; and Dougherty.

Works Cited

Abdullah, Sharif. "The Soul of a Terrorist: Reflections on Our War with the 'Other.'" In *The Psychology of Terrorism*, vol. 1: *A Public Understanding*, ed. Chris E. Stout, 129–141. Westport, CT: Praeger, 2002.

Abelson, Robert P. "Psychological Status of the Script Concept." *American Psychologist* 36, 7 (July 1981): 715–729.

Aldama, Frederick Luis. *Why the Humanities Matter: A Commonsense Approach.* Austin: University of Texas Press, 2008.

Altman, Neil. "Manic Society: Toward the Depressive Position." *Psychoanalytic Dialogues* 15 (2005): 321–346.

———. *The Analyst in the Inner City.* 2nd ed. New York: Routledge, 2009.

Ammons, Elizabeth. *Brave New Words: How Literature Will Save the Planet.* Iowa City: University of Iowa Press, 2010.

Anderson, Craig A., and James J. Lindsay. "The Development, Perseverance, and Change of Naïve Theories." *Social Cognition* 16.1 (1998): 8–30.

Appiah, Kwame Anthony. *In My Father's House: Africa in the Philosophy of Culture.* New York: Oxford University Press, 1992.

Ardila, Rubén. "The Psychology of the Terrorist: Behavioral Perspectives." In *The Psychology of Terrorism*, vol. 1: *A Public Understanding*, ed. Chris E. Stout, 9–15. Westport, CT: Praeger, 2002.

Aron, Arthur, and Tracy McLaughlin-Volpe. "Including Others in the Self: Extensions to Own and Partners' Group Membership." In *Individual Self, Collective Self, Relational Self*, ed. Constantine Sedikides and Marilyn B. Brewer, 89–108. Philadelphia: Psychology Press, 2001.

Atran, Scott. *In Gods We Trust: The Evolutionary Landscape of Religion.* New York: Oxford University Press, 2002.

Balkin, J. M. *Cultural Software: A Theory of Ideology.* New Haven: Yale University Press, 1998.

Bastian, Brock, and Nick Haslam. "Psychological Essentialism and Stereotype Endorsement." *Journal of Experimental Social Psychology* 42 (2006): 228–235.

Batson, C. Daniel, et al. "Empathy and Attitudes: Can Feeling for a Member of a Stigmatized Group Improve Feelings Toward the Group?" *Journal of Personality and Social Psychology* 72 (1997): 105–118.

304 Literature and Social Justice

Batson, C. Daniel, Johee Chang, Ryan Orr, and Jennifer Rowland. "Empathy, Attitudes, and Action: Can Feeling for a Member of a Stigmatized Group Motivate One to Help the Group?" *Personal and Social Psychology Bulletin* 28 (2002): 1656–1666.

Bazelon, David L. "The Morality of the Criminal Law." *University of Southern California Law Review* 49 (1976): 385–405.

Beck, Aaron T. *Prisoners of Hate: The Cognitive Basis of Anger, Hostility, and Violence*. New York: Perennial, 1999.

Begley, Sharon. *Train Your Mind, Change Your Brain*. New York: Ballantine, 2008.

Bellah, Robert N., Richard Madsen, William M. Sullivan, Ann Swidler, and Steven M. Tipton. *Habits of the Heart: Individualism and Commitment in American Life*. Updated ed. Berkeley: University of California Press, 1996.

Benforado, Adam, and Jon Hanson. "The Great Attributional Divide: How Divergent Views of Human Behavior Are Shaping Legal Policy." *Emory Law Journal* 57.2 (2008): 311–408.

———. "Legal Academic Backlash: The Response of Legal Theorists to Situationist Insights." *Emory Law Journal* 57.5 (2008): 1087–1145.

———. "Naïve Cynicism: Maintaining False Perceptions in Policy Debates." *Emory Law Journal* 57.3 (2008): 499–574.

Betancourt, Hector. "Attribution-Emotion Processes in Whites' Realistic Empathy Approach to Conflict and Negotiation." *Peace and Conflict: Journal of Peace Psychology* 10.4 (2004): 369–380.

Blair, Irene V., Jennifer E. Ma, and Alison P. Lenton. "Imagining Stereotypes Away: The Moderation of Implicit Stereotypes through Mental Imagery." *Journal of Personality and Social Psychology* 81 (2001): 828–841.

Bless, Herbert, Klaus Fiedler, and Fritz Strack. *Social Cognition: How Individuals Construct Social Reality*. New York: Psychology Press, 2004.

Bok, Sissela. *Common Values*. Columbia: University of Missouri Press, 1995.

Bower, Gordon H. "Affect and Cognition." *Philosophical Transactions of the Royal Society of London* 302 (1983): 387–402.

Bower, Gordon H., and Joseph P. Forgas. "Mood and Social Memory." In *Handbook of Affect and Social Cognition*, ed. Joseph P. Forgas, 95–120. Mahwah, NJ: Erlbaum, 2001.

Boyd, Brian. *On the Origin of Stories*. Cambridge, MA: Harvard University Press, 2009.

Bracher, Mark. "How to Teach for Social Justice: Lessons from *Uncle Tom's Cabin* and Cognitive Science." *College English* 71 (2009): 359–384.

———. *Social Symptoms of Identity Needs: Why We Have Failed to Solve Our Social Problems and What to Do About It*. London: Karnac, 2009.

———. "Teaching for Social Justice: Reeducating the Emotions through Literary Study." *JAC* 26 (2006): 463–512.

Brewer, Marilynn. "Reducing Prejudice through Cross-Categorization: Effects of Multiple Social Identities." In *Reducing Prejudice and Discrimination*, ed. Stuart Oskamp, 165ff. Mahwah, NJ: Erlbaum, 2000.

Brewer, Marilynn B., and Amy S. Harasty Feinstein. "Dual Processes in the Cognitive Representation of Persons and Social Categories." In *Dual-Process*

Theories in Social Psychology, ed. Shelly Chaiken and Yaacov Trope, 255–270. New York: Guilford, 1999.

Britch, Carroll, and Cliff Lewis. "Growth of the Family in *The Grapes of Wrath*." In *Critical Essays on Steinbeck's* The Grapes of Wrath, ed. John Ditsky, 97–108. Boston: G. K. Hall, 1989.

Bucci, Wilma. *Psychoanalysis and Cognitive Science*. New York: Guilford, 1997.

Cain, Herman. Statement on Occupy Wall Street. ABC News. http://abcnews.go.com/Politics/cain-tells-occupy-wall-street-protesters-blame/story?id=14674829#.TshCQmC4Iy4 (accessed Nov. 29, 2011).

Callero, Peter L. *The Myth of Individualism: How Social Forces Shape Our Lives*. New York: Rowman and Littlefield, 2009.

Carlston, Donal E. "Associated Systems Theory: A Systematic Approach to Cognitive Representations of Persons." In *Associated Systems Theory: A Systematic Approach to Cognitive Representations of Persons*, ed. Robert S. Wyer Jr., 1–78. Hillsdale: Erlbaum, 1994.

Carpenter, Frederic I. "The Philosophical Joads." In *The Grapes of Wrath: Texts and Criticism*, ed. Peter Lisca and Kevin Hearle, 562–571. New York: Penguin, 1997.

Casey, Janet Galligani. "Dis/Locating the Radical in *The Grapes of Wrath*." In The Grapes of Wrath: *A Reconsideration*, ed. Michael J. Meyer, 1:261–276. New York: Rodopi, 2009.

Chen, Ronald, and Jon Hanson. "Categorically Biased: The Influence of Knowledge Structures on Law and Legal Theory." Harvard Public Law Working Paper 08-43.

———. "The Illusion of Law: The Legitimating Schemas of Modern Policy and Corporate Law." *Michigan Law Review* 103 (2004): 1–149.

Choi, Incheol, Reeshad Dalal, Chu Kim-Prieto, and Hyekyung Park. "Culture and Judgment of Causal Relevance." *Journal of Personality and Social Psychology* 84 (2003): 46–59.

Choi, Incheol, and Richard E. Nisbett. "Situational Salience and Cultural Differences in the Correspondence Bias and Actor-Observer Bias." *Personality and Social Psychology Bulletin* 24 (1998): 949–960.

Choi, Incheol, Richard E. Nisbett, and Ara Norenzayan. "Causal Attribution across Cultures: Variation and Universality." *Psychological Bulletin* 125 (1999): 47–63.

Chorover, Stephan L. *From Genesis to Genocide: The Meaning of Human Nature and the Power of Behavior Control*. Cambridge, MA: MIT Press, 1979.

Cialdini, Robert B., Stephanie L. Brown, Brian P. Lewis, Carol Luce, and Steven L. Neuberg. "Reinterpreting the Empathy–Altruism Relationship: When One into One Equals Oneness." *Journal of Personality and Social Psychology* 73 (1997): 481–494.

Clarke, Simon. *Social Theory, Psychoanalysis, and Racism*. New York: Palgrave, 2003.

Clore, Gerald L., and Karen Gasper. "Feeling Is Believing: Some Affective Influences on Belief." In *Emotions and Beliefs: How Feelings Influence Thoughts*, ed. Nico H. Frijda, Antony S.R. Manstead, and Sacha Bem, 10–44. New York: Cambridge University Press, 2000.

306 Literature and Social Justice

Clore, Gerald L., and Andrew Ortony. "Cognition in Emotion: Always, Sometimes, or Never?" In *Cognitive Neuroscience of Emotion*, ed. Richard D. Lane and Lynn Nadel, 24–61. New York: Oxford University Press, 2002.

Cohen, Geoffrey L., Joshua Aronson, and Claude M. Steele. "When Beliefs Yield to Evidence: Reducing Biased Evaluation by Affirming the Self." *Personality and Social Psychology Bulletin* 26 (2000): 1151–1164.

Conder, John J. "Steinbeck and Nature's Self: *The Grapes of Wrath*." In The Grapes of Wrath: *Texts and Criticism*, ed. Peter Lisca and Kevin Hearle, 625–642. New York: Penguin, 1997.

Crawford, Mary, and Roger Chaffin. "The Reader's Construction of Meaning: Cognitive Research on Gender and Comprehension." In *Gender and Reading: Essays on Readers, Texts, and Contexts*, ed. Elizabeth A. Flynn and Patrocinio P. Schweickart, 3–30. Baltimore: Johns Hopkins University Press, 1986.

Crockett, H. Kelly. "The Bible and *The Grapes of Wrath*." *College English* 24 (1962): 193–199.

Crockett, Walter H. "Cognitive Complexity and Impression Formation." *Progress in Experimental Personality Research* 2 (1965): 47–90.

Cupchik, Gerald. "Emotional Effects of Reading Excerpts from Short Stories by James Joyce." *Poetics* 25 (1998): 363–377.

Currie, Elliott. *Crime and Punishment in America*. New York: Picador, 1998.

Darley, John M., and C. Daniel Batson. "'From Jerusalem to Jericho': A Study of Situational and Dispositional Variables in Helping Behavior." *Journal of Personality and Social Psychology* 27 (1973): 100–108.

Dasgupta, Nilanjan, and Anthony G. Greenwald. "On the Malleability of Automatic Attitudes: Combating Automatic Prejudice with Images of Admired and Disliked Individuals." *Journal of Personality and Social Psychology* 81 (2001): 800–814.

Davis, Mark H., Laura Conklin, Amy Smith, and Carol Luce. "Effect of Perspective Taking on the Cognitive Representation of Persons: A Merging of Self and Other." *Journal of Personality and Social Psychology* 70 (1996): 713–726.

Delgado, Richard. "'Rotten Social Background': Should the Criminal Law Recognize a Defense of a Severe Environmental Deprivation?" *Law and Inequality* 3 (1983): 9–90.

DeMott, Robert. "Introduction." In *Working Days: The Journals of* The Grapes of Wrath, ed. Robert DeMott, xxiii–xxiv. New York: Penguin, 1989.

DeSteno, David, and Piercarlo Valdesolo. *Out of Character: Surprising Truths about the Liar, Cheat, Sinner (and Saint) Lurking in Each of Us*. New York: Crown, 2011.

de Waal, Frans. *The Age of Empathy: Nature's Lessons for a Kinder Society*. New York: Three Rivers Press, 2009.

Diamond, Jared. *Guns, Germs, and Steel: The Fates of Human Societies*. New York: Norton, 1999.

Ditsky, John. "The Ending of *The Grapes of Wrath*: A Further Commentary." In *Critical Essays on Steinbeck's* The Grapes of Wrath, ed. John Ditsky, 116–124. Boston: G. K. Hall, 1989.

Dodge, Kenneth, and Nikki Crick. "Social Information-Processing Bases of Aggressive Behavior in Children." *Personality and Social Psychology Bulletin* 16 (1990): 8–22.

Doris, John M. *Lack of Character: Personality and Moral Behavior*. New York: Cambridge University Press, 2002.

Dougherty, Charles T. "The Christ-Figure in *The Grapes of Wrath*." *College English* 24 (1962): 224–226.

Drewery, Wendy, and John Winslade. "The Theoretical Story of Narrative Therapy." In *Narrative Therapy in Practice*, ed. Gerald Monk, John Winslade, Katie Crockett, and David Epston, 32–51. New York: Jossey-Bass, 1996.

Dreyfus, Hubert L., and Paul Rabinow. *Michel Foucault: Beyond Structuralism and Hermeneutics*. 2nd ed. Chicago: University of Chicago Press, 1983.

Dundes, Alan. "Binary Opposition in Myth: The Propp/Lévi-Strauss Debate in Retrospect." *Western Folklore* 56 (1997): 39–50.

Eagleton, Terry. *The Function of Criticism*. London: Verso, 1984.

———. *The Idea of Culture*. New York: Wiley-Blackwell, 2000.

———. *Literary Theory: An Introduction*. Minneapolis: University of Minnesota Press, 1983.

Ekman, Paul. "What We Become Emotional About." In *Feelings and Emotions*, 119–135. New York: Cambridge University Press, 2004.

Elbow, Peter. "The Uses of Binary Thinking." *Journal of Advanced Composition* 13 (1993): 51–78.

Elliott, Emory. "Afterword to *The Jungle*." In *Upton Sinclair's* The Jungle, ed. Harold Bloom, 95. Philadelphia: Chelsea House, 2002.

Erikson, Erik. *Identity: Youth and Culture*. New York: Norton, 1968.

Fabick, Stephen D. "Us & Them: Reducing the Risk of Terrorism." In *The Psychology of Terrorism*, vol. 2: *Clinical Aspects and Responses*, ed. Chris E. Stout, 225–241. Westport, CT: Praeger, 2002.

Falk, Patricia J. "Novel Theories of Criminal Defense Based upon the Toxicity of the Social Environment: Urban Psychosis, Television Intoxication, and Black Rage." *North Carolina Law Review* 74 (1996): 731–811.

Felski, Rita. 2008. *Uses of Literature*. New York: Blackwell.

Fetterley, Judith. *The Resisting Reader*. Bloomington: Indiana University Press, 1978.

Fineman, Martha Albertson. *The Autonomy Myth: A Theory of Dependency*. New York: New Press, 2004.

Fiske, Susan T. "Schema-Triggered Affect: Applications to Social Perception." In *Affect and Cognition: The Seventeenth Annual Carnegie Symposium on Cognition*, ed. Margaret S. Clarke and Susan T. Fiske, 56–78. Hillsdale, NJ: Erlbaum, 1982.

Folsom, Michael Brewster. "Upton Sinclair's Escape from *The Jungle*: The Narrative Strategy and Suppressed Conclusion of America's First Proletarian Novel." In *Upton Sinclair's* The Jungle, ed. Harold Bloom, 21–47. Philadelphia: Chelsea House, 2002.

Forgas, Joseph P. "Feeling Is Believing? The Role of Processing Strategies in Mediating Affective Influences on Beliefs." In *Emotions and Beliefs: How Feelings Influence Thoughts*, ed. Nico H. Frijda, Antony S. R. Manstead, and Sacha Bem, 108–143. New York: Cambridge University Press, 2000.

308 Literature and Social Justice

Försterling, Friedrich. *Attribution: An Introduction to Theories, Research and Applications.* Philadelphia: Taylor and Francis, 2001.

Foucault, Michel. *The Archaeology of Knowledge.* Trans. A. M. Sheridan Smith. New York: Pantheon, 1981.

———. *Discipline and Punish.* Trans. Alan Sheridan. New York: Vintage, 1979.

———. *The History of Sexuality,* vol. 1: *An Introduction.* Trans. Robert Hurley. New York: Vintage, 1980.

Frank, Robert H. *Passions within Reason: The Strategic Role of the Emotions.* New York: Norton, 1988.

———. *What Price the Moral High Ground?* Princeton: Princeton University Press, 1995.

French, Warren. *John Steinbeck.* New York: Twayne, 1961.

Frenkel-Brunswik, Else. "Intolerance of Ambiguity as an Emotional and Perceptual Personality Variable." *Journal of Personality* 18 (1948): 108–143.

———. "Tolerance towards Ambiguity as a Personality Variable." *American Psychologist* 3 (1949): 268.

Frijda, Nico H., and Batja Mesquita. "Beliefs through Emotions." In *Emotions and Beliefs: How Feelings Influence Thoughts,* ed. Nico H. Frijda, Antony S. R. Manstead, and Sacha Bem, 45–77. New York: Cambridge University Press, 2000.

Gaertner, Samuel L., and John F. Dovidio. "Categorization, Recategorization, and Intergroup Bias." In *On the Nature of Prejudice,* ed. John F. Dovidio, Peter Glick, and Laurie A. Rudman, 71–88. Malden, MA: Blackwell, 2005.

Galinsky, Adam D., Gillian Ku, and Cynthia S. Wang. "Perspective-Taking and Self–Other Overlap: Fostering Social Bonds and Facilitating Social Coordination." *Group Processes and Intergroup Relations* 8 (2005): 109–124.

Garbarino, James. *Lost Boys: Why Our Sons Turn Violent and How We Can Save Them.* New York: Free Press, 1999.

———. *Raising Children in a Socially Toxic Environment.* San Francisco: Jossey-Bass, 1995.

Garber, Marjorie. *A Manifesto for Literary Studies.* Seattle: Walter Chapin Simpson Center for the Humanities, 2003.

Gardiner, Judith Kegan. *Rhys, Stead, Lessing, and the Politics of Empathy.* Bloomington: Indiana University Press, 1989.

Gawronski, Bertram. "Implicational Schemata and the Correspondence Bias: On the Diagnostic Value of Situationally Constrained Behavior." *Journal of Personality and Social Psychology* 84 (2003): 1154–1171.

Gelman, Susan A. *The Essential Child: Origins of Essentialism in Everyday Thought.* New York: Oxford University Press, 2003.

Gelman, Susan A., Gail D. Heyman, and Christine H. Legare. "Developmental Changes in the Coherence of Essentialist Beliefs about Psychological Characteristics." *Child Development* 78 (2007): 757–774.

Gibson, John, Wolfgang Huemer, and Luca Pocci, eds. *A Sense of the World: Essays on Fiction, Narrative, and Knowledge.* New York: Routledge, 2007.

Gilbert, Daniel T. "Speeding with Ned: A Personal View of the Correspondence Bias." In *Attribution and Social Interaction,* ed. John M. Darley and Joel Cooper, 5–36. Washington, DC: American Psychological Association, 1998.

Gilbert, Daniel T., and Patrick S. Malone. "The Correspondence Bias." *Psychological Bulletin* 117 (1995): 21–38.

Gilligan, James. *Preventing Violence.* New York: Thames and Hudson, 2001.

———. *Violence: Reflections on a National Epidemic.* New York: Vintage, 1997.

Goleman, Daniel. *Emotional Intelligence.* New York: Bantam, 1995.

———. *Social Intelligence.* New York: Bantam, 2006.

Grand, Sue. *The Reproduction of Evil.* New York: Routledge, 2002.

Greenberg, Martin S., David R. Westcott, and Scott E. Bailey. "When Believing Is Seeing: The Effect of Scripts on Eyewitness Memory." *Law and Human Behavior* 22, 6 (1998): 685–694.

Greenblatt, Stephen. "Towards a Poetics of Culture." In *The New Historicism,* ed. H. Aram Veeser, 1–14. New York: Routledge.

Greenwald, Glenn. *A Tragic Legacy: How a Good versus Evil Mentality Destroyed the Bush Presidency.* New York: Crown, 2007.

Griesbach, Daniel. "'The Whole Texture of the Country at Once': Steinbeck's General Chapters in *The Grapes of Wrath.*" In The Grapes of Wrath: *A Reconsideration,* ed. Michael J. Meyer, 2:579ff. New York: Rodopi, 2009.

Guimond, Serge, Guy Begin, and Douglas L. Palmer. "Education and Causal Attributions: The Development of 'Person-Blame' and 'System-Blame' Ideology." *Social Psychology Quarterly* 52 (1989): 126–140.

Halpern, Faye. "In Defense of Reading Badly: The Politics of Identification in 'Benito Cereno,' *Uncle Tom's Cabin,* and Our Classrooms." *College English* 70 (2008): 551–577.

Hamilton, David L. "A Cognitive-Attributional Analysis of Stereotyping." *Advances in Experimental Social Psychology* 12 (1979): 53–84.

Hancock, Ange-Marie. *The Politics of Disgust: The Public Identity of the Welfare Queen.* New York: New York University Press, 2004.

Haney, Craig. "Making Law Modern: Toward a Contextual Model of Justice." *Psychology, Public Policy, and Law* 8 (2002): 3–63.

Hansen, Michael D. "The Power of Strange Faces: Revisiting *The Grapes of Wrath* with the Postmodern Ethics of Emmanuel Levinas." In *The Moral Philosophy of John Steinbeck,* ed. Stephen K. George, 107–129. Lanham, MD: Scarecrow Press, 2005.

Hanson, Jon, and Kathleen Hanson. "The Blame Frame: Justifying (Racial) Injustice in America." Harvard Public Law Working Paper no. 08-47.

Hanson, Jon, and Michael McCann. "Situationist Torts." *Loyola of Los Angeles Law Review* 41 (2008): 1345–1453.

Hanson, Jon, and David Yosifon. "The Situation: An Introduction to the Situational Character, Critical Realism, Power Economics, and Deep Capture." *University of Pennsylvania Law Review* 152 (2003): 129–346.

———. "The Situational Character: A Critical Realist Perspective on the Human Animal." *Georgetown Law Journal* 93 (2004): 1–142.

Harpham, Geoffrey Galt. "Foucault and New Historicism." *American Literary History* 3 (1991): 360–375.

———. *The Humanities and the Dream of America.* Chicago: University of Chicago Press, 2011.

———. *Shadows of Ethics: Criticism and the Just Society*. Durham, NC: Duke University Press, 1999.

Harrison, Kristen. "Scope of Self: Toward a Model of Television's Effects on Self-Complexity in Adolescence." *Communication Theory* 16 (2006): 251–279.

Haslam, Nick. "Dehumanization: An Integrative Review." *Personality and Social Psychology Review* 10 (2006): 252–264.

Haslam, Nick, Brock Bastian, Paul Bain, and Yoshihisa Kashima. "Psychological Essentialism, Implicit Theories, and Intergroup Relations." *Group Processes and Intergroup Relations* 9 (2006): 63–76.

Haslam, Nick, Brock Bastian, and Melanie Bissett. "Essentialist Beliefs about Personality and Their Implications." *Personality and Social Psychology Bulletin* 12 (2004): 1661–1673.

Haslam, Nick, and Sheri R. Levy. "Essentialist Beliefs about Homosexuality: Structure and Implications for Prejudice." *Personality and Social Psychology Bulletin* 32 (2006): 471–485.

Hatfield, Elaine, John T. Cacioppo, and Richard L. Rapson. *Emotional Contagion*. New York: Cambridge University Press, 1994.

Henry, P. J., Christine Reyna, and Bernard Weiner. "Hate Welfare but Help the Poor: How the Attributional Content of Stereotypes Explains the Paradox of Reactions to the Destitute in America." *Journal of Applied Social Psychology* 34 (2004): 34–58.

Herman, David. "Narrative Theory after the Second Cognitive Revolution." In *Introduction to Cognitive Cultural Studies*, ed. Lisa Zunshine, 155–175. Baltimore: Johns Hopkins University Press, 2010.

Hicks, Kathleen. "'It ain't kin we? It's will we?': John Steinbeck's Land Ethic in *The Grapes of Wrath*." In The Grapes of Wrath: *A Reconsideration*, ed. Michael J. Meyer, 1:397–416. New York: Rodopi, 2009.

Hochschild, Jennifer L. *Facing Up to the American Dream: Race, Class, and the Soul of the Nation*. Princeton: Princeton University Press, 1995.

Hoffman, Martin L. *Empathy and Moral Development: Implications for Caring and Social Justice*. Cambridge: Cambridge University Press, 2000.

Hogan, Patrick Colm. *Cognitive Science, Literature, and the Arts: A Guide for Humanists*. New York: Routledge, 2003.

———. *The Culture of Conformism*. Durham, NC: Duke University Press, 2001.

———. *The Mind and Its Stories: Narrative Universals and Human Emotion*. New York: Cambridge University Press, 2003.

———. "Stories and Morals: Emotion, Cognitive Exempla, and the Arabic Aristotelians." In *The Work of Fiction: Cognition, Culture, and Complexity*, ed. Alan Richardson and Ellen Spolsky, 31–50. Aldershot, UK: Ashgate, 2004.

———. *Understanding Nationalism: On Narrative, Cognitive Science, and Identity*. Columbus: Ohio State University Press, 2009.

———. *What Literature Teaches Us about Emotion*. New York: Cambridge University Press, 2011.

Holland, Norman N. "Why This Is Transference, Nor Am I Out of It." *Psychoanalysis and Contemporary Thought* 5 (1982): 27–34.

———. "Unity Identity Text Self." *PMLA* 90 (1975): 813–822.

Honderich, Ted. *After the Terror*. Edinburgh: Edinburgh University Press, 2002.

Hoover, Kenneth. *The Future of Identity*. Lanham, MD: Lexington, 2004.

Horowitz, Mardi. *Cognitive Psychodynamics*. New York: Wiley, 1998.

———. "Person Schemas." In *Person Schemas and Maladaptive Interpersonal Patterns*, ed. Mardi J. Horowitz, 13–31. Chicago: University of Chicago Press 1991.

Hudley, Cynthia, and Sandra Graham. "An Attributional Intervention to Reduce Peer-Directed Aggression among African-American Boys." *Child Development* 64 (1993): 124–138.

Huesmann, L. Rowell. "The Role of Social Information Processing and Cognitive Schema in the Acquisition and Maintenance of Habitual Aggressive Behavior." In *Human Aggression: Theories, Research, and Implications for Social Policy*, ed. Russell G. Geen and Edward Donnerstein, 73–109. New York: Academic Press, 1998.

Hunt, Lynn. *Inventing Human Rights*. New York: Norton, 2007.

Iacoboni, Marco. *Mirroring People: The Science of Empathy and How We Connect with Others*. New York: Picador, 2009.

Jameson, Fredric. "Imaginary and Symbolic in Lacan: Marxism, Psychoanalytic Criticism, and the Problem of the Subject." In *Literature and Psychoanalysis*, ed. Shoshana Felman, 338–395. Baltimore: Johns Hopkins University Press, 1982.

———. *The Political Unconscious: Narrative as a Socially Symbolic Act*. Ithaca: Cornell University Press, 1981.

Jayaratne, Toby Epstein, Oscar Ybarra, Jane P. Sheldon, Tony N. Brown, Merle Feldbaum, Carla A. Pfeffer, and Elizabeth M. Petty. "White Americans' Genetic Lay Theories of Race Differences and Sexual Orientation: Their Relationship with Prejudice toward Blacks, and Gay Men and Lesbians." *Group Processes and Intergroup Relations* 9 (2006): 77–94.

Johnson, Mark. *Moral Imagination: Implications of Cognitive Science for Ethics*. Chicago: University of Chicago Press, 1993.

Jones, James M. *Prejudice and Racism*. 2nd ed. New York: McGraw-Hill, 1997.

Jost, John T., Jack Glaser, Arie W. Kruglanski, and Frank J. Sulloway. "Political Conservatism as Motivated Social Cognition." *Psychological Bulletin* 129 (2003): 339–375.

Juergensmeyer, Mark. "The Logic of Religious Violence." In *Inside Terrorist Organizations*, ed. David C. Rapoport, 172–193. Portland, OR: Frank Cass.

Katz, Jack. *Seductions of Crime*. New York: Basic, 1990.

Keen, Suzanne. *Empathy and the Novel*. New York: Oxford University Press, 2007.

———. "A Theory of Narrative Empathy." *Narrative* 14 (2006): 207–236.

Keller, Johannes. "In Genes We Trust: The Biological Component of Psychological Essentialism and Its Relationship to Mechanisms of Motivated Social Cognition." *Journal of Personality and Social Psychology* 88 (2005): 686–702.

Kirby, Lisa. "A Radical Revisioning: Understanding and Repositioning *The Grapes of Wrath* as Political 'Propaganda.'" In The Grapes of Wrath: *A Reconsideration*, ed. Michael J. Meyer, 1:245–260. New York: Rodopi, 2009.

Kristeva, Julia. *Revolution in Poetic Language*. Trans. Margaret Waller. New York: Columbia University Press, 1984.

312 Literature and Social Justice

———. *Strangers to Ourselves*. Trans. Leon S. Roudiez. New York: Columbia University Press, 1991.

Lakoff, George. *The Political Mind*. New York: Viking, 2008.

Lancaster, Ashley Craig. "Subverting Eugenic Discourse: Making the Weak Strong in John Steinbeck's *Their Blood Is Strong* and *The Grapes of Wrath*." In The Grapes of Wrath: *A Reconsideration*, ed. Michael J. Meyer, 2:421–444. New York: Rodopi, 2009.

Larsen, Stephen. *The Fundamentalist Mind: How Polarized Thinking Imperils Us All*. Wheaton, IL: Quest, 2007.

Lazarus, Richard S. *Emotion and Adaptation*. New York: Oxford University Press, 1991.

———. "Progress on a Cognitive-Motivational-Relational Theory of Emotion." *American Psychologist* 46, 8 (1991): 819–834.

Lazarus, Richard S., and Bernice N. Lazarus. *Passion and Reason: Making Sense of Our Emotions*. New York: Oxford University Press, 1994.

Lentricchia, Frank. *Criticism and Social Change*. Chicago: University of Chicago Press, 1983.

———. "Foucault's Legacy: A New Historicism?" In *The New Historicism*, ed. H. Aram Veeser, 231–242. New York: Routledge, 1989.

Lerner, Richard M. *Final Solutions: Biology, Prejudice, and Genocide*. University Park: Pennsylvania State University Press, 1992.

Levy, Sheri R. "Reducing Prejudice: Lessons from Social-Cognitive Factors Underlying Perceiver Differences in Prejudice." *Journal of Social Issues* 55 (1999): 745–765.

Levy, Sheri R., and Carol S. Dweck. "Trait- versus Process-Focused Social Judgment." *Social Cognition* 16 (1998): 151–172.

Levy, Sheri R., Antonio Freitas, and Peter Salovey. "Construing Action Abstractly and Blurring Social Distinctions: Implications for Perceiving Homogeneity Among, but Also Empathizing with and Helping Others." *Journal of Personality and Social Psychology* 83 (2002): 1224–1238.

Levy, Sheri R., Jason E. Plaks, and Carol S. Dweck. "Modes of Social Thought: Implicit Theories and Social Understanding." In *Dual-Process Theories in Social Psychology*, ed. Shelly Chaiken and Yaacov Trope, 179–202. New York: Guilford, 1999.

Levy, Sheri R., Jason E. Plaks, Ying-yi Hong, Chi-yue Chiu, and Carol S. Dweck. "Static versus Dynamic Theories and the Perception of Groups: Different Routes to Different Destinations." *Personality and Social Psychology Review* 5 (2001): 156–168.

Levy, Sheri R., Steven J. Stroessner, and Carol S. Dweck. "Stereotype Formation and Endorsement: The Role of Implicit Theories." *Journal of Personality and Social Psychology* 74, 6 (1998): 1421–1436.

Lewis, Michael. *The Culture of Inequality*. 2nd ed. Amherst, MA: University of Massachusetts Press, 1993.

Lewontin, R. C., Steven Rose, and Leon J. Kamin. *Not in Our Genes: Biology, Ideology, and Human Nature*. New York: Pantheon, 1984.

Linville, Patricia W., and Gregory W. Fischer. "Exemplar and Abstraction Models of Perceived Group Variability and Stereotypicality." *Social Cognition* 11 (1993): 92–125.

Lisca, Peter. "The Dynamics of Community in *The Grapes of Wrath*." In *Critical Essays on Steinbeck's* The Grapes of Wrath, ed. John Ditsky, 87–97. Boston: G. K. Hall, 1989.

———. "*The Grapes of Wrath* as Fiction." In *The Grapes of Wrath: Texts and Criticism*, ed. Peter Lisca and Kevin Hearle, 572–588. New York: Penguin, 1997.

———. *The Wide World of John Steinbeck*. New Brunswick, NJ: Rutgers University Press, 1958.

Lisca, Peter, and Kevin Hearle. "Editors' Introduction." In The Grapes of Wrath: *Texts and Criticism*, ed. Peter Lisca and Kevin Hearle, 547–561. New York: Penguin, 1997.

Lopez, Gretchen E., Patricia Gurin, and Biren A. Nagda. "Education and Understanding Structural Causes for Group Inequalities." *Political Psychology* 19 (1998): 305–329.

Lukes, Steven. *Individualism*. London: Blackwell, 1985.

Mack, John E. "Looking beyond Terrorism: Transcending the Mind of Enmity." In *The Psychology of Terrorism*, vol. 1: *A Public Understanding*, ed. Chris E. Stout, 173–184. Westport, CT: Praeger, 2002.

Mayo, Clara W., and Walter H. Crockett. "Cognitive Complexity and Primacy-Recency Effects in Impression Formation." *Journal of Abnormal and Social Psychology* 68 (1964): 335–338.

McCauley, Clark. "Psychological Issues in Understanding Terrorism and the Response to Terrorism." In *The Psychology of Terrorism*, vol. 3: *Theoretical Understandings and Perspectives*, ed. Chris E. Stout, 3–29. Westport, CT: Praeger, 2002.

McConachie, Bruce. "Toward a Cognitive Cultural Hegemony." In *Introduction to Cognitive Cultural Studies*, ed. Lisa Zunshine, 134–150. Baltimore: Johns Hopkins University Press, 2010.

McKinnon, Susan. *Neo-Liberal Genetics: The Myths and Moral Tales of Evolutionary Psychology*. Chicago: Prickly Paradigm Press, 2005.

McNamee, Stephen J., and Robert K. Miller Jr. *The Meritocracy Myth*. 2nd ed. New York: Rowman and Littlefield, 2009.

Mergler, Nancy, and Ronald Schleifer. "Cognition and Narration: Binary Structures, Semiotics, and Cognitive Science." *New Orleans Review* 18 (1991): 64–75.

Meyers, Diana Tietjens. *Subjection and Subjectivity: Psychoanalytic Feminism and Moral Philosophy*. New York: Routledge, 1994.

Milgram, Stanley. *Obedience to Authority: An Experimental View*. New York: HarperCollins, 1974.

Miller, Dale T. "The Norm of Self-Interest." *American Psychologist* 54 (1999): 1053–1060.

Miller, Joan G. "Culture and the Development of Everyday Social Explanation." *Journal of Personality and Social Psychology* 46 (1984): 961–978.

Miller, Matthew. *The 2 Percent Solution*. New York: Public Affairs, 2003.

Mills, Nicolaus. *The Triumph of Meanness*. New York: Houghton Mifflin, 1997.

Monk, Gerald. "How Narrative Therapy Works." In *Narrative Therapy in Practice*, ed. Gerald Monk, John Winslade, Katie Crockett, and David Epston, 3–31. New York: Jossey-Bass, 1996.

Monroe, Kristen Renwick. "Explicating Altruism." In *Altruism and Altruistic Love: Science, Philosophy, and Religion in Dialogue*, ed. Stephen G. Post, Lynn G. Underwood, Jeffrey P. Schloss, and William B. Hurlbut, 106–122. New York: Oxford University Press, 2002.

———. *The Heart of Altruism: Perceptions of a Common Humanity*. Princeton: Princeton University Press, 1996.

Montrose, Louis A. "Professing the Renaissance: The Poetics and Politics of Culture." In *The New Historicism*, ed. H. Aram Veeser, 15–36. New York: Routledge.

Mookerjee, R. N. *Art for Social Justice: The Major Novels of Upton Sinclair*. Metuchen, NJ: Scarecrow Press, 1988.

Morris, Michael W., and Kaiping Peng. "Culture and Cause: American and Chinese Attributions for Social and Physical Events." *Journal of Personality and Social Psychology* 67 (1994): 949–971.

Moskowitz, Gordon B. "On Schemas and Cognitive Misers: Mental Representations as the Building Blocks of Impressions." *Social Cognition: Understanding Self and Others*, 153–192. New York: Guilford, 2005.

Newman, Leonard S., Tracy L. Caldwell, Brian Chamberlin, and Thomas Griffin. "Thought Suppression, Projection, and the Development of Stereotypes." *Basic and Applied Social Psychology* 27 (2005): 259–266.

Nisbett, Richard E. "Essence and Accident." In *Attribution and Social Interaction*, ed. John M. Darley and Joel Cooper, 171–197. Washington, DC: American Psychological Association, 1998.

———. *The Geography of Thought: How Asians and Westerners Think Differently . . . and Why*. New York: Free Press, 2003.

Norris, Christopher. *Truth and the Ethics of Criticism*. New York: Manchester University Press, 1994.

Nussbaum, Martha C. *Cultivating Humanity: A Classical Defense of Reform in Liberal Education*. Cambridge, MA: Harvard University Press, 1997.

———. *Not for Profit: Why Democracy Needs the Humanities*. Princeton: Princeton University Press, 2010.

———. *Poetic Justice: The Literary Imagination and Public Life*. Boston: Beacon Press, 1995.

———. *Upheavals of Thought: The Intelligence of Emotions*. New York: Cambridge University Press, 2001.

Oatley, Keith. *Such Stuff as Dreams: The Psychology of Fiction*. Malden, MA: Wiley-Blackwell, 2011.

Ochsner, Kevin N. "Characterizing the Functional Architecture of Affect Regulation: Emerging Answers and Outstanding Questions." In *Social Neuroscience: People Thinking about Thinking People*, ed. John T. Cacioppo, Penny S. Visser, and Cynthia L. Pickett, 245–268. Cambridge, MA: MIT Press, 2006.

Olweean, Steve S. "Psychological Concepts of the 'Other': Embracing the Compass of the Self." In *The Psychology of Terrorism*, vol. 1: *A Public Understanding*, ed. Chris E. Stout, 113–128. Westport, CT: Praeger, 2002.

Owens, Louis. "The Culpable Joads: Desentimentalizing *The Grapes of Wrath*." In *Critical Essays on Steinbeck's* The Grapes of Wrath, ed. John Ditsky, 108–116. Boston: G. K. Hall, 1989.

Works Cited   315

————. The Grapes of Wrath: *Trouble in the Promised Land*. New York: Twayne, 1996.

————. *John Steinbeck's Re-Vision of America*. Athens, GA: University of Georgia Press, 1985.

Padesky, Christine A. "Schema Change Processes in Cognitive Therapy." *Clinical Psychology and Psychotherapy* 1 (1994): 267–278.

Palmer, Alan. "Storyworlds and Groups." In *Introduction to Cognitive Cultural Studies*, ed. Lisa Zunshine, 176–192. Baltimore: Johns Hopkins University Press, 2010.

Parker, David. "The Turn to Ethics in the 1990s." *Critical Review* 33 (1993): 3–14.

Perlman, Diane. "Intersubjective Dimensions of Terrorism and Its Transcendence." In *The Psychology of Terrorism*, vol. 1: *A Public Understanding*, ed. Chris E. Stout, 17–47. Westport, CT: Praeger, 2002.

Phillips, Stephen T., and Robert C. Ziller. "Toward a Theory and Measure of the Nature of Non-Prejudice." *Journal of Personality and Social Psychology* 72 (1997): 420–434.

Pinker, Steven. *The Blank Slate: The Modern Denial of Human Nature*. New York: Penguin, 2002.

Piven, Jerry S. "On the Psychosis (Religion) of Terrorists." In *The Psychology of Terrorism*, vol. 3: *Theoretical Understandings and Perspectives*, ed. Chris E. Stout, 119–148. Westport, CT: Praeger, 2002.

Plaks, Jason E., Carol S. Dweck, Steven J. Stroessner, and Jeffrey W. Sherman. "Person Theories and Attention Allocation: Preferences for Stereotypic Versus Counterstereotypic Information." *Journal of Personality and Social Psychology* 80 (2001): 876–893.

Plaks, Jason E., Sheri R. Levy, Carol S. Dweck, and Steven J. Stroessner. "In the Eye of the Beholder: Lay Theories and the Perception of Group Entitativity, Variability, and Essence." In *The Psychology of Group Perception*, ed. Vincent Yzerbyt, Charles M. Judd, and Olivier Corneille, 127–146. New York: Psychology Press, 2004.

Pollard-Gott, Lucy. "Attribution Theory and the Novel." *Poetics* 21 (1993): 499–524.

Post, Jerrold M. "Terrorist Psycho-logic: Terrorist Behavior as a Product of Psychological Forces." In *Origins of Terrorism: Psychologies, Ideologies, Theologies, States of Mind*, ed. Walter Reich, 25–40. Washington, DC: Woodrow Wilson Center Press, 1998.

Railsback, Brian E. "The Darwinian *Grapes of Wrath*." In *The Critical Response to John Steinbeck's* The Grapes of Wrath, ed. Barbara A. Heavilin, 225–229. Westport, CT: Greenwood Press, 2000.

Railton, Stephen. "Pilgrim's Politics: Steinbeck's Art of Conversion." In *New Essays on* The Grapes of Wrath, ed. David Wyatt, 27–46. New York: Cambridge, 1990.

Reed, John R. "*The Grapes of Wrath* and the Esthetics of Indigence." In The Grapes of Wrath: *Texts and Criticism*, ed. Peter Lisca and Kevin Hearle, 603–615. New York: Penguin, 1997.

Reeder, Glenn D. "Trait-Behavior Relations and Dispositional Inference." *Personality and Social Psychology Bulletin* 19 (1993): 586–593.

Reyna, Christina, P. J. Henry, William Korfmacher, and Amanda Tucker. "Examining the Principles in Principled Conservatism: The Role of Responsibility Stereotypes as Cues for Deservingness in Racial Policy Decisions." *Journal of Personality and Social Psychology* 90 (2005): 109–128.

Richardson, Alan. *The Neural Sublime: Cognitive Theories and the Science of the Mind.* Cambridge: Cambridge University Press, 2010.

Robins, Robert S., and Jerrold M. Post. *Political Paranoia: The Psychopolitics of Hatred.* New Haven: Yale University Press, 1997.

Rorty, Amelie. "What It Takes to Be Good." In *The Moral Self,* ed. Gil G. Noam and Thomas E. Wren, 28–55. Cambridge, MA: MIT Press, 1993.

Rorty, Richard. "Ethics without Principles." *Philosophy and Social Hope,* 72–90. New York: Penguin, 1999.

———. "Human Rights, Rationality, and Sentimentality." In *The Politics of Human Rights,* ed. Obrad Savic, 67–83. New York: Verso, 1999.

———. "Justice as a Larger Loyalty." In *Justice and Democracy,* ed. Ron Bontekoe and Marietta Stepaniants, 9–22. Honolulu: University of Hawaii Press, 1997.

Ross, Lee. "Comment on Gilbert." In *Attribution and Social Interaction,* ed. John M. Darley and Joel Cooper, 53–66. Washington, DC: American Psychological Association, 1998.

Ross, Lee, and Donna Shestowsky. "Contemporary Psychology's Challenges to Legal Theory and Practice." *Northwestern University Law Review* 97 (2003): 1081–1114.

Ross, Lee, and Richard E. Nisbett. *The Person and the Situation.* New York: McGraw-Hill, 1991.

Rubin, David C. "The Basic-Systems Model of Episodic Memory." *Perspectives on Psychological Science* 1 (2006): 277–311.

Russell, Robert L., and Paul van den Broek. "Changing Narrative Schemas in Psychotherapy." *Psychotherapy* 29 (1992): 344–354.

Ryan, William. *Blaming the Victim.* New York: Pantheon, 1971.

Salter, Christopher L. "John Steinbeck's *The Grapes of Wrath* as a Primer for Cultural Geography." In *Critical Essays on Steinbeck's* The Grapes of Wrath, ed. John Ditsky, 138–152. Boston: G. K. Hall, 1989.

Schank, Roger. *Dynamic Memory Revisited.* 2nd ed. New York: Cambridge University Press, 1999.

Scheuer, Jeffrey. *The Sound Bite Society: Television and the American Mind.* New York: Four Walls Eight Windows, 1999.

Schmitt, Manfred, Robert Behner, Leo Montada, Lothar Müller, and Gisela Müller-Fohrbrodt. "Gender, Ethnicity, and Education as Privileges: Exploring the Generalizability of the Existential Guilt Reaction." *Social Justice Research* 13 (2000): 313–337.

Schneider, Daniel J. "Schema Theories." *The Psychology of Stereotyping,* 120–172. New York: Guilford, 2004.

Schweickart, Patrocinio P. "Reading Ourselves: Toward a Feminist Theory of Reading." In *Gender and Reading: Essays on Readers, Texts, and Contexts,* ed. Elizabeth A. Flynn and Patrocinio P. Schweickart, 31–62. Baltimore: Johns Hopkins University Press, 1986.

Shapiro, Brian P., Paul van den Broek, and Charles R. Fletcher. "Using Story-Based Causal Diagrams to Analyze Disagreements about Complex Events." *Discourse Processes* 20 (1995): 51–77.

Shaw, Patrick W. "Tom's Other Trip: Psycho-Physical Questing in *The Grapes of Wrath*." In The Grapes of Wrath: *Texts and Criticism*, ed. Peter Lisca and Kevin Hearle, 616–624. New York: Penguin, 1997.

Shockley, Martin. "Christian Symbolism in *The Grapes of Wrath*." *College English* 18 (1956): 87–90.

Shrum, L. J. "Media Consumption and Perceptions of Social Reality: Effects and Underlying Processes." In *Media Effects: Advances in Theory and Research*, ed. Jennings Bryant and Dolf Zillman, 69–95. Mahwah, NJ: Erlbaum, 2002.

Sinclair, Upton. "Art and Propaganda." In *The Jungle*, ed. Clare Virginia Eby, 354–356. New York: Norton, 2003.

———. *The Jungle*, ed. Clare Virginia Eby. Norton, 2003.

———. "What Life Means to Me." In *The Jungle*, ed. Clare Virginia Eby, 348–353. New York: Norton, 2003.

Singer, Jerome L., and Peter Salovey. "Organized Knowledge Structures." In *Person Schemas and Maladaptive Interpersonal Patterns*, ed. Mardi J. Horowitz, 33–79. Chicago: Chicago University Press, 1991.

Singer, Peter. *A Darwinian Left: Politics, Evolution, and Cooperation.* New Haven: Yale University Press, 1999.

———. *The Expanding Circle: Ethics, Evolution, and Moral Progress.* Princeton: Princeton University Press, 2011.

Sklar, Howard. "Breaking Bread: The Sympathetic Effects of Sharing Food in *The Grapes of Wrath*." In The Grapes of Wrath: *A Reconsideration*, ed. Michael J. Meyer, 2:509–530. New York: Rodopi, 2009.

Slap, Joseph W., and Laura Slap-Shelton. *The Schema in Clinical Psychoanalysis.* Hillsdale, NJ: Analytic Press, 1991.

Smith, Adam. *The Theory of Moral Sentiments.* Amherst, NY: Prometheus, 2000.

Smith, Craig A., and Leslie D. Kirby. "Putting Appraisal in Context: Toward a Relational Model of Appraisal and Emotion." *Cognition and Emotion* 23 (2009): 1352–1372.

Smith, Eliot R. "Mental Representation and Memory." In *The Handbook of Social Psychology*, 4th ed., vol. 1, ed. Daniel T. Gilbert, Susan T. Fiske, and Gardner Lindzey, 391–445. New York: Oxford University Press, 1998.

Smith, Eliot R., and Jamie DeCoster. "Dual-Process Models in Social and Cognitive Psychology: Conceptual Integration and Links to Underlying Memory Systems." *Personality and Social Psychology Review* 4 (2000): 108–131.

Sookman, Debbie, and Gilbert Pinard. "Integrative Cognitive Therapy for Obsessive-Compulsive Disorder: A Focus on Multiple Schemas." *Cognitive and Behavioral Practice* 6 (1999): 351–362.

Spolsky, Ellen. "Darwin and Derrida: Cognitive Literary Theory as a Species of Post-structuralism." In *Introduction to Cognitive Cultural Studies*, ed. Lisa Zunshine, 292–310. Baltimore: Johns Hopkins University Press, 2010.

Staub, Ervin. *The Roots of Evil: The Origins of Genocide and Other Group Violence.* New York: Cambridge University Press, 2003.

Stein, Karen Farchaus. "Complexity of the Self-Schema and Responses to Disconfirming Feedback." *Cognitive Therapy and Research* 18 (1994): 161–178.

Steinbeck, John. *The Grapes of Wrath: Texts and Criticism.* Ed. Peter Lisca and Kevin Hearle. New York: Penguin, 1997.

———. "John Steinbeck's Acceptance Speech for the Nobel Prize for Literature in 1962." In *A Casebook on* The Grapes of Wrath, ed. Agnes McNeill Donohue, 293–295. New York: Thomas Y. Crowell, 1968.

Stern, Daniel. *The Interpersonal World of the Infant.* New York: Basic, 1985.

Stewart, Tracie L., Ioana M. Latu, Kerry Kawakami, and Ashley C. Meyers. "Consider the Situation: Reducing Automatic Stereotyping through Situational Attribution Training." *Journal of Experimental Social Psychology* 46 (2010): 221–225.

Strean, Herbert S., and Lucy Freeman. *Our Wish to Kill: The Murder in All Our Hearts.* New York: Avon, 1993.

Stowe, Harriet Beecher. *Uncle Tom's Cabin.* 2nd ed. Ed. Elizabeth Ammons. New York: Norton, 2010.

Swan, Kenneth. "The Enduring Values of John Steinbeck's Fiction: The University Student and *The Grapes of Wrath.*" In *The Critical Response to John Steinbeck's* The Grapes of Wrath, ed. Barbara A. Heavilin, 297–307. Westport, CT: Greenwood Press, 2000.

Taylor, Charles. *The Ethics of Authenticity.* Cambridge, MA: Harvard University Press, 1992.

———. "The Politics of Recognition." In *Multiculturalism: Examining the Politics of Recognition*, ed. Amy Gutman, 25–74. Princeton: Princeton University Press, 1994.

Taylor, Shelley E. *The Tending Instinct.* New York: Henry Holt, 2002.

Taylor, Shelley E., and Jennifer Crocker. "Schematic Bases of Social Information Processing." In *Social Cognition: The Ontario Symposium*, ed. E. Tory Higgins, C. Peter Herman, and Mark P. Zanna, 89–134. Hillsdale, NJ: Erlbaum, 1981.

Teasdale, John D. "Clinically Relevant Theory: Integrating Clinical Insight with Cognitive Science." In *Frontiers of Cognitive Therapy*, ed. Paul M. Salkovskis, 26–47. New York: Guilford, 1996.

Teasdale, John D., and Philip J. Barnard. *Affect, Cognition, and Change: Re-Modeling Depressive Thought.* Hillsdale, NJ: Erlbaum, 1993.

Tesser, Abraham. "Self-Generated Attitude Change." In *Advances in Experimental Social Psychology*, vol. 11, ed. L. Berkowitz, 289–338. New York: Academic Press, 1978.

Todorov, Tzvetan. *Life in Common: An Essay in General Anthropology.* Trans. Katherine Golsan and Lucy Golsan. Lincoln: University of Nebraska Press, 2001.

Trope, Jaacov. "Dispositional Bias in Person Perception: A Hypothesis-Testing Perspective." In *Attribution and Social Interaction*, ed. John M. Darley and Joel Cooper, 67–97. Washington, DC: American Psychological Association, 1998.

Turner, Mark. *The Literary Mind: The Origins of Thought and Language.* New York: Oxford University Press, 1996.

Works Cited **319**

Turpin, Jeff P. "Making and Breaking Golden Rules: Adaptationist Analysis of John Steinbeck's *The Grapes of Wrath*." In The Grapes of Wrath: *A Reconsideration*, ed. Michael J. Meyer, 1:377–396. New York: Rodopi, 2009.

Tyson, Lois. *Critical Theory Today*. 2nd ed. New York: Routledge, 2006.

Vaughan, Susan. *The Talking Cure: The Science behind Psychoanalysis*. New York: Diane, 1997.

Vermeule, Blakey. "Machiavellian Narratives." In *Introduction to Cognitive Cultural Studies*, ed. Lisa Zunshine, 214–230. Baltimore: Johns Hopkins University Press, 2010.

———. *Why Do We Care about Literary Characters?* Baltimore: Johns Hopkins University Press, 2010.

Visser, Nicholas. "Audience and Closure in *The Grapes of Wrath*." In *The Critical Response to John Steinbeck's* The Grapes of Wrath, ed. Barbara A. Heavilin, 201–219. Westport, CT: Greenwood Press, 2000.

Volkan, Vamik D. *The Need to Have Enemies and Allies*. Northvale, NJ: Aronson, 1988.

Warren, Elizabeth. Statement on class warfare. http://www.cbsnews.com/8301-503544_162-20110042-503544.html (accessed Oct. 5, 2011).

Weiner, Bernard. *Judgments of Responsibility: A Foundation for a Theory of Social Conduct*. New York: Guilford Press, 1995.

———. *Social Motivation, Justice, and the Moral Emotions*. Mahwah, NJ: Erlbaum, 2006.

Wells, Adrian. *Emotional Disorders and Metacognition: Innovative Cognitive Therapy*. New York: Wiley, 2000.

Wertsch, James V. "A Clash of Deep Memories." *Profession* (2008): 46–53.

Wessells, Michael. "Terrorism, Social Injustice, and Peace Building." In *The Psychology of Terrorism*, vol. 4: *Programs and Practices in Response and Prevention*, ed. Chris E. Stout, 57–73. Westport, CT: Praeger, 2002.

Westen, Drew. *The Political Brain: The Role of Emotion in Deciding the Fate of the Nation*. New York: Public Affairs, 2007.

Westen, Drew, and Amy Kegley Heim. "Disturbances of Self and Identity." In *Handbook of Self and Identity*, ed. Mark R. Leary and June Price Tangney, 643–664. New York: Guilford, 2005.

Westervelt, Saundra. *Shifting the Blame*. Piscataway, NJ: Rutgers University Press, 1998.

White, Michael. "Folk Psychology and Narrative Practice." In *The Handbook of Narrative Psychotherapy: Practice, Theory, and Research*, ed. Lynne E. Angus and John McLeod, 15–51. Thousand Oaks, CA: Sage, 2004.

Wittenbrink, Bernd, Pamela L. Gist, and James L. Hilton. "Structural Properties of Stereotypical Knowledge and Their Influences on the Construal of Social Situations." *Journal of Personality and Social Psychology* 72 (1997): 526–543.

Wolf, Ernest. *Treating the Self*. New York: Guilford, 1988.

Wolgast, Elizabeth. *The Grammar of Justice*. Ithaca, NY: Cornell University Press, 1987.

Wright, R. George. "The Progressive Logic of Criminal Responsibility and the Circumstances of the Most Deprived." *Catholic University Law Review* 43 (1994): 459–504.

Wright, Richard. "How 'Bigger' Was Born." *Native Son*, 431–462. New York: Perennial, 1998.

———. *Native Son*. New York: Perennial, 1998.

Young, Jeffrey E., Janet S. Klosko, and Marjorie E. Weishaar. 2003. *Schema Therapy: A Practitioner's Guide*. New York: Guilford, 2003.

Zillman, Dolf, and Hans-Bernd Brosius. *Exemplification in Communication*. Mahwah, NJ: Erlbaum, 2000.

Zimbardo, Philip. *The Lucifer Effect: Understanding How Good People Turn Evil*. New York: Random House, 2007.

Zinn, Howard. 1995. *A People's History of the United States, 1492–Present*. Rev. and updated ed. New York: HarperPerennial.

Zunshine, Lisa. "Introduction: What Is Cognitive Cultural Studies?" In *Introduction to Cognitive Cultural Studies*, ed. Lisa Zunshine, 1–33. Baltimore: Johns Hopkins University Press, 2010.

———. *Strange Concepts and the Stories They Make Possible: Cognition, Culture, Narrative*. Baltimore: Johns Hopkins University Press, 2008.

———. *Why We Read Fiction*. Columbus: Ohio State University Press, 2006.

Zuwerink, Julia R., and Patricia G. Devine. "Attitude Importance and Resistance to Persuasion: It's Not Just the Thought That Counts." *Journal of Personality and Social Psychology* 70, 5 (1996): 931–944.

Index

Italic page numbers refer to diagrams.

Abdullah, Sharif, 150
Abu Ghraib prison abuses, 44–46
Achebe, Chinua, 160
action scripts: and atomism schema,
137; and autonomy schema, 74,
169, 178; and essentialism schema,
100; and exemplars, 18, 20, 72; as
form of knowledge, 10; and heterogeneity schema, 161–162, 220–
221, 274–275; and homogeneity
schema, 161; and information-
processing routines, xii–xiii; and
literary texts, 29, 72; and malleability schema, 100, 101, 102, 184,
215, 267–268; and prototypes, 16,
18; and situationism schema, 71, 72,
74, 178, 203–205, 240–241, 251–
252; and solidarity schema, 137,
191–192, 230–234, 235, 282–
283
Aldama, Frederick Luis, ix, 298n3
Alger, Horatio, 159
Allport, Gordon, 89, 129
Altman, Neil, 146–147
altruism: and atomism schema, 104,
118, 120, 123, 124; and heterogeneity schema, 217; and situationism
schema, 40; and solidarity schema,
107–108, 120, 123, 230, 234
American Dream, 35, 36, 62

Ammons, Elizabeth, ix, xiv
Appiah, Kwame, 109
Ardila, Rubén, 144
Aristotle, 94
Aron, Arthur, 301n1
associated systems theory (AST),
299n10
Assommoir, L' (Rougon-Macquart),
97–98
atomism schema: absolutization of,
121, 126, 128; description of, xi–
xii, 8, 15, 103–106; and eliminating basis for criticism, 125–127;
and exemplars, 134–135; falseness
of, 106–118, 128; and *The Grapes
of Wrath*, 193, 221, 229, 231, 233;
harmful consequences of, 118–
127; and identity-needs, 107; and
information-processing routines,
31, 127, 134, 137–139, 290; and *The
Jungle*, 185–186; and *Native Son*,
238, 250, 280; and patriarchy, 131;
and preventing care for others,
118–123; and pride, 130, 136–137;
and proprioceptive feedback, 128–
129; replacing, 127–139, 233, 235,
280; and simplification, 129, 130,
133; sources of, 128–134; and television, 132–136. *See also* solidarity
schema

attention and focus: and altering schemas, 287–288; and atomism schema, 137, 138; and autonomy schema, 205; and essentialism schema, 91; and heterogeneity schema, 275; and homogeneity schema, 162, 163; and information-processing routines, xii, 21, 27; and malleability schema, 101, 215, 269; and plasticity of brain, 80; and situationism schema, 69, 205, 249; and solidarity schema, 139

autonomy schema: costs of, 49–50; and culture, 61–66; description of, x–xi, 8, 14–15; and egocentrism, 59–60; and emotions, 18, 30, 74, 169; essentialism schema compared to, 75–76, 300n1, 300n2; evidence of operation of, 46–57; and exemplars, 19–20, 67, 72–74, 168, 169; falseness of, 37–46, 49; faulty judgments produced by, 35–36, 57; and geography, 64; and *The Grapes of Wrath*, 193, 194, 207, 208, 210; hegemony of, 36–37, 56, 68; and identity-needs, 60–61; and information-processing routines, 22–23, 24, 31, 35–36, 62–63, 67, 68–72, 171, 208, 210, 290; and *The Jungle*, 19–20, 168–169, 171; and language, 65–66; in legal system, 50–53, 54, 66, 67; and *Native Son*, 237, 238, 239, 240, 241, 251; and perception, 58, 68; and propaganda, 66–67; and prototypes, 17–18, 20, 72–74, 169; replacing, xi, 36, 57–68, 238, 239, 240, 251; sources of, 58–68; and television, 67, 68; and visibility, 58–59. *See also* situationism schema

Balkin, J. M., 6–7, 22, 297n2
Bastian, Brock, 300n1
Batson, Daniel, 27–28
Bazelon, David, 84
Beck, Aaron, 143, 144, 156
Begley, Sharon, 77, 301n3

behavior: and autonomy schema, 47, 49–50, 51, 53, 198, 300n2; and essentialism schema, 75; and situationism schema, 39–46, 52–53, 57, 150, 170–172, 197, 199, 239
Bellah, Robert, 36–37, 104, 134
Benforado, Adam, 49, 54, 57, 58–59, 64
Binet, Alfred, 96
bin Laden, Osama, 149–150, 160
biological determinism, 87–90, 95
Bissett, Melanie, 300n1
"blaming the victim" syndrome, 55, 56, 57, 121–122
body images: and atomism schema, 135–136; and autonomy schema, 17, 73, 169, 176; and essentialism schema, 99; as form of knowledge, 10; and heterogeneity schema, 160–161; and homogeneity schema, 160; and malleability schema, 99, 182, 253–254; and situationism schema, 73, 176–177, 201–202, 249–251; and solidarity schema, 136, 189–190, 280–281
Bok, Sissela, 113, 114
Book of Job, 72
bottom-up information processing, 15–16, 21
brain: amygdala, 153, 156; and emotional-psychological-neurological solidarity, 114–118; and homogeneity schema, 153–154, 156; and mirror neurons, 29, 116–118, 129, 188–191, 201–202, 282, 299n14; plasticity of, 79–80, 301n3
Bucci, Wilma, 112
Bush, George W.: and atomism schema, 138–139; and autonomy schema, 45, 67, 292; and homogeneity schema, xii, 15, 142, 145–146, 156, 158

Cacioppo, John T., 153
Camus, Albert, 135
capitalist system: and *The Grapes of Wrath*, 197–198, 204–205, 231, 233,

235; and *The Jungle*, 173–174, 177, 178, 192; laissez-faire capitalism, 124, 173, 174, 178, 180
Capra, Frank, 136
Carnegie, Andrew, 124
Casey, Janet Galligani, 94
Catullus, 158
character: and atomism schema, 122, 291; and autonomy schema, x–xi, 8, 17, 19, 20, 23, 35, 39, 46–47, 48, 49, 52, 55, 59, 61, 62, 67, 69–73, 167, 171, 175, 239, 291; and essentialism schema, xi, 8, 15, 75–77, 85, 86, 87, 90, 95, 97–99, 167, 180, 252, 266, 291; and heterogeneity schema, 140, 141, 142, 147, 148–151, 154, 157, 159–161, 163, 164, 184–185, 219–221, 271, 273, 275; and homogeneity schema, 15, 140, 141, 142, 143, 147–148, 150, 152, 157–159, 161, 162, 283; and information-processing routines, 7, 21–23, 27; and malleability schema, xi, 76, 77–80, 83–84, 92, 98–102, 180–184, 214–217, 219, 252–255, 259–260, 262–266, 267, 268, 269, 283, 293; and situationism schema, 40, 45, 46, 49, 51, 52, 53, 56–57, 71–72, 150, 171–177, 178, 179–180, 193, 194–195, 199, 200–201, 206–209, 235, 239, 241, 246, 247, 249, 283
Chomsky, Noam, 111
Chorover, Stephan, 8–9, 82
Cialdini, Robert B., 119
circumstances: and life outcomes, 172, 177, 197, 239; and situationism schema, 170–178, 179, 194–195, 197, 199, 200, 205–206, 238, 250, 291
Clarke, Simon, 143, 146, 151
Clinton, Bill, 11
Clore, Gerald L., 30
cognitive miserliness, 129
cognitive schemas: altering faulty schemas, xii, xiii, xiv, 10–11, 16, 25–27, 32, 288, 294; construction of new schemas, 288–289; defini-

tion of, 14, 298n8; and faulty information processing, 24, *24*, 294; as functional constructs, 14, 298n9; and fundamental attribution error, 46–47; naïve theory as, 299–300n1; protest novels as schema-altering apparatuses, xiii, xiv, 27–31, *31*, 32; and stereotypes, x. *See also* person-schemas
cognitive science, x, 7, 13
cognitive therapy, 25
competition: and atomism schema, 104, 118, 124, 128, 133–134, 136, 137, 229, 291; and autonomy schema, 67, 68, 73, 170
concepts: and autonomy schema, 17, 72–73, 169; and essentialism schema, 98; as form of knowledge, 10; and heterogeneity schema, 159; and homogeneity schema, 159; and malleability schema, 98, 252–253; and situationism schema, 73, 177, 196, 239; and solidarity schema, 276–278
Confessions (Rousseau), 105
confirmation bias, 22
crime and criminals: and atomism schema, 123; and autonomy schema, 39, 67, 71, 73, 239; and essentialism schema, 82; and heterogeneity schema, 147–148, 275, 293; and homogeneity schema, 144, 146, 160, 161; and malleability schema, 78, 79, 182, 211, 212, 252–253, 264, 293; and prototypes, 16, 73; and situationism schema, 51, 52, 53, 56, 173, 205, 239, 251–252, 293
criminal justice system: and autonomy schema, 50, 51, 52; and essentialism schema, 83, 85, 97, 291; and malleability schema, 84, 85; and schema criticism, x, 293. *See also* legal system
Crocker, Jennifer, 298n8
Crockett, Walter H., 141, 142
cultural relativism, 109, 125

324 Literature and Social Justice

Dahmer, Jeffrey, 159
Davids, Fakhry, 144
dehumanization: and atomism schema, xi, 15, 104; and essentialism schema, 88, 89, 92, 181–182; and heterogeneity schema, 273; and homogeneity schema, xii, 15, 142, 146; and malleability schema, 261; and situationism schema, 43; and solidarity schema, 233
Derrida, Jacques, 126–127
DeSteno, David, 147, 148, 150–151
Diamond, Jared, 80–81
Dickens, Charles, 97, 106
dispositionism, 47–50, 53, 57
distributed cognition, 118
Doris, John, 39, 147–148, 150
Dweck, Carol S., 76, 88, 300n2

Eagleton, Terry, 3–4, 110–111, 113, 114, 125–126, 300n3, 301n2
East Asian cultures: and atomism schema, 105; and autonomy schema, 61–65; and essentialism schema, 76, 81, 94–95; and homogeneity schema, 155–156
education: atomism schema in, 119, 131–132; and autonomy schema, 53, 66; and essentialism schema, 86–87, 96; and heterogeneity schema, 273; and homogeneity schema, 146; and human nature, 9–10; and malleability schema, 78, 79, 83, 92, 100, 101, 184; and schema criticism, x, 288, 290, 292; and situationism schema, 38, 167–168, 178, 192, 205; and solidarity schema, 110, 192, 231–233, 234, 278–279
Elbow, Peter, 155
Emerson, Ralph Waldo, 106
emotions: and atomism schema, 136–137; and autonomy schema, 18, 30, 74, 169; and essentialism schema, 99–100; and exemplars, 18, 20, 29–30, 72; as form of knowledge, 10, 11–12; and heterogeneity schema, 161, 220–221, 273–

274; and homogeneity schema, 153, 155–156, 161, 163; and information-processing routines, xii, 29–30; and literary texts, 29–31, 299n16, 299n17; and malleability schema, 100, 101, 102, 183–184, 215, 255–259, 261, 263–264, 266–267; and prototypes, 16, 17; and situationism schema, 70–71, 72, 74, 177–180, 200–203, 206–207, 240, 241, 246, 251; and solidarity schema, 114–118, 137, 187–191, 225, 229–230, 234–235, 275, 277, 281–282
empathic arousal: and heterogeneity schema, 270, 273; and malleability schema, 257–258, 259–261, 262, 265; and situationism schema, 177, 201–203, 242, 251; and solidarity schema, 115–117, 123, 188–189, 234, 235, 276, 278–279, 282, 301n3
entity theory, 76, 90–91, 300n2. See also essentialism schema
environmental forces: and atomism, 121–122; and essentialism schema, xi, 8, 15, 83, 86, 88, 89, 91, 95–100, 237; and genetics, 76–78, 82, 85, 86, 89, 96, 98, 121–122, 300n3; and heterogeneity schema, 150, 270; and malleability schema, xi, 75, 76–78, 79, 80, 82, 83–84, 91, 98–100, 101, 102, 180, 182–184, 193, 210, 214, 235, 237, 252, 253–255, 258, 259, 261, 262–266, 267, 269, 291, 293, 301n3; and plasticity of brain, 79–80; and schema criticism, 290; and situationism schema, 38, 53, 56, 57, 60, 62; socially toxic environments, 78–79, 182, 255, 267, 269; and solidarity schema, 118, 186, 276, 281
episode scripts: and atomism schema, 136; and autonomy schema, 17, 73, 169, 172; and epiphanic experiences, 211, 212–213, 259–263; and essentialism schema, 99; as form of knowledge, 10; and heterogeneity schema, 159, 217–219, 271–

273; and homogeneity schema, 159; and malleability schema, 99, 211–213, 259–263; and quotidian experiences, 211; and situationism schema, 73, 168, 171–174, 197–199, 240–248; and solidarity schema, 136, 188–189, 223–227, 234–235, 278–280; and traumatic experiences, 211–212

episodic memory: and exemplars, 19, 26, 28, 174, 175, 177, 295; and information-processing routines, xiii; and prototypes, 13, 26

Erikson, Erik, 235, 273

essentialism schema: autonomy schema compared to, 75–76, 300n1, 300n2; core qualities of, 76, 300n1; and culture, 76, 81, 94–95; description of, xi, 8, 15, 75; evidence of operation of, 90–92; falseness of, 76–82; and fatalistic views, 85–90; and geography, 81–82; and *The Grapes of Wrath*, 193, 210; harmful consequences of, 82–90; and identity-needs, 95; individual differences in, 95; and information-processing routines, 31, 90–92, 98, 290; and language, 94; and *Native Son*, 237, 238, 252, 263, 266; and prototypes, 98–100; replacing, 92–100, 180, 252–253, 263, 266–267; sources of, 93–98; and television, 97. *See also* malleability schema

evolutionary psychology, 96–97, 107–108, 153

exemplars: and altering faulty person-schemas, 16, 25–26, 27, 58, 288–289; and atomism schema, 134–135; and autonomy schema, 19–20, 67, 72–74, 168, 169; and emotions, 18, 20, 29–30, 72; and episodic memory, 19, 26, 28, 174, 175, 177, 295; and essentialism schema, 98; and heterogeneity schema, 152, 158–162, 184–185, 272, 273, 275; and homogeneity schema, 157; and infor-

mation processing routine, xii–xiii; literature operating on, xiii, xiv, 27–28, 74, 93, 287, 288; and malleability schema, 98–101, 181–182, 211–217, 253–259, 263, 264; and metacognition, 25; and schema criticism, 289, 290, 295; and situationism schema, 68, 72–74, 168, 171, 172–177, 200, 202, 207, 241, 243, 245, 246, 249; and solidarity schema, 127, 134–137, 139, 187–188, 227–228, 229, 231, 233, 278; as type of knowledge, 13, 18–21

expectation and notice: and essentialism schema, 90; and heterogeneity schema, 163; and homogeneity schema, 162; and information-processing routines, xii–xiii, 27, 29; and malleability schema, 91, 101, 269; and situationism schema, 68–69, 179, 205

Federalist Society, 67
Felski, Rita, 4
feminist criticism, 3
Fetterley, Judith, 3
Fineman, Martha, 37, 55–56
Foucault, Michel, 3–7, 298n4
Frank, Robert H., 8, 114, 132
Freeman, Lucy, 148–149
Frenkel-Brunswik, Else, 140–141, 142, 156, 162
fundamental attribution error: and atomism schema, 121; and autonomy schema, xi, 35, 39, 46–47, 49, 205; and essentialism schema, 89; and literary texts, 29; prevention of, 57; and public policy, 54; sources of, 58–60, 63

Gaddafi, Muammar, 160
Gage, Rusty, 80
Garbarino, James, 77–78, 301n3
Gardner, Chris, 19
Gaspar, Karen, 30
Gates, Bill, 39
Gelman, Susan, 93–94, 95, 96

326 Literature and Social Justice

genetics: and environmental influences, 76–78, 82, 85, 86, 89, 96, 98, 121–122, 300n3; and essentialism schema, 89–90, 96, 97–98
Gilbert, Daniel, 55, 59
Gilligan, James, 79
Goleman, Daniel, 117, 255–256
Good Samaritan experiment, 40, 48
Grapes of Wrath, The (Steinbeck): and actions, 203–205, 230–234; and atomism schema, 193, 221, 229, 231, 233; and autonomy schema, 193, 194, 207, 208, 210; and body images, 201–202; and concepts, 196; and emotions, 200–203, 225, 229–230; and episodes, 197–199, 208, 211–213, 217–219, 223–227, 234, 241; and essentialism schema, 193, 210; and heterogeneity schema, 184, 193, 217–221, 232; and homogeneity schema, 193; and identity-needs, 214, 216, 227; and information-processing routines, 205–210, 214–216, 218; and life stories, 199–200, 213–217, 219–220, 228–229; and malleability schema, 193, 210–217, 232; and propositional knowledge, 194–196, 210–211, 221–223; and prototypic individuals, 200, 227–228; and revolution, 195, 211; and situationism schema, 193, 194–210, 232, 241; and solidarity schema, 193, 221–236, 282, 283
Greenspan, Alan, 124–125
Greenwald, Glenn, 145–146
Grylls, Bear, 135

Haney, Craig, 51–53
Hanson, Jon, 39, 49, 50, 53–54, 56–59, 64, 66, 66–67
Hanson, Kathleen, 50
Hard Times (Dickens), 106
Harrison, Kristen, 157
Hartwell, Steven, 41
Haslam, Nick, 300n1
Hatfield, Elaine, 115–116

Henry, O., "The Gift of the Magi," 230
Herman, David, 118
heterogeneity schema: and common humanity, xii; diachronic heterogeneity, 219, 270; and exemplars, 152, 158–162, 184–185, 272, 273, 275; and *The Grapes of Wrath*, 184, 193, 217–221, 232; and information-processing routines, 31, 151, 152, 162–164, 218, 275; and intra-individual diversity of character, 140, 141, 148–150, 154, 164, 273; and *The Jungle*, 162, 184–185; and *Native Son*, 160–161, 162, 184, 237, 269–275, 283; replacing homogeneity schema with, 151–164, 270, 275; synchronic heterogeneity, 270
Hitler, Adolf, 86, 142, 160, 279
Hobbes, Thomas, 104, 105, 124, 185
Hochschild, Jennifer, 54–55, 62
Hoffman, Martin, 115, 301n3
Hogan, Patrick, 18, 109, 298n8, 299n12, 299n16
Holland, Norman, 4
Holocaust, 42–44, 147
homogeneity schema: costs of, 141–147, 152; and culture, 155–156; description of, xii, 8, 15; essentialism schema compared to, 300n1; and exemplars, 157; falseness of, 147–151, 152; and good–bad dichotomy, 140–146; and identity-needs, 143, 153–155, 161, 301n1; and information-processing routines, 31, 151, 152, 162–164, 290; and language, 155; and projection, 141, 142–143, 145, 146, 162–163; and projective identification, 145, 146–147, 162–163, 246; replacing, 151–164, 270, 275; sources of, 152–158; and television, 156–158, 160. *See also* heterogeneity schema
human agency, model of, 56–57
human nature: assumptions concerning, 8–10, 14, 16, 21, 238; and homogeneity schema, 155; and prop-

ositional knowledge, 26–27; and universalism, 109–114, 119, 125, 126; and women's experience, 131
Hussein, Saddam, 160

Iacoboni, Marco, 116–118, 119, 129, 130, 299n14
ideology: and atomism schema, 130; and homogeneity schema, 143; ideology critique, 3–4, 5; and information-processing routines, 22; and situationism schema, 199, 205; and solidarity schema, 233
"implicit person" theories. *See* person-schemas
incremental theory, 76, 90, 91. *See also* malleability schema
individualism, 104, 117–118, 130, 131–132, 134, 233
inequality, 36, 57, 86–88
inference: and atomism schema, 137, 138; and autonomy schema, 71–72; and essentialism schema, 90, 93; and heterogeneity schema, 163, 275; and homogeneity schema, 162; and information-processing routines, xii, 21, 23, 27, 29; and malleability schema, 101, 215, 264; and prototypes, 16; and situationism schema, 69–70, 179, 205, 206, 209, 249
information-processing scripts or routines: and altering faulty person-schemas, 16, 22, 24, 25–26, 27, 289; and atomism schema, 31, 127, 134, 137–139, 290; and autonomy schema, 22–23, 24, 31, 35–36, 62–63, 67, 68–72, 171, 208, 210, 290; and essentialism schema, 31, 90–92, 98, 290; and heterogeneity schema, 31, 151, 152, 162–164, 218, 275; and homogeneity schema, 31, 151, 152, 162–164, 290; knowledge produced by, 7; literature operating on, xiii, xiv, 28–31, 74, 287, 288; and malleability schema, 31, 90–92, 100–102, 184, 214–216,

235, 263–264, 268–269; and metacognition, 25; as micro-cognition, xii–xiii; and schema criticism, 289, 290, 295, 296; and situationism schema, 22–23, 30, 31, 36, 58, 68–72, 172, 179–180, 203, 205–209, 235, 241–242, 245, 251; and solidarity schema, 31, 137–139, 191, 234–235, 236, 283; as type of knowledge, 13, 21–24
information search: and atomism schema, 137; and heterogeneity schema, 163, 275; and homogeneity schema, 162; and information-processing routines, xii, 21, 29; and malleability schema, 101, 264, 269; and situationism schema, 69, 249
infrahumanization: and atomism schema, xi, 15, 104; and essentialism schema, 88–89, 92; and heterogeneity schema, 273; and homogeneity schema, xii, 15, 152; and situationism schema, 43
injustice. *See* social injustice
inseparability thesis, 147
interactive cognitive subsystem theory (ICS), 299n10
involuntary mimicry, 201, 225–226
Ito, T. A., 153
It's a Wonderful Life (film), 135, 136, 137

Jakobson, Roman, 155
James, William, 148
Jameson, Frederic, 3, 4, 298n4
Jayaratne, Toby Epstein, 86, 89
Jefferson, Thomas, 120
Jeurgensmeyer, Mark, 156
John M. Olin Foundation, 66
Johnson, Dwayne "The Rock," 135
Johnson, Mark, 111–112
Jungle, The (Sinclair): and actions, 178, 184, 191–192, 231; and atomism schema, 185–186; and autonomy schema, 19–20, 168–169, 171; and body images, 176–177, 182, 189; and concepts, 177; and emotions,

328 Literature and Social Justice

Jungle, The (Sinclair) (*continued*)
 177–178, 183–184, 187–191; and episodes, 171–174, 188–189, 241; and heterogeneity schema, 162, 184–185; historical reception of, 287; and information-processing routines, 179–180, 184; and life stories, 174–175, 182–183; and malleability schema, 180–184, 192; and propositional knowledge, 169–171, 180–181, 186–187; and prototypic individuals, 175–176, 181–182, 184–185, 187–188; and situationism schema, 168–180, 192, 200, 241; and social class, 167–168, 170; and socialism, 170, 181, 183, 186–187, 188, 191, 192, 283; and solidarity schema, 185–192, 231, 282, 283

Kakutani, Michiko, 45
Kant, Immanuel, 105
Keller, Johannes, 88, 95
Kleinian psychoanalysis, 142–143, 145, 151, 154
knowledge: faulty knowledge, xii–xiii, 4, 7, 8–13, 22, 295, 297–298n3; forms of, 10–13, 287, 295, 298n4, 298–299n10; types of, 13–14, 16–24. *See also* cognitive schemas; propositional knowledge
Kristeva, Julia, 4, 112–113, 301n2

La Bruyère, Jean de, 105
Lacan, Jacques, 4, 111, 112
Lakoff, George, 11, 12, 14
La Rochefoucauld, François de, 105
Larsen, Stephen, 153, 154, 156
Lee, Harper, 152
legal system: atomism schema in, 119; autonomy schema in, 50–53, 54, 66, 67; essentialism schema in, 83–85. *See also* criminal justice system
Lentricchia, Frank, 3
Lerner, Richard, 82–83, 88, 89–90, 95
Levi, Primo, 148
Levinas, Emmanuel, 126–127
Lévi-Strauss, Claude, 155

Levy, Sheri R., 88, 300n2
Lewis, Michael, 36
Lewontin, R. C., 76, 87
life outcomes: and autonomy schema, 46; and malleability schema, 263; situational determinants of, 37–39, 57, 170–171, *172*, 177, 179, 197, 200, 240, 248–249
life scripts: and atomism schema, 136, 229; and autonomy schema, 17, 73, 169, 174, 175; and essentialism schema, 99; as form of knowledge, 10; and heterogeneity schema, 159–160, 219–220; and homogeneity schema, 159; and malleability schema, 99, 182–183, 213–217, 263–266; and situationism schema, 73, 174–175, 199–200, 248–249; and solidarity schema, 136, 228–229
literary texts: and altering faulty person-schemas, 74; and atomism schema, 134–135; and cognitive schemas, 27–31, *31*, 32; and emotions, 29–31, 299n16, 299n17; and essentialism schema, 97–98; and exemplars, xiii, xiv, 18, 27–28, 74, 93; and heterogeneity schema, 157, 158, 160–161, 162, 163; and homogeneity schema, 152, 159; and information-processing routines, xii, xiv, 28–31, 74, 287, 288; and malleability schema, 100, 101–102; potential to produce socially transformative psychological changes in readers, ix, xiii, xiv, 3–4, 5, 6, 27–28, 31–32, 164, 167, 233–234, 288; and schema criticism, 288–290; and situationism schema, 71–72; and solidarity schema, 139. *See also* protest novels
Locke, John, 104
Lukes, Steven, 130

Machiavelli, Niccolò, 105
Mack, John, 144–145, 156
malleability schema: and environmental forces, xi, 75, 76–78, 79, 80, 82,

83–84, 91, 98–100, 101, 102, 180, 182–184, 193, 210, 214, 235, 237, 252, 253–255, 258, 259, 261, 262–266, 267, 269, 291, 293, 300–301n3, 301n3; and exemplars, 98–101, 181–182, 211–217, 253–259, 263, 264; and *The Grapes of Wrath*, 193, 210–217, 232; and identity-needs, 216; and information-processing routines, 31, 90–92, 100–102, 184, 214–216, 235, 263–264, 268–269; and *The Jungle*, 180–184, 192; limits of human malleability, 300–301n3; and *Native Son*, 252–269, 283; and prototypes, 98–100, 253–259; replacing essentialism schema with, 92–100, 180, 252–253, 263, 266–267; and social justice, 76; and stereotypes, 88, 91–92

Malone, Patrick, 55
Manichean worldview, 145–146
Marx, Karl, 125–126
Marxism, 3, 4, 5, 6, 214
McCann, Michael, 66
McCauley, Clark, 144, 150
McDermott, Terry, 45
McKinnon, Susan, 90, 96–97
McNamee, Stephen, 36, 38–39
Meany, Michael, 77
media: and atomism schema, 132–134; and autonomy schema, 67, 205; and essentialism schema, 97, 252–253; and exemplars, 18; and homogeneity schema, 156–158, 160; and schema criticism, 290; and situationism schema, 243–244
memory: and atomism schema, 137, 138; encoding of, 70, 287; and essentialism schema, 90–91; and exemplars, 18–19, 21, 295; and heterogeneity schema, 218, 275; and homogeneity schema, 157, 160, 163; and information-processing routines, xii, 21, 23, 289, 295; and literary texts, 29, 31, 72, 287–288; 299n17; and malleability schema, 91, 101, 102, 213, 259, 263–264,

266; and mood-congruent recall, 72; procedural memory, xiii, 21, 22, 295; semantic memory, xiii, 13, 295; and situationism schema, 70, 171, 176, 179–180, 200, 202, 206, 246, 249; and solidarity schema, 190, 233, 235. *See also* episodic memory
Mengele, Josef, 148
meritocracy, 36
metacognition: and atomism schema, 127, 186–187; development of, xiii, 7, 25, 26–27, 58, 68, 152, 288, 289; and essentialism schema, 93; and heterogeneity schema, 218–219, 275; and homogeneity schema, 152; literature aiding in development of, 28–29, 74, 288; and malleability schema, 100, 180–181, 213; and revisions to procedures, 13; and schema criticism, 288, 289, 290, 294, 295; and situationism schema, 169–171, 195–196, 207–209, 248; and solidarity schema, 127, 234–235
Meyers, Diana Tietjens, 11
Milgram, Stanley, 40–41, 48
Miller, Dale, 131–132
Miller, Joan, 56, 62
Miller, Robert, 36, 38–39
Mills, Nicolaus, 124
mindfulness, 79–80
mirror neurons, 29, 116–118, 129, 188–191, 201–202, 282, 299n14
mood-congruent recall, 72
Moskowitz, Gordon B., 298n8
multiculturalism, 119, 122
Mussolini, Benito, 279

naïve theory, 299–300n1
nationalism, 156
Native Son (Wright): and actions, 240–241, 251–252, 274–275, 282–283; and atomism schema, 238, 250, 280; and autonomy schema, 237, 238, 239, 240, 241, 251; and body images, 249–251, 253–254, 280–281; and concepts, 239, 252–253, 276–278; and emotions, 240,

330 Literature and Social Justice

Native Son (Wright) (*continued*)
241, 246, 251, 255–259, 261, 263–264, 266–267, 273–274, 281–282; and episodes, 240–248, 259–263, 271–273, 278–280; and essentialism schema, 237, 238, 252, 263, 266; and fear, 241–248, 249, 251, 256, 257, 258, 259; and fight/flight response, 241–242, 245–248; and heterogeneity schema, 160–161, 162, 184, 237, 269–275, 283; and homogeneity schema, 238, 270, 275; and identity-needs, 242–244, 251, 259, 267, 271, 274, 279; and information-processing routines, 241, 275, 283; and life stories, 248–249, 263–266; and malleability schema, 252–269, 283; and perception, 59; and propositional knowledge, 238–239, 252, 270–271, 276–278; and prototypic individuals, 249, 269–270, 278; and racism, 237, 243–244, 254, 255, 261, 265, 267, 273, 274; and situationism schema, 238–252, 283; and solidarity schema, 237, 250, 275–283; and threats, 241–245, 246, 247, 248, 249, 250, 262
neural systems, 153. *See also* brain
New Historicist criticism, 5–6
Newman, Leonard S., 142
Nietzsche, Friedrich, 105
Nisbett, Richard E., 39–40, 64–65, 94–95, 105
Norris, Christopher, 126–127
Nussbaum, Martha, ix, 29, 106, 119, 267, 294

Oatley, Keith, 30
Oliver Twist (Dickens), 97
Olweean, Steve, 138–139

Palmer, Alan, 118
paranoid-schizoid position, 142–143, 151, 154
Pascal, Blaise, 105
Pascal-Leone, Alvaro, 80
Perlman, Diane, 145

person-schemas: and bottom-up information processing, 15–16, 21; and conservatism, 300n1; corrective measures for, xiii, 16, 24, 25–26, 27, 58, 74, 235, 287, 289, 294–295; general person-schemas, xii, 14–16; and social injustice, x–xi, 294. *See also* atomism schema; autonomy schema; essentialism schema; homogeneity schema
perspective taking, 201, 203, 251, 261
Phillips, Steven, 120–121
Pinker, Steven, 9–10, 109–110, 125, 149, 151, 300–301n3
Piven, Jerry S., 149–150
Plaks, Jason E., 300n2
Plato, 9, 89
Pollard-Gott, Lucy, 71
Post, Jerrold M., 143, 154–155
prejudice, 11, 88–89, 92, 120, 142, 143
procedural memory, xiii, 21, 22, 295
propositional knowledge: and atomism schema, 186–187; and autonomy schema, 169; as determinant of perception, 7; and faulty knowledge, 10, 11, 12, 21–22, 26; and heterogeneity schema, 270–271; and homogeneity schema, 158; and human nature, 26–27; and information-processing routines, xii; and literature, 28–29; and malleability schema, 180–181, 210–211, 252; and metacognition, 25; and situationism schema, 169–171, 194–196, 238–239; and social criticism, 295; and solidarity schema, 221–223, 276–278; as type of knowledge, 13
protest novels: and cognitive schemas, xiii, xiv, 27–31, *31*, 32; and radical cognitive politics, 31, 32, 164; as schema-altering apparatuses, xiii, xiv, 27–31, *31*, 32; and schema criticism, x, 289; social justice promoted by, 31–32, *31*, 167. See also *The Grapes of Wrath* (Steinbeck); *The Jungle* (Sinclair); *Native Son* (Wright)

prototypes: and altering faulty person-schemas, 16, 25–26, 27, 289; and autonomy schema, 17–18, 20, 72–74, 169; and essentialism schema, 98–100; forms of, 17–18; and heterogeneity schema, 158–162; and information-processing routines, xii–xiii; literature operating on, xiii, xiv, 27–28, 287, 288; and malleability schema, 98–100, 253–259; and metacognition, 25; and schema criticism, 289, 290, 295; and situationism schema, 72–74, 171, 242; and solidarity schema, 134–137; and stereotypes, 16–17, 299n11; as type of knowledge, 13, 16–18, 298n7

prototypic individuals: and atomism schema, 134–135; and autonomy schema, 17, 73, 169; and essentialism schema, 98; as form of knowledge, 10; and heterogeneity schema, 98–99, 160, 184–185, 269–270; and homogeneity schema, 160; and malleability schema, 181–182, 253–259; and situationism schema, 73, 175–176, 200, 249; and solidarity schema, 135, 187–188, 227–228

psychoanalysis: Kleinian psychoanalysis, 142–143, 145, 151, 154; and social criticism, 4, 5, 6

public policy: and atomism schema, 119, 137, 138, 139, 291, 292–293; and autonomy schema, 29, 35, 49, 50, 54–56, 57, 291, 292–293; and essentialism schema, 82–83, 88, 89–90, 100, 291, 292–293; and heterogeneity schema, 291, 293, 296; and homogeneity schema, 141, 142, 291; and information-processing routines, 24, 236; and in-group/out-group relations, 290, 291; and malleability schema, 92, 100, 291, 292, 293, 296; and protest novels promoting social justice, 31–32, 31; and prototypes, 16, 17, 74; and schema criticism, 289, 290–

294, 296; and situationism schema, 291, 292, 293, 296; and solidarity schema, 139, 283, 291, 292, 293–294, 296

Pursuit of Happyness (film), 19

racism: and correcting faulty knowledge, 10–11; and essentialism schema, 81, 86–87, 237; and heterogeneity schema, 273, 274; and homogeneity schema, 143; and malleability schema, 254, 255, 261, 265, 267; and situationism schema, 243–244

radical cognitive politics: and protest novels, 31, 32, 164; and social justice, xiv, 12–13, 164

Rand, Ayn, 124

rational choice theory, 106

readers, literary texts producing changes in, ix, xiii, xiv, 3–4, 5, 6, 27–28, 31–32, 164, 167, 233–234, 288

Reagan, Ronald, 149

religion: and autonomy schema, 36–37, 50, 53, 64–65; and forms of knowledge, 10; and heterogeneity schema, 218–219; and homogeneity schema, 144–145, 156, 160; and solidarity schema, 228, 229, 231, 279–280, 282–283

Rice, Condoleezza, 45

Robins, Robert S., 143, 154–155

Rockefeller, John D., 124

Rorty, Richard, 119–120, 128

Ross, Lee, 39–40, 45, 46, 50–51, 64–65

Rougon-Macquart, Zola, 97–98

Rousseau, Jean-Jacques, 104, 105, 107

Rumsfeld, Donald, 45

Ryan, Paul, 125

Ryan, William, 37, 55, 56

Salovey, Peter, 298n8

schema criticism: and cognitive retraining activities, 295–296; and examination of faulty schemas, 291–292; and extending schema-

332 Literature and Social Justice

schema criticism (*continued*)
altering processes, 288, 296; methodology of, 32, 74, 288–289; negative form of, 289–290; positive form of, 289; and promotion of social justice, x, xiv, 32, 294, 296; and public policy, 289, 290–294, 296; and refuting faulty knowledge, 12; social criticism distinguished from, 295; and solidarity schema, 139
Scheuer, Jeffrey, 67–68, 132–133, 134
Schwartz, Jeffrey, 79–80
Schwarzenegger, Arnold, 135
Schweickart, Patrocinio, 3
semantic memory, xiii, 13, 295
Shestowksy, Donna, 45, 50–51
Sinclair, Upton, 167–168. See also *The Jungle* (Sinclair)
Singer, Jerome L., 298n8
Singer, Peter, 108, 113, 300n3
situationism schema: and culture, 61–64; and exemplars, 68, 72–74, 168, 171, 172–177, 200, 202, 207, 241, 243, 245, 246, 249; and *The Grapes of Wrath*, 193, 194–210, 232, 241; and information-processing routines, 22–23, 30, 31, 36, 58, 68–72, 172, 179–180, 203, 205–209, 235, 241–242, 245, 251; invisibility of situations, 40, 45, 58, 67, 71, 240, 241, 248; and *The Jungle*, 168–180, 192, 200, 241; and *Native Son*, 238–252, 283; replacing autonomy schema with, xi, 36, 57–68, 238, 239, 240, 251; situational causes of behavior, 39–46, 52–53, 57, 150, 170–172, 197, 199, 239; situational determinants of life outcomes, 37–39, 57, 170–171, *172*, 177, 179, 197, 200, 240, 248–249
Smith, Adam, 106, 114–115
social change, 3–7, 56, 268
social cognition: and cognitive retraining activities, 295–296; and essentialism schema, 93; features of, 7; and heterogeneity schema, 152; and information-processing

routines, 235–236, 296; and prototypes, 28
social criticism: cognitive therapy compared to, 25; deficiencies of, 3–7, 294; schema criticism distinguished from, 295; and social injustice grounded in faulty cognitions, ix–x, xii, 12. *See also* schema criticism
Social Darwinism, xi, 15, 87–88, 104, 124–125, 180, 187, 192
social injustice: and atomism schema, 119–120; and autonomy schema, 49, 56; cognitive roots of, x, xiii, 8; and consequences of faulty information processing, 24, *24*, 294; and essentialism schema, 88; grounded in faulty knowledge, ix–x, xii, 4, 12; and homogeneity schema, 146; psychological roots of, 164; in social order, x, xiv, 8, 14–15
social justice: and malleability schema, 76; protest novels promoting, 31–32, *31*, 167; and radical cognitive politics, xiv, 12–13, 164; and schema criticism, x, xiv, 32, 294, 296; and solidarity schema, 233, 235
social order: and autonomy schema, xi, 53–57, 64–65; and essentialism schema, 82, 83–85, 96; and homogeneity schema, 141, 142; and legal system, 50–53, 54; and protest novels, 27; and schema criticism, 289, 290–294; social injustice in, x, xiv, 8, 14–15; and solidarity schema, 233, 283
social roles, 41–42
social toxins, 78–79, 84, 182, 255, 267, 269
solidarity schema: and connectedness, xi–xii; emotional-psychological-neurological solidarity, 114–118, 123, 135, 136, 138, 187, 221, 222, 224–227, 230, 233, 275–276, 278, 279, 281, 283, 293; and emotions, 114–118, 137, 187–191, 225, 229–230, 234–235, 275, 277, 281–282;

and ethics, 113–114, 126; and exemplars, 127, 134–137, 139, 187–188, 227–228, 229, 231, 233, 278; and *The Grapes of Wrath*, 193, 221–236, 282, 283; and identity-needs, 107, 113, 123, 135; and information-processing routines, 31, 137–139, 191, 234–235, 236, 283; and in-group loyalties, 128; and *The Jungle*, 185–192, 231, 282, 283; and language, 111–112, 301n3; and *Native Son*, 237, 250, 275–283; ontological solidarity, 106, 109–114, 126, 127, 135, 136, 138, 187, 221, 222–223, 226–227, 228, 233, 275, 276, 278, 279, 281, 282, 283, 293; practical solidarity, 106, 107–109, 135, 136, 138, 187, 188, 221–224, 226–227, 228, 233, 275–278, 279, 281, 283, 292, 293; replacing atomism schema with, 127–139, 233, 235, 280; and self–other merging, 106, 121, 127, 227, 301n1
Soper, Kate, 125
Soviet Union, 138
Spencer, Herbert, 87–88
Stalin, Josef, 160
Stallone, Sylvester, 135
Stanford Prison Experiment, 41–42, 45–46
Stein, Karen Farchaus, 163
Steinbeck, John, 193, 204, 212, 219, 230–231. See also *The Grapes of Wrath* (Steinbeck)
stereotypes: and essentialism schema, 83, 88, 91; and exemplars, 19, 28; and faulty knowledge, 7; and homogeneity schema, 143, 146; and injustice, x, xii, 14; and malleability schema, 88, 91–92; and person-schemas, 14, 15–16; and prototypes, 16–17, 299n11
Stern, Daniel, 112, 128–129
Stoics, 105
Stowe, Harriet Beecher, *Uncle Tom's Cabin*, 72, 159–160
Strean, Herbert, 148–149
stress: and essentialism, 77–78; and

homogeneity schema, 151, 152, 155; and malleability schema, 253, 259; and solidarity schema, 110–111, 190
Stroessner, Steven J., 88
Stroud, Les, 135
subjectivity theory, 3, 4, 5, 7
supposition: and autonomy schema, 70, 71–72, 241; and essentialism schema, 253; and heterogeneity schema, 163, 275; and homogeneity schema, 159, 162; and information-processing routines, xii, 21, 23, 27, 29; and malleability schema, 101, 264, 269; and situationism schema, 70, 179, 206, 249

Taylor, Charles, 113
Taylor, Shelley E., 108–109, 131, 298n8
terrorist attacks of 9/11, 44–45, 144–145, 156, 158
terrorists and terrorism, 138, 144–145, 150
Thurow, Lester, 39
Tocqueville, Alexis de, 130
Todorov, Tzvetan, 105, 106, 107, 113, 130
To Kill a Mockingbird (Lee), 152
top-down information processing, 15–16, 21
Trope, Yaacov, 46–47
Trump, Donald, 135
24 (television series), 97
Two and a Half Men (television series), 133

United States: and atomism schema, 105, 106, 130, 138–139; and autonomy schema, 35, 36–37, 61–66; and essentialism schema, 76, 81, 83, 94; and homogeneity schema, 142, 144–146, 155–156
universalism, 109–114

Valdesolo, Piercarlo, 147, 148, 150–151
violence: and atomism schema, 104, 105, 134, 138; and autonomy schema, 237; and essentialism schema, 83, 85–86, 89, 237; and

334   Literature and Social Justice

violence (*continued*)
heterogeneity schema, 270, 271–272; and homogeneity schema, 143, 146, 147, 156; and malleability schema, 180–181, 183, 255–257, 258, 259, 262–263, 264, 269; and situationism schema, 173, 198, 240–241, 245, 246–249, 251–252; as social toxin, 78, 79; and solidarity schema, 276
Volkan, Vamik, 154–155

Warren, Elizabeth, 292–293
Wells, Adrian, 298n8
Westcott, Brooke Foss, 104
Westen, Drew, 11–12
white supremacy, 237, 243, 255, 259, 269

Wirths, Eduard, 148
Wolgast, Elizabeth, 104, 106
Wordsworth, William, 136
Wright, George, 84–85
Wright, Richard, 237–238, 251, 255. See also *Native Son* (Wright)

Yosifon, David, 39, 49, 53–54, 56–57, 64, 66–67

Ziller, Robert, 120–121
Zimbardo, Philip, 41–42, 44, 45–46, 53, 65
Zinn, Howard, 37
Zizek, Slavoj, 4, 301n2

Lightning Source UK Ltd.
Milton Keynes UK
UKOW03f0235231014

240527UK00004B/243/P